POETRY AT STAKE

POETRY AT STAKE

LYRIC AESTHETICS AND THE CHALLENGE OF TECHNOLOGY

Carrie Noland

PRINCETON UNIVERSITY PRESS PRINCETON, NEW JERSEY

Library of Congress Cataloging-in-Publication Data
Noland, Carrie, 1958–
Poetry at stake : lyric aesthetics and the challenge of technology / Carrie Noland.
p.   cm.
Includes bibliographical references and index.
ISBN 0–691–00416–1 (cloth : alk. paper).—ISBN 0–691–00417–X
(pbk. : alk. paper).
1. French poetry—19th century—History and criticism. 2. French
poetry—20th century—History and criticism. 3. Lyric poetry—History and criticism. 4. Literature and technology—United States. 5. Literature and technology—France. 6. Aesthetics, Modern. I. Title.

PQ433.N65 1999

841'.0409091—dc21 99–25333

This book has been composed in Sabon

The paper used in this publication meets the minimum
requirements of ANSI/NISO Z39.48-1992 (R1997)
(*Permanence of Paper*)

http://pup.princeton.edu

Printed in the United States of America

10 9 8 7 6 5 4 3 2 1

10 9 8 7 6 5 4 3 2 1

(Pbk.)

A section of chapter four has been published as "Poetry at Stake:
Blaise Cendrars, Cultural Studies, and the Future of Poetry in the Literature Classroom" in *PMLA (Publications of the Modern Language
Association in America)* 112, no. 1 (1997). Chapter five was published previously as "High Decoration: Blaise Cendrars, Sonia Delaunay, and the Poem as Fashion Design" in *Journal X: A Journal in Culture and Criticism* 2, no. 2 (1998). And an earlier version of chapter
seven appeared as "Rimbaud and Patti Smith: Style as Social Deviance" in *Critical Inquiry* 21, no. 3 (1995). © 1995 by The University
of Chicago Press. All rights reserved. Permission for republication
has been granted.

You're walking . . . and you don't always realize it but you're always falling. With each step . . . you fall. You fall forward a short way and then catch yourself. Over and over . . . you are falling . . . and then catch yourself. You keep falling and catching yourself falling. And this is how you are walking and falling at the same time.
　Laurie Anderson, *Words in Reverse*

In principle, philosophy can always go astray, which is the sole reason why it can go forward.
　Theodor W. Adorno, *Negative Dialectics*

Contents

ROSES

To

The National Endowment for the Humanities, for a year-long Fellowship for University Teachers that allowed me to write large portions of this book;

The Columbia University Council of Humanities and the University of California, Irvine, School of Humanities, for awarding me a series of summer grants that permitted consultation of rare documents, manuscripts, and letters housed in the Fonds Robert Delaunay at the Bibliothèque nationale and the Fonds Jacques Doucet at the Bibliothèque Sainte-Geneviève in Paris, the BBC Radio Written Archives in Reading, England, the Fonds Blaise Cendrars in Berne, Switzerland, the Musée de la Résistance in Fontaine-la-Vaucluse, France, and the Visual Arts Library at the University of California, Santa Barbara;

Renée Riese Hubert, for facilitating research contacts in Europe and for her generous loan of rare books;

Miriam Cendrars and Mme. René Char, for granting me access to archival materials;

Aaron Noland, for providing the best research assistance a daughter could ever hope to have;

Marjorie Beale, for her invaluable intellectual comradery, her sense of discernment, and her faithful friendship;

Victoria Silver, for her well-placed constructive criticism and numerous stimulating conversations on Adorno;

Leslie Rabine and Richard Terdiman, for taking the time to read and comment insightfully on the entire manuscript;

Gerald Fetz, John Smith, and Mark Katz, for helping me to decipher Adorno's German;

David Carroll and Ellen Burt, for the advice and support they offered during the many phases of this book's preparation;

Frank Banton (United Nations International School), Arnold Weinstein, Edward Ahearn (Brown University), and Richard Sieburth (Harvard University), for the gift of their inspired teaching of poetry;

Barbara Johnson and Susan Suleiman (Harvard University), for nourishing my enthusiasms, challenging my boundaries, and disciplining my voice;

Bahamin Yazdanfar and Ganiat Alao, for providing excellent care to my children, Julian and Francesca, while I was occupied with such enthusiasms, boundaries, and disciplines;

Dorothy Noland, for exposing me at an early age to experimental art and for always getting me the best aesthetic instruction she could find;

and Christopher Beach, my soulmate and partner in poetic subversion, for manifesting a quality and magnitude of generosity that I may never fully repay.

Abbreviations

The following abbreviations are used for frequently cited texts:

AT   Theodor W. Adorno. *Aesthetic Theory*. Translated by Robert Hullot-Kentor. Minneapolis: University of Minnesota Press, 1997.

Ill   Arthur Rimbaud. *"Illuminations" and Other Prose Poems*. Translated by Louise Varèse. Rev. ed. New York: New Directions, 1957.

MM   Theodor W. Adorno. *Minima Moralia: Reflections from Damaged Life*. Translated by E.F.N. Jephcott. London: Verso, 1996.

ND   Theodor W. Adorno. *Negative Dialectics*. Translated by E. B. Ashton. New York: Continuum, 1992.

POETRY AT STAKE

Introduction

Poetry at Stake: Lyric Aesthetics
and the Challenge
of Technology

NEARLY a century before performance poet Laurie Anderson released her CD-ROM *Puppet Motel*, the French poet Guillaume Apollinaire declared that poetic activity could indeed be pursued in more overtly commercial and industrial realms. At a time when the French avant-garde was by no means united in its estimation of mass cultural forms, Apollinaire openly encouraged poets to abandon the page in favor of modern transmission technologies, the same technologies that would eventually be deployed by performance poets such as Anderson. As early as 1917, Apollinaire predicted in "L'Esprit nouveau et les poètes" (Poets and the new spirit) that it would only be a matter of time before poets, more "refined" than the general public, would take hold of the means of production provided by the phonograph or the cinematic apparatus in order to apply them to the ends of subjective expression.[1] Encouraged by the recent success of theatrical spectacles such as *Parade* and *Les Mamelles de Tirésias*, Apollinaire had good reason to feel that the future of poetry lay increasingly in its collaboration with other arts and other domains.[2] He zealously envisioned a new wing of the avant-garde prepared to realize hybrid poetic forms "unimaginable until now" (*OC*, 944). But when Apollinaire delivered his lecture in 1917 he could not have known how prescient his words would in fact turn out to be. Apollinaire died the following year and therefore missed the opportunity to witness the birth of a large range of innovative poetic practices that would revolutionize the way lyric poetry would be written and read in the twentieth century.

In "L'Esprit nouveau et les poètes" Apollinaire was able to profess an affirmative attitude toward technology because he believed that poetry already contained within itself an incipient technological apparatus. If, as Apollinaire claimed, the entire evolution of poetry had been governed by experimentation on the level of form, an experimentation made possible, moreover, by the invention and multiplication of print technologies, then more advanced technologies of reproduction and transmission merely realized rather than displaced the inner dynamic of the poetic genre. Apollinaire even suggested that the barrier so carefully guarded between symbolic and commercial fields did not necessarily have to remain intact. He cheerfully enjoined his peers to create poems with machines, then claimed that these mechanically produced poems might successfully compete in a more broadly defined cultural market. Anticipating the adventurous performance artists of the 1970s and 1980s, Apollinaire proposed that poetry treat popular technologies not as a threat to its subsistence but as a potential extension of its own compositional means. According to Apollinaire's logic, lyric poets would be able to mobilize the epistemological and aesthetic potential of technology precisely because poetry had always been in large part controlled by a conventionalized rhetoric and a set of repeatable formal constraints. The rhetorical power of Apollinaire's "L'Esprit nouveau et les poètes" derived from his decision to accompany a call for poets to recuperate reproductive technologies with an acknowledgment that the technological was already presupposed by the compositional dialectics of the poetic text.

In presenting poetry in this manner, Apollinaire broke decisively with a critical and poetic tradition that had consistently situated poetry, and especially lyric poetry, in direct opposition to all forms of technological mediation. This tradition had enjoyed almost unchallenged dominance both in the academy and in the most respected literary journals of Apollinaire's day. Early-twentieth-century debates concerning the impact of industrialization on human consciousness typically portrayed lyric poetry as an ally in the fight against the mechanization, standardization, and commodification of human activity. It is not surprising, then, that Apollinaire's celebration of modern technologies and his faith in their aesthetic potential had the effect of alienating him from both his poetic contemporaries and his future critics. These critics would almost unanimously declare "L'Esprit nouveau et les poètes" the work of a futurist opportunist, a *blessé de guerre* who had lost sight of the harsh realities of capitalist industrialization.[3] To this day very few literary historians have taken Apollinaire's proposals seriously; in fact, the general trend in French poetry criticism has continued to be to oppose lyric expression to all technologically mediated forms of signifying practice. But by choosing to ignore the influence of other media upon poetic production, and by denying the implication of poetry in the rationalization of culture, twentieth-century poetry critics (especially those who embraced the Heideggerian ontology of the fifties) have created a false vision of the poetic genre. Promoting an ideology of the poetic object as radically free of technological contamination, these critics have exiled poetry from consideration within a broader cultural and historical context.[4]

My intention in this book is to demonstrate that Apollinaire was, at least in part, correct. Not only did he predict that poets would increasingly turn to modern technological means in order both to reinvigorate forms of poetic expression and to expand their audience base but he intuitively seized a truth of poetic composition that avant-garde poets would consistently foreground in their later works, namely, that "external" threats to subjectivity such as technology and commodification actually play an instrumental role in the composition of the lyric text and, as a corollary, in the construction of the autonomous (lyric) subject. Further, implicit in Apollinaire's manifesto was the notion that the commodifying practices of industry would not prove detrimental to poetry in the long run. Instead, he suggested, these same commodifying practices would help poetry to realize one of its most romantic aims: to be read, heard, recited, and perhaps even written by the many.

This book pursues the full implications of Apollinaire's decision to ally lyricism with the technological means and promotional strategies of modern capitalism. I explore the dialectical basis of Apollinaire's contentions while examining concrete examples of modern and postmodern poetic practice. If poetry critics have conventionally assumed that the poetic is by definition the very contrary of the mechanization and commodification of the human voice, the poets I consider in the first chapters of this book—Arthur Rimbaud, Blaise Cendrars and René Char—reject the strict dualism of this traditional opposition. Arthur Rimbaud, for instance, ignores the barrier separating high art from popular culture when he models his lyric subject on the mechanical creations of the nineteenth-century theatrical spectacle known as the *féerie* (fairy play). Similarly, Blaise Cendrars explores the distinction between symbolic and economic fields of production when he identifies thematically and displays formally the affinities between poetic strategies and those developed by modern advertising and fashion design. Finally, by adopting radio transmission as an analog for the lyric voice, René Char jeopardizes the Heideggerian poetics of presence with which his works have long been identified. For all three poets, the analogies they discern between lyric devices and mechanical processes are far from accidental; they indicate, rather, that poetry bears within itself a technical component, an "integrative machinery," in Theodor Adorno's terms, that can be mobilized, as any technology can, for a variety of contradictory ideological and commercial purposes.

Yet if Rimbaud, Cendrars, and Char explore the relation between technology and poetry on the level of analogy, the poets I study in the last chapters of this book work to *materialize* this analogy by applying industrially generated technologies to the development of hybrid poetic forms.

In order to follow the itinerary of an experimental poetic tradition I trace back to the works of Rimbaud, I focus in the last section on American performance poets who, along with the group of poets associated with Poésie Sonore, have attempted to advance the debate concerning poetry and technology to the point where even the operative criteria distinguishing one from the other no longer hold.[5] The poets I treat in the final chapters, punk rock poet Patti Smith and performance artist Laurie Anderson, depend explicitly upon lyric conventions, such as densely figurative language and a confessional rhetoric that identifies the speaking subject closely with the author, to create poems produced and disseminated through the technological means and promotional strategies of the music, video, and computer industries. Smith and Anderson both demonstrate that text-based poetic strategies can collaborate with industrial technologies to form a third, rarely theorized public. An analysis of this public and the type of works it supports may alter our understanding of the role high art plays in the postmodern cultural environment, an environment in which poetry mediates technological processes and, in turn, is increasingly subjected to their mediation.

Thus, in order to broaden the context in which French poetry has traditionally been studied, I move from an analysis of French lyric poets to an exploration of recent performance poetries produced in the United States. Certainly, France has long harbored its own experimental tradition, one engaged in developing either aleatory techniques (dada) or mathematical formulas (OULIPO) for the purposes of poetic production; however, it is American and not French culture that has produced the most radical cross-media experimental forms.[6] Poets such as William Burroughs, John Giorno, Brian Gysin, and Richard Kostelanetz began in the 1960s to combine poetry—as both oral and written text—with video and audio technologies.[7] During the 1970s and 1980s American record companies and television broadcasters offered limited but unexpected support to poets seeking to ally traditional, text-based poetic practices with advanced transmission technologies. The 1990s has seen an explosion of hybrid poetic forms—MTV poetry, Slam poetry, and CD-ROM hypertext poetry—that exploit to an even greater extent the promotional venues of the culture industry. Yet if France, for various economic and cultural reasons, has not led the way for poets seeking "machiner la poésie comme on a machiné le monde," as Apollinaire predicted it would in 1917 (OC, 954), the example of the French lyric tradition has nonetheless played a crucial role in inspiring the most promising manifestations of what we may tentatively call a popular poetic subculture. Anderson and Smith can justifiably be said to be the foremost inheritors of a distinct poetic tradition whose origins they situate, as do I, in the works of late romantic and early avant-garde lyricists. Both are engaged in transforming what the situationists called "the discoveries of modern [French] poetry" into innovative, critical, and yet widely disseminated forms.[8]

My strategy in this book is twofold. First, I resituate these poetries in their respective cultural and social contexts in order to provide an alternative critical discourse on lyric poetry as well as an alternative account of its evolution into the plurivocal poetries of the twentieth-century avant-garde. I seek to understand how lyric poetry envisions its own relation to history, how it depicts and confesses to its participation in the great industrial transformations altering daily life. In the course of my argument I mount a defense of the study of poetry; however, this defense is based not on poetry's difference, its hypothetical immunity and thus irrelevance to the study of broader cultural transformations, but rather on poetry's absolute pertinence, its impact on and implication in the formation of other, often opposed cultural practices. My aim is to reveal the existence of extensive ties, both practical and epistemological, linking capitalist expansion and its corollaries, modern industrialization and electronic information processing, to poetic forms of subjective expression. Reading poems in the context of other types of signifying practice, I compare specific rhetorical techniques with the standardizing processes developed by commercial industries (fashion design and advertising); the military-industrial complex (radio transmission and cryptography); the culture industry (stagecraft technologies and popular music); and the computer industry (CD-ROM hypertext technologies). No other book has attempted to broaden to such an extent the context in which modern poetry is read and theorized.

Further, I work to expose the dialogue that has occurred repeatedly between poetic and mechanical modes of reproduction in the hope that the study of poetry will once again be regarded as crucial to an understanding of the evolution of both subversive and popular cultural forms. I argue here that poems both nourish and draw sustenance from the realm of the mechanically reproduced. In certain cases it may even be impossible to explicate either popular cultural forms or print-based poetic forms if they are studied in isolation from one another. It would be historically inaccurate and theoretically obtuse to insist that poems reflect technological innovations in any direct or predictable manner. What can be demonstrated, however, is that lyric poets of modernity are acutely aware of their situation within a broader field of cultural practices and that, moreover, certain lyricists are willing to employ phonographic, electronic, and cybernetic technologies in order to broaden the range of the lyric voice. In a gesture mingling admission and defiance these lyric poets display their consciousness of heteronomous mediations through a controlled use of figural, formal, and sometimes extratextual means. I therefore apply the techniques of close reading to both texts and hybrid works to show that in certain cases it is only by studying the printed poem alongside instances of industrialized cultural expression that we may begin to discern the compositional dialectics by which they both achieve form.

My study begins with Rimbaud, a nineteenth-century, exclusively *text*-based poet, because he is the first to assess the situation of poetry in a disenchanted world in affirmative as well as negative terms. Rimbaud confronts a late-nineteenth-century cultural market in which new technologies are placing the prophetic function of poetry at stake by offering rare glimpses into types of experience and modes of fabrication foreign to reified lyric notions of what the self—or poetry—can be. But unlike other members of his generation, Rimbaud does not repudiate the new world that surrounds him. He expresses instead an incipient awareness that the capitalist market responsible for generating new technologies also holds the potential to inspire alternative conceptions of human subjectivity, conceptions that may eventually nourish a lyric poetry exhausted with the romantic conception of the self. His poetry suggests further that the bourgeois market's emphasis on the innovative and the flashy engenders not only machines that restrict vision but also machines facilitating vision's extension into previously unknown realms.[9] And yet Rimbaud is by no means as confident about the unalloyed benefits of technology as the futurists will soon come to be. Expressing an ambivalence that is paradigmatic of the entire tradition under study, Rimbaud remains unsure whether to celebrate the opportunities for innovation that capitalism offers or to mourn the loss of autonomous creativity that its mechanics seem to forbid. Rimbaud clearly recognizes, that is, the dialectical nature of the "progress" Apollinaire later exalts. He understands that the very markets and machines promising liberation from reified images of the human subject can, unless radically mediated in turn, submit this subject to even more rigorous forms of determination.

Thus, if Rimbaud and the other poets treated in this study acknowledge the degree to which expression and even modes of apperception are modified by the introduction of new technologies into daily life, they also recognize that these new technologies are generated within the context of a particular economy or aggregate of social conditions. They realize, that is, that means of production are embedded in a network of relations of production and cannot easily be materially extracted—or conceptually abstracted—from these relations. Although the dream of many of the

poets considered here is to employ technologies in a fashion *not* determined by their conditions of manufacture, they rarely blind themselves
(as Apollinaire did) to the link between industrial support and the possibilities offered for creative reappropriation. The following chapters therefore proceed to situate modern and postmodern lyricists not only in the
context of the dominant technologies of their respective periods but also
in the context of the larger historical conditions within which these technologies were developed. Poems are read in relation to the bourgeois cultural market of the nineteenth century, the youth and global markets of
the twentieth, or, in the case of Char, the conditions of World War II
military communications. Chapters 1, 4, 5, and 7 center on the place
of poetry within a particular economic milieu; chapters 2, 6, and 8 are
concerned more exclusively with the way in which an individual poet
reinterprets lyric expression when challenged by a given industrial practice. Chapter 3 departs somewhat from the strict emphasis on lyric poetry
per se and provides a close reading of Theodor Adorno's *Negative Dialectics as* a lyric utterance. I choose *Negative Dialectics* because it models a
persuasive theory of the modern lyric, mirroring this lyric's dialectical
momentum in the very evolution of its argument. While approximating a
lyric confession of mediation in the austere context of philosophy, *Negative Dialectics* also clarifies the extent to which markets, technologies,
and truth discourses are all inextricably intertwined. Thus, each chapter
of *Poetry at Stake* treats a distinct and idiosyncratic instance of subjective
expression. All chapters, however, focus on what I consider to be the
quintessentially lyric moment, the moment when the lyric subject is forced
to divulge that its voice is not entirely its own.

The poets examined here can thus be considered confessional poets, poets
striving to locate the mechanical, heteronomous element that inhabits and
situates their subjective speech. *Heteronomy* is a term derived from Kantian philosophy that I employ in this book to refer to the contingent forces
responsible for shaping instances of individual expression. Each chapter
defines heteronomy in a slightly different manner according to the context
at issue. The heteronomous element is identified as a market-inspired rhetorical or compositional means (e.g., synesthesia or assemblage); as a topical, historically determined content or diction (e.g., pastoral diction or the
idiom of advertising); and as a particular time-bound vision of subjective
agency (e.g., the subject as autonomous or as technologically mediated).

My claim in this book is that lyric poets of the avant-garde not only
recognize that self-expression is saturated with contingency but also seek
to disclose these contingencies through a variety of confessional tactics.

Critics in the past have been surprisingly reluctant to analyze subjective discourses in terms of their heteronomous mediations even when these mediations have been foregrounded by the authors themselves. Yet if the immanence of lyric expression has not received the critical attention it demands, the profound heteronomy of the visual arts, in contrast, has been the major preoccupation of a number of critical discourses on modern and postmodern art. Peter Bürger's *Theory of the Avantgarde*, published first in Germany in 1974 and translated into English ten years later, initiated a reading of dada and surrealism that brought the issue of aesthetic autonomy and its discontents to the fore. In the wake of Bürger's influential book, a wide variety of critics began to analyze how artists from Tristan Tzara to Hans Haacke succeeded in revealing the influence of market preferences and exhibition policies on supposedly independent aesthetic choices. Responding to Bürger's book soon after it appeared, Andreas Huyssen moved to refocus the discussion on avant-garde art, asking in *After the Great Divide* not whether the attack on aesthetic autonomy had been successful but rather why it had been attempted in the first place.[10] Unfortunately, Huyssen's provocation was somewhat overwhelmed at the time by debates centering attention on the "death" of the avant-garde, the disappointment of its aspirations, and the absorption of its techniques into popular culture.[11]

But Huyssen's question was a good one. What, indeed, prompted the artists of modernity to reappraise the function of art within a technology-driven consumer culture? In terms that will prove essential to the argument of this book, Huyssen suggests that the avant-garde's rejection of aesthetic autonomy, its critique of art as an institution, was attributable not only, and not even primarily, to a mistrust of such institutions per se but rather to an ambivalent or "bipolar" experience of the increasingly technologized European landscape (10). "No other single factor," he insists, "influenced the emergence of the new avantgarde art as much as technology, which . . . penetrated to the core of the work itself" (9). By shifting the focus from the relationship between the artwork and the aesthetic institution to the artist's conflicted experience of productive conditions *beyond* the aesthetic institution, Huyssen in effect altered the terms of the debate. Because Bürger chose to look exclusively at the artist's relationship to the institutions of the art world, his model suffered from a tendency to conflate surrealism with dada, the works of Pablo Picasso with those of Kurt Schwitters. In actuality, the positions these artists maintained vis-à-vis the aesthetic institution were quite different, in part because they were influenced by contacts with reproductive technologies beyond the aesthetic field that were far more varied than Bürger allowed.[12]

But if, as Huyssen argues, technology "sparked" avant-garde production—both to new innovative heights and to new self-reflexive depths—

it would fall to other critics to determine, in each individual case, how technology could be said to "reside" at "the core of the work itself" (9). For although Huyssen imagines a study whose goal would be to analyze the effect of a "bipolar" experience of technology on the production and distribution of art, he never actually examines an avant-garde painting, poem, or event in this context. Of course, *After the Great Divide* has been followed by a number of provocative studies resituating avant-garde works in the context of the technologies informing them. These studies include Kirk Varnedoe and Adam Gopnik's *High and Low: Modern Art and Popular Culture*, Jeffrey Weiss's *The Popular Culture of Modern Art: Picasso, Duchamp and Avantgardism*, Robert Jenson's *Marketing Modernism in Fin-de-Siècle Europe*, Johanna Drucker's *The Visible Word: Experimental Typography and Modern Art*, Thierry de Duve's *Pictorial Nominalism: On Marcel Duchamp's Passage from Painting to the Readymade*, and Hal Foster's *Compulsive Beauty*.[13] But these studies of modern and in some cases postmodern cultural production focus almost exclusively on the *visual* arts: on systems of gallery promotion, on pictorial themes, and on the popular spectacles of the nineteenth and twentieth centuries. In general, the field of poetry studies has refused to follow the path opened by critics of visual culture. Notable exceptions are Marjorie Perloff's *Radical Artifice: Writing Poetry in the Age of Media* and Michael Davidson's *Ghostlier Demarcations: Modern Poetry and the Material Word*,[14] both of which analyze how contemporary American poets position their craft vis-à-vis the advanced reproductive technologies available to them. These works can be said to inspire and complement my own, for they establish that reproductive technologies do indeed "penetrate" the compositional practices of contemporary American lyricists. Still, the broad strokes of Huyssen's argument indicate that the origins of a contemporary American lyricism have yet to be located in the poetics of an earlier European avant-garde.

Locating such a poetics, however, requires that we break new ground, for poetry criticism, especially in France, has been singularly resistant to the kind of materialist approach that regularly informs studies devoted to contemporary American poetry or European avant-garde art. In the French context, Richard Terdiman's *Discourse/Counter-Discourse: The Theory and Practice of Symbolic Resistance in Nineteenth-Century France* cleared the stage for a materialist approach to avant-garde lyric poetry by drawing attention to Mallarmé's critical appropriation of modern typographical technologies for the composition of poetic texts.[15] Mallarmé's response to modernity, however, was less multifaceted than Rimbaud's; as Terdiman's study confirms, Mallarmé's vigorous repudiation of market forces could not have inspired the celebratory gestures of poets such as Apollinaire or Cendrars.[16] The tradition of avant-garde poets that would go on to explore Rimbaud's profound ambivalence toward modernity still requires further delineation and theoretical treatment.

Alternative discourses on poetry's relation to technology have been difficult to reconstruct, largely because the vein of criticism prefigured by Apollinaire's "L'Esprit nouveau et les poètes" has found so few supporters among critics of modern French poetry. And yet the call for poets to reappropriate technological means for the extension and fulfillment of lyric's potential did produce an echo in an entirely foreign context, namely, in the early texts Walter Benjamin composed on cinematic and photographic technologies and their role in modern experience. In "One-Way Street," for instance, Benjamin idealistically envisions a reconciliation between advanced reproductive technologies and the prophetic power traditionally associated with auratic forms marked by the hand or traversed by a vocal tremor. Looking back to Apollinaire, Benjamin also forecasts that once poets master the new representational technologies "they will renew their authority in the life of peoples."[17] As in "A Small History of Photography," of 1931, Benjamin suggests that what guarantees the enduring aesthetic value of a work, and thus its "aura," is the artist's "*attitude* to his techniques" and not the provenance of the techniques themselves. Benjamin even entertains the possibility that "the most precise technology" may provide its products with a "magical value."[18] The camera lens, for instance, might offer a new perspective, one that opens up onto the unconscious, or onto what Apollinaire called somewhat enigmatically the "inhuman."[19] This "inhuman" perspective, beyond the grasp of illusionist techniques or the consciousness of a unified subject, would become available when the artist adopted a technique—in Rimbaud's terms, a "méthode"—originating outside the realm of romantic subject-centered discourses. With the aid of this photographic, phonographic, or filmic technique, the artist could then work to dislodge reified images of the lyric subject that had up to that point limited rather than enlarged the range of available expressive modes. But of course for this to happen, these technologies would have to be severed from their current relations of production and placed in qualitatively different hands.

In these early essays, Benjamin provides in embryo a highly suggestive dialectical theory of the relation between technology and poetry, a theory that finds amplification in the later works of Adorno. In his unfinished *Aesthetic Theory*, of 1970, Adorno acknowledges that it is indeed possible to "produce artistically by manipulating means that originated extra-aesthetically" (*AT*, 33). But this possibility presents itself only because the artwork is already informed by techniques that dictate formal patterns against which the individual artist must constantly struggle. Confirming Apollinaire's own diagnosis of art as an intrinsically technical medium,

Adorno writes that all artistic conventions, even those belonging to the earliest "auratic" genres (e.g., cave painting or incantation) already contain the seed of more advanced procedures generated "extra-aesthetically." In Adorno's view, the "authentic" lyric poet is one who draws attention to the historical immanence of these procedures, revealing that they both facilitate and limit the expression of the self.

It may seem paradoxical to some that I evoke Adorno in order to defend the relevance of industrial or popular culture to the analysis of lyric poetry. To be sure, Adorno's general reputation in the academy would discourage one from turning to his works for an objective theory of capitalist technologies and their relation to high art. But I would argue that cultural critics have too frequently reduced Adorno's account of culture under capitalism to a wooden description of two discrete and mutually exclusive forms: the thoroughly autonomous work of art on the one hand and the thoroughly heteronomous product of the culture industry on the other.[20] Adorno's most telling blind spot may indeed be his refusal to conceive of the technologically reproduced cultural product as pervious to dialectical mediation; however, one need only glance at *Aesthetic Theory* to see how thoroughly he dismisses the concept of art's intrinsic autonomy: "it is impossible to insist on a critique of the culture industry that draws the line at art" (*AT*, 18). Just as Beethoven turns out to be the consummate businessman in *Dialectic of Enlightenment*, avant-garde works emerge in Adorno's essays as subject to a wide variety of heteronomous interventions. Thus, although Adorno does not look kindly upon the productions of Hollywood or Tin Pan Alley, there is nonetheless one way in which he invites us to take popular culture seriously as an object of study. The study of popular culture is relevant to Adorno if only because it helps to shed light on the generative processes of art. The aspect of Adorno's aesthetics that surely has not "outlived its usefulness," as Huyssen puts it in *After the Great Divide*, "is Adorno's suggestion that mass culture [is] not imposed on art *only from the outside*" (42, emphasis added). Since lyric poetry has traditionally been considered beyond the pale of mass culture, it appears particularly vital that the boundary separating the "inside" from the "outside" of the lyric form be retraced. Adorno's materialist poetics encourages us to ask how each *specific* technology (as opposed to a general, dehistoricized concept of *technē*) inflects historical forms of subjective expression and their modes of reflexive self-awareness. How might the rise of a commodity culture, the advent of cinema, the invasion of radio technologies, or the intrusion of cybernetics into everyday life nuance a poet's understanding of subjectivity and challenge the viability of lyric forms?

Adorno thus remains an important source of inspiration for a cultural approach to poetry because for him an autonomous work of art is only autonomous insofar as it is free to confront, confess, and even thematize its profound heteronomy. The immanence of the heteronomous, according to Adorno, is the knowledge that art seeks to impart. And it is only art's dialectical negativity, its willingness to place itself at stake, that potentially redeems art and prevents it from becoming pure ideology. Thus, for Adorno the confessional moment—which he links specifically to lyric poetry—stands as a potential model for cultural resistance. What Adorno fails to recognize, however, is that such resistance can take place in less elite cultural realms as well.

This book is intended neither as an apology for capitalism nor as a celebration of modern technology; rather, it is meant to be an exploration of the often contradictory ways in which avant-garde poets have responded to both. The poets studied here recognize at once the creative possibilities and the destructive tendencies of a material situation entirely different from that into which the lyric form was initially introduced. Adorno's treatment of avant-garde poets in works such as *Aesthetic Theory* is schematic and illustrative; he does not provide, nor does he aim to provide, a full portrait of the lyricist's reaction to the modern world. His approach does, however, raise important questions concerning the nature of the relations between lyric poetry and its changing material contexts. *Aesthetic Theory* makes frequent and strategic allusions to symbolist and cubist poets, yet the crucial role played by French poetry in the development of Adorno's aesthetic theory has never received the attention it deserves.[21] A related objective of this book is thus to reestablish a dialogue between Adorno and the avant-garde poetry that informed his aesthetics. My readings of specific poems attempt to show in what way the poet's "crisis of experience" (*AT*, 34) both corresponded to and differed from Adorno's own.

As Apollinaire foresaw, the moment of dialectical self-consciousness provoked by the avant-garde's confrontation with capitalism by no means led to poetry's demise. On the contrary, the technologies depicted as menacing poetry's existence—from the printing press to electronic communications—have turned out to be vital, rather than fatal, to poetry's evolution as an aesthetic form. Early avant-garde poets were among the first to apprehend that modern conditions of production could actually allow poetry to evolve toward new forms requiring new audiences or interpretive communities whose culture could not be contained within the traditional antipodal categories of heteronomous and autonomous art. Apollinaire's "rappel à l'ordre" in "L'Esprit nouveau et les poètes" was also a reminder that poetry would have to acknowledge the changing conditions in which it would be composed, that poetry could not "shelter itself from the world that surrounds it," or "se cantonner hors de ce qui l'entoure" (OC, 954).

And yet the risk poetry runs by pretending to ignore its supposedly external conditions is matched by another risk, that of embracing these conditions all too tightly and thus losing the integrity of poetry as a language-based and voice-generated genre. This integrity is related to a certain vision of the subject—the subject as spontaneous, unpredictable, and indeterminate—that modern culture may need, after all, to preserve. For it is by no means clear that poetry can extend itself beyond the page without forfeiting what the situationists took to be the other significant discovery of modernity, namely, the subversive indeterminacies of literary textuality, the political potential of graphemic and phonetic signifying play, whose untotalizable field of effects may reflect and sustain what is irreducible about subjectivity itself. The poets treated in this book explore fully the contradiction between two opposed exigencies: on the one hand the need to confess mediation and on the other the need to modify forms of mediation in order to register the irregularities and indeterminacies of personal experience too easily smoothed out by standardizing grids. Technology turns out to be an image of what poetic writing *is*: a set of compositional practices and conventions evolving according to the logic of a specific market. Yet technology is simultaneously an image of what poetry *must not be*: a combinatory mechanism, a self-sufficient and self-sustaining language incapable of grasping what has been excluded by the rules of its own system.

One

Traffic in the Unknown: Rimbaud's Interpretive Communities, Market Competition, and the Poetics of *Voyance*

RIMBAUD has been at the center of some of the most vigorous literary battles of our time. As René Etiemble noted in 1952, even before his death in 1891 Rimbaud had already entered the literary community's "machine for making gods" [machine à faire des dieux],[1] inspiring a prodigious number of appraisals, testimonials, and portraits of sometimes questionable authority. Passing rapidly through the mythmaking machine, "Rimbaud" emerged fully processed into forms that might gain him the "affection," as Etiemble puts it, of the twentieth century's "collective imaginary" (55). Over the course of a few decades, thanks to the efforts of reviewers, biographers, and enthusiasts, Rimbaud came to personify a wide variety of mutually contradictory archetypes, from the Christian to the heretic, the angel to the demon, the fascist to the communard. The variety of these archetypes reveals more than the ideological preoccupations of twentieth-century interpretive communities; it points to the fact that a poetic corpus, even one supposedly committed to *dérèglement* as a compositional principle, can be pressed into the service of specific political and nationalist agendas.

Although there were many critical discourses on Rimbaud circulating at the turn of the century, the most influential was one that sought to disengage Rimbaud's poetry from any ideological interest whatsoever. This critical discourse, invested in a vision of Rimbaud as a pure, isolated spark of creativity, has proved remarkably durable, nourishing some of the most tenacious clichés of current French poetry criticism, such as the historical transcendence of the lyric poem and the autonomy of the lyric subject.[2] In order to present Rimbaud's poetry as untainted by interests of any kind, however, neoromantic critics had to suppress certain features of his poetry as well as certain aspects of his literary career. Effecting their own brand of ideological obfuscation, these critics recognized neither Rimbaud's entrepreneurial spirit (the degree to which he sought literary success) nor his technical mastery (the extent to which he self-consciously strove to develop a highly sophisticated technique). Rimbaud's Parnassian predecessors may have succeeded in establishing the model of lyric as a self-generating, self-sustaining project, but it was Rimbaud who provided the definitive example of a poet capable of sacrificing social communication in order to transcend all forms of contingency.

This chapter explores the twentieth-century invention of a Rimbaud divorced from history. By tracing the genealogy of the neoromantic discourse on Rimbaud I hope to provide one account of how lyric poetry came to hold its unique status in literary studies, how it came to represent, against a background of contesting voices, the exemplary virginal and monoglossic utterance. A study of Rimbaud's historiography also suggests why the lyric has recently fallen out of favor, why it has failed to arouse interest in an academy increasingly given over to the pursuit of the heterogeneous and the openly ideological. For the very features earlier critics attributed to Rimbaud's poetry, and to lyric poetry in general—such as autonomy, univocality, and transcendence—are the features that render it inimical to the context-oriented materialist scholarship of contemporary cultural studies. However, a closer look at those aspects of Rimbaud's poetry that neoromantic critics suppressed in their exegetical and biographical enterprises reveals that Rimbaud's poetry can serve as the locus of an alternative understanding of the lyric and of its relation to history, an understanding that may allow us to reread lyric poems in relation to the "internal dialogism" that characterizes their verbal texture.[3] In the chapter that follows, I examine the underlying assumptions of early Rimbaud scholarship, arguing that the figure of the poet stood for a definition of poetry as autonomously generated that his texts, in fact, consistently problematize. Rimbaud's poems hold the key to a critical approach capable of reconciling materialist and formalist approaches: on the one hand, their topical diction and repeated parabases harbor a critique of aesthetic ideology; on the other, their elaborate figural networks oblige us to attend to the rhetorical devices that distinguish specifically *lyric* modes of critique from rival forms.

What I call the dominant, or mainstream, discourse on French lyric poetry emerged around 1910 from the pages of that highly influential arbiter of early-twentieth-century taste, *La Nouvelle Revue Française*.[4] The *NRF*, whose neoromanticism was epitomized in its "classicisme moderne,"[5] presented Rimbaud as a poet of pure intuition, rejecting all things Western in an effort to return language to its innocent, primal state. As the early-twentieth-century avant-garde drifted toward a more self-critical and ironical approach to aesthetic distinction, critics of the *NRF* were increasingly anxious to preserve the link between poetic language and a superior order of truth.

The *NRF*'s coverage of modern poetry was initiated under the sign of Paul Claudel, whose preface to the 1912 edition of Rimbaud's works trapped the lyric within an entirely metaphysical frame. The neoromantic critical discourse of the *NRF* was not entirely inadequate to the poetry it offered to the public; however, it is clear that such a discourse neglected certain features of poetic writing that avant-garde poets were interested in bringing to the fore. Critics of the *NRF* were for the most part unable to account for features of poetic language that drew attention either to poetry's graphemic materiality or to its purely phonetic patterning. They conducted little formal analysis, and absolutely no sociological analysis, as a quick glance at Michel Arnauld's "Du Vers Français" or André Gide's "Baudelaire et M. Faguet" confirms.[6]

The presence of Paul Valéry on the literary scene may have inspired in poetry critics a preoccupation with the mechanics of textual production. However, Valéry's proposition that poetic writing was a métier was virtually drowned out in the early twenties, not only by the clamor of surrealist manifestoes but also by writings of critics dedicated to a romantic vision of the poet as Nature's child. Albert Thibaudet, who wrote for the *NRF*, exemplified this tendency to privilege inspiration over technique; in *Paul Valéry* Thibaudet flatly refused the notion that an inspired poet might also be involved in a form of *labor*.[7] In response, Henri Brémond led an effort to reconcile Valéry's emphasis on production with Thibaudet's faith in inspiration, claiming that all poetry, inspired or not, inevitably emerges from a "usine" [factory]; "Pas d'usine, pas de poème," Brémond concludes decisively in *La Poésie pure* of 1926.[8] But such a balanced (and suggestive) revision of the dominant critical paradigm does not seem to have affected the reception of Rimbaud's work in particular. From the moment Rimbaud emerged as a major poet in the early part of the twentieth century, his name served neoromantic critics as a synonym for a form of writing that most successfully resisted manufacture in the linguistic "usine."

One can begin to ascertain precisely what was at stake in the reception of Rimbaud and in the cultural positioning of poetry in general by studying more closely the aesthetic ideology of the dominant critical discourse as it was elaborated in essays on modern poetry composed by the review team of the *NRF* between 1909 and 1914. The most influential poetry critics at the dawn of the century, Jacques Rivière and his reviewers Henri Ghéon, Jean Schlumberger, the orientalist Raymond Schwab, and Albert Thibaudet, all sought in their prewar essays to capture Rimbaud within the wide net of an idealist, vitalist-inspired discourse on the lyric genre.[9] These critics depicted Rimbaud as anything but a focused social critic or patient linguistic technician; he was instead a prophet, a "mystique à l'état sauvage" [savage mystic] as Claudel would write in his preface of 1912.[10]

With the *NRF* as their privileged forum, critics promoting the "classi-cisme moderne" of Claudel, Jammes, Fargue, Verhaeren, Vielé-Griffin, and Valéry imposed a vision of Rimbaud as, in the words of Henri Ghéon, "one who abdicates his reason and proscribes all logical processes."[11]

In 1914 Jacques Rivière published a set of seminal essays containing perhaps the first analyses of Rimbaud's poems (as opposed to anecdotal synopses of his life).[12] In these early essays Rivière reads Rimbaud's work as a demonstration of what poetry, according to an idealist aesthetics, ought to be: a pure voice of presocial innocence and primal subjectivity rebelling against the constraints of ordinary language use. Transcending his own portrait of Rimbaud as untutored innocent, however, Rivière manages to present a vision of Rimbaud far more nuanced than the ver-sions offered by his contemporaries. Applying a greater degree of formal analysis to Rimbaud's texts than they had previously known, Rivière com-pares the drafts of two sections of *Une Saison en enfer* (*A Season in Hell*) with the versions published in the 1912 *Complete Works*. Ironically, even though Rivière offers a precious glimpse of a Rimbaud at work, a Rim-baud concerned with producing verbal effects, he nevertheless concludes his study with the assertion that changes in the manuscript were *not* the result of "une simple mise au point technique" [a mere technical adjust-ment] but rather signs of the poet's effort to render the scene "plus vraie" [truer to life].[13] The opposition Rivière establishes between attention to verbal technique on the one hand and the search for greater truth on the other is one that would be sustained by a wide variety of critics, from Rolland de Renéville and André Breton to Albert Béguin.[14] Further, the aesthetic program fostered by the *NRF* (and exemplified, according to them, by Rimbaud) would soon find amplification in the works of the prominent critics of the forties and fifties: Gabriel Bounoure, Georges Poulet, Jean-Pierre Richard, Maurice Blanchot, Georges Bataille, and Jules Monnerot.[15] The latter, especially, tended to reiterate the neoroman-tic distinction between poetry and technical mastery. Immediately after World War II Monnerot would write that poetry instantiates "the pure, inventive element of the arts, an element present in all creation but entirely effaced in technology, for instance, where there is nothing but industry and fabrication."[16] Although subtly different in orientation, all six of these postwar critics would press Rimbaud into the service of a similar ideal, through their analyses of his work forging a theory of modern po-etry that would have a more lasting effect on aesthetic discourses than might have been expected.

Rivière's estimation of Rimbaud was linked to the journal's approach to modern poetry in general. Although generously inclusive at first, the *NRF* soon rejected poets too closely linked to the avant-garde, especially, as it would turn out, those who claimed to be the foremost inheritors of Rimbaud. In 1910 the editors of the *NRF* published a summary of contemporary poetic movements entitled "La Génération nouvelle et son unité" [The new generation and its unity], an assessment composed by one of the most influential leaders of the protofuturist avant-garde, Jules Romain. But the unity asserted by the title of the piece would soon be belied both by the factionalism of the poets gathered under the title's umbrella and by the intolerance of the *NRF* critics assigned to review their works. Some of the poets grouped under the vague heading "Génération nouvelle" would remain in the *NRF* pantheon up until the war; Goethe, Hugo, Rimbaud, Verhaeren, Claudel, Gide, and Charles-Louis Philippe all continued to receive praise from critics like Ghéon and Schwab. But other poets who had appeared on the initial list—Walt Whitman, Apollinaire, Max Jacob, and the poets of L'Abbaye—either disappeared altogether from the review's pages or provoked less and less enthusiasm as time went on. Why was the *NRF* able to accommodate the avant-garde, at least as it was represented by Jules Romain, in 1909 but unable to appreciate the development of its tendencies a year later?

A survey of the journal's articles on poetry printed during the prewar years reveals two major factors responsible for alienating *NRF* critics from the poetic avant-garde. First, the *NRF*'s resistance to viewing Rimbaud as a self-conscious technician was consistent with the journal's attitude toward the most technically oriented aesthetic of the period, that of cubist painting. The advent of cubism dramatized the incompatibility between avant-garde and modernist approaches to aesthetic production. The movement introduced by Apollinaire as "more cerebral than sensual" and by Blaise Cendrars as the product of "cold reason" was received by the *NRF* reviewers of the 1911 Salon d'Automne with a hostility bordering on hysteria.[17] The principal accusation the *NRF* made against cubist canvasses was, significantly for our purposes, that they resulted from an "invention mécanique";[18] they displayed "a crass will to construct" and suffered from a lack of "direct contact with things."[19] But the technical approach to objects derided by the *NRF* was precisely the aspect of cubist practice Apollinaire praised in his 1913 *Peintres cubistes*.[20] For Apollinaire, Picasso's tendency to study an object "as a surgeon dissects a cadaver" (13) suggested an entirely different "contact with things," one that could admit and even thematize rather than obscure the techniques (such as perspective and chiaroscuro) responsible for the *illusion* of "direct" contact. Apollinaire drew attention to that aspect of cubist practice concerned with disclosing the *means* by which contact with things is initiated, the various procedures by which a vision of the world is attained. The literary circles of the *NRF*, on the other hand, had no epistemological investment in illuminating mediation, as their hostility toward avant-garde preoccupations makes clear. The idea of interrogating representation per se seems to have been regarded with considerable suspicion. By the same token, the self-reflexive procedures of a Mallarmé were also deemed "assez dangereux" by André Gide in an *NRF compte rendu*, "Contre Mallarmé."[21] Any suggestion that aesthetic composition might be dominated by a coldly analytical, highly rational process, one dissecting not only the object but also the technical means by which that object is evoked in representation, seems to have been antithetical to the spirit of the *NRF*, and, by extension, to the dominant tradition of poetry criticism they supported. The lack of any sustained critical discussion of Mallarmé in the early pages of the *NRF* should suggest why Rimbaud was feted as a wild child come to purify, without method or even irony, the words of the tribe.

The *NRF*'s dismissal of avant-garde aesthetics, and, as a corollary, of a portrait of Rimbaud as avant-garde technician, can also be attributed to the arrival of futurism on the French cultural scene. The publication of F. T. Marinetti's "Futurist Manifesto" in the *Figaro* of 20 February 1909 produced a schism in the literary community that virtually created the French avant-garde as an oppositional movement within modernism. Futurist *provocateurs* not only praised the new technologies that critics of the *NRF* had disparaged but openly celebrated the market that had stimulated the invention of these technologies. The futurists adopted the unabashed pursuit of profit and fame as a compulsory element of their aesthetic ethos.[22] Whereas Apollinaire immediately seized the aesthetic significance of futurism's satire of symbolic capital, Jacques Copeau, the *NRF*'s man on the scene, condemned Marinetti's manifesto as pure hype, "incoherent and ridiculous."[23] "Marinetti's provocation," wrote Copeau, "betrays either a great lack of reflection or a great thirst for fame" (83). Ironically, it was Marinetti's focus on fame ("réclame") in particular that would inspire the most defining gestures of avant-garde practice over the next eighty years. Not only were the *NRF* critics blind to the significance of futurism for the future of European aesthetics but they were unable to acknowledge specifically those aspects of Rimbaud's work that evoke the productive relations of poetic writing during his own period. In rejecting both cubism and futurism, the *NRF* manifested its resistance to art forms that were self-consciously attempting to place in relief both the representational techniques they deploy and the debt these techniques owe to heteronomous pressures exerted upon art from within and beyond the cultural market.

In sum, to maintain the neoromantic discourse network that presented Rimbaud as an originary "demigod," critics of the *NRF* were compelled to ignore a certain number of facts concerning the conditions under which Rimbaud wrote as well as the sensitivity he exhibited vis-à-vis the impact of these conditions on the nature of his own poetic practice. And yet the question concerning Rimbaud's putative investment in fame and technical mastery seems to have continued to plague his critics and admirers. The critical community's very earliest assessments of Rimbaud in fact center on his relation—or rather, on his *non*relation—to writing as a métier. Perhaps the first attempt to deal with Rimbaud as a professional writer (as opposed to a curiosity) was undertaken by Paul Verlaine in his 1883 essay "Rimbaud," originally published in the review *Lutèce* and reprinted the following year in *Les Poètes maudits*.[24] Anxious to wrest the legacy of Rimbaud from Verlaine's grip, Isabelle Rimbaud and her husband, Paterne Berrichon, soon produced two highly sentimentalized accounts of the poet's life.[25] Although the two versions, Verlaine's and the family's, differed in significant ways (Verlaine of course preserved Rimbaud's resistance to organized religion intact, whereas Berrichon and Isabelle converted the invalid on his deathbed), there is one point on which they all converged. Verlaine, Isabelle, and Berrichon alike insisted that Rimbaud had never made any attempt whatsoever to sell his works. As Verlaine puts it in *Les Poètes maudits*, Rimbaud's work suffered during his lifetime from a "monstrous oblivion" because he never promoted his work *in any way* ("ne l'ayant pas 'lancée' *du tout*") (40, Verlaine's emphasis). Likewise, although scandalized by Verlaine, Isabelle, in her own imaginative biography, "was in complete agreement with the legend propagated by Verlaine confirming that her brother never had the idea of publishing his verses, nor did he seek to gain from them either recompense or celebrity."[26] The Rimbaud family and Verlaine both supported a vision of the young poet as commercial ignoramus, thoroughly innocent of any motive beyond that of revealing Truth (whether a savage or a spiritual one). At the end of the century, to be a demigod meant not being able to put a price on things, an implication Rimbaud himself would parody in "Solde" (Sale).

Ironically, Verlaine's *Poètes maudits* is now considered one of the earliest examples of what would become the major promotional genre of the late nineteenth century, the *portrait littéraire*. The *portrait littéraire* served a specific marketing function: a critic would introduce an audience to the author's life as a means of stimulating interest in his writings. According to Robert Jouanny, after 1870 the book market was reinvigorated by an abundance of these *portraits* and *comptes rendus* featuring the personality of the author rather than the attributes of the text. "A potential public existed," asserts Jouanny. "One merely had to find it and excite its curiosity." In order to excite this curiosity, writes Jouanny, authors resorted to "professional tricks" such as special editions, unusual formats, manifestoes, and, most often, *portraits littéraires*, "which disguised behind an apparent 'scorn for the vulgar' an evident desire to attract attention."[27]

Paradoxically, however, the transformation of the author into a *vedette* or profitable commodity was achieved precisely by denying the author's literary ambition. What publishers discovered, in other words, was that the romantic conception of the antisocial poet *sold*.

Not all literary critics of the late nineteenth century, however, were blind to the "charismatic ideology" governing literary production. Soon after Verlaine's treatment appeared, Ferdinand Brunetière delivered a withering critique of the romantic conception of Rimbaud, arguing that "there is no one that Rimbaud didn't solicit, between 1869 and 1871, to obtain publication. Able to mold himself to conform to all disciplines, all styles, he virtually wrote on command, delivering to each review, to each newspaper, whatever he thought might please."[28] In a somewhat more sympathetic vein, another would-be biographer, Georges Izambard, seconded Brunetière's assessment of the young poet's ambition. In his *Arthur Rimbaud à Douai et à Charleville*, of 1927, Izambard describes how Rimbaud, during a brief sojourn at Izambard's aunts' house, devoted his time entirely to recopying the verses he had written on the road: "He copies verses. . . . The slightest mistake makes him begin again, after first requesting large sheets of classroom paper. When one hand is blackened with ink, he comes to us and says: 'I have no more paper'—and he does this several times a day. We give him money [les quelques sous nécessaires] to get more. 'Write on the back,' suggests one of my aunts. Totally scandalized, he replies, 'For the printer you never write on the back.' As you can see, he clearly intended to get published [à se faire imprimer]."[29]

Obviously, the point here is not to determine the veracity of either Verlaine's version or Izambard's; of more interest is that Rimbaud's relation to publication became an important issue, one that would contribute substantially to the dynamics of his reception. Apparently, Verlaine and the Rimbaud family felt that writing to get published ("à se faire imprimer") sullied the venture itself. They found it more tolerable to have sheltered "un mystique à l'état sauvage" than to have abetted a literary *career*. Their attitude reflects an idea implicit in the nineteenth-century romantic discourse network, namely, that if the poet is to achieve social validation, he has to reject all ties to a commercial field. Given Rimbaud's second career as a sales representative, it must have seemed even more urgent to his admirers that the break between poetry (pronouncing a message) and commerce (packaging that message) be complete. By proclaiming the poet's innocence, even his savagery, critics could save his corpus from assuming a value *relative to other values*. In this way Rimbaud's poetry could remain for all time priceless, or, as the poet would write in "Solde," "sans prix."

Of course, desiring fame, or at least publication, is not quite the same as seeking economic remuneration. However, the pursuit of either one would require making concessions, if only partial, to a market over which the poet could have little control. Countering the dominant mode of Rimbaud criticism, Steve Murphy also has shown to what a great extent Rimbaud acknowledged the influence of the market both explicitly (in letters) and implicitly (in poems). According to Murphy, Rimbaud cleverly tailored the pieces he wrote between 1869 and 1870 to suit the journal to which he submitted them.[30] This practice indicates an acute understanding on Rimbaud's part of the conditions of the symbolic market of his period as well as a willingness to conform (often parodically) to them.

If we read Rimbaud's correspondance with sufficient care, we find that Rimbaud was obsessed with packaging from very early on. There could be nothing more transparent, for instance, than his attempt to promote himself *(se lancer)* in a letter to Théodore de Banville of 24 May 1870:

> Que si je vous envoie quelques-uns de ces vers,—et cela en passant par Alph. Lemerre, le bon éditeur,—c'est que j'aime tous les poëtes, tous les bons Parnassiens,—puisque le poëte est un Parnassien,—épris de la beauté idéale.

> If I send you some of these verses—and this thanks to Alph. Lemerre, that good publisher—it is because I love all poets, all good Parnassians—since the poet is a Parnassian—entranced with ideal beauty.[31]

Entranced with ideal beauty or not, Rimbaud still demands that Banville "make a bit of room for 'Credo in unam' among the Parnassians."[32] And references to publication are by no means confined to his professional correspondence. In his early letters to friends, Rimbaud's favorite subject—aside from the severities of his mother and his own boredom— is his work, his work *as work*, that is, as a quantity of effort and time expended in the pursuit of a particular project. In a letter of May 1873 to Ernest Delahaye, for instance, Rimbaud writes: "Je travaille pourtant assez régulièrement; je fais de petites histoires en prose, titre général: Livre païen ou Livre nègre" [Yet I work fairly steadily; I am writing little stories in prose, entitled: Pagan Book, or Negro Book].[33] Moreover, Rimbaud often asks Delahaye for books or for catalogs of books. As would most aspiring poets exiled from the cultural center of Paris, Rimbaud struggles to keep abreast of new publications in his field. That is, he clearly demonstrates in his letters a *professional* interest in poetic writing.

In brief, one of Rimbaud's most obsessive epistolary preoccupations is the publication of his work. Even in his later letters to Verlaine he demands to know the whereabouts of manuscripts, he suggests methods for passing them from one hand to another, and he comments on their state of completion or incompletion. Rimbaud's correspondence with Verlaine combines affectionate bantering with the exchange of news pertaining to their shared profession. "Je suis ton *old cunt open* or *opened*, je n'ai pas là mes verbes irréguliers [!]" [I am your *old cunt open* or *opened*, I haven't quite got my irregular verbs (!)], writes Verlaine, then: "Reçu lettre de Lepelletier (affaires); il se charge des ROMANCES,—Claye et Lechevallier. Demain, je lui enverrai manusse" [Received letter from Lepelletier (business); he's looking into the ROMANCES—Claye and Lechevallier. Tomorrow, I'll send him the manuscript] (Verlaine to Rimbaud, May 1873, *OC*, Verlaine's emphasis). Verlaine's manuscripts in particular are referred to with a surprising persistence, leading one to suspect that Verlaine's career as a poet was often a subject of their conversation (i.e., they spoke frequently about the *Romances* as well as their own romance). Indeed, letters exchanged after their breakup in London concern the location of certain manuscripts as much as they do the terms of an eventual reunion. Rimbaud often reveals the marketing savvy of a veteran poet, as in a letter written to Ernest Delahaye in May 1873:

> Verlaine doit t'avoir donné la malheureuse commission de parlementer avec le sieur Devin, imprimeur du *Nôress*. Je crois que ce Devin pourrait faire le livre de Verlaine à assez bon compte et presque proprement. (S'il n'emploie pas les caractères emmerdés du *Nôress*. Il serait capable d'en coller un cliché, une annonce!)

> Verlaine must have given you the wretched commission of negotiating with Lord Devin, the printer of the *Nôress*. I believe this Devin could put out Verlaine's book at a good rate and almost as it should be. (If he doesn't use the shitty characters of the *Nôress*. He could stick on an illustration, or an ad!)[34]

Rimbaud's early correspondence is convincing testimony both to his grasp of the means by which symbolic objects are promoted ("Il serait capable d'en coller un cliché, une annonce!") and to his desire to use these means to commercial ends (*se lancer*). One wonders, then, what would have led literary critics of the next generation to suppress any mention of Rimbaud's aggressive approach to the literary métier. Why would Rolland de Renéville and Jules Mouquet, who edited the Pléiade edition of Rimbaud's complete works in 1954, begin their introduction with the familiar portrait of the poet as one who "abandoned" his "slender but fulgurating corpus . . . without trying to publish any of it" (*OC*, x)? And why would a critic as subtle and theoretically informed as Kristin Ross state that Rimbaud "categorically refuses the choice of *métier*"?[35] Perhaps these critics have been impressed by the story of Rimbaud's dramatic auto-da-fé, in which, as Isabelle Rimbaud would have it, the poet burned the unsold copies of *Une Saison en enfer*. It nevertheless seems surprising that despite all epistolary proof to the contrary critics would repeatedly insist upon Rimbaud's professional insouciance, his disregard for all the dirty little details of marketing. The most striking example of such critical mystification is surely provided by Jacques Rivière himself, who writes in an essay published in the same issue as the letter to Delahaye cited above that Rimbaud was utterly disinterested in literature as a means of gaining symbolic and economic capital. "Writing was never anything more to him [than] a way of unburdening his soul," states Rivière a few pages before the Delahaye letter appears. "Compared with this formidable desire, what sense could literature have for him? As soon as *A Season in Hell* was published, he destroyed it, just as one might throw away an instrument that no longer served."[36]

Thus, although Rivière is one of Rimbaud's most insightful critics, he nevertheless fails to consider a significant aspect of the latter's poetic production, namely, the degree to which a highly developed market awareness may, in his case, have *stimulated* rather than discouraged greater differentiation. For Rivière, the poet's pursuit of the unknown is by definition a lonely, autonomous pursuit, the unknown being an absolute rather than a relational and thus exchangeable entity. It does not occur to Rivière that there might be "trafficking in the unknown," to quote an expression Rimbaud himself invents in a letter of 4 May 1881 when referring to the economic exploitation of uncharted territories. "La récolte du café aura lieu dans six mois," he explains in a letter from Harar. "Pour moi, je compte quitter prochainement cette ville-ci pour aller *trafiquer dans l'inconnu*" [The coffee harvest will take place in six months. . . . For my part, I intend to leave this city in the near future to go *trafficking in the unknown*] (OC, 340, emphasis added). It is difficult to resist the analogy Rimbaud's diction tacitly establishes between exploring the conceptual unknown and returning with images to sell (poetry) and exploring the geographical unknown and returning with goods to sell (commerce). Even in the famous 15 May 1871 "Lettre du voyant" to Paul Demeny Rimbaud suggests that the unknown, like any other distributable product of commerce, is a quantifiable commodity, precious, most likely, because it is the object of desire of many other poets as well. "Le poète définirait la quantité d'inconnu s'éveillant en son temps dans l'âme universelle," writes Rimbaud. "Enormité devenant norme, absorbée par tous, il serait vraiment *un multiplicateur de progrès*!" [The poet would define the quantity of unknown awakening in his time in the universal soul. Enormity transformed into norm, absorbed by all, the poet would surely be a *multiplier of progress*!] (OC, 271–72, Rimbaud's emphasis).

By introducing the unknown as a quantity and not a quality Rimbaud already produces a false ring. Intertwining a traditional romantic discourse of discovery ("inconnu," "éveiller," "âme universelle") with a contemporary discourse on capitalist expansion ("quantité," "multiplicateur," "progrès"), Rimbaud anticipates his later enigmatic reference to "trafficking in the unknown" as well as the complex ironies of "Solde." The redundancy of Rimbaud's lexicon can only draw poetry and trade into implicit comparison. This comparison works to destabilize the authenticity of the unknown—after all, the geographic unknown is only unknown to a European—while highlighting the heteronomous motivations determining literary as well as commercial "traffic." But Rimbaud's perhaps accidental pun is not the only clue to his radical insight. Rimbaud's correspondence indicates time and again that in contrast to his early critics, he indeed seizes the essential hybridity of the poetic enterprise, the manner in which heteronomy and autonomy, enterprise and impulse, are imbricated in the creative design. The poet may be a "voyant," as Rimbaud says in the "Lettre du voyant," but he still must *se faire voyant*, make himself a seer according to a process at once calculated ("raisonné"), full of risks ("Qu'il crève dans son bondissement"), and, last but not least, requiring funds (*OC*, 270–71).

Consider, for instance, the manner in which Rimbaud interrupts the ecstatic exclamations of his letter to Demeny to refer to the penury that prevents him from disseminating his verse:

> Voilà. Et remarquez bien que, si je ne craignais de vous faire débourser plus de 60 c. de port,—moi pauvre effaré qui, depuis sept mois, n'ai pas tenu un seul rond de bronze!—je vous livrerais encore mes "Amants de Paris", cent hexamètres, Monsieur, et ma "Mort de Paris", deux cent hexamètres!—
>
> Je reprends:
> Donc le poëte est vraiment voleur de feu.

> There. And take note that were I not afraid of making you put out more than 60 centimes in postage—poor timid me who for seven months hasn't had a brass farthing!—I would also send you more of my "Lovers of Paris," one hundred hexameters, Sir, and my "Dead Man of Paris," two hundred hexameters!—
>
> I recommence:
> Therefore the poet is truly the thief of fire.[37]

Critics seldom, if ever, quote this particular passage of the "Lettre du voyant," although the lines immediately preceding and following it have been the object of almost obsessive interest.[38] At the very least one might have expected some analysis of Rimbaud's "Je reprends," an expression vaguely evocative of the classroom but conjuring forth even more vividly the rehearsal on stage. As Anne-Emmanuelle Berger has noted, references to theatrical staging are scattered throughout the "Lettre du voyant."[39] Rimbaud takes an intermission in the middle of the letter, "La suite à six minutes" [To be continued in six minutes], and the first poem he sends to

Demeny, "Mes Petites Amoureuses," is presented as a musical overture: "J'ai l'archet en main, je commence" [Bow in hand, I begin] (*OC*, 271). Recopied verses are presented with the fanfare of a performance, and his poetics ("Le Poëte se fait *voyant* par un long, immense et raisonné *dérèglement* de *tous les sens*" [The Poet makes himself a *seer* by a long, immense, and reasoned *derangement* of *all the senses*]) are delivered with all the panache of a superior student in complete control of his teacher's discourse (*OC*, 270, Rimbaud's emphasis). Demeny, the addressee of the letter, is a fellow fledgling poet; he shares with Rimbaud the same romantic-symbolist-Parnassian inheritance and is thus capable of appreciating Rimbaud's added flourishes. Rimbaud's tone is a mixture of the earnest prophetic and the exaggerated oratorical; he performs his poetics before an audience he knows will recognize this performance as simultaneously serious and in jest. The aside concerning his financial condition is therefore essential rather than accidental to the poetics proposed. For Rimbaud, poems may be "stolen fire," but they also weigh (and cost) a certain amount per hexameter. True, Rimbaud is not confessing any mercenary motives in this letter; he does not say that he will shape and package his poems so that they might interest a larger public. In the "Lettre du voyant" Rimbaud is merely concerned with sharing his enthusiasm while recognizing the cost of its transmission. And yet even in this early forum he displays the two attributes that will virtually define his poetic success: an ability to master dominant poetic rhetorics and a tendency to reformulate them ironically by referring to the material conditions of their utterance and distribution. True to form, Rimbaud proves himself capable of parabasis ("Je reprends") in the midst of hyperbole ("le poëte est vraiment voleur de feu").

The tonal hybridity exhibited in this letter is characteristic of Rimbaud's work in general. Poetry is always, for him, both a quality and a quantity, a "chant pieux" [pious chant] (*OC*, 273) and an object to be weighed, counted, recopied, packaged, and sold. Rimbaud does not need to read Baudelaire's "Conseils aux jeunes littérateurs" (Advice to young writers) to know that literature is, above all, "un remplissage de colonnes" [a filling of columns].[40] If we consider the circumstances of Rimbaud's poetic production in the 1870s, it becomes clear that the material conditions of creative labor would have weighed just as heavily on Rimbaud's shoulders as they had on Baudelaire's. Pierre Bourdieu and Robert Jouanny have both established that the decade of the 1870s was a period of dramatic change in French cultural life. In the years following the Commune increased literacy, a weakening of censorship laws, new technologies in printing, and the formation of new libraries combined to create an atmosphere conducive to the expansion of the literary field.[41] According to Bourdieu, the "relative opening up of the field of cultural production

due to the increased number of positions offering basic resources to producers" resulted in two interrelated phenomena: an immigration of
would-be poets from the provinces to the French capital and thus a more
centralized circulation of rapidly evolving poetic styles.[42] In other words,
the last quarter of the nineteenth century saw an unprecedented degree
of "trafficking in the unknown." Seen in the light of general trends governing the literary market of Rimbaud's time, his long walk from Charleville to Paris was probably not the aimless and subversive vagabondage
that Kristin Ross claims it to have been. On the contrary, the itinerary of
his *errance* seems to have retraced the calculated steps of a Rastignac or,
even more to the point, of a Théodore de Banville.[43]

Read in sequence, Rimbaud's continual references to the cost of mailing
and recopying, as well as his frequent allusions to the lures of Paris, begin
to paint a portrait of the young poet as parvenu, but a parvenu for whom
the lack of material resources posed a very vivid obstacle indeed. During
his early years Rimbaud was concerned primarily with acquiring the basic
rudiments—books, paper, stamps, influential friends—necessary for the
pursuit of a literary career. Put simply, Rimbaud lived in a world in which
capital (material resources) produced more capital (fame and eventually
remuneration). The distinct quality of his poetic language, I believe, reflects the depth of precisely this experience of the material, geographical,
and social underpinnings of symbolic success. The fresh quality of Rimbaud's verse can be attributed in part to his unique ability to mime but
also intensify received poetic discourses by tempering them with a commercial discourse fully lived and therefore lit from within.

———————

Rimbaud was not alone in attempting to define the precise nature of lyric's
relation to a rapidly evolving cultural market. Many poets of his period
thematized the market, allegorizing it through the figure of the clown, the
prostitute, or the histrion. Whereas poetries of circumstance never sought
to disguise their contingency, lyric poetry had historically claimed distinction on the basis of the autonomy of its form and content. Paradoxically,
however, almost at the very moment the subjective voice began to speak,
its alleged autonomy and purity were placed under suspicion. And it was
lyric poets, not literary critics, who raised the specter of heteronomous
determination; critics of the *NRF* would never have spoken as openly of
market conditions as lyric poets themselves did—even during the period
of high romanticism. Prefiguring the cynicism of Baudelaire, Alfred de
Musset suggested as early as 1830 that the motives of the confessional
enterprise might be less circumspect than they first appeared. For instance,
Musset's "Les Voeux stériles" [Sterile vows] begins by evoking the analo-

gies between poet and prostitute, confession and exhibitionism, that play
such a crucial role in symbolist poetics. (These analogies, of course, would
find no place in the dominant discourse on lyric poetry formulated in the
early years of the twentieth century.)

> Puisque c'est ton métier de faire de ton âme
> Une prostituée, et que, joie ou douleur
> Tout demande sans cesse à sortir de ton coeur;
> Que du moins l'histrion, couvert d'un masque infâme,
> N'aille pas, dégradant ta pensée avec lui,
> Sur d'ignobles tréteaux la mettre au pilori.

> Since it is your profession to make of your soul
> A prostitute, and since, joy or sadness,
> Everything flows incessantly out of your heart;
> At least the histrion, covered with an infamous mask,
> Should not degrade your thoughts,
> Exposing them to ridicule on the ignoble stage.[44]

Musset's cleverly placed enjambment between "ton âme" and "Une
prostituée" evokes the gap separating the soul from the market, subjectivity from commerce, a gap intended to ensure the reputation of lyric expression and simultaneously define its unique position within the cultural
field. The genius of Musset's strategy consists, however, in transforming
the admission of heteronomy—"L'artiste est un marchand, et l'art est un
métier" [The artist is a merchant, and art a métier] (86)—into a renewed
dedication to truth. By abdicating the stage, Musset seems to suggest, the
lyric monologue can find its raison d'être in the clear air of a higher truth:
"Que ta muse, brisant le luth des courtisanes, / Fasse vibrer sans peur l'air
de la liberté / Qu'elle marche pieds nus, comme la Vérité" [May your
muse, breaking the courtesans' lute, fearlessly sound the song of liberty,
May she walk with nude feet, like Truth] (85).

Three decades later, in 1862, Charles Marie Leconte de Lisle would
take the opportunity to retrace the boundary between poetry and métier
that Musset's verses had subtly begun to dismantle. In "Les Montreurs"
[Showmen], from *Poèmes barbares*, Leconte de Lisle refuses the role of
confessional poet paid by the rowdy mob so that he might freely express
his more intimate "wishes." Leconte de Lisle's departure from the stage
of the confessional histrion implies a disdain for the popular audience
romantic poets had previously sought to engage. The poet of art for art's
sake chooses silence over speech, self-effacement over histrionics, and
thereby avoids admitting any contingency whatsoever. Leconte de Lisle
begins his first tercet by refusing all concessions to his imagined reader
("tu"):

Dans mon orgueil muet, dans ma tombe sans gloire,
Dussé-je m'engloutir pour l'éternité noire,
Je ne te vendrai pas mon ivresse ou mon mal,

Je ne livrerai pas ma vie à tes huées,
Je ne danserai pas sur ton tréteau banal
Avec tes histrions et tes prostituées.

In my silent pride, in my tomb without glory,
Even swallowed up by black eternity
Still I would not sell you my rapture or my pain,

I will not deliver my life over to your heckling
I will not dance on your banal stage
With your histrions and your prostitutes.[45]

Proudly, the poet consigns himself to oblivion, resisting the temptation to perform "[s]on ivresse ou [s]on mal." Of course, the very existence of "Les Montreurs" belies the poet's declaration, for silence and oblivion are hardly the poem's own aspirations. In effect, the transcendence of contingency, the refusal of fame and remuneration, promises an even greater notoriety to the hermetic poet: an "éternité noire" that distinguishes him from the banal "histrion" and the compromised "prostituée."

Rimbaud's own relation to performance and, thus, to symbolic success should be analyzed in the context of a more general preoccupation with confessional theatrics he shares with other nineteenth-century poets. A student of Musset, Baudelaire, and Leconte de Lisle, Rimbaud is fully aware that the lyric gesture flirts dangerously with a vain search for effects. At times Rimbaud appears to be following Leconte de Lisle's precedent, as when he refuses a "métier" in "Mauvais Sang" [Bad blood]: "J'ai horreur de tous les métiers" (OC, 220). Elsewhere, however, his poems echo the ironies of "Les Voeux stériles," in which a rejection of the seductive muse ("le luth des courtisanes") leads him to an even greater exhibitionism ("Qu'elle marche pieds *nus* . . ."). Rimbaud's oeuvre is full of poems that satirize even while indulging in the confessional gesture. As in "Le Coeur volé" [The stolen heart], also titled "Le Coeur du pitre" [The clown's heart], the intimate anecdote recounted by the poet reveals itself on closer inspection to be a metacritique of confessional language as allegorical exercise. Confession is recast as a young poet's rite of passage, one that serves to demonstrate, paradoxically, his mastery of the "métier" of confession. There is no poetic utterance, Rimbaud seems to imply, that does not demand attention, that does not strive to be noticed. In this connection it is worth considering Steve Murphy's claim that Rimbaud's "se faire voyant" refers not only to a desire to *see* (in the strong sense of the word) but also to a desire to *be seen*. "The grammatical status of the word *seer*," notes Murphy, "is undecidable. If one takes this word to be an adjective, and not simply a substantive, then the entire logic of the passage shifts. The poet would be *voyant* in the same way one might qualify a color as *voyante*, as attracting attention."[46] *Se faire voyant*, in other words, can be read as synonymous with *se faire remarquer* [to get oneself noticed] or *se faire imprimer*. Confession is not only a means to self-knowledge but also a requirement of symbolic success.

Irony and double entendre do not, however, constitute Rimbaud's only—or even his most original—responses to the market and its influence on poetic composition. Nor are the "pitre" and "comédien" as they appear in his verse merely figures for loss or capitulation. In the fully evolved poetics of *Illuminations* Rimbaud comes to recognize the mutual interdependence of poetic "progrès" and market competition, the fundamentally dialectical structure of aesthetic practice that transforms heteronomy into an impetus for technical invention. As if to mark a break with the poetic solutions proposed by Leconte de Lisle and Musset, Rimbaud enters into dialogue with his contemporary Charles Cros, whose 1879 preface to *Le Coffret de santal* [The sandalwood case] refers directly to the poet's implication in market exchange. Here the speaker of the poem not only sells his poetic wares but, further, uses the money he earns to buy fresh ones, "de fraîches roses." Thus, after inventorying the bric-à-brac of a poet's traditional stock of figures—"Bibelots," "Fleurs mortes," "Bijoux," "chiffons," and so on—Cros exclaims:

> Quel encombrement dans ce coffre!
> Je vends tout. Accepte mon offre,
> Lecteur. Peut-être quelque émoi,
>
> Pleurs ou rire, à ces vieilles choses
> Te prendra. Tu paieras, et moi
> J'achèterai de fraîches roses.
>
> What a jumble in this case!
> I sell it all. Accept my offer,
> Reader. Perhaps some sentiment,
>
> Laughter or tears, towards these old things
> Will move you. You will pay, and as for me,
> I'll go buy fresh roses.[47]

It would seem at first glance that the poet is merely reestablishing the same relation between lyric poetry and exhibitionism, exposing and selling, as that maintained in earlier poems by Leconte de Lisle and Musset. As the poem progresses, however, the degradation of production is acknowledged by the poet and reinvented as resource. That is, buying and selling, pleasing and performing, are treated metaphorically as elements of a necessary and creative exchange ("vieilles choses" can, after all, be traded for "fraîches roses"). The ambiguity of Cros's last verse suggests that the economic renumeration the poet receives affords him both practical assistance (he can now acquire the bare necessities of the craft) and rhetorical assistance (inspiration or "fraîches roses"). To buy ("j'achèterai") represents here a transformative, even a creative act through which the poet manipulates a competitive market in such a way that it provides him with the basic materials he requires.

Rimbaud's "Solde" can be fruitfully reread through the lens provided by Cros's preface. In "Solde" what is important, finally, is not that the poet sells his "illuminations"—"Les Voix reconstituées" [Revived voices], "les corps sans prix" [priceless bodies], and so on—but that "Les vendeurs ne sont pas à bout de solde!" [Salesmen have not reached the end of their stock!] (*OC*, 208). As Rimbaud exultantly tells us, the poet always has more to sell because having to sell is itself a state that—in the best of circumstances—can stimulate the production of new verse. In Rimbaud's poetry, writes Maurice Blanchot, "the degradation that makes being into an inert and produced thing . . . must be borne, taken on by the poet . . . poetry, drawing from this essential weakness, gives itself the task of transforming lack into resource."[48] The portrait Rimbaud paints for us in "Solde" is thus a portrait of an exchange system that is infinitely iterative rather than saturated and self-enclosed. The market offers the poet ever more opportunities to refill his inspirational "coffre" with a crowd of flowers or tropes ["une foule des jeunes et fortes roses"] ("Fleurs," *OC*, 195).

One of the sharpest ironies of literary history is that a poet centrally concerned with the material conditions of the literary occupation should have become the idol of critics devoted to saving poetry from the taint of the commercial. The problem with appraisals such as those offered by Rivière, Verlaine, Monnerot, and even Ross (aside from the fact that they involve the projection of some dubious cultural fantasies) is that they deny the agency of market pressures, obscure the potentially constructive role of competition, and prevent readers from seizing in Rimbaud the complex play of capitulation and resistance that renders his work such a fascinating illustration of cultural dynamics.

The critical discourse on poetry exemplified in particular by the early essays in the *NRF* is one that still holds sway today, informing a large body of work on French poetry despite the interventions of formalist, structuralist, and poststructuralist paradigms. Clearly, approaches to

French poetry have greatly evolved since 1914; yet, strangely, Rimbaud's texts have remained for the most part beyond the purview of the radically revised critical apparatus developed in France and America since the cold war.[49] To be sure, the strain of criticism associated with Paul Valéry, one that presents poetic writing as governed by the application of technique and the rhythms of revision, bore its fruits in the 1960s as critics focused increasingly on "devices" of defamiliarization productive of poetic effects (rather than metaphysical truths). Still, such a change in orientation does not seem to have radically altered Rimbaud's place in the literary pantheon. In 1978, for instance, Shoshana Felman noted the presence of a commercial subtext in Rimbaud's work but added firmly that "this inflationist economy of the new is of course alien to Rimbaud's spirit."[50] And for Berger, writing in 1992, Rimbaud demonstrates that poetry subsists "sans support marchand" [without market support], owing nothing "to progress in printing and modes of communication favored by [industrial] development."[51] Berger's conclusion, which echoes Rivière's, does not permit us to consider how the capitalist market and the advanced technologies it introduces might in fact inform the evolution of poetic technique.

Lest a misunderstanding arise, I should make clear at this point that I do not believe Rimbaud's poetry to be entirely deducible from the conditions of the literary market of his time. And yet, as Michael Baxandall has cogently argued with respect to cubist painters and their milieu, all artists develop their work within a "circumstantial frame" that offers an array of resources to be exploited and obstacles to be surmounted.[52] This frame constitutes, in Baxandall's terminology, the artist's "Brief," a set of challenges facing the artist that are grounded in "local conditions" (30), "cultural circumstances" that precede the artist's appearance on the scene (47). As poems by Cros, Leconte de Lisle, and Musset indicate, one of the foremost tasks composing the poet's "Brief" in the mid to late nineteenth century was to define the lyric's relation to more overtly commercial, or "prostituted," cultural forms. Another task had to do with maintaining individuality within a broadened literary market that tended to fracture into submarkets or cliques (such as the Parnassians or the Zutistes). The market is only one of the many circumstances by which poetic production is framed, but it is a circumstance that can exact innovations in diction, figural mode, and form, areas that are traditionally conceived as independent, evolving autonomously within their own sphere, and mediated primarily by individual interests or skills. Baxandall's comments on the role of the market in the painter's world can illuminate Rimbaud's predicament as well: "The [poet] registers his individuality very much by his particular perception of the circumstance he must address. Indeed, if one is to think of a [poet] 'expressing himself,' it is most of all here, in the analysis of his environment which schematically speaking . . . precedes the process of [writing] itself, that one can most securely locate an individuality" (46–47).

Clearly, Rimbaud never "sold out" to market pressures, to a particular audience's passion for confessional rhetoric. Further, the late, bitterly ironic poems of *Illuminations* suggest that he fully seized the menace that a capitalist literary market might present for poetic expression. Rimbaud may indeed have demystified the cult of aesthetic autonomy operating during his generation, but this demystification did not lead him—nor should it lead us—to demonize in turn the forces of reification a competitive market imposes on creativity and individuation. In the best of scenarios the standardizing tendencies of the market can stimulate a particularly violent resistance, one to which we might owe, in Rimbaud's case, the birth of an irreducibly distinct voice.

Finally, it should be recalled that the relationship between poets and their circumstances is never a one-way street; rather, it is reciprocal and evolving. Rimbaud's interventions in the poetic field of production irreversibly altered that field, just as his generic and rhetorical innovations transformed the lyric genre, whose altered problematic his successors then had to address. Again, Baxandall's words are suggestive: "the [poet's] complex problem of good [poetry writing] becomes a serial and continually self-redefining operation" (73). In a sense, Rimbaud made the problem of the artist's relation to circumstances, the "continually self-redefining operation" of literary individuation, one of the central themes of his own work.

In conclusion, I would maintain that modern French poetry criticism has failed to provide tools with which to identify and analyze the influence of market pressures on poetic composition. Since these pressures have conventionally been considered uniformly negative, any admission that they might indeed exert an influence has been seen as denigrating poetry itself. But a distinction needs to be made between works that listen only to the voice of commerce and works that attempt to harmonize this voice with the complex melodies of individual expression. Rimbaud's poetry persuades us to take another look at how market pressures engage dialectically with other exigencies of compositional practice. But before we can begin to theorize this dialectical process we need to obtain a better view of what the market itself may have looked like to a nineteenth-century poet such as Rimbaud. As a number of cultural historians have documented, by the end of the nineteenth century the conventional cultural market had been flooded with new forms of literary and visual entertainment made possible through the development of increasingly sophisticated technological means.[53] Poets no longer competed only with other poets or with other purely literary forms. Available forms of culture suddenly included the *roman feuilleton*, the diorama, the panorama, and, most important for our purposes, the protocinematic theatrical spectacle known as the *féerie*. If critics (and many poets too) regarded these market-generated, popular forms with unalloyed contempt, there were others who looked with no little fascination upon the spectacle of a literature—or, more broadly, a culture—entirely responsive to only one type of demand. That is, if it was true for Baudelaire that "badly applied technological advances brought about by photography greatly contributed, like all purely material forms of progress, to the impoverishment of the French artistic genius," it does not follow that all authors of the period saw the rise of reproductive technologies in quite the same way.[54] Photographic, dramatic, and incipient film technologies did not at that time, nor do they today, presage for all high-cultural producers a weakening or "impoverishment" of traditional aesthetic forms. The "denunciation of 'industrial literature' " so frequently heard from the mouths of aesthetes has obscured the fact that, in Bourdieu's words, "while the [commercial] field is a source of constraints, *it is also liberating*, inasmuch as it enables new categories of producers to subsist without constraints other than those of the market."[55] More recent histories of modern culture have provided numerous examples of the ways in which the capitalist market, and the impulse toward diversification inherent within it, have contributed significantly to the creation of new types of poetry and to the consolidation of new audiences capable of enjoying the verbal arts.[56]

Perhaps Rimbaud, scornful of Izambard's "poésie subjective," instinctively seized the liberating as well as the detrimental aspects of economic determination, although of course he did not succumb to this determination alone. Rimbaud was obviously fascinated by more commercial as well as by more popular or folk-based forms. In his poetry he makes frequent references to vaudeville and popular theater, the two "up and coming" genres Bourdieu situates at the antipodes of poetry in his graphic rendering of nineteenth-century literary production.[57] Such references indicate that fully heteronomous forms operated a seduction on Rimbaud's thought; in his effort to find the key or method to the unknown, Rimbaud may very well have envied the freedoms enjoyed by more commercial forms. These forms were indeed constrained by the pressures of an audience in search of a specific type of thrill. But precisely because they labored under these constraints, early avatars of the cinema such as vaudeville, the *opéra-comique*, and the *féerie* were the breeding ground of technological innovations that, as I argue in the next chapter, took hold of the poet's imagination, offering a different variety of inspiration from that provided by Hugo, Baudelaire, Gautier, and Musset.

Two

A Poetry of Attractions: Rimbaud's Machine and the Theatrical *Féerie*

ALTHOUGH reviewers for the *NRF* set the tone for poetry criticism for decades to come, a strong revisionist reading of Rimbaud did appear soon after the inaugural issue of the *NRF* was published in 1909. This reading was articulated by the artists of cubism, *simultanéisme*, constructivism, and other allied movements of the avant-garde. Departing radically from the preoccupations of the *NRF*, the avant-garde discourse emphasized not the spontaneity of Rimbaud's writing but rather the degree to which it depended upon a technique or rational method. This second critical discourse, which eventually provided the impetus for neo-Marxist critical paradigms, lacked rigorous development and wide academic acceptance up until at least the mid twentieth century. In the meantime, avant-garde and neoromantic discourses coexisted uncomfortably within poetry criticism until World War II (although the latter enjoyed dominance both within the academy and in the most widely distributed literary reviews). Not until the publication of Jacques Gengoux's *Le Symbolique de Rimbaud: Le Système des sources* in 1947 did a Rimbaud fully in command of an evolving method finally appear in critical discourse.[1] A long hiatus would then separate Gengoux's work from Theodor Adorno's "George-Hofmannsthal Correspondance," of 1967, in which Rimbaud is described as the poet who "delivers the poem over to technique."[2] Adorno's estimation of Rimbaud was eventually elaborated on by Antoine Raybaud in his *Fabrique d' "Illuminations,"* of 1989, the definitive critical rendering of Rimbaud as an "engineer, inventor of (poetic) objects."[3]

Confronting each other in the early battles concerning Rimbaud's reception were two opposed philosophies of language, or what Friedrich A. Kittler has suggestively named two distinct and incommensurable "discourse networks."[4] Rimbaud entered the field of European culture just as one discourse network, represented by critics whose tastes and generic expectations were formed by nineteenth-century romanticism, was giving way to the second network, one disseminated not by critics but by the emerging experimental avant-gardes of Italy, Russia, and France. Rimbaud appeared at the cusp, so to speak, of these two discourse networks, and perhaps for this reason he became such a rich site of myth. Whereas the discourse network of 1800 was underwritten by phonologists and romantic philosophers, who associated poetry with "natural" maternal rhythms, the discourse network of 1900 received its legitimacy through the research of psycho-physiologists, who were rapidly discovering the enculturated, arbitrary and differential (graphic) rather than organic and motivated (phonic) structure of human speech patterns. Kittler spells out in clear terms the dangers the avant-garde discourse network held out for received romantic conceptions of poetry: "When the alphabetization-made-flesh gave way to technological media [at the turn of the century] . . . Poetry also disintegrated" (178); what the avant-garde discovered was that "the ersatz sensuality of Poetry could be replaced, not by Nature, but by technologies" (245–46). Apollinaire said as much in "L'Esprit nouveau et les poètes" when he urged poets to surround the human voice with the cacophony of modern machinery, confident that the new harmonies of the modern world would produce an equivalent if not more intense aesthetic effect.

Thus, when Apollinaire presented Rimbaud in this same text as the "first" poet of "l'esprit nouveau"—the first poet of the new discourse network—he placed all subsequent experimentation, from the functionalism of the constructivists to the montage practices of Cendrars, under the aegis of a rather different Rimbaud from that championed by Rivière and the NRF.[5] One would be hard-pressed to reconcile Rivière's Rimbaud of primal innocence with either the Rimbaud of Fernand Léger (for whom Rimbaud's work "contains the cinema of the future")[6] or the Rimbaud of Cendrars (for whom Rimbaud's work anticipates the spirit of modern advertising). If Rimbaud represented for these members of the avant-garde the "first" poet of *l'esprit nouveau*, it was not because he had left poetry behind or initially sought a pagan language but because he had approached poetry as a kind of linguistic manufacturing. This is not to say that Apollinaire and Cendrars rejected the type of lyric *élan* traditionally associated with Rimbaud. On the contrary, they linked this *élan* to the dynamism of the machine, thereby establishing a continuity between the physiological energy fracturing syntax and establishing rhythmic patterns and the physical energy propelling the machines of the modern world.[7]

L'esprit nouveau is a term Apollinaire adopted in 1917 to form a conceptual umbrella under which he hoped to reunite the splintering postwar avant-garde. According to Apollinaire, poets of *l'esprit nouveau* were those who instinctively seized the continuity between the lyric *élan* and the energy of modernity; these poets were attempting to bring this continuity to the reader's attention by means of rhythmic, thematic, and figural innovations. Apollinaire expected that in the future poets of *l'esprit nouveau* would place advanced reproductive technologies, such as radio transmission, the phonograph, and the film camera, at the service of lyric creation. The technological "marvels" of modernity, Apollinaire stated in

1917, imposed on poets the "task" of keeping the "subtle poetic imagination" up to date; poets could not allow themselves to fall behind engineers
(des artisans), who, for their part, were constantly ameliorating and upgrading their machines.[8]

Apollinaire's lecture of 1917 openly contradicted the mood of nihilism
dominating wartime and postwar art movements. His positive attitude
toward the rising industries of mass culture (as well as his strident nation-
alism and his rather embarrassing "rappel à l'ordre") caused him to lose
much of the respect he had previously enjoyed. Younger writers, students
of dada and Reverdy, were disappointed by the futurist orientation of
Apollinaire's ideas. While the surrealists were busy defending poetry
against the onslaught of industrialized culture, Apollinaire was insisting
that poetry could only regain its status as prophetic oracle if poets con-
sented to submit their medium to a kind of technical upgrade and "machiner la poésie comme on a machiné le monde" [mechanize poetry the
way they've mechanized the world].[9]

The surrealists, then, would not be the ones to celebrate the increased
mechanization of the lyric voice Apollinaire had associated with Rimbaud. Apollinaire's vision did, however, exert an influence on another
aesthetic discourse, one that was alien to that of modern poetry criticism.
The image of Rimbaud (and indeed of the poet in general) as "the complement of the natural scientist"[10] emerged in the 1920s in a place where
even Etiemble would not have thought to look for it, namely, in the pages
of Le Corbusier's purist journal entitled, appropriately, *L'Esprit nouveau*.
It is crucial to an understanding of European modernism to register Le
Corbusier's reception of Rimbaud, for it constitutes an important
exception to the rule governing the destiny of Rimbaud's works (as well
as the destiny of modern poetry in general). Whereas literary critics almost
invariably allied Rimbaud with the modernism of the fragment, the
occult, and the unconscious (in brief, with romantic modernism), purist
aestheticians identified Rimbaud with the opposed modernism of the machine aesthetic, Bauhaus, and the functionalism of Le Corbusier.

In the statement of purpose included in the first issue of *L'Esprit nouveau* the editors, Paul Dermée, Amédée Ozenfant, and Charles-Edouard
Jeanneret (Le Corbusier), openly reaffirmed the continuity between Rimbaud's poetic experiments and the "esthétique mécanique" they intended
to champion.[11] Yoking together the names of Rimbaud and Mallarmé
perhaps for the first time, the editors proceeded to lay out an industrial
aesthetic they believed to be entirely consonant with the experimental
ethos of these two late-nineteenth-century writers. If it seems somewhat
odd that Rimbaud was called on to underwrite the purists' celebration of
industrial design, it should be remembered that precisely during this period the conceptual barriers separating the spontaneous from the mechan-

ical, the aesthetic from the industrial, were in the process of eroding. Psychological theories revealing the mechanical element of the irrational (the supposed seat of creativity) were permeating the domain of aesthetics, revising the traditional opposition between independent aesthetic taste and instinctual motor reflex. *L'Esprit nouveau* inaugurated its first two issues by running an article by the academic aesthetician Victor Basch, who was attempting to impose the new science of sensation on traditional Kantian aesthetic theory. In "Esthétique nouvelle et une science de l'art" Basch argues that if there is indeed a universal recognition of the beautiful, then the aesthetician must determine its biological and neurological bases: "If Aesthetics intends to become a science, it will have to replace subjective impressions with objective, verifiable, and measurable principles *[notions]*."[12]

The efforts of academics such as Basch, as well as the works of the psycho-physiologists Pierre Janet, Jean-Marie Charcot, Théodule Ribot, and Henri Bergson, left a strong imprint on the purists' theory of aesthetic creation.[13] All areas of artistic activity had to be rethought in terms of recent discoveries in psycho-physiology. Paul Dermée, the purists' in-house poet and literary critic, was given the task of expounding a theory of the lyric that would take the physiological basis of aesthetics into account. In "Découverte du Lyrisme," an article printed in the first issue of *L'Esprit nouveau*, Dermée strove to achieve the necessary reconciliation between lyric spontaneity and a purist aesthetics of physical laws. For Dermée, the "lesson" of Rimbaud's poetry in particular was identical to that taught by Bergson, Janet, and Ribot, namely, that the sensory apparatus (the source of "lyrisme") could be considered a mechanism as well as a muse, an intricate system of calculable responses as well as a seat of fluctuating impulses. But Dermée emphasized that the motor of lyricism had to dictate its own laws; it could not be subordinated to the intelligence, which derives images and meters from artificial rather than organic patterns of stimuli and response. According to Dermée, the "flux lyrique" is tied to the very rhythms of biological life; attention to this fluctuating but rhythmic "song" would yield the true lyric of the self, or *moi intérieur.*[14]

Implicitly, Dermée was arguing that the "spirit of construction" promoted by purist artists and engineers had to obtain its principles from a source more profound than the intelligence. The roots of an "esthétique mécanique" were located in a layer of experience underlying (and sometimes veiled by) cerebral ruminations. Thus, if the "spirit of construction" was "as necessary to create a painting or poem as it was to build a bridge," as the editors of *L'Esprit nouveau* asserted, it was only because paintings, poems, and bridges found their appropriate constructive principles in a set of profound psychic laws uncovered by experimental psychology and, for some purists, through research in the physical sciences.[15] This was the "lesson" the editors of *L'Esprit nouveau* attributed to Rimbaud and Mallarmé: these poets did not impose technique from without but derived procedures from the very apparatus generating and coordinating the energies of expression.[16]

The purist's vision of Rimbaud as the originator of an "esthétique mécanique" does not seem to have inspired any revisionist readings of the poet's work. Similarly, Apollinaire's presentation of Rimbaud as engineer would soon be eclipsed in the decades that followed, first by a surrealist poetics of the unconscious, then by neoromantic theories of poetic production promulgated by Resistance ideology. However, while the question of Rimbaud's technique preoccupied few literary critics of the twenties, the peculiarities of Mallarmé's method were emerging as a subject of almost obsessive interest. Contrasted repeatedly with Rimbaud, Mallarmé emerged as the poetic technician par excellence, the modern poet who had most successfully mechanized ("machiné") the lyric "I" by "ceding the initiative" to that other apparatus, words ("les mots").[17] It is to the credit of the editors of *L'Esprit nouveau* that they avoided the opposition between Rimbaud and Mallarmé so favored by literary critics of the same generation.[18] The purists provided the impetus for a new history of lyric poetry when they placed the names of Mallarmé and Rimbaud side by side on the masthead of their promotional journal for constructivist principles.

Adorno offered further grounds for this revisionist literary history when he published his *Aesthetic Theory* in 1970. Until that point, few critics since the purists had identified Rimbaud with Mallarmé on the basis of their shared interest in constructive principles and sophisticated verbal technique. Yet, in *Aesthetic Theory* it is Rimbaud's poetry and not Mallarmé's that stands as the exemplary instance of poetic modernity. Rimbaud owes his privileged place in Adorno's corpus to the fact that he not only derives the intimacies of the lyric from the complexities of technique but also explicitly relates these techniques to the productive conditions in which they were forged. Adorno's reading of Rimbaud differs from that of the purists, although he extends their understanding of the technical component of lyricism in significant ways. For Adorno, Rimbaud is the poet who not only seeks "la formule" of lyricism in the laws of the perceptual apparatus but also—and this nuance is crucial—intuitively grasps the degree to which this apparatus is historically mediated rather than transcendentally given. Adorno takes Marx's dictum that consciousness is a historical phenomenon to mean that the epistemologies and perceptual grids informing consciousness are immanent as well. The psychophysiologist's *moi intérieur* is thus not a constant from which universal and timeless laws can be deduced. Productive conditions influence both sensuous experience and the ways in which it is processed into cognitive forms.[19]

Rimbaud is Adorno's exemplary modern poet because he acknowledges the role played by productive conditions in the constitution of subjectivity. Rimbaud's art, Adorno contends, emanates from an "advanced [subjective] consciousness" inflected by industrial procedures "developed under the given relations of production" (*AT*, 33). This consciousness is "advanced," however, only insofar as it is self-reflexive, capable of seizing the ways in which it is itself penetrated by (reflective of) objective conditions. An art that does not acknowledge the extent to which advanced technologies "radiate into areas of life far removed from them, deep into the zones of subjective experience," can never achieve the required degree of self-consciousness (*AT*, 34). Such a non-self-reflexive art cannot measure technology's influence adequately, and thus it fails to create a viable cultural alternative to technological forms. Non-self-reflexive art is not, in Adorno's words, "equal" in sophistication to the "high industrialism" it abjures (*AT*, 33). This art remains to some extent mystified, ignorant of its own formal, rhetorical, and epistemological debts to conditions whose constitutive influence it can never completely evade.

Adorno distinguishes Rimbaud from Mallarmé (and implicitly from Valéry as well) on the grounds that the latter buries the historical conditions that inform his work, whereas the former highlights these conditions, recuperating them as a thematic and formal resource. According to Adorno, Mallarmé acknowledges advanced industrialization only negatively, that is, by resisting the onslaught of alternative forms of production and transmission in an attempt to derive all utterances from the potentialities of print culture. Mallarmé aims to accomplish precisely what Apollinaire proscribes: he wishes to "shelter himself from his surroundings" [se cantonner de ce qui l'entoure]. He therefore becomes haunted, according to one critic, by the fear of "possession by an utterance not [his] own," experiencing the anxiety of "*involuntary re/citation.*"[20] In contrast, Rimbaud discerns within the very technologies threatening poetry's cultural dominance a means of challenging reified notions of the lyric subject and the sovereignty of printed forms. That is, he seeks out the "utterance not [his] own" in an effort to relocate a latent aspect of the subject congealed in alienated objectifications. To the extent that Rimbaud denies the transcendence Mallarmé desires, he achieves Adorno's ideal of the modern, demystified, self-reflexive poet. However, to the extent that he embraces technologically generated popular forms and celebrates the demise of the unified lyric subject he goes beyond Adorno's ideal of the melancholic confessional poet and prefigures the futurists and constructivists, whose solutions to the crisis of modernity Adorno ultimately rejects. But the very features of Rimbaud's *esprit nouveau* that Adorno finds objectionable are those that would win him admirers among members of the twentieth-century European—and later, American—avant-garde. Poets from Blaise Cendrars to Patti Smith would come to identify Rimbaud with a more "bipolar" approach to modernity than that advocated by Mallarmé. For them, Rimbaud suggested ways of crossing not only semantic fields but also cultural spheres; he prophesied the end of poetry's isolation, imaginatively projecting it across the Great Divide separating the sophisticated rhetorical techniques of the lyric from the equally sophisticated technological procedures and promotional strategies developed within the popular realm.

————————

As a poet actively seeking an alternative to the defunct "poésie subjective" of the Parnassians and the romantic symbolists,[21] Rimbaud was clearly vulnerable to the seductions of technologically generated forms of popular culture. Rimbaud's biographers have made us aware that his exposure to these modern technological forms was quite extensive.[22] Moreover, Rimbaud's poems themselves indicate the poet's overt interest not only in "street signs," "popular engravings," and "erotic books with bad spelling"[23] but also in peculiarly modern forms of visual, technologically generated spectacle. The procedural innovations and perceptual distortions introduced by popular technologies offered Rimbaud a new resource, namely, the potential to evoke latent aspects of the subject that a more conventional poetic language of human emotions (a "poésie subjective") had failed to express. The poems of *Illuminations* in particular suggest that the procedures Rimbaud emulated were not those of print culture and, further, that the subject images he wished to adopt were not those of the traditional first-person lyric. Rimbaud's privileged figures for poetic practice are in fact the *opéra-comique* and the *féerie*, forms that are less evocative of the syntactic, paronomasiac, and rhetorical procedures associated with literature than of the highly sophisticated precinematic stage technologies blossoming in the broadened cultural realm of the mid-nineteenth century.

In essence, of course, Rimbaud's response to these spectacles was entirely verbal; no Rimbaldian dioramas, panoramas, or *féeries* are known to exist. However, thematic references to the *féerie* and the *opéra-comique* do not limit their field of effects to the thematic order; they begin, as I argue in the next section, to dictate formal and rhetorical operations as well. In his own domain, then, Rimbaud appears to have explored the most radical implications of Adorno's own form of argumentation: he confronted the popular spectacle as a dialectical entity, capable of oppressive redundancy in the worst (and least mediated) of circumstances, but also, in the best, capable of suggesting procedural innovations and alternative images of subjectivity that a poet in search of the latent mechanics of the psyche—"la formule," "méthode," or "clef" of the lyric *élan*—might well have hastened to claim for his own use.

———————

As many critics have noted, Rimbaud's allusions to nineteenth-century theater usually center on the figure of the lyric subject as *comédien*.[24] The poems in *Illuminations*, for example, are filled with various costumed figures for what James Lawler has aptly named Rimbaud's "theatre of the self."[25] Several of these figures, such as "Bottom" and "Hélène," appear to identify the image of the poetic subject with the actor; other figures, most notably that of the "Génie," have been read as evoking allegorically the power of representation itself. But instead of exploring the connections between these theatrical figures and the specific representational technologies to which they belong, critics have tended to view them as embodying a transformative energy transcendent and autonomous of history. The eponymous hero of the poem "Génie," for instance, has not been read as a contingent incarnation, a stock figure drawn from the nineteenth-century *féerie*, but rather as a vision of the creative subject unmoored from history, infused with the power of infinite metamorphosis.

In this regard, Roger Munier's interpretation of Rimbaud's "Génie" is entirely typical. Munier's *"Génie" de Rimbaud* reflects the Heideggerianism of the fifties while rehearsing many of the critical commonplaces established by Rivière as early as 1914.[26] In his reading of "Génie" Munier treats the heroic figure as the "élan pur" of a transformative energy implicitly associated with Heideggerian Being (4). The Genie, writes Munier, is "the origin," but also "the Absolute" [le Tout], "Being . . . not as a concept, but dynamically, poetically, as impulse [élan]," "beyond the world," "beyond the self" (11).

Munier's reading is, of course, permitted by Rimbaud's text, which describes the Genie as that quality lending to each temporal incarnation its "charm" [délice]. In the opening lines, for instance, the Genie appears as the very essence of agitation, the pulse of movement, or, as he will later be called, the "fécondité de l'esprit" [fecundity of the mind]:

> Il est l'affection et le présent puisqu'il a fait la maison ouverte à l'hiver écumeux et à la rumeur de l'été, lui qui a purifié les boissons et les aliments, lui qui est le charme des lieux fuyants et le délice surhumain des stations. (*OC*, 205)

> He is affection and the present since he has made the house open to foamy winter and to the murmur of summer, he who has purified food and drink—he who is the charm of the fleeing places and the superhuman delight of stations. (*Ill*, 135)

In support of Munier's thesis one might note that many of the poem's images suggest a link between the Genie and a transcendent force whose promise is always realizable in the present but projected into the future. The "stations" evoke, for instance, the stations of Christ, eternity-filled incarnations of deity's appearance on earth. Further, an allusion in the third stanza to the "promesse" that replaces the Adoration solidifies the identification of the Genie with a superhuman force. Rimbaud would appear to be describing in "Génie" a dynamic of ultimate salvation, an epiphany of understanding, or the *jouissance* of a "santé essentielle" [essential health] as described in "Conte" [Tale].

But although Munier successfully captures the Genie as a process rather than a state, he nonetheless neglects to explore one of the less consistent figures of the poem, the comparison between the Genie and a "machine." Perhaps because the promise of the Adoration is somewhat difficult to reconcile with an allusion to the mechanical, Munier pursues more than forty pages of exegesis without ever citing in its entirety the stanza in which the allusion to the machine appears:

Il est l'amour, mesure parfaite et réinventée, raison merveilleuse et imprévue, et l'éternité: machine aimée des qualités fatales. (*OC*, 205)

He is love, perfect measure reinvented, marvelous and unlooked-for reason, and eternity: loved instrument [machine] of fatal qualities. (*Ill*, 135)

That Munier suppresses the second half of this sentence (although he spends a good deal of time analyzing the first) indicates the difficulty a certain strain of contemporary poetry criticism continues to have with references to the mechanical nature of the dynamic the poet solicits. To be sure, the reference is not as self-evident as those to the Adoration and the stations of Christ. Rimbaud's use of the diacritical colon is equivocal throughout "Génie," which only compounds the apparent obscurity of the phrase. But Munier misses a valuable clue in his reading of the poem when he neglects to observe the grammatical similarity of the title, "Génie," to the "machine": like the "Génie" of the title, "machine aimée des qualités fatales" also lacks an article of any kind (as do "mesure" and "raison," with which the Genie is also identified). The "syntactic armature" of the sentence, as Atle Kittang would have it, is that of the predicative, or the dictionary definition.[27] The "machine aimée" and the "Génie," "mesure" and "raison," are alike in their grammatical construction as virtual onomastics. In brief, they are synonyms for one another.

In "H," another poem in *Illuminations*, the "machine aimée" returns as a "mécanique érotique" [erotic mechanics] (*OC*, 202) possessing a "porte . . . ouverte à la misère" [door . . . open to penury] (*OC*, 203) that unequivocally echoes "Génie" 's "maison ouverte à l'hiver" (*OC*, 205). "H" is another version of "Génie," part of the cycle (including

"Being Beauteous," "Barbare," and "Conte") in which a force blasts apart "[l]es apparences actuelles" [present appearances] ("Jeunesse, IV," *OC*, 208). The purificatory labors of "Génie," for instance, reappear in "H" as "l'ardente hy*giène* des races" (*OC*, 203), a function that will be evoked again in the destructive rituals of "Conte." Perhaps if Munier had cited "H" as a significant intertext for "Génie" instead of relying entirely on "Conte" he would have been led to make more of the recalcitrant figure of the Genie as machine. The association of Hortense (the heroine of "H") with a "mécanique érotique" is, after all, far more difficult to avoid than the passing reference to the Genie as a "machine aimée." Still, it seems somewhat remarkable that Munier neglects to note how the punctuation of the latter poem works to establish that the "élan" in its eternal incarnation resembles not a god, not Heideggerian "Being," but a machine.

The representation of power—mystical, creative, or erotic—as mechanical in nature is consistent with images found throughout Rimbaud's *Illuminations*. In "H," "Being Beauteous," and other poems of the cycle the "mécanique érotique" wields a power to transform that destroys even as it reconstitutes: "O terrible frisson des amours novices" [Oh terrible shudder of new loves], writes the poet in "H" (*OC*, 203); "O . . . terrible célérité de la perfection des formes" [O . . . terrible velocity of perfecting forms] in "Génie" (*OC*, 206). In the space the Genie provides—"Là, [où] la moralité des êtres actuels se décorpore" [There, (where) the morality of real beings dematerializes] (*OC*, 203)—there occurs the eclipse of all "apparences actuelles." But this eclipse is not the result of an impersonal coup de grâce; on the contrary, the power of the Genie becomes available as the result of a calculation. To set the erotic, transformative machine in motion, one must discover the formula, invent the procedure, find the key. The quest after the empowering formula or key is one of the central themes organizing Rimbaud's entire corpus. In "Vies, II," for instance, the speaker announces nostalgically: "J'ai trouvé quelque chose comme la clef de l'amour" [I found something like the key to love] (*OC*, 182). And in "Alchimie du verbe," in *Une Saison en enfer*, the hero describes his past adventures in similar terms: "Depuis longtemps je me vantais de posséder tous les paysages possibles" [For a long time I prided myself on possessing every landscape imaginable] (*OC*, 232); "je tiens le système" [The system is mine] (*OC*, 237).

Interestingly, the "door" ("H") or "house" ("Génie") that such a key might open does not lead to ultimate contact with the denuded appearance of Being. Instead, the key the poet seeks is one that allows him access to all appearances, all representational systems, *simultaneously*. The "machine aimée" described in "Génie" is inclusive and synesthetic; it controls not only the genres of the musical and the literary but all forms

of visual representation as well. Likewise, the Genie is not Christ in his
apparition as pure spirit but rather Christ as the all-powerful carpenter,
a kind of "Génie-ingénieur." This "ingénieur" can produce anything, as
in "Jeunesse, IV," where he is responsible for "*toutes* les possibilités harmoniques et architecturales" [*all* harmonic and architectural possibilities]
(*OC*, 208, emphasis added). A divine *metteur en scène*, the "Génie-ingénieur" also stages all the scenes of history; possessing his key allows the
poet to rule over representation itself, as in "Vies, I," where he exclaims
that he once had "une scène où jouer les chefs-d'oeuvres dramatiques de
toutes les littératures" [a stage upon which to play the dramatic master-
pieces of all literatures] (182). The romantic genius (another meaning of
génie) returns in Rimbaud's work as the ultimate creative machine,
capable of generating a seemingly limitless number of "scènes." Clearly,
then, the poems in *Illuminations* do not reject representational languages in favor of a purity of speech but seek instead their regulated repro-
gramming, a "*réglage* des textes," which is, according to Antoine Raybaud, "le moyen du *dérèglement* des *sens*" [the means of *deregulating* the
senses].[28]

In a provocative footnote to her *Banquet de Rimbaud: Recherches sur
l'oralité*, Berger has suggested that Rimbaud's key, the one he exhorts us
to find in "H" ("Trouvez Hortense!"), is nothing other than the key to
the procedure he applies for rewriting the entire corpus of nineteenth-
century French literature. Rimbaud's machine, in other words, is a kind
of montage machine, severing the "original" links between signifiers in
order to recirculate them. "Several *Illuminations* are in fact secret glosses
on other works," claims Berger, "sacred texts, certainly, but also novels
by Hugo, perhaps by Flaubert and others."[29] Scrutinizing one poem in
particular, Bruno Claisse has caught Rimbaud in the act of recycling one
text to make another, in this case using Michelet to construct "Barbare."[30]
Advancing one step further, Jean-Louis Baudry elaborates a *telquelian*
theory of Rimbaud as *scripteur*, playing with—to evoke Barthes—the
body of his mother (text).[31] "Every text is the rewriting of another," announces Baudry (34). The procedure by which one text is generated is the
"mechanism of textual production" (45), responsible for what one might
call "l'effet du sujet" [the subject effect].

There is much to be said for an approach to Rimbaud as a telquelian
scripteur. Indeed, one often suspects that a key to Rimbaud's procedure
of "rewriting" would solve many of the "complications" of Rimbaud's
texts.[32] But it is also important to ask why, at this precise moment in
history, Rimbaud would insist upon figuring his procedure—intertextual,
synesthetic, paronomasiac, or otherwise—as specifically *mechanical* in
nature. Baudelaire, after all, rewrites Hugo, Poe, and Gautier, but he does
not overtly present his poetic procedure as a "machine aimée." Further,

as Baudry's comments suggest, Rimbaud's procedure is not simply a recycling machine for creating new texts out of the old; for Rimbaud, new
texts present the possibility of new subjective states ("effets du sujet"), or
rather, new images for what a subject potentially could be. Rimbaud states
in "Alchimie du verbe" that "plusieurs *autres* vies me semblaient dues"
[several *other* lives seemed due me] (*OC*, 237, Rimbaud's emphasis), ex-
plaining in this way his motive for searching out "un verbe poétique accessible, un jour à l'autre, à tous les sens" [a poetic word accessible, one
day, to all the senses] (*OC*, 233). To be a "maître de fantasmagories," as
Rimbaud calls himself in *Une Saison en enfer,* is also to be a subject that
has mastered its own continual transformations. And indeed, representational systems are only significant to Rimbaud to the extent that they
furnish alternative forms of subjectivity, to the extent that they provide a
space in which to perform subjectivity differently.

To nuance Baudry's structuralist paradigm, then, one might say
that Rimbaud's practice aims not merely to demonstrate how texts
produce subjectivities as effects but also to propose these subject
effects as inhabitable alternatives. In this reading the Genie is a kind of
manufacturer of postures, costumes, and masquerades, a *metteur en scène*
of plays in which "tous les caractères nuanc[ent] ma physionomie" [all
characters nuance my physiognomy] ("Guerre," *OC*, 205). The Genie
allows Rimbaud, in other words, to impersonate all the characters of
"un opéra fabuleux" ("Alchimie du verbe," *OC*, 237). If in "Conte" the
Genie appears as the "promesse d'un amour multiple et complexe," in
"H" he is a "mécanique érotique," a keyboard of organs and erogenous
zones that can be played to produce an infinite variety of gendered positions. In "Antique," moreover, the Genie-machine reappears once again,
but this time explicitly in the guise of an androgyne. A "Gracieux fils de
Pan" [Graceful son of Pan], the Genie possesses all sexual organs and
dispositions: "Ta poitrine ressemble à une cithare" [Your breast is like a
lyre], the poet says to his androgynous machine; "Ton coeur bat dans ce
ventre où dort le *double sexe*" [Your heart beats in that belly where sleeps
the *double sex*] (*OC*, 180; *Ill*, 25, emphasis added). Here, the idealized
love object (the "machine aimée") is clearly a cyborg, half human ("poitrine," "coeur") and half instrument ("cithare," "bat[terie]"). The "ventre" of the cyborg Pan boasts, appropriately, a "double sexe." All sexual
experiences are available to this mechanical Tiresias, whose erotics of simultaneity produces images of gender confusion and hybridity. Because
the Genie-machine places himself at the service of the lyric speaker, he
permits this speaker in turn to create for himself an infinite number of
dramas, an infinite number of gendered subjectivities. Like a computer
programmed with all utterances, the Genie-machine also possesses all attributes—of gender as well as of appearance. "[S]on corps" is simply the

aggregate of all bodies combined: "*les* formes, *les* sueurs, *les* chevelures et *les* yeux" [forms, sweat, long hair, and eyes] ("Barbare," *OC*, 198, emphasis added; *Ill*, 103). Only the Genie-machine offers the poet the opportunity to reconceptualize the body, to play the keyboard of human attributes, and thus to realize the ultimate "dégagement rêvé" ("Génie," *OC*, 206).

If it is true, as Michel Foucault, Jonathan Crary, and others have argued, that what a subject can consciously experience is limited and administered by historical apparatuses, then it stands to reason that Rimbaud would seek as his ideal machine an apparatus capable of transcending history, capable, that is, of affording him every subjectivity imaginable. Rimbaud's multiple allusions to the machine testify to his awareness that a subject's perspective, and thus its identity, is always historically circumscribed, that the individual observer always experiences "within a prescribed set of possibilities" determined by specific technologies and their theoretical, scientific, or ideological bases.[33] This "prescribed set of possibilities" is responsible not simply for how or what the subject sees. In addition, technologies governing observation and discrimination help constitute the dominant definition of subjectivity, presenting it either as unified and self-present or, alternatively, as fragmented between a conscious and unconscious life. Rimbaud's theory of *voyance* reflects the poet's grasp of the technological underpinnings of epistemological shifts, his understanding that what one sees and knows—in fact, what one *is*— can be regulated by more than pharmaceutical or alchemical modes of interference. The form of subjectivity to which Rimbaud wishes to accede in *Illuminations* is figured, accordingly, as the product of the most advanced technological apparatus imaginable. The Genie-machine, the "mécanique érotique," and the various keys, formulas, and procedures mentioned throughout the Rimbaud corpus are valued by the poet for the very reason that their possession would allow him to inhabit every point of view, to articulate every potential utterance regardless of all preexisting institutional, discursive, or technological constraints.

However, because Rimbaud is himself a historically situated subject, the poetic figures by which he represents his ideal machine cannot appear without bearing their own historical stamp. That is, in order for Rimbaud to envision what his ideal machine might look like, he must extrapolate from the existing technological apparatuses that frame his vision. Rimbaud thus associates his "machine aimée" not with an electronic synthesizer or with the possibilities of subject formation offered by the internet but rather with a specifically nineteenth-century technology, to be precise, the theatrical technology responsible for the special effects of the popular *féerie*.

As we have seen, Rimbaud's ideal machine is belovèd ("aimée") primarily because of its combinatory powers, its capacity to mix and match attributes of appearance and gender. But whereas critics of the structuralist generation have defined the "machine aimée" as a specifically textual procedure, one that recycles and recombines passages from preexisting literary works, Rimbaud himself rarely evokes a literary model to describe either the machine's workings or its field of effects. Instead, Rimbaud draws his metaphors for textual practice from the example of popular theatrical forms. These metaphors are in keeping with Rimbaud's emphasis on the performative, since theater literalizes the transformations a text can only describe. In *Une Saison en enfer* Rimbaud compares his "machine aimée" to an "opéra fabuleux," presumably because he considers opera, especially the Wagnerian spectacle, to be the most synthetic and inclusive dramatic form of the period.[34] In *Illuminations*, however, the operatic is a less exemplary model than the *féerie*, which, because of its multiple transformation scenes and sophisticated *machines à trucs*, approximates more accurately the type of representational apparatus Rimbaud has in mind.

The *féerie*, or, in its adjectival form, the *féerique*, is alluded to numerous times in *Illuminations*. The *féerie* is consistently related to images of ecstatic or even painful transformation, a "jouissance" by which a subject achieves its own annihilation. ("Génie," *OC*, 205). In "Matinée d'ivresse," for instance, the speaker places himself on the "Chevalet féerique" [the fairylike rack] upon which the "promesse surhumaine" made to our created body and soul is to be fulfilled (*OC*, 184). Or again in "Ornières" [Ruts] the dawn is met by a "Défilé de féeries" [Wonderland procession] (*OC*, 188; *Ill*, 59), suggestive of the "merveilleuses images" of "Après le déluge" (*OC*, 175). There is even a poem named "Fairy," in which the poet evokes a scene of tumultuous genesis similar to that found in "Aube" [Dawn].[35]

It is by no means accidental that Rimbaud chooses the example of the *féerie* to suggest the workings of his "machine aimée." Raybaud has noted in passing that Rimbaud alludes to the *féerie* because it represents an alternative to the bourgeois theater of narrative propriety, a middle-brow form typically derided by nineteenth-century authors.[36] But the question still remains why Rimbaud chooses to privilege the *féerie* instead of the pantomime or the *opéra-comique*, other popular forms he could have mentioned if he had merely desired to convey his interest in popular spectacle. During the nineteenth century bourgeois theater in general was closely linked to social and didactic purposes; it did not require the representation of alternative realities, dream sequences, and fantasy narratives such as those found in the popular sphere of the *fête foraine* (rural fairground).[37] The demands of bourgeois realism could not, then, provide a forum for the development of advanced stage technologies such as the revolving backdrop, the trap door, and other *trucs*, or mechanical devices, associated with the *féerie*. The evolution of theater as a set of representational technologies, as opposed to a set of specifically verbal practices, could only occur in the domain of the *fête foraine*, where religious and social constraints did not apply to the same extent.

Rimbaud's fascination with the *féerie* can be explained, then, by the peculiar role it played in the developmental history of those scenic technologies that would eventually be appropriated by early cinema. As a popular form, the *féerie* had to respond to the audience's ever-increasing demand for dramatic visual effects. Accordingly, it was in the more popular and increasingly commercialized forms that autonomous principles of technical development were allowed to operate. If the development of the *féerie* genre was constrained by market pressures, it was also liberated from other types of demands, such as those of realistic portrayal, ethical propriety, and classical coherence. The *féerie* was thus by no means one popular form among a host of others from which Rimbaud could have selected his figure for the ideal subject-producing machine. Rather, it was the most technologically sophisticated cultural form of the nineteenth century, one that relied entirely upon advanced technical innovations in stagecraft and engineering to produce its startling visual effects.

Although numerous critics and cultural historians have established the centrality of the *féerie* both to the nineteenth-century experience of modernity and to its subsequent critique, it is worth recalling here how a theatergoer of Rimbaud's own day would have responded to the spectacle.[38] Théophile Gautier's *Histoire de l'art dramatique en France depuis vingt-cinq ans*, a vast compendium of theater reviews, typifies the nineteenth-century reaction to the *féerie*, confirming that the genre stood at the vanguard of theatrical innovation precisely because it provided seductive images of the subject's emancipation from spatial and temporal bonds. Gautier's review of *Bijou* [Jewel], a *féerie* performed at the Cirque-Olympique in 1838, reveals to what a great extent the genre was associated with the development of stagecraft technologies capable of subverting the conventions of theatrical realism. Here Gautier attempts to convey the excitement of the various technical *coups* introduced in *Bijou* but then adds:

> Il est impossible de rendre compte, scène par scène, de pareilles billevesées; *tout le mérite en revient au décorateur et au machiniste*; le public a bien compris cela, que, sans vouloir entendre le nom des auteurs, il a redemandé le machiniste à grands cris. On lui a apporté le machiniste, qui se nomme M. Sacré [!].

> It is impossible to record, scene by scene, such unlikely twists of fate; *all praise goes to the stage designer and the machinist*. The public has caught on: ignoring the authors, the public called loudly for the machinist. The machinist was brought out; his name was Mr. Sacred [!].[39]

As Gautier observes, it is clearly the complex technologies of stagecraft and not the text of *Bijou* that most interest the audience. The appeal of the genre, in other words, lies in its ability to provide a "spectacle oculaire."[40] Engineering, not the authorial imagination, is able to realize the spatial and temporal displacements that approximate Rimbaud's "dégagement rêvé." In the same vien, Gautier's review of *La Poule aux oeufs d'or* [The hen with the golden eggs] describes how the spectator is transported from a French village to the Isle of Harmony and then to a temple of proto-Baudelairean "grottes basaltiques," all by means of a complex system of mechanized curtains and trap doors.[41] In fact, whenever Gautier attends a *féerie* he is sure to evoke the fantastic *changements à vue*, the sudden scene changes and transformation acts that afford the genre its unique identity.

Moreover, as Gautier notes, the type of subject found in the *féerie* is profoundly different from that presented in the psychological drama of the same period. Whereas in the latter the subject is limited both by the unities of the Greek stage and by the bourgeois definition of subjective agency, the subject of the former is often given a key—a golden egg or a genie's bottle—awarding it absolute control over the scene changes themselves. (Thus, the subject truly becomes a "maître de fantasmagories.") In a sense, the *féerie* represents the ultimate fantasy, the fantasy of being able to perform one's own fantasies continuously, "without interruption," as Gautier writes, and "without pause."[42]

Gautier's testimony explains why the term *féerie* is favored in Rimbaud's *Illuminations*, why the poet might have nurtured an ambition to rival this early modernist contribution to the next century's "société du spectacle." The *féerie*, although a theatrical rather than a cinematic form, drew from advances in engineering in a manner that anticipated the *cinéma d'attractions*, destined to replace the *féerie* by the end of the century. The *féerie* was an incipient reproductive technology, reliant upon machines to an unprecedented extent for its visual, epistemological, and psychological effects. It thus constituted a technology of subject production significant to Rimbaud in two ways: on the one hand, it posited a subject continually susceptible to radical transformation, while on the other, it provided the model of an advanced procedure promising this protean subject's eventual realization. The fantastic transformations of the stage, as well as the physical metamorphoses of the performers, worked in the service of a particular vision of human subjectivity, one to which Rimbaud, in *Illuminations*, implicitly appeals.

Clearly, then, for Rimbaud, the most alienating subject images were not those generated by mechanical means of reproduction; rather, what Rimbaud found most oppressive was the outmoded lyric subject of Izambard's "poésie subjective," (*OC*, 268), a subject he considered "fadasse" [insipid] because not incessantly metamorphic. With respect to Izambard's more traditional lyricism, Rimbaud's poems exhibit, in Atle Kittang's words, "a deep-seated anti-lyricism, a refusal to place the writing subject on stage as the origin" of his own text."[43] For Rimbaud, the traditional subject of the lyric must have represented closure and limitation, while the metamorphic subject of a "low," heteronomous form—the *féerie*—offered the opportunity to explode the parameters of the reified subject and its limited stage. In sum, the *féerie* was paradigmatic of an art form capable of evolving independently toward the realization of the most sophisticated representational techniques and, consequently, toward the realization of the most innovative and varied images of the human subject as well.

Obviously, however, Rimbaud could not directly apply to poetic writing the stagecraft technologies of a *féerie*. What he could do, though, was evolve an analogous textual apparatus as disruptive as that found on the *féerie* stage. Insofar as Rimbaud's rhetorical "upgrading" tends to make his texts more hermetic and therefore less available to popular audiences, he merely succeeds in distancing his poetry from the cultural forms that inspired it. But insofar as Rimbaud recasts the romantic self-generating subject as a subject that reinvents itself with the aid of complex visual technologies and precinematic machines, Rimbaud can be said to anticipate the work of future multimedia poets, such as Laurie Anderson and Patti Smith. Rimbaud's accomplishment in *Illuminations* is to have translated the industrially realized *trucs* of the *féerie* into a set of highly advanced poetic techniques. In doing so, he combines a purely technical demand (to produce a *féerique* effect through verbal as opposed to visual means) with other exigencies, such as the need to succeed within a field governed by strictly defined aesthetic conventions and values. Thus, if the *féerie* uses set changes and lighting to transport characters from one locale to another, Rimbaud develops instead a rhetorical procedure for destabilizing all references to place. As Marjorie Perloff has observed, in *Illuminations* "the sense of place becomes more and more elusive."[44] Rimbaud's cityscape is a "phantasmagoria"; "It is the landscape of fairytale, of calculated artifice" (54). Asserting improbable contiguities, Rimbaud manages to invert spatial relations and distort proportions. "Pour l'étranger de notre temps," he concedes, "la reconnaissance est impossible" [For a stranger of our time recognition is impossible] ("Villes [II]," OC, 191).

Rimbaud's technique is transparent but daring. In poems such as "Les Ponts" Rimbaud employs self-contradictory stage directions to complicate and undermine the consistency of his own descriptions. Repeated reticulations—*dans* [in, into], *sur* [on], *devant* [before], *derrière* [behind]—create the impression of a descriptive hypertrophy while the laws governing space become irrecuperable. If Baudelaire navigates us smoothly from armchair to Cythera by respecting the laws of realist description,[45] Rimbaud's multiplied conjunctions, comparisons, and prepositional constructions violently lurch us from place to place, from temporality to temporality, as in "Promontoire":

> "L'aube d'or *et* la soirée frissonante trouvent notre brick *en* large *en* face de cette villa et de ses dépendances, qui forment un promontoire *aussi* étendu *que* l'Epire et le Péloponnèse *ou que* la grande île du Japon, *ou que* l'Arabie! (*OC*, 199)

> Golden dawn *and* shivering evening find our brig lying by *opposite* this villa and its dependencies, which form a promontory *as* extensive *as* Epirus and the Peloponnesus, *or as* the large island of Japan, *or as* Arabia! (*Ill*, 105, emphasis added)

The "aussi . . . que" that introduces the final chain of place names functions somewhat like Lautréamont's "beau comme"; it too anticipates the surrealist *métaphore filée* (based on an abuse of *de* and *en*), producing absurd comparisons (Arabia a promontory?) that annul verisimilitude entirely. These conjunctions and comparisons act as *changements à vue* only to the extent that they destabilize vision; what they present is less "a landscape of fairytale" than a landscape of landscapes, a kind of postmodern agglomeration of disparate styles. In "Parade," for instance, the scenes shift so violently that even the bodies of the players eventually burst and overflow: "Les yeux flambent, le sang chante, les os s'élargissent" [Eyes flame, blood sings, bones swell] (*OC*, 180; *Ill*, 23). Or again in "Barbare," dashes and exclamation points break up sentences, transporting the reader rapidly from one fantastic glittering tableau to another. Before this jumble the eye seizes not its stable reincarnation in *one* elsewhere or *one* other; rather, the eye is hypostatized as pure organ, subjectless and free to lose itself in every group of passing "Chinois, Hottentots, bohémiens, niais, hyènes, Molochs . . ." [Chinese, Hottentots, gypsies, simpletons, hyenas, Molochs . . .] ("Parade," *OC*, 180; *Ill*, 23). In short, Rimbaud responds to a theater of attractions with a poetry of attractions. To quote Leo Bersani: "Everything [in *Illuminations*] is designed—as in a spectacularly vulgar circus number—to fascinate our eyes, to make it impossible for us to turn our glutted vision away from the hypnotic scene."[46]

Rimbaud seems to consider the *féerique* technique by which his "dégagement rêvé" is achieved to be the ultimate textual technology, one that transcends all vicissitudes of fashion, all historical change. Rimbaud invites this interpretation of the apparatus as permanently up-to-date ("absolument moderne"): he describes his "machine aimée" as "eternel[le]," implying that it possesses all the necessary accessories with which to represent every imaginable variety of being. The "machine" coveted by the poet is by definition all-encompassing, capable of generating an infinite number of performative selves. His is a "[r]êve intense et rapide de groupes sentimentaux avec des êtres de *tous* les caractères parmi *toutes* les apparences" [intense quick dream of sentimental groups with people of *all* possible characters amidst *all* possible appearances] ("Veillées" [Vigils], OC, 192–93; Ill, 77, emphasis added). This ideal of self-sufficiency, plenitude, and ahistorical transcendence is evoked continuously throughout the Rimbaldian corpus, and yet, strangely, it is an ideal that Rimbaud himself parodies in the final poems of *Illuminations*.

While many poems present the "machine aimée" (or Genie figure) in transcendent terms, there remains one poem of the cycle in which even an erotic mechanics proves to be fully contingent and bounded by temporality. This poem is "Conte," a rewriting of "Génie" in which a union between a human subject (in the guise of the "Prince") and his "mécanique érotique" is explicitly narrated. The "machine aimée des qualités fatales" reappears in the sixth stanza of "Conte" as a machine promising "un amour multiple et complexe, . . . un bonheur indicible, insupportable même!" [a complex and multiple love, . . . an indescribable happiness, unendurable even] (OC, 179; Ill, 19). In the form of a Genie, the "machine aimée" is annihilated as it fuses (fatally) with the (human) Prince. "Le Prince était le Génie," reads the penultimate stanza. "Le Génie était le Prince" [The Prince was the Genie, the Genie was the Prince] (OC, 179; Ill, 19).

Critics have traditionally interpreted this ultimate identification of Prince and Genie as signaling a moment of disillusionment; that the Genie turns out to be (merely) the Prince is taken to mean that he was nothing more than a figment of the Prince's imagination in the first place. This is admittedly one level upon which the text, as self-designated fairy tale, is working. But given Rimbaud's protofuturist visions of a miraculous fusion between man and machine, it is possible to read the final lines as alluding to an entirely different order of disillusionment. It is not so much that the Genie is simply an imagined release, a putative key to *dérèglement* that fails to transform the human being into a keyboard of unlimited subjectivities. Rather, the Genie succeeds all too well: he transforms the Prince—by fusing with him—into an advanced technology of metamorphosis. However, this technology of metamorphosis is itself limited, for no machine can transcend history. It is in this sense that the Prince and the Genie must both die.

"Conte," in fact, provides two discrete death scenarios. In the first death scene the Prince and the Genie experience a kind of *jouissance*, an ultimate fusion that removes them from temporality: "Le Prince et le Génie s'anéantirent probablement dans la santé essentielle. Comment n'auraient-ils pas pu en mourir? Ensemble donc ils moururent" [The Prince and the Genie annihilated each other probably in essential health. How would they have helped dying of it? Together then they died]. In the second scene, however, both meet their death by submitting to the natural processes of decay: "Mais ce Prince décéda, dans son palais, à un âge ordinaire. Le Prince était le Génie. Le Génie était le Prince" [But this Prince died in his palace at an ordinary age, the Prince was the Genie, the Genie was the Prince] (*OC*, 179; *Ill*, 19). How are we to understand these two endings, these two different types of fatality?

On the one hand, the Genie of "Conte" is represented as the very mechanism of *dérèglement*. The Genie is eternal, and thus logically it would be impossible to come up with a new and improved model to replace the old one. On the other hand, as the poems themselves intimate, even the most advanced technology, even a *féerie* capable of anticipating every combinatory possibility, is limited by the historically specific set of engineering skills that it epitomizes. The "machine aimée" ultimately fails the Prince, then, not because the machine exists only in the Prince's mind but because the mind and thus its machines exist only *in history*. They are, to put it bluntly, merely mortal. A procedure may be the most advanced and differentiated of its moment; it may, in fact, be "absolutely modern." But a procedure can only be as "modern" as the historical evolution of technology allows. Like the Prince, then, the *féerique* Genie-machine is also dated, situated with respect to space and time: "ce Prince décéda, dans son palais *à un âge ordinaire*." It is as temporally and geographically bounded creations, and not as beings transcendent in annihilation, that the Prince and his machines die together.

Paradoxically, given its title, "Conte" is the poem that marks the poet's lucid capitulation to history. For it is here that the poet observes the redundancy of the creative drive and the historicity of the technologies through which it is (temporarily) satisfied. The language of the poem betrays this historicity even when it seems to be yearning toward its own annihilation in the sublime.

> Un Génie apparut, d'une beauté ineffable, inavouable même. De sa physionomie et de son maintien ressortait la promesse d'un amour multiple et complexe! d'un bonheur indicible, insupportable même! (*OC*, 179)

> A Genie appeared, of ineffable beauty, unavowable even. In his face and his bearing shone the promise of a complex and multiple love! of an indescribable happiness, unendurable even. (*Ill*, 19)

The Genie is beyond beauty, the poem tells us, beyond speech even ("même"). A typical figure of the romantic sublime, the Genie is experienced as even beyond bearing: "insupportable même!" But the superlative exclamation "même," itself appearing twice, does more than simply mark the excessiveness of the Genie's beauty; it is a word that turns back on itself, suggesting both the exceptional and, paradoxically, the redundant ("le même," meaning "the same"). In other words, at the heart of the description that would establish the Genie's radical otherness we are reminded instead of the Genie-machine's similarity to earlier textual mechanics, its redundancy as a (soon to be outmoded) technology of the (anti)sublime. What is "unendurable," finally, is not the blinding otherness of the Genie-machine but its sameness, its "insupportable *même.*" Rimbaud's "Conte" thus points toward the final recuperation of the Genie figure in "Solde," a poem in which the figures of *Illuminations* are inventoried and put up for sale. The "*élan* de nos facultés" [the soaring of our faculties] described in "Génie" (*OC*, 205; *Ill*, 135) reappears in "Solde" as an "*Élan* insensé et infini" [Wild and infinite flight (soaring)] (*OC*, 209; *Ill*, 149). The "barque de deuils *sans prix*" [priceless mourning boat] of "Fairy" (*OC*, 204; *Ill*, 131) returns as a "corps *sans prix*, hors de toute race, de tout monde, de tout sexe, de toute descendance" [Bodies without price, outside any race, any world, any sex, any lineage] (*OC*, 208; *Ill*, 147). The "délice surhumain" of "Génie" is recast as a circus attraction (a process already initiated by "Parade"), while the techniques applied by the performers are inventoried as a "stock d'études" [stock of studies] ("Mouvement," *OC*, 202; *Ill*, 118). "Solde" sets up a ricochet of allusions joining each poetic promise to its commodified form. Even the *féerie* winds up on the sale rack: "A vendre, les habitations et les migrations, sports, féeries et conforts parfaits, et le bruit, le mouvement et l'avenir qu'ils font!" [For sale, colonizations and migrations, sports, fairylands and incomparable comforts, and the noise and the movement and future they make!] (*OC*, 208; *Ill*, 149). Finally, "Solde" makes us suspect that what the Genie offers, the "occasion, unique, de dégager les sens" [the unique occasion to release our senses] (*OC*, 208), may be "à l'occasion," a secondhand trick whose secrets have already been revealed ("S[old]e").

According to romantic thought, the goal of the aesthetic is to transcend the limits of the historically determined, to remain, in some sense, "indicible" and thus "sans prix." But Rimbaud's modernity inheres in his intuition that procedures developed in the domain of high art may eventually prove susceptible to market appropriation, commodification, and eventual obsolescence, just like those developed in the domain of popular culture. Rimbaud, in effect, anticipates the outmoding of his own advanced procedures, bound, as they are, to the temporality of their inception. Similar to a theatrical *machine à trucs* rendered obsolete by its next incarnation, modern cinema, Rimbaud's "machine aimée" is also the victim of history, too soon "antique" as it undergoes the "terrible velocity" of time.

It must be added, however, that the Genie's failure is also the Prince's chance. True, no technology, no machine, no textual practice, can transcend history and exhaust all the self-conceptions that human beings will ever require. But the very fact that productive modes and the subject images they construct are transient rather than absolute ensures that they will be susceptible to modification. In other words, the threat that a textual (or mechanical) practice may be limited in terms of the representations it can achieve is simultaneously the guarantee that new subject images and new procedures will be conceived at a later date. The Prince may die, but he cannot be reified if the machines generating his self-images also become obsolete. Paradoxically, then, the technique's historicity, its temporal limitation, also constitutes its mana, the substance that allows it to register the struggle of real, situated historical subjects attempting to find means of expression within the confines of their material conditions. Even the continually metamorphic *sujet féerique* may become a gimmick (as it has, for instance, in the modern cinema of special effects), a hardened form that denies the subject's carnal vulnerability, its necessarily limited response to events. Thus, a technology that is not used self-reflexively to reveal its implication in history, to reveal its mortality as a reflection of the human self, is a technology that loses contact with the life that sustained and inspired it. If a technique or technology insists upon its transcendence of history, if it denies that its subject images are transient and situated, and if it seeks to promote these subject images as the reality and not the representation of being, then the mana the technique or technology once contained becomes all the more difficult to detect and revitalize. The slight gap between the subject and its (conceptual, discursive, and technological) mediations promises that the transfer of mana will indeed take place. Once that gap is eliminated, once image coincides with existence and machine with the endless peregrinations of human desire, then the human perishes, trapped in a world of machines without death. Thus, the most important moment of *Illuminations* is the moment in "Conte" when the Genie-machine—now one with the Prince—dies. This death signifies that even the most beloved representational machines, even the most coveted concepts of the self, are imperfect and can lose their pertinence. Paradoxically, the confession of immanence is precisely what preserves in the lyric a bit of the humanity it once addressed.

On the one hand, then, Rimbaud's vision of an ideal "machine aimée" prefigures the frighteningly complete and all-encompassing technovisions of the futurists. But on the other, Rimbaud's "fairytale" ("Conte") of a machine that confesses its own fall into temporality effectively challenges a futurist poetics convinced of the unalloyed advantages of the machine. When Rimbaud acknowledges that the "promesse d'un amour multiple et complexe" fails in relation to the ambition of desire—"la musique savante manque à notre désir" (OC, 179)—he inaugurates a lyric tradition dedicated to exposing both the necessity and the inadequacy of mediation, the promise and the impossibility of authentic self-presentation. Although Rimbaud himself never creates a multimedia hybrid lyric form, although he fails, that is, to combine the stage technologies of the *féerie* with a textual practice, he does at least suggest that new subject images, and the new means for producing them, may emerge not from the preexisting conventions of the Book but rather from the domain of market-dominated, industrially produced popular culture. The continuing recirculation of energies, rationalities, images, and procedures that Rimbaud tacitly advocates in *Illuminations* is essential to the "santé essentielle" of the modernity his poems allow us to envision. A field that is not nourished by exigencies other than those that have dominated it in the past is a field that can only reproduce death in the form of "le même."

Three _____

Confessing Philosophy: *Negative Dialectics* and/as Lyric Poetry

> The poet can learn little from the philosopher, but the philosopher much from the poet.
> *(Friedrich Schlegel)*

NEGATIVE DIALECTICS, despite its philosophical thematic, represents Adorno's lyric moment, a lyric moment raised, so to speak, to the second power. Like the poems of *Illuminations*, *Negative Dialectics* also exhibits a concern with the expressive articulations of a subject while simultaneously reminding its readers of the machinery through which such articulations are both realized and denied. Paradoxical as it might seem, *Negative Dialectics* resembles more closely than any of Adorno's other works a late romantic lyric revelation: it manipulates a highly abstract philosophical discourse (rather than a sophisticated poetic rhetoric) for the purpose of instantiating a moment of self-exposure.

Negative Dialectics is, after all, written under the sign of the confessional. In the preface the author clearly informs us that he is "prepared for the attacks to which *Negative Dialectics* will expose him" now that, finally, he is "confessing" [geständig].[1] *Negative Dialectics* claims to tell us a fundamental truth about its first-person pronoun, but this truth will be attained through the exercise of an ironic self-consciousness stalking the immanence of the other in every apprehension—and disclosure—of the self. Because *Negative Dialectics* respects the subject's articulations while nonetheless remaining suspicious of the forms into which they have been congealed, it bears a resemblance to the modern lyric in both design and tone.

Out of the pages of *Negative Dialectics*, then, I intend to unfold a theory of lyric expression more adequate to the self-reflexive poetry of the Rimbaldian and post-Rimbaldian avant-garde tradition I have been delineating. Adorno's explicit theoretical statements concerning lyric poetry, such as those found in *Aesthetic Theory*, "Lyric Poetry and Society," and related essays in *Prisms*, coincide fairly consistently with what the philosopher in fact illustrates in *Negative Dialectics*. Adorno's essays on aesthetics deserve sustained consideration; however, *Negative Dialectics* arguably offers a more provocative theory of lyric production than the former works insofar as it exemplifies the theory it adumbrates. Although *Negative Dialectics* announces itself as a confessional project only in the final section, "Meditations on Metaphysics," the text nevertheless aims throughout toward a moment of self-exposure, a lyric moment in which the speaking subject openly reflects upon its own deeply historicized—and technically mediated—mode of being.

Negative Dialectics presents itself as a confessional lyric, the speaking subject's revelation of mediation, in order to draw attention to the method, rhetorical structure, technique, or hidden interest intervening in even the most sustained effort to relay an "unregimented experience," either of phenomena or of the self (*ND*, 123). As in many lyric poems, a complex machinery is mounted for the purpose of expressing that ineffable "remainder," the "inhuman" or unvoiced subject of discourse (*ND*, 5). Adorno simply widens what is often perceived in lyric poetry as a gap between the subject's spontaneous exclamations and the poem's complex rhetoric. In *Negative Dialectics* the disproportion between the conceptual apparatus—here a rehearsal of the history of Continental philosophy—and the intimate, first-person confessional mode marks the limit of a certain practice that has been labeled alternately lyric or idealist.[2] If the lyric as conventionally defined is the expression of strong emotions and idealism is the enterprise launched to rescue the individuated subject of these emotions, then *Negative Dialectics* is the culmination and, simultaneously, the reversal of both traditions. Since in Adorno's historical narrative the discourse of the subject has become susceptible to mechanical repetition (reified first by romantic and then by popular discourses) the task of defending particularized experience falls to a different type of discourse, one borne by a voice that is not recognizably that of an idiosyncratic individual subject. Like Rimbaud before him, Adorno accuses subjective discourses of reifying the very object of their concern and thus of conforming secretly to the historical forces of standardization they were meant to resist.[3] *Negative Dialectics* thus appears as a kind of *cas extrême* of lyricism, one in which the conventional figures of lyric address have been evacuated in the name of the very subject they are intended to protect.

The near disappearance of the first-person singular within a text written under the sign of the confessional is symptomatic of a primordial "fall" of man into self-consciousness, a fall that allows man to seize himself as a mediated object instead of a source of expression. According to Adorno, the confession of mediation constitutes the redemptive gesture both of philosophy and of art. "Authentic" art, like "authentic" philosophy, necessarily involves a moment of self-exposure, an avowal of the method by which the philosophical or poetic rhetoric arrives at and delivers its revelations. Confessional discourses are by definition self-reflexive; the speaking subject must assume a degree of distance vis-à-vis a past state of consciousness, a past utterance or act. In the context of philosophy the self-reflexive moment entails the acknowledgment of an embedded conceptual system, one that has provided tools but also limited the scope of what a philosophical consciousness can apprehend. Adorno conjugates his ambivalence toward method by approaching the question of mediation from three distinct but interrelated perspectives: he praises the method by which revelation is achieved; he acknowledges the degree to which method mediates or deforms the truth it reveals; and he conducts a self-reflexive examination of method's entanglement in particular interests. These three moments, structurally separated in *Negative Dialectics*, are condensed and rendered simultaneous in the most evolved rhetoric of lyric poetry. Adorno simply extends across the geography of argument an experience typically collapsed in lyric poetry into brief, allusive, and therefore less didactic forms.

The lyric poem holds a privileged place in Adorno's philosophical system largely because it has served as a major site for the development and maturation of confessional, subject-centered discourses. Confession is not, of course, solely the concern of lyric poetry; self-exposure is a popular generic feature of eighteenth- and nineteenth-century narrative as well.[4] Nevertheless, it is in the modern lyric that confession achieves its most condensed and dialectical form. As early as 1856, for instance, Victor Hugo establishes definitively the link between the confession and the lyric. In his preface to *Les Contemplations* he announces that from that point on the lyric subject's primary function will be to contemplate its own flaws.[5] The moral terms in which Hugo casts his project are not foreign to a negative dialectics as conceived by Adorno. Contrition for one's past errors becomes an analog for the atonement of intellection as it recognizes its blindness to the hidden need that had compelled it. But while Hugo's moral rigor stands as a model for the project of *Negative Dialectics*, Adorno's dialectics of self-exposure owes a far greater debt to the exemplary irony, the "poison tutélaire" of Charles Baudelaire.[6] Baudelaire puts a new spin on the confessional, sending it from the sure terrain of illuminating self-revelation to the troubling no-man's-land of perpetual error. In Baudelaire's hands the lyric no longer promises a moment of epiphany in which the subject triumphantly attains its true nature (or union with God). Instead, the lyric is redefined as a discourse in which a subject comes to recognize and then negate its past delusions, revealing each succeeding figuration of subjectivity, each effort to assume a voice of sincerity, to be histrionic, mediated by objectifying forms previously taken for the substance itself. The subject of the Baudelairean confession experiences itself as a kind of empty container, a fragile shell easily broken by the force of retrospective insight. The contrast between Hugo's mode of revelation as redemption and Baudelaire's mode of self-exposure as performance indicates a tension at the heart of the confessional enterprise that Adorno will exploit both in *Negative Dialectics* and *Minima Moralia: Reflections from Damaged Life*, his other major confessional work. This tension concerns the function of confession itself, which is theoretically to posit a speaking subject capable not only of insight but also of self-incarnation in language. The functional ambiguity arises at the very moment when the speaking subject affirms its newfound authenticity, for as Baudelaire implies repeatedly in his prose and poetic works, there is no reason to believe that the purity and self-knowledge gained through a confession are quite thorough enough. The confessional gesture is, then, somewhat like irony in that it tends to require its own repetition in order to realize its epistemological claims.

At first glance, confession would appear to be the most personal and least universalizing form of expression, the very antithesis of a discursive mode (such as philosophy) intent upon ascertaining an absolute and *general* truth. But one of Adorno's most successful "ruses" is to link a philosophical enterprise with the intimate confession of an individual subject. This juxtaposition of discursive modes works to suggest the generality, the historical rather than personal nature, of the individual subject's truth. (At the same time, the juxtaposition implies the subjective—self-involved and self-interested—character of universalizing, axiomatic thought.) By "confessing" in *Negative Dialectics*, Adorno self-consciously associates his own project with works of nineteenth-century lyricism in which the subject's autonomy from social forces (as well as the universal legitimacy of its truth discourses) is specifically what has been placed at stake. For in nineteenth-century lyricism the self-knowledge gained by introspection is precisely not a knowledge limited to the author's self. Although dependent upon an excessive use of the first-person pronoun and a tone of intimate self-disclosure, confession is in fact a highly public gesture, defining, by means of an "I" that has become a mere figure of speech, consciousness as a rhetorically and historically overdetermined rather than transcendental form. The nineteenth-century poet places the lyric "I" at stake, confessing that its favored pronominal category obfuscates the historical nature of the subjectivity it conveys.[7] Confession at its most self-reflexive is the ambiguous form a discourse takes when it wants simultaneously to affirm that a subjective remainder exists and to deny that its unmediated expression has been achieved.

It is thus not difficult to understand why Adorno chooses to frame both *Negative Dialectics* and *Minima Moralia* as confessional works. If the impulse generating each is to unveil the objectivity inhabiting the subject, the historical conditions and rhetorical forms constraining even the most intimate and personal of apprehensions, then it stands to reason that both works should begin by focusing on the technologies responsible for the production of what is commonly taken to be the self. One might easily object that were one to compare a text by Adorno to a subject-centered utterance, *Minima Moralia* would provide a more appropriate candidate than *Negative Dialectics*. *Minima Moralia* presents itself openly as a set of autobiographical reflections. Whereas *Negative Dialectics* proceeds with considerable reticence, waiting until its conclusion to explode into personal memoire, *Minima Moralia* commits the impertinence of referring to its subjective source of articulation throughout. The tension between the drive to speak as a subject and the drive to illustrate this speaking subject's dependence upon atrophied forms determines *Minima Moralia*'s bitterly ironic tone. Clearly, *Minima Moralia*, which confesses to "the shame of still having air to breathe, in hell" (*MM*, 23), conforms more readily to the model of the lyric confession proposed by Baudelaire.[8] Like the subject of "Spleen, II," the author of *Minima Moralia* finds himself in the predicament of remaining an amorphous "matière vivante," an unnameable subjective excess, in a desert of objectifying forms or subject positions that have lost their signifying value (they are now "surannées," out of style).[9] The guilt of the author of *Minima Moralia* is that of someone who still manages to breathe, thus continuing to animate—and perpetuate—a contaminated "I."

However, the confessional tone of *Negative Dialectics* is quite different from that sounded in *Minima Moralia*. *Negative Dialectics* cannot be placed as securely in the tradition of the Baudelairean "Spleen" poem but must be compared to lyric works whose confidence in rational and linguistic means has not yet been utterly destroyed. Rotating just slightly the angle from which he views his philosophical constellation, Adorno focuses *Negative Dialectics* more closely on the process involved in self-reflexivity, on the movement from one objectified form of subjectivity to the next, rather than on the objectifying cases or shells the subject inhabits along the way. In *Negative Dialectics* the admission of the inadequacy of concepts, personal pronouns, and other objective means is presented not as an endless spiraling downwards or a degrading fall but as an incremental advance entailing the acquisition of an "infinitesimal freedom" (*MM*, 26). The vertiginous displacements of the demystifying consciousness lead not to despair, or at least not immediately to despair; instead they engender an appreciation of the process by which a heightened consciousness has been achieved. Confession may not expose the "true" self, but as a cognitive act it at least implies a deepening of insight, a progressive introspection.

Negative Dialectics has more of an affinity, then, with a poem like Rimbaud's "Matinée d'ivresse," in which a voice calls out with conviction, "Nous t'affirmons, méthode!"[10] If Baudelaire presents a scenario in which all means are corrupt, Rimbaud's poetry suggests that adequate means, propitious sites ("le lieu et la formule"), might still be found ("Vagabonds," *OC*, 190). The first part of *Negative Dialectics* reads as a kind of hymn to method, a celebration of the process by which the confessional, self-reflexive turn can indeed be made. Objectifying means must be retained, Adorno argues in the introduction, if only because there is no knowledge to be gained without them: "thinking without a concept," without a "conceptual machinery" [Begriffsapparatur],[11] "is not thinking at all" (*ND*, 98). True, Adorno continues, Hegel may have failed to "use philosophical concepts for coping with all that is heterogeneous to those concepts" (*ND*, 4), but this very failure indicates a path for dialectics to follow in the future. As a method, dialectics may register its own distortions and in that way (i.e., negatively), protect the heterogeneous "remainder" it knows it cannot attain (*ND*, 5). Just as Rimbaud uses the lyric "I" to reveal its "other," so Adorno retains method in order to approach the unknown lying beyond method's boundaries.[12] Adorno calls his continuing faith in method—his belief that "the concept can transcend the concept . . . and can thus reach the nonconceptual"— a "naive" although "inalienable" feature of speculative thinking (*ND*, 9). This "naive" commitment to method can be said to distinguish the Adorno of *Negative Dialectics* (or the poet of *Illuminations*, for that matter) from the philosopher of *Minima Moralia*, who abandons himself to spleen. But it is also this commitment to method, this reliance on a distorting apparatus, to which Adorno, in *Negative Dialectics*, is guiltily confessing.

As might be expected, Adorno's English translator, E. B. Ashton, has approached the confessional aspect of *Negative Dialectics* from a rather different angle. Having in mind, no doubt, Adorno's engagement with Lukács and other Marxist thinkers, Ashton reads *Negative Dialectics* as a massive "apologia," a mea culpa for a fall from Marxist grace. "At bottom, this book is an apologia for deviationism," writes Ashton, "a Marxist thinker's explication of his inability to toe the lines laid down today for proper Marxist thinking" (*ND*, xi). The "sins" to which Adorno admits, according to Ashton, "are epitomized in one: in the contention that history, all reinterpretations to the contrary, has failed to take the course predicted for it as a scientific necessity." Although Ashton's reading arguably makes sense within the context of doctrinal Marx-

ism, it does not satisfy other considerations, such as why a good deal of
Negative Dialectics is devoted to demonstrating that Hegelian idealism,
and not Marxist teleology, is the resounding failure of post-Kantian
thought. The dialogue with Hegel informs any dealings Adorno might
have with Marx; indeed, as the title of the volume confirms, it is Hegel,
not Marx, who is the principal authority figure to be challenged, and
challenged from within his own system rather than by means of references
to objective conditions alien to his thought. It would aid Adorno little to
accuse Hegel (or Marx, for that matter) of the guilt of false prophecy;
the accusation of such guilt has to come from within the Hegelian
corpus itself. It is Hegel, in other words, who must confess to the flaws
in the idealist system, and confess, in Adorno's hands, is precisely what
he will do.

In fact, as it turns out, Adorno's privileged model for the confessional
mode will be Hegel himself, the philosopher who "confess[es] compulsively," according to Adorno, in the course of developing his conceptual
materials (*ND*, 324).[13] Referring to Hegel's *Philosophy of History*,
Adorno observes how the author, unbeknownst to himself, admits the
very truth his entire philosophical system is designed to deny, namely,
that dissonance between individual and state, particular and universal,
still exists. Even in the act of asserting the contrary, Hegel lets it be
known, through what Adorno calls a "philosophical slip of the pen" (*ND*,
310), that the synthesis or reconciliation anticipated by his system has
not occurred.

But if Hegel confesses "compulsively" and inadvertently to the sin of
his thought (the desire for reconciliation), Adorno wants his own confessional gesture to be conscious and explicit; in fact, he wants confession
to become the new form assumed by the philosophical enterprise. For
only confession can be considered the act of reflexive consciousness—
reason's own self-criticism—appropriate to an age in which all intellection manifests guilt. In a sense, then, Ashton is correct when he points
to the failure of teleology as the crucial problem to be faced in *Negative
Dialectics*; but what concerns Adorno is less the failure of a Marxist materialist teleology than a flaw at the heart of the dialectical system as a
whole: the degree to which dialectics imposes reconciliation upon "unregimented experience," thereby distorting the substance of what it should
preserve intact.

To return to Adorno's prefatory remarks, it would seem that what
Adorno's readers "knew . . . all the time" is that despite his radical suspicion of the dialectical process, it is to dialectics that he will nonetheless
adhere (*ND*, xxi). Dialectics is to be preferred to any other available device or "conceptual machinery" because it is uniquely equipped to
conduct "the self-critique of the concept" (*ND*, 136). Even "while doing

violence to the object of its syntheses," Adorno claims, dialectics "heeds a potential that waits in the object," making "amends"—through astringent self-critique—"to the [dismembered] pieces for what it has done" (*ND*, 19).

Adorno's figurative language—dialectics "makes amends" [gutzumachen], it "heeds a potential" [gehorcht]—suggests the possibility, even within method, of what he calls elsewhere an "affinity" or "mimetic" relation between thinking and the particular object of thought.[14] Like the word *mimesis*, *affinity* [Affinität] implies in Adorno's texts an exchange of knowledge or power (mana) between entities belonging to distinct and incompatible spheres.[15] If it is true that "without affinity there is no truth" (*ND*, 270), then the validity of Adorno's project hinges on the possibility of this affinity, on the slight chance, that is, that the generalizing concept might "heed a potential" immanent in the object. Adorno's appeal to affinity tacitly establishes another link between lyric poetry and dialectics. For the lyric also builds its hopes on the slight chance that tropological systems might accommodate the forms of the object world. The operative model, however, both of lyric poetry and of dialectics, is not that of adequation but that of consubstantiality. The concept, like the trope, must be possessed by, without actually coinciding with, the object it conjures forth. Philosophy can once more be rendered "mimetic" if it encourages a transfer of force or affect from that which is deprived of language (the inanimate, vegetal, bestial, or somatic) to that which may come to speak in its place (the concept, formula, or figure). Thus, the act of philosophical discrimination, like that of poetic figuration, entails a kind of miming, a somatic or subjective moment in which a subject recapitulates the other in its own (objectifying) terms. For the mimetic moment to inhere, the objectifying terms must be recognized as both identical and nonidentical to that which they name, continuous with the other in one respect, discontinuous with it in another. Through constant self-correction and elimination of the noncoincident, the outmoded, or "suranné," dialectical method can rediscover even within hardened concepts "moments of the reality that require[d] their formation" (*ND*, 11).

Thus, in spite of his reservations, Adorno still places his faith in method, in a conceptual system and therefore in a set of operations, a *techne*, of thought. Method is both necessary and facilitating, allowing the subject to approach, albeit "asymptotically," the object of its reflections (*ND*, 407). That the massive introduction to *Negative Dialectics* is devoted to an affirmation of method as, precisely, *mediating*, as communicating a message, implies that there is more to a confessional philosophy than an admission of error, blindness, or defeat. "When we contemplate philosophical history," writes Adorno, "[we perceive] how superior the system, whether rationalistic or idealistic, has been to its opponents for

more than two centuries" (*ND*, 20). With respect to Heidegger in particular, Adorno warns that the rejection of Western philosophical method
produces the very opposite of emancipation. Any effort to reject dialectics, to find a "new beginning at an alleged zero point," requires that one
don the "mask of strenuous forgetfulness" (*ND*, 71). Heidegger's "noble
turn away from science finally serves only to confirm the universal rule
of science, not unlike the way irrationalist slogans under fascism served
as a counterpoint to scientific-technological activities" (*ND*, 74). The philosopher who would abjure all systems in the name of immediate truth,
warns Adorno, simply ends up imposing the authority of his own, the
terms of which have not yet passed through the flames of critical self-
reflection.

Yet if all Adorno hoped to achieve was a critical analysis of the terms,
models, and methods that make up the toolbox of Western philosophy,
then *Negative Dialectics* would be self-reflexive without being confessional, deconstructive without being materialist. What makes it a work
of materialist philosophy (as well as an act of personal confession) is the
author's insistence upon examining the historical conditions out of which
conceptual systems emerge, the needs to which they respond, and the
temptations by which they are seduced. Adorno's passing reference to
the resemblance between Heidegger's "turn away from science" and the
"irrationalist slogans" of fascism is by no means incidental to his argument. Clearly, Adorno's first move in *Negative Dialectics* is to establish a
critical "relation to ontology" in the chapter of the same name; he wants
to defend dialectics against Heidegger's dismissal by portraying dialectics
as the self-reflexive method uniquely suited to exposing the irreducible
"gap," the moment of *non*synthesis, between the concept and the nonconceptual.[16] Kant and Hegel remain "models" despite their faults because
they provide means for apprehending the very gap that ontology would
like to close (although they do so only at moments of inattention, through
occasional lapses and "slip[s] of the pen"). A fully confessional philosophy must drive a wedge even deeper into this gap. For Adorno this wedge
is historical materialism. As a method that analyzes the conceptual system
in light of its material context, historical materialism reveals the heteronomous motivations (economic and ideological) informing that system's
construction: "It is when things are being read as a text of their becoming
that idealistic and materialistic dialects touch" (*ND*, 52). The author's
second move in *Negative Dialectics* thus involves a search for the hidden
connections between universalizing truth discourses and the particular
motives of self-interest they disguise. Conceptual systems, as Adorno proposes, may indeed preserve a moment of the reality that "requires their
formation" (*ND*, 11); it is up to an idealistic dialectics to strive for an
ever closer approximation of this moment. Meanwhile, it is materialism's

task to observe how that "moment of reality" is mediated heteronomously, how it is syncopated by the contingent rhythms of thought as it
unfolds in a man-made world.

The first target of Adorno's dialectical materialism is the unavowed
heteronomy of Heidegger's ontology, the philosopher's refusal to examine
the way his *"prima philosophia* [is] crassly compromised by the contingency of material things" (*ND*, 75). Adorno argues that Heidegger's "ontological need" for an authoritative truth reflects not only a philosophical
imperative but also a drive on the part of a privileged elite (to which
Heidegger, of course, belongs) to find a myth legitimating its own domination. Adorno admits to sharing this same "ontological need" or philosophical imperative; in contrast to Heidegger, however, Adorno struggles
to avow the immanent historicity of the forms in which this need is articulated. Because Heidegger lacks the kind of historical self-reflexivity that
Adorno strives to achieve, his ontology tends to promote unself-conscious
"slave thinking" (*ND*, 89). According to Adorno, Heidegger "categorically dictate[s]" to his followers (90), disguising his own historically, geographically, and ethnically conditioned voice as that of Being.

Predictably, the next target of Adorno's attack is Kant's earlier version
of the Heideggerian project: his effort to erect a transcendental subject
autonomous of social (and thus historical) determinations. In the first
section of part 3, "Freedom: On the Metacritique of Practical Reason,"
Adorno takes up Kant's model of subjective freedom, revealing not only
that the notion of freedom itself has historical roots (*ND*, 218) but, further, that its exfoliation in Kantian idealism cannot be separated from the
rise of the bourgeoisie and the increasing dominance of its (self-)interests.
Just as Heidegger's theory of Being answers fascism's ideological needs,
so Kantian idealism, argues Adorno, responds to "an unexpressed mandate from the bourgeoisie to find transparent grounds for [its own eco-
nomic] freedom."[17] In the same vein, Adorno argues in the second half of
part 3, "World Spirit and Natural History," that Hegel too "was in bond-
age to his class, a class forced to perpetuate its dynamic categories lest it
perceive the bounds of its continued existence" (*ND*, 342).

Admittedly, Adorno's materialist analyses of conceptual models are
brief, schematic, and therefore somewhat unsatisfying. Their brevity is
due, perhaps, to the force and inclusiveness of the larger argument they
support, an argument that is anthropological rather than narrowly historical in orientation. At bottom, *Negative Dialectics* seeks to disclose the
"need," the physically derived intellectual *hunger*, compelling each instance of speculative thought.[18] However, the irreducible presence of need
in human existence is not the immediate object of Adorno's analysis. It
cannot be, for need is synonymous with suffering, an experience that can
only receive mediated, provisional, and contingent forms of expression.

Instead Adorno is interested in these expressive contingencies, in history's various and twisted ways of responding to need such that it might be harnessed and directed in ways beneficial to a particular race or ruling class. As a historian, Adorno presents us with a narrative in which need, perverted by barter, bourgeois capitalism, and eventually racist totalitarianism, comes to contort metaphysics as well, producing in turn the nascent individualism of Enlightenment thought, transcendental idealism, and the fundamental ontology of Heidegger. There is no method, no mechanics, that does not respond to a need, that does not, in the very act of responding, pervert this need into something that can be momentarily fulfilled and thus betrayed. Finally, however, the insight into method's imbrication in historically specific modes of yearning does not provide an argument for method's suppression. That is why, deficient as they may be, earlier philosophical systems still furnish viable models for future speculation. As Adorno stresses repeatedly, "the fact that thinking is mediated by objectivity does not negate thinking" (*ND*, 233).

> The need is what we think from, even where we disdain wishful thinking. The motor of the need is the effort that involves thought as action. The object of critique is not the need in thinking, but the relationship between the two. (*ND*, 408)

In this penultimate paragraph of *Negative Dialectics*, Adorno depicts thought not as pure and autonomous speculation but rather as a kind of action, a transformation of the *donné* whose "motor" is insatiable need. Need cannot be eradicated, for "a thought without need, a thought that wished for nothing, would be like nothing," abstract and disinterested, yes, but also hollow and inhuman (*ND*, 93). Adorno suggests that ultimately there is only one way for thought to alter its "relationship" to need, for thought to *think need*. Since thought cannot transcend need entirely, it must throw off the domination of need *insofar as this need is manifested in a precise historical form*. Thought can do so precisely by reflecting upon this form's historicity. Treated sequentially, these distorted, historicized forms of need, from the need for reconciliation and individual rights to the need for commodities such as stockings, produce a narrative of the subject in history. Negative dialectics can locate this "implicit history" by analyzing the images of need human subjects generate over time. History is readable, in other words, as a story of need's distortions. The most one can expect of a self-reflexive philosophy, Adorno concludes, is that it will reject all "palliatives" or false images of need (*ND*, 66) and "lend a voice" to a "suffering" that is more authentic because inappropriable, inconsolable, and unrelenting (*ND*, 17).

Unfortunately, however, philosophy cannot speak for the suffering that impels it except in its own, admittedly distorting idiom. Thus, Adorno's final gesture, one that can only be made after the pattern of affirmation and confession has been firmly set in place, is to save mediation once again, to acknowledge method's ability to "lend" its voice, to give or sacrifice something of itself for the sake of another.[19] As a corollary, one important to the larger argument of this book, Adorno also decides to save along with dialectics the mediation he calls the "sinful" [sündhaft] body of language.[20] But the language to which Adorno refers, the language he wants to save, is not merely demonstrative language, the philosophical terminology of dialectics; it is also, or perhaps even especially, *poetic* language, the form of language whose task, we are told, is to express "perennial suffering" (*ND*, 362). Because it insists upon the particular, the individuality of the speaking subject, poetic language constitutes philosophy's mimetic element, that element of argument that strains to set the concept within a new constellation.[21] This poetic element alone can stage affinity, can "lend" a voice to suffering, even if this voice is ultimately not suffering's own. The poetic, "sinful" body of language is the mediation that seduces as it communicates, the film, veil, or tinted transparency (*ND*, 57) that thought lays gingerly upon the world and without which this world would never attain visibility at all. But this film, this "sinful" body of language, is also a variety of "semblance" [Schein], an aesthetic illusion or epistemological ruse "bound to become entangled" in contingencies of need yet again (*ND*, 393). The Adorno of "Meditations on Metaphysics" knows he cannot do without this "naive," poetic element, and yet it is specifically for this element that he must atone.

As the reader may already have surmised, *Negative Dialectics* constitutes Adorno's most sustained and self-conscious response to Benjamin's theory of the dialectical image.[22] If for Benjamin empathetic gazing at the worn commodity allows the observer access to the "implicit history" of a living, subjective desire, for Adorno it is the "conceptual machinery" of a negative dialectics that most successfully teases out the historical distortions of need. In *Negative Dialectics* Adorno praises Benjamin's attempt to combine rationality with intuition, "incomparable speculative skill" with a collagelike "proximity" to the particular (*ND*, 18). But he also criticizes Benjamin for his "impermissible 'poetic' element" (*ND*, 18), his tendency to lend currency to names as if they were not concepts but inalienable truths (*ND*, 52). Ironically, this impermissibly "poetic" faith in a mimetic philosophy is one that Adorno ends up tentatively— and guiltily—embracing in his last chapter, "Meditations on Metaphysics." Recognizing that poetry's promise of reconciliation and transcendence reflects an ineluctable "metaphysical need" (*ND*, 371), Adorno concludes uncharacteristically by permitting philosophy to be seduced by that which it seeks, through reason, to demystify: the dream of immediacy and the realm of aesthetic semblance. Faith in poetic language, in a language of subjectivity and immediacy, causes the "fall" [Sturzes] of metaphysics; yet at the same time such a faith remains "in solidarity with metaphysics" (*ND*, 408), consonant with metaphysics's most profound desire to render the "absolute otherness terribly defying thought" (*ND*, 407). In the very last line of *Negative Dialectics* Adorno accepts this "fall"; the philosopher succumbs to the impermissibly "poetic" as he yields to the Siren's song.

––––––––––

Adorno's *Negative Dialectics* assigns lyric poetry the paradoxical task of simultaneously positing and denying the validity of its own voice. The (cautious) faith the lyricist places in language is echoed in *Negative Dialectics* in the philosophical imperative to use conceptual tools to transcend the concept. At the same time, the lyricist's doubt, the suspicious attitude toward rhetoric, finds its correlative in the philosopher's careful reappraisal of the dialectical instruments he wields. *Negative Dialectics* is lyrical to the extent that it preserves "the micrological view" (*ND*, 408), the discriminatory impulse, even while acknowledging the conceptual and rhetorical machines by which that impulse is betrayed.

The question remains, however, whether a lyric poem can be shown to resemble, in its own fashion and according to its own scale, the epistemological structure of self-reflexion, confession, and reaffirmation that Adorno presents in *Negative Dialectics*. Closer examination of a specific poem can draw out the parallels between Adorno's negative dialectics as a method for ascertaining knowledge and lyric poetry as a rhetorical language that also strives to gain access to a higher, more immediate truth. As I argued previously, Rimbaud is better suited than Baudelaire to provide an ideal illustration of Adorno's dialectical philosophy, a philosophy that manages to celebrate method—the *techne* conditioning its own conclusions—even as it confesses to the imbrication of this method in a set of heteronomous interests. The cyclical pattern of *Une Saison en enfer* could be interpreted, and indeed has been, in light of its dialectical structure. However, I want to turn to a shorter pastoral lyric entitled "Aube" (Dawn) since it offers a more concise demonstration of how lyric admits the heteronomy of its own tools. One of the most romantically inspired poems of *Illuminations*, "Aube" reproduces the argument of *Negative Dialectics* in the equivocations of a specifically lyric language. Here, faith in language's body is replaced by an admission of language's "sinful" contingency, an admission that in turn is supplanted by the realization that even a contingent language produces its own form of truth.

On a first reading, "Aube" appears to be a straightforward depiction of a scene in which contact between a subject and an object, consciousness and nature, is consummated. In terms evoking a sexual union between a masculine aggressor and a feminized dawn or "déesse," the poet imagines the immediate transmission of a knowledge that, like a scent, emanates from a more primal, visceral order of experience. "Alors je levai un à un les voiles . . . ," the speaker recounts, "et j'ai senti un peu son immense corps" [Then, one by one, I lifted up her veils . . . and I felt a little her immense body]. However, "Aube" only superficially evokes a scene in which direct contact is pursued and won; as we shall see, the well-worn cliché of the heterosexual seduction scene obscures a number of elements that in fact undermine its habitual function.

AUBE

J'ai embrassé l'aube d'été.

Rien ne bougeait encore au front des palais. L'eau était morte. Les camps d'ombres ne quittaient pas la route du bois. J'ai marché, réveillant les haleines vives et tièdes, et les pierreries regardèrent, et les ailes se levèrent sans bruit.

La première entreprise fut, dans le sentier déjà empli de frais et blêmes éclats, une fleur qui me dit son nom.

Je ris au wasserfall blond qui s'échevela à travers les sapins: à la cime argentée je reconnus la déesse.

Alors je levai un à un les voiles. Dans l'allée, en agitant les bras. Par la plaine, où je l'ai dénoncée au coq. A la grand'ville, elle fuyait parmi les clochers et les dômes, et, courant comme un mendiant sur les quais de marbre, je la chassais.

En haut de la route, près d'un bois de lauriers, je l'ai entourée avec ses voiles amassés, et j'ai senti un peu son immense corps. L'aube et l'enfant tombèrent au bas du bois.

Au reveil il était midi. (OC, 194)

DAWN

I embraced the summer dawn.

Nothing yet stirred on the face of the palaces. The water was dead. The shadows still camped in the woodland road. I walked, waking quick warm breaths; and gems looked on, and wings rose without a sound.

The first venture was, in a path already filled with fresh, pale gleams, a flower who told me her name.

I laughed at the blond wasserfall that tousled through the pines: on the silver summit I recognized the goddess.

Then, one by one, I lifted up her veils. In the lane, waving my arms. Across the plain, where I notified the cock. In the city, she fled among the steeples and the domes; and running like a beggar on the marble quays, I chased her.

Above the road near a laurel wood, I wrapped her up in her gathered veils, and I felt a little her immense body. Dawn and the child fell down at the edge of the wood.

Waking, it was noon. (Ill, 81–83)

In "Aube" the speaker's privileged relation to nature is indicated by the figure of prosopopoeia; here, as the speaker passes by, it is the flowers of the natural world that assume voice: "La première entreprise fut . . . une fleur qui me dit son nom." While the line can be read as simply reiterating a familiar topos of French romanticism, one in which the natural world speaks to man through an anthropomorphizing trope, here the purity, spontaneity, and immediate character of the transmission is challenged by the peculiar use of the word *entreprise* at the beginning of the line ("La première entreprise fut . . ."). The choice of this word seems awkward for several reasons, not the least of which is that the grammar of the sentence does not allow the reader to know with precision who or what is the agent undertaking the adventure that produces the flower's name. The vision of an Adamic universe in which man knows nature as it wishes to be known (or in which words are coterminous with the natural objects they name) is thus displaced by an equivocation: it is unclear whether the flowers independently undertake to name themselves for the speaker— who would at that point be the mute witness of their ritual—or whether the speaker, as he walks through and awakens the world to his consciousness, is engrossed in an attempt (an "entreprise") to make nature speak its being.

Ultimately, determining who or what produces the name or the speech of flowers is of subordinate concern. In fact, the grammatical ambiguity is itself significant, suggesting that in the moment of mimetic transfer— when nature speaks directly to the subject—the distinction between subject and nature collapses and they become one and the same. Rimbaud appears to be describing a spontaneous contact, the "first" and singular meeting of the speaker with the awakening world (note the use of the past absolute), a mimetic transfer of mana or knowledge from the natural world to human consciousness. However, the scenario is more complicated than it initially appears, for in "Aube" we cannot know whether we are witnessing the communion of two entities or a scene of conquest. According to the *Petit Robert*, the Old French meaning of *entreprendre* was *attaquer*, "to attack"; that is, the word belonged originally to a military vocabulary.[23] If we consider further that it was precisely during the period in which Rimbaud was writing that the word *entreprise* was acquiring new uses, uses related specifically to industry and commerce, it becomes evident to what a great extent his poem revises the topos of originary contact.[24] By linking prosopopoeia with enterprise, "Aube" evokes the very intervention of social forces the narrative of mimetic contact would seem to deny. Dictionaries printed during the course of the nineteenth century attest to the increasing association of *entreprise* with commercial and industrial (rather than military, royal, or romantic) conquests. Although the term had long been associated with "rapports marchands" [market relations] (*Petit Robert*, 700), idiomatic spin-offs, such as *entrepreneur* and the expression *l'esprit d'entreprise* emerge only in the nineteenth century.[25] The obsessive question animating the intellectual life of the time was, after all, how to define the distinction, if indeed there was one, between commercial and other, "disinterested" enterprises. The distinctly commercial character of the word "entreprise," when juxtaposed with a traditional romantic rhetoric, causes tension within the poem, the very tension that defines *Illuminations* as a study of urbanization as opposed to a book of pastoral odes. "Aube," like many other poems in the volume, depicts not an unmediated contact with nature but rather nature's original exploitation for human use. The poem thus contains its own confessional moment, one in which the very word used to indicate a mimetic transfer ends up divulging the work of instrumental reason and, as a corollary, the coercive influence of a hidden interest or "need." The word "entreprise" makes it impossible to determine whether the speech of flowers is a simple and innocent gesture ("entreprise" as a beginning or initial effort undertaken by "une fleur") or, alternatively, the result of a calculation, a project undertaken by the speaking subject for recompense.

What we can know for sure from Rimbaud's other works is that contact with the natural world is never a simple matter; it is a complex, hermetic, and even academic matter involving a "formule," a "méthode," or, as he writes in "Mouvement," a "stock d'études" [a stock of studies] (*OC*, 202). When in "Aube" Rimbaud describes the speech of flowers as the result of an "entreprise," he intimates that even the most mimetic form of knowledge—the flower's communication of its own name—involves industry, effort, the application of a technique. If we read "une fleur" as a flower of rhetoric (a reading Rimbaud's previous usages more than allow), then poetry emerges as the originary undertaking, the "première entreprise," virtually creating the world it awakens. In this scenario, what speaks to the poet is poetry itself; "I am a flower of rhetoric speaking *as* a flower," says the flower, simultaneously confessing its real name, which is rhetoric.

Another traditional image for rhetoric also plays an important role in the poem, namely, the image of the veil. In keeping with the ambiguity established by the impersonal construction "La première entreprise fut . . . ," the image of the veil returns twice in the poem, each time framed in a significantly different way. The first time it appears (in the fifth paragraph), the author implies that the veil (of rhetoric) can be lifted: "Alors je levai un à un les voiles." Here, recognition of "la déesse" ("à la cime argentée je reconnus la déesse") leads immediately to the speaker's attempt to remove her "veils." However, it turns out that the speaker will not achieve the absolute nudity of (the sun's) truth by lifting veils; rather, this speaker will end by embracing these veils, sensing by means of their accumulated mass the body beneath: "je l'ai entourée *avec* ses voiles amassés, et j'ai senti un peu son immense corps." The move from "*les* voiles" in the fifth paragraph ("Alors je levai un à un les voiles") to "*ses* voiles" in the next ("je l'ai entourée avec ses voiles amassés") indicates, as Karen Dillman has proposed, that the primary revelation recounted in "Aube" is not that veils can be lifted but rather that "veils are an important aspect of *elle* and that without them *elle* disappears."[26] Further, if we read the connective "et" in the line above as causative, then we can conclude that for Rimbaud veils are specifically that which allows intimacy; contact is never a matter of hearing the spontaneous voice of the other or of directly touching the body of the sun (knowing nature *in itself*). For epistemological contact to occur (*embrasser* as both physical intimacy and perceptual apprehension) intervention is required. And intervention is rarely innocent. In this case, the goal of the "entreprise" turns out to be to stage a seduction that reiterates itself, to create ever more veils, ever more names, and thus, ultimately, to arrive "près d'un bois de lauriers." If the poet's wish is to reach the summit of his literary career ("En haut de la route"), at the point where the "lauriers" grow, then it is indeed enterprising on his part to amass flowers and to learn their proper names. "Aube" suggests that the sensual knowledge its speaker fleetingly apprehends ("j'ai senti un peu son immense corps") derives from an enterprise that may be more than simply spiritual in character; in fact, the subject's privileged experience is indebted to a very worldly venture indeed: an effort to achieve "lauriers."

The grammar and the diction of "Aube" subtly remind us that there is no Eden without effort, no perfect knowledge disinterestedly given. The choice of the word "entreprise" is by no means fortuitous. Ultimately, the figuration of mimesis as an "entreprise" disrupts the closure of "Aube," placing it in communication with poems in the volume that more overtly thematize the encroachment of standardizing processes associated with capitalist enterprise and democratization. The adventures of modernity that Rimbaud describes in poems such as "Promontoire"— "Les plus colossales constructions de l'Italie, de l'Amérique et de l'Asie" [the most colossal edifices of Italy, America, and Asia] (*OC*, 199; *Ill*, 106–7)—and "Villes [II]"—"les conceptions de la barbarie moderne les plus colossales" [the most colossal conceptions of modern barbarity] (*OC*, 191; *Ill*, 69)—are not alien to the enterprises of the strolling poet. "Aube" in effect implicates the poetic enterprise in the larger economic trends of bourgeois Europe, trends it is difficult, the poet admits, to transcend. "La même magie bourgeoise à tous les points où la malle nous déposera!" [The same bourgeois magic wherever the mailtrain (trunk) sets you down], he exclaims in "Soir historique" (*OC*, 201; *Ill*, 115). The poet's means ("malle" and "mal") always accompany him as he travels from poem to poem, in other words, to essentially the same place. Despite all efforts to leave worldly things behind, these means—the "mal," method, or enterprise—in fact assume agency, determining where the poet will go and what he will be able to see ("à tous les points où la malle *nous* déposera").

And yet Rimbaud never renders explicit the nature of the relations between his own "entreprise" and those other, more overtly commercial enterprises governing the forward march of nations. This other type of forward march makes a dramatic appearance in "Démocratie" as nothing less than the *true* march—"La *vraie* marche" [The *real* advance], "au service des plus monstrueuses exploitations industrielles ou militaires" [at the service of the most monstrous exploitations, industrial or military] (*OC*, 204; *Ill*, 129, emphasis added). In *Illuminations* the link between "Aube" and "Démocratie," between the pastoral idyll and the conquest of territories, is evoked solely by the pressure of one discourse—"J'ai *marché*, réveillant les haleines vives et tièdes" ("Aube")—as it rubs up against another—"C'est la vraie *marche*. En avant, route!" ("Démocratie"). Rimbaud's texts allow us to establish a relation between poetic practice and expansionism that is, in the first instance, lexical. But further, both types of walking, or *marches*, are depicted as advances, one geographical, the other cognitive. Whatever irony might be intended by the citational quality of "Démocratie," it is clear that "la vraie marche" still constitutes an appropriative act, one in which the *promeneur solitaire* senses in Rousseauesque fashion his mastery over nature, just as the advancing soldier might sense the imminence of conquest. The redundancy of the figure of walking (the *marche matinale*, or promenade at dawn; the military advance, or *avant-garde*) suggests an equivalence between poetic ratiocination and the degree of sophistication exhibited by technologies responsible for the gradual expansion of colonialism, trade, and industrial standardization. The pastoral landscape of "Aube," which Jacques Plessen calls "féerique," belies a scene of labor, one in which the poet toils at a "chantier," or work space (as Rimbaud puts it in "Being Beauteous"), in an effort to "awaken" a somnolent world.[27] At no moment does Rimbaud imply that the communion poetry recounts might occur without method, without the intervention of technique. The speaker's project in "Aube" is to use rhetorical flowers as machines—like those of hydraulics or metallurgy—to animate a somatic universe, a universe of "haleines vives et tièdes," which, without the spirit of enterprise, might remain forever silent, "sans bruit."[28]

   It would be a mistake, however, to conclude that "Aube" is simply a
poem about mediation and the way it forces nature to assume an artificial
speech. The richness of Rimbaud's text, as well as its resemblance to
Adorno's own, resides in its ambiguous stance toward the "undertaking"
("entreprise"), the quest for affinity and for authentic communication.
The poem may admit that the "première entreprise" has something to
do with the acquisition of "lauriers," the promise of symbolic and even
pecuniary success, but it does not by the same token refuse the knowledge
that has been achieved or repudiate the new voice that has been heard.
The confession of impurity, in other words, fails to negate the value of
the revelation. To be sure, rhetoric is an imperfect tool with which to
approach a somatic universe, and yet it is only by applying this tool that
the subject manages to "[sentir] un peu son immense corps."

―――――――――

   "Aube" displays a peculiarly poetic mode of confession by exploiting
the historically specific multiaccentuality of words such as "entreprise,"
"lauriers," and "fleurs." *Negative Dialectics*, albeit in an entirely different
genre and idiom, exploits a similar technique, using the single word
Produziertes, for example, to refer both to the product of technology
(the commodity or factory product) and the product of thought.[29] And
yet the analogy between Rimbaud's confessional project and Adorno's
own would be misleading if the historical specificity of each were not
also brought into focus. A question that needs to be addressed, then, is
how this historical specificity affects the confession's contents (and not
just the form alone). The short lyric and the extended philosophical
treatise may share certain varieties of confessional wordplay, but what,
precisely, is the nature of the heteronomy to which each author feels he
must confess?
   Rimbaud's allusion to "entreprise" and to the pursuit of "lauriers" (a
metonym for symbolic capital) suggests that for him the desire for recognition, the desire for self-gratification and distinction through literary
achievement, constitutes the primary "sin" to be acknowledged. (This
"sin," the poet implies further, is complicit with the abuses of capitalism
in general; the complicity of Rimbaud's individual "sin" with material
conditions is of course its objective component.) Adorno's "sin," however, is more, or at least other, than a desire for distinction, although he
too knows that market pressures are never entirely foreign to philosophical speculation.[30] By the time Adorno takes up his pen to write *Negative
Dialectics* the significance of the phenomenon Rimbaud's poetry once registered—the increasing hegemony of capitalism—has been eclipsed by a

more singular event, namely, the Holocaust. As Adorno tells us, he is writing "after Auschwitz." His lyric mode of confession as well as the contents of his confession are necessarily marked by a trauma different from that registered in Rimbaud's texts. If *heteronomy* in Rimbaud's context refers to the poet's need to compete in a cultural market, a need that drives him to use (rhetorical) machines, in Adorno's context *heteronomy* refers to the disciplinary pressures that require him to rely on concepts and methods drawn from a philosophical tradition whose guiding principle has, after Auschwitz, become highly suspect.

This guiding principle is none other than the principle of "hidebound" self-preservation (*ND*, 298), an exacerbated version of the *esprit d'entreprise* acknowledged in Rimbaud's works.[31] After Auschwitz philosophy is closer to the most unalloyed manifestations of self-interest in that it remains engaged in preserving the subject from the objectivity by which it is threatened. This task obliges philosophy to rely on "models"—conceptual systems and categories—that are themselves tainted by the contingencies of the post-Holocaust "situation." According to the broad lines of the narrative Adorno offers in *Negative Dialectics*, philosophy, and more particularly the idealist tradition, merely completes the most primitive gesture of self-protection when it promotes the individual subject to the state of autonomy. The supposed "emancipation of individuality" (*ND*, 42) achieved by Enlightenment thought is fully dialectical, for it ends up producing a model of resistance to coercion that becomes coercive in turn. That is, in order to conform to its philosophical ideal, the autonomous subject must ward off all objective mediations, prove itself self-identical and immune to internal contradiction and change. The philosophical ideal of individual subjectivity, Adorno demonstrates, is a concept that actually oppresses the mobility—the very life—of the empirical subject in whose name this concept's formation was required. In brief, philosophy's cardinal "sin" is to have defended the category of the subject while simultaneously sacrificing the subjective substance this category was meant to protect. This sin becomes increasingly heinous as history progresses, for, as Adorno's analysis of Auschwitz suggests, the twentieth-century twist on the transformation of the living subject into a category is the transformation of this same subject into an indistinguishable, nugatory, and finally dispensable thing. An idealist philosophy based on the defense of the individual, Adorno gloomily concludes, anticipates not only this individual's reification but also its logically consistent demise as Holocaust "specimen" (*ND*, 362). Paradoxically, the more the category of the subject is idealized, the less the empirical individual has a right to differ from its ideologically determined mold.

Of course, philosophy does not produce fascist totalitarianism as a logical consequence of its idealism; philosophy cannot determine the composition of the forces that will employ and distort its ideational forms. But
neither has philosophy set up obstacles to the reification of the subject by
interrogating autonomous subjectivity as a conceptual category. In
Adorno's eyes, this failure to attack the sacrosanct category of the autonomous subject has incapacitated philosophy as it has sought to reconceptualize its cultural function in a post-Holocaust world. Although, as Adorno
notes, philosophy is indeed capable of struggling against its own "motor,"
of advocating self-sacrifice and even pure negativity, the major thrust of
Western systems has been toward the affirmation of human domination,
the justification of the "I" 's conquest over the world.[32]

Adorno feels his own project to be compromised, then, by philosophy's
historical role as defender of the category of the individual. Adorno's guilt
consists in continuing to speak *for* the subject in a tainted language *of* the
subject. If Rimbaud's "sin" is to seek to distinguish himself, Adorno's
"sin" is to perpetuate a tradition that champions the self as worthy of
distinction.[33] The problem Adorno faces in "Meditations on Metaphysics" is how to speak for the human subject—indeed, how to speak at all—
without evoking the hardened category of the speaking subject and, as a
corollary, without seeking the preservation of the individuated subject
who speaks.

To get to the heart of Adorno's confessional enterprise, as well as to
seize the peculiar modality of his dialectical lyricism, I propose to analyze
"After Auschwitz," the famous passage near the end of *Negative Dialectics* in which Adorno admits his guilt for, quite simply, surviving.
Strangely, Adorno's lyric moment is framed not by the first-person singular, as might be expected, but rather by passive constructions and third-
person pronouns, which attenuate what is nonetheless an obvious connection between the author and "him who was spared."

> Even in its formal freedom, the individual is as fungible and replaceable as
> under the liquidators' boots.
>
> But since, in a world whose law is universal individual profit, the individual
> has nothing but this self that has become indifferent, the performance of the
> old familiar tendency [der Vollzug der altvertrauten Tendenz] is at the same
> time the most dreadful of things. There is no getting out of this, no more than
> out of the electrified barbed wire around the camps. Perennial suffering has as
> much right to expression as a tortured man has to scream; hence it may have
> been wrong to say that after Auschwitz poems could no longer be written [nach
> Auschwitz liesse kein Gedicht mehr sich schreiben].[34] But it is not wrong to
> raise the less cultural question whether after Auschwitz it is permissible to go

on living—especially whether one who escaped by accident, one who by rights should have been killed, may go on living. Mere survival calls for the coldness, the basic principle of bourgeois subjectivity, without which there could have been no Auschwitz; this is the drastic guilt of him who was spared [drastische Schuld des Vershonten].[35]

Although Adorno's translator faithfully conveys the general meaning of the passage, he nevertheless fails to do justice to the precise syntax, to the contorted passive constructions, that the author's abhorrence of personal pronouns causes him to produce. These repeated passive constructions indicate that the one thing a subject absolutely cannot do after Auschwitz (even if this subject can return to writing poetry) is unselfconsciously say "I." To speak in the first-person singular is to commit a kind of rhetorical crime against specificity, to subsume the subject's substance in what Adorno calls a "linguistic generality" (ND, 126). However, saying "I," like living, is a habit, an "old familiar tendency" that is hard to relinquish. The "performance [Vollzug] of the old, familiar tendency" may be "dreadful," but striking the set of subjectivity would be consistent with the most genocidal impulses of repression. The "I," then, must go on inscribing itself in discourse—like a placeholder, a sign of hope held out for that which it cannot incarnate. Similarly, lyric poetry, the poetry of the "I," must go on being written. But this writing will always be a "performance," a strangely passive "being written," by writing itself. Still, if the "I" can self-consciously submit the terms of its own presentation to renewed examination, then it might model for philosophy an antidote to reason's dominion. This is Adorno's wager: that a lyric poetry willing to place itself at stake, willing to interrogate the source of its own vigor, might offer a partial solution to philosophy's aporetical condition. Poetry, as well as that "impermissible" poetic element of philosophy, might find absolution through the expression of "perennial suffering"; but after Auschwitz this suffering will include the agony of expression itself, the agony, that is, of having one's own suffering depersonalized, already written out.

Adorno's proposed antidote to affirmative dialectics is one he derives at least in part from the self-reflexive poetries of the late nineteenth century. Of course, in "After Auschwitz" Adorno is describing a crisis he identifies solely with his own historical period. It is possible nonetheless to seize a premonition of this crisis in the lyrics Rimbaud composed almost a century earlier. Adorno's confession in the (plural) third person (the German reads literally, "the drastic guilt of *the spared ones*") is anticipated by Rimbaud in "Aube" at the moment when the first-person singular ("*J'ai embrassé l'aube d'été*") gives way in the final lines to the third-

person "enfant" ("L'aube et *l'enfant* tombèrent au bas du bois"). Shifting
from first to third person, the speaking subject of "Aube"—like Adorno's
demystified performer—takes a step backward to observe the artificiality
of its own gesticulations. According to Adorno, this step is one all "thinking men and artists" have taken.[36] It is not incidental that at the very
moment the subject steps backward to assume the stance of the "spectator," this subject also looses footing and *falls*: "L'aube et l'enfant *tombèrent* au bas du bois." For the depersonalization of spectatorship is also a
kind of sin, the sin of privileging distance and objectification over participation and one's own subjective (and thus potentially empathetic) experience of suffering.[37] The fact that "Aube" terminates in an entirely impersonal construction ("Au reveil *il était midi*") is suggestive of the inversion
of the lyric condition, one in which the subject acknowledges mediation,
yields to the third person, and thus risks its total evacuation as a unique
human presence. In the final lines of "Aube" Rimbaud's subject takes this
plunge: a pastoral universe of nymphs and lovers is replaced by a landscape that allows no subjective description since it can be better rendered
in the precise language of chronometrics. But the question still remains
whether this replacement of the subject with a purely scientific objectivity
is the solution Adorno's negative dialectics requires. To be sure, the language of subjectivity is bound to be tainted, but would anyone want to
awaken to a world without mediation, a world without shadows or veils?

Ultimately, as Adorno implies in "After Auschwitz," the lyric "I" must
be preserved as a kind of reminder of the resistance to total standardization it represents. In the right hands the "I," or the category of the subject,
may become a thoroughly dialectical entity. As the poets of the twentieth
century discover, the "I" is both "the product of pressure," a distorted,
already "written" thing, and "the energy center for resistance to this pressure," the potential agent of its own rewriting (*ND*, 283).

But if, as Adorno repeatedly insists, even the most self-reflexive languages
fall short of their ideal, then in what sense can they still be called "authentic" or "valid"? Why should poetic conduct—as the subject's resistance
to the pressure of standardization—be saved if it is nothing more than
"the performance of the old, familiar tendency," "the most dreadful of
things"?

Problematic as it may seem, terms such as *authentic* and *valid* play an
extremely important role in Adorno's aesthetic and philosophical meditations. From his early work on Kierkegaard all the way through to his last
unfinished work, *Aesthetic Theory*, the question of authenticity returns
to haunt Adorno's most affirmative or at least most resigned moments.

The persistence of *authenticity* as a critical term seems curious, given its polemical use in *The Jargon of Authenticity*, of 1964. Adorno is obviously aware that in the German cultural context of the thirties and forties (and even after Auschwitz) to speak of authenticity is to invoke a fascist discourse concerned with cynically promoting the centrality and autonomy of the self.[38] The fact that Adorno recuperates the term and uses it so widely in *Aesthetic Theory* indicates that he perceives even within its fascist appropriation the distortion of an irrepressible "ontological need" for some type of transcendent experience. Validating the need but not the form it has taken, Adorno opts to rescue the term but, in true dialectical manner, strategically reverses Heidegger's usage: *authenticity* will now be redefined as lyric's grasp of its own immanence to, rather than transcendence of, historical contingencies. Dialectically reconstituted, the opposition between *authenticity* (the knowledge of immanence) and *inauthenticity* (the illusion of transcendence) comes to serve as a significant principle structuring Adorno's corpus.

This opposition is also one that informs the work of Paul de Man, a literary critic whose theory of subjective expression arguably offers the most persuasive alternative to Adorno's more historically oriented model. The comparison between de Man's deconstruction of the cognitive moment and Adorno's redemption of the same is a fruitful one, for it highlights the crucial difference between a critical approach that terminates in a totalizing vision of loss and one that alternates incessantly between a vision of loss and a glimpse of potential gain. In many respects, de Man's theory of poetic language reflects Adorno's darker, Baudelairean side, but it does not cover the full ground of Adorno's materialist aesthetics.[39] For Adorno, the "authentic" consciousness—artistic, critical, or philosophical—is one that denies transcendence and yet retains faith in its eventual realization. In contrast, de Man refuses the term *authenticity* altogether but nonetheless reintroduces the distinction between the two modes of consciousness at a higher level. An "authentic" consciousness is replaced in de Man's constellation by a language that "asserts the knowledge" of its own inauthenticity; meanwhile, the blindly "inauthentic" consciousness continues to exist in a state of "mystified adjustment."[40] Confessing its inauthenticity does not ensure the authenticity of either the subject or its language: "to know inauthenticity," de Man underlines, "is not the same as to be authentic" (214). Recounting Baudelaire's story of the Sage from "De l'essence du rire" [The Essence of the Comic], de Man insists that the poet's error, or "fall," is a demystifying moment entailing pure anguish, an acute sense of impotence or loss (the loss, specifically, of the illusion of autonomy, self-mastery, and mastery over nature through language).[41] Characteristically, de Man denies that this anguish, this self-reflexive *dédoublement*, can lead to anything other than a heightened consciousness of one's own irremediable factitiousness. It is worthwhile, de Man seems to suggest, to acknowledge the need that makes us long for domination of the unknown (our need to dominate nature, for instance, our need for autonomy and the transcendence of mediation, our need, even, for "reference"), but there can be nothing gained (except allegory) from an analysis of this need's historical modes of appearing.

However, if for de Man there is no fully "authentic" stance available to the modern subject, Adorno, in contrast, rescues the term to refer to a specific variety of self-reflexive artistic practice. This practice involves a self-reflexive moment, one in which the artist attempts to seize the historical forms into which need has been distorted. For Adorno, the distorting element that prevents consubstantiality between name and thing, the conceptual and the nonconceptual, is neither historically uniform nor exclusively rhetorical. It is for this reason that a confessional dialectics must lead to immanent critique.

De Man seems to fear that the subject's grasp of mediation (its "assertion of inauthenticity") might reinforce an equally mystified belief in its own transcendence of this mediation. By refusing the term *authentic* as a qualifier for any conscious stance whatsoever de Man hopes to discourage the remystification of the cognitive moment. But Adorno cannot entirely deny the desire for a transcendent or demystified state of consciousness; ultimately, for him, the ideal of transcendence expresses an authentic or constitutive aspect of human longing. Adorno thus chooses to honor the naiveté of idealism and risk reintroducing ideology. As a result, he ends up embracing a set of poets that de Man never even allows into the purview of his critical gaze, poets who ecstatically envision the acquisition of a "transfigured body" and mind (*ND*, 400). This utopian transfiguration may indeed be a creation of language itself, but if so, it is a creation of that part of language that is consubstantial with a longing for truth. "*Aux sots je préfère les fous*," quips Adorno. "Folly is truth in the form which men are struck with as amid untruth they will not let truth go" (*ND*, 404).

Clearly, for Adorno the confession of mediation constitutes a kind of "fall," an instance of the subject's demotion and loss of stature. However, this fall is also potentially a liberating moment, one in which the subject discards the yoke of solipsism by acknowledging its debt to conditions it can never fully control. Confession may lead merely to its own repetition; however, there is always the chance that confession will also provide an experience in which the subject's bounded, reified identity is, for a vital instant, productively weakened. At this instant the subject would not find itself above its surroundings but rather coextensive with them. In other words, the "promesse" of harmony between name and being would be realized not by name's transmutation into pure subjectivity; rather, the subject would achieve consubstantiality with the objective (the name, the concept, or the machine) by seizing *itself* as a partially objective being. The "transfigured body" attained would then be similar to the yogic body, which loosens its boundaries to experience its continuity with all earthly things. This is specifically the experience Adorno prescribes as an "antidote" to philosophy's hypostatization of the subject, for it allows this subject to reappraise itself as objectively mediated, that is, as part of the natural history it once hoped to tame (*ND*, 13). The confessional moment in Adorno emerges, then, both as a relapse into despair, a state in which the subject observes itself as a dead (linguistic) thing, and, conversely, as an advance toward freedom, a state in which the subject is reborn as historically constituted rather than bounded and isolated. For as the subject relinquishes the illusion of an isolated, autonomous consciousness, a pure subjectivity, it can also be reconciled with a social collectivity, a collectivity defined not by some shared demystified experience of the present but rather by a set of historically specific epistemologies and discursive formations by which a generation seizes the unassimilable, irreducible real.

It would seem, then, that Adorno offers a third option unavailable within de Man's binary system (in which one is either mystified or aware that one is mystified). For Adorno the alternative is not to overcome inauthenticity, to achieve a pure experience of the self (just as one can never unmediatedly express suffering), but rather to seize the self as a historically constituted being. On the pragmatic level, then, Adorno's third option involves analyzing the distinct properties of the various, probably infinite veils and allegories the subject spins. For these veils, these modes of being, are not independent or serendipitous creations either of the subject or of language (understood as a static, self-identical, uninflected entity). These veils are borrowed instead from an ever-changing succession of collective discourses, images, and epistemologies available to the speaker at a particular moment in time. The "authentic" lyricist uses the occasion of the "I" 's dissolution to examine the historical content of the rhetorical, conceptual, or mechanical veils the "I" has worn. For like any instance of apparel, these veils possess a "temporal nucleus" (*AT*, 192), a constitutive bond with lived time. Of course, such a project of examination will always lead the subject to generate yet more veils, yet more allegories. Ultimately, it is up to the critic to decide whether these veils manage to capture "a bit of the reality"—"un peu [de l']immense corps"—that once required their formation.

If philosophy were to follow the arc of the lyric's "fall," it might succeed in completing a "Copernican turn" that Adorno considers long overdue (*ND*, 66). This Copernican turn would unseat the subject from its position at the center of the universe, confronting it finally with a less self-serving vision of its only partial and perhaps secondary role in a dialectical interchange with first and then second nature. But the "prevailing trend in epistemological reflection," Adorno reminds us, has been instead to solidify the subject's domination, "to reduce objectivity more and more to the subject" (*ND*, 176). In opposition to this trend, Adorno calls for a form of reflection—and a form of art—that would reverse philosophy's momentum, placing the subject in jeopardy but at the same time recalling this subject's essential mobility, its unstable nature: its slave's freedom.

Thus, if de Man experiences the exposure of heteronomy, the subject's "thingness," as an occasion for anguish and despair, Adorno recognizes in the confession of heteronomy the opportunity to revise idealist conceptions of both the subject and the nature of its freedom or authenticity. In sum, Adorno rescues the term *authenticity* to designate an artistic consciousness that confesses mediation (that "asserts" a knowledge of its own "inauthenticity") but seeks in this very confession a redefinition of the subject and a reconceptualization of that subject's relation to objective conditions. *Negative Dialectics* reflects the guarded optimism of this second approach, for even as it proposes a critique of *techne* (as method, rhetoric, or even technology) it celebrates *techne* as providing the only potential bridge to a new, always historically framed knowledge of the self *as* historically framed.

It is for this reason that Adorno's dialectical approach appears more appropriate to the larger corpus of poetic modernism than does de Man's deconstruction of the cognitive moment. De Man's theory of literature as allegory is a persuasive tool for studying a wide variety of romantic and early modernist texts; however, it fails to account adequately for the full evolution of twentieth-century avant-garde lyricism. Within de Man's perspective there is no way to address the significance of avant-garde pastiche, dadaist institutional critique, the futurist machine aesthetic, or the hybrid poetries of postmodernism.[42] Writers such as Rimbaud, Apollinaire, and Cendrars may confess to the "inauthenticity" of a language that aspires to be utterly subjective, but in their works this confession rises above the order of lament and self-mockery to assume a tone of exultation. These poets, that is, do not invariably take the revelation that the traditional idealist subject is mediated, and thus "inauthentic," to be crippling; on the contrary, they sometimes experience the exposure of the subject's heteronomy as lyric's greatest potential. After all, the fall from the height of autonomy brings the poet down to the level of the street, and the street, if we are to believe André Breton, is the only place where things (like history) are really happening.[43] For Cendrars too, falling into the street, into the arms of the impersonally generated discourses of the billboard or the *affiche*, rewards the poet with the discovery not only that these discourses are eloquent with "implicit history" but that this history may potentially reveal a previously inarticulate element of the poet's own being. By embracing the many discourses—from the romantic to the commercial—informing the subject's own, avant-garde poets imply that they harbor a variety of longing unavailable to a "significative language," a traditional lyric idiom: "Emphatically modern art breaks out of the sphere of the portrayal of emotions and is transformed into the expression of what no significative language can achieve" (*AT*, 60).

The art historian Johanna Drucker has suggested with particular reference to Apollinaire that the avant-garde poet manages to raise the question how a subjectivity is constituted precisely by integrating mechanically reproduced languages that apparently do not emanate from a single bounded subject. "The leap Apollinaire is making," states Drucker, "is not merely toward a different source of poetic language, but toward a different concept of subjectivity, one more fully conscious of the *social component of subject formation*."[44] The revelation that lyric expression bears a "social component," that it is shot through and through not only with literary but also with "public" languages, is experienced by many avant-garde poets as the very opportunity for the artist to conduct critical cultural work. For as much as the failure of the romantic subject to produce itself and its own discourses might appear at first as a "fall" back into a dependent state of animality, this same failure can also be conceived as the event that promises the end of the metaphysical isolation of the subject that idealism had imposed. Poets of *le travail nouveau*, from Rimbaud to Laurie Anderson, understand the declaration "JE est un autre" to mean not simply that the self relies upon alien means in order to generate itself but, further, that these means may be manipulated like so many knobs and buttons on a subject-producing machine. For them, that is, the heterogeneous nature of self-generation might offer the occasion for a pastiche reconstruction of the self. In this second, decidedly more affirmative scenario the self declares that it will learn something about its own nature by allowing the other to speak in its place. The impersonal discourses of the random, of advertising, of newsprint, of computer-generated speech, and even of a negative dialectics are cherished rather than repudiated as "inauthentic," for they promise, despite their heteronomy and their historical limitations, to reveal a latent truth about the nature of human subjectivity. The wager the twentieth-century lyricist makes is that if there is no discourse "born exclusively of the subject" (*AT*, 24), then neither is the heteronomous born exclusively of the objective other.

Finally, the demise of the romantic performative subject opens up new vistas for lyric poetry while altering in significant ways its formal and thematic character. This is not to say that avant-garde poets are uniformly sanguine concerning the intertextual, paratextual, commercial, and technological mediations that challenge the autonomy of the lyric subject. One can easily find moments in the work of Rimbaud, Apollinaire, Cendrars, Char, or Smith and Anderson, for that matter, when a nostalgia for the romantic image of subjective plenitude is clearly expressed. But I would argue in conclusion that it is precisely this alternation between affirmation and regret, faith and suspicion, that most successfully characterizes the distinct voices of the poetic avant-garde. The discovery of mediation, of the self's implication in the public domain, can inspire a joyous inventiveness even while rekindling fears of technological determinism and bureaucratic control. Adorno's dialectical aesthetics helps us to account for the aporetic condition of the subject after romanticism; his *Negative Dialectics* is the testament of the human subject as cyborg, a creature who must write through a distorting apparatus in order to achieve, paradoxically, an authentic voice.

Four

Blaise Cendrars and the Heterogeneous Discourses of the Lyric Subject

BLAISE CENDRARS is arguably Rimbaud's most direct poetic heir. The attitude toward modern technology that Rimbaud exhibits in his poems is explicitly assumed by Cendrars, who manifests his debt by extrapolating from the earlier poet's dialectical confessions a set of experimental techniques. The pastiche quality of Rimbaud's "Paris," for instance, a poem composed entirely of advertisements appearing on the city's walls,[1] anticipates the mature technique of Cendrars's *Dix-neuf poèmes élastiques* (Nineteen elastic poems), of 1919, a volume that juxtaposes in collage fashion a number of discourses drawn from mechanically reproduced popular forms of the early twentieth century. Both the irony and the excitement conveyed by a poem such as "Paris" reemerge in Cendrars's early works, indicating that he too felt ambivalence in the face of a world undergoing dramatic economic, social, and epistemological transformations.

Like those of Rimbaud, the works of Cendrars have also produced a schism within the critical community. Anxious to distinguish Cendrars from Marinetti, to whom he has often been compared, one group of scholars has denied the poet's futurist tendencies. They insist that Cendrars's poetics were fundamentally nostalgic, evoking modern mechanization only to deride it or to reveal its dangers. Others, however, believe that Cendrars embraced the modern world wholeheartedly, promoting capitalist expansion in Brazil, for instance, or unabashedly celebrating the protosociety of the spectacle.[2] The difficulty Cendrars's critics have had reaching a consensus on the poet's relation to modernity indicates that a fundamental tension resides within his corpus, a tension responsible, I would suggest, for his ambiguous status within the French modernist canon. Was Cendrars a futurist, a dadaist, or a nostalgic high modernist? Did he celebrate modernity or, conversely, regard it with acute skepticism?

Cendrars's lyric poetry is of particular interest for a study of modernity's influence, for, in the absence of Apollinaire (who died in 1918), he remains the only major French poet to have wrestled with the full implications of futurist thought. As opposed to a futurist like Marinetti, however, Cendrars never abandoned the lyric "I," although he did, as we shall see, interrogate its autonomy in a way few others have attempted.[3] Echoing

Rimbaud, Cendrars registered both the promise and the threat that the machine held out for a textual practice invested in the integrity of the subject. Cendrars thus provides an illuminating example of a modern lyricist at odds with the very dynamism he emulates. His ambiguous position with regard to modern technology reflects a tension peculiar to the lyric's confrontation with the machine.

———————

In a recent article on Cendrars's futurist novel, *Moravagine*, Jay Bochner reproduces two contradictory versions of a brief text by Cendrars in which the issue of modern technology and its potentially pernicious role in everyday life is explicitly addressed.[4] The text concerned is the "Lettre en guise de postface" (Letter in place of a postface), an epistolary stamp of approval that Cendrars was asked to provide for Jean Epstein's *La Poésie d'aujourd'hui: un nouvel état d'intelligence* [Poetry today: a new state of awareness].[5] The first version of the missive, which Bochner ratifies, reads as follows:

> Brisure nette. Nouveau départ direct sur ligne d'acier.
> Il y a l'époque: tango, ballets Russes, cubisme, Mallarmé, bolchévisme intellectuel, insanité.
> Puis la guerre: un vide.
> Puis l'époque: construction, simultanéisme, affirmation. Calicot: Rimbaud: changement de propriétaire. Affiches. La façade des maisons mangées par les lettres. La rue enjambée par le mot. *La machine moderne dont l'homme sait se passer.* Bolchévisme en action. Monde.

> Clean break. A new departure, straight ahead on a line of steel.
> There is the epoch: tango, Russian ballet, cubism, Mallarmé, intellectual bolchevism, madness.
> Then the war: a void.
> Then the epoch: construction, simultaneity, affirmation. Salesman: Rimbaud: a change of ownership. Posters. The facade of buildings eaten by letters. Words spanning the street. *The modern machine that man can do without.* Bolchevism in action. World.[6]

The second version, proposed by Claude Leroy in "Inédits et documents" [Unpublished works and documents], resembles the first in every respect except its rendering of the third to last line, which reads: "La machine moderne dont l'homme *ne* sait se passer" [The modern machine that man *cannot* do without].[7] Leroy justifies his addition of the negative "ne" by referring to the context in which the "postface" was written: "The context, as well as everything we know about the Cendrars of 1920, obliges us, in our opinion, to make this correction" (182). It is true, as

Leroy points out, that the essays Cendrars wrote during the late teens and early twenties—"Profond aujourd'hui" (Profound today [1917]), "J'ai tué" (I have killed [1918]), and "L'ABC du cinéma" (The ABCs of cinema [1917, revised 1921])—tend to display a relatively positive attitude toward the mechanical. And yet his tone in these essays is always slightly ironical. A glance at the literary context cannot, then, tell us precisely what Cendrars was trying to suggest in his letter to Epstein. Did he intend to present machines as essential or incidental, beneficial or potentially dangerous, to human existence?

Taking up the question of Cendrars's attitude toward modern means of reproduction in "Blaise without War," Bochner insists that the latter interpretation is the correct one. In reference to *Moravagine* and, more particularly, to that curious hymn to the machine later anthologized as "Le Principe de l'utilité" [The utility principle], Bochner hypothesizes that for Cendrars, machines "in that first context of love, are the purveyors of freedom, loving and flying, but in the context of imprisonment, they are agents of repression" (56). Cendrars advocates mechanical means, Bochner concludes, but only as long as they serve to prolong rather than direct the artisan's will. Against Leroy's version of the "Lettre en guise de postface," Bochner calls to his defense the finale of *Moravagine*, in which the machine, once touted for its creative potential, now falls into the hands of conflicting but equally destructive nationalisms.

There are many reasons to adopt Bochner's perspective. His theory explains, for instance, Cendrars's growing disenchantment with the ideals of the machine aesthetic and, more generally, with a democratic capitalism he describes mischievously in the "Lettre en guise de postface" as a "Bolchévisme en action." As several critics have remarked, Cendrars's mature novel of 1949, *Le Lotissement du ciel* [Parceling out the sky], explicitly associates a "machinisme impitoyable" with slavery and mass genocide rather than with progress and the equal distribution of goods.[8] In a similar about-face Cendrars laments in 1954 the domination of the very commercial iconographies he praises earlier in the "Lettre en guise de postface." The *affiches* that are seen in 1921 as decorative elements reanimating the dull cityscape are now accused of destroying the unique identity of the local environment.[9] But the linear development that critics want to attribute to Cendrars's assessment of modernity belies what I believe to be a more dialectical approach, evident even in his earliest descriptions of modern life. In the "Lettre en guise de postface," for instance, Cendrars intimates that the colorful "affiches" that poetically span the street ("La rue *enjambée* par le mot") contain a hidden menace. By describing the facades of urban habitations as "mangées par les lettres" [eaten by letters], Cendrars suggests that commercially inspired inscriptions in effect perpetrate a form of violence on the cityscape even as they render it spectacular, theatrical, aesthetic.

Aestheticization is often associated with violence in Cendrars's work. To transform the city into a surface of inscriptions, to link *(enjamber)* one street to another as poetic syntax might link two verses, is also to injure in some way an original visual identity. In contrast to his futurist contemporaries, Cendrars does not merely celebrate the violence of aestheticization; he is highly concerned with the ethical consequences of aesthetic choices. Cendrars's approach to the machine is far more nuanced than that of the futurists, for he realizes that by adopting mechanical means or, alternatively, by assimilating mechanical languages and iconographies the art object stands both to gain and to lose. Forms of artistic expression cannot evolve, cannot widen the range of their influence, without disabling other, equally significant functions. The machine is thus a fully dialectical entity for Cendrars: it threatens to obliterate certain forms of experience while simultaneously providing humans with visual and verbal languages they would not otherwise have at their disposal. For Cendrars, then, the violence of industrialization produces a new and vital aesthetic of the everyday, just as the aesthetic of the everyday inflicts a certain form of violence on other expressive modes (such as the pastoral, the lyric, the elegy) and the forms of subjective experience associated with them (tranquillity, intimacy with nature, the monolingualism of solitude).

Cendrars's logic as it is exposed in "Le Principe de l'utilité" explains a good deal about his approach not only to mechanical forms of reproduction but also to the discourses they engender. Here, Cendrars appears almost uniformly sanguine (the essay is even dedicated to Henry Ford). He insists, for instance, that the principle responsible for the spread of industrialism, colonialism, and capitalist enterprise is also the inspiration for a highly valued "langage nouveau,"[10] the language of the ubiquitous *affiche* that Cendrars, like other artists of his time, finds "liberating."[11] This "langage nouveau" of the advertisement, dangerous as it may prove to be, nonetheless appeals to Cendrars. He refuses to associate industrial expansion and its corollary, advertising, solely with the profit motive but claims instead that they represent the previously unappreciated voice of "le peuple." Because "le principe de l'utilité" hypothetically functions to provide the most people with the most wares, it can be said to incarnate the will of the people ("la personnalité populaire").[12] Artists who would condemn industrial expansionism live in ignorance ("vivent à côté") of the people and their material and sensual needs:

> Les intellectuels ne s'en rendent pas encore compte, les philosophes l'ignorent toujours . . . les artistes vivent à côté, seul l'immense peuple des ouvriers a assisté à la naissance quotidienne de ces nouvelles formes de la vie, a travaillé à leur éclosion, a collaboré à leur propagation . . . a pris le volant en mains.

Intellectuals don't yet understand and philosophers never will . . . artists too miss the point. Only the immense population of workers witness the daily birth of these new forms of life; only they have worked to see them blossom; only they have collaborated in their propagation . . . only they have taken things into their own hands. (50)

To be sure, Cendrars's vision of a "Bolchévisme en action" is far removed from the reality of industrial domination he apprehends later on. Nevertheless, his naive depiction of modern life contains in embryo a theory of commercial discourses that was in fact adopted by a surprisingly wide variety of early-twentieth-century artists and writers.[13] This theory receives elaboration in Cendrars's longer essays, where commercial languages, although industrially produced, nonetheless appear to be both popular and populist in orientation. The "bel optimisme" [beautiful optimism] of the machine and its exultant self-advertisements are not oppressive and dehumanizing but rather constitute "le prolongement de la personnalité populaire, . . . la réalisation de ses pensées les plus intimes . . . de ses appétits les plus forts" [the extension of the will of the people, . . . the realization of its most intimate thoughts . . . its sharpest appetites].[14] Cendrars wants to be the poet who listens to this language of the appetites; more than that, he wishes to weave this language into the very fabric of his own song. In Adorno's terms, Cendrars discerns in popular discourses a reflection of legitimate human appetites, or "needs"; what he does not yet perceive is the extent to which these needs have been distorted into exploitative forms.

These "new" languages of "the people" are actually quite diverse in nature; they embrace not only the idioms of advertising—"les affiches multicolores et les lettres gigantesques"—but also a vast set of industrially produced discourses that Cendrars will appropriate for poetic use, such as "le code des signaux, la T.S.F." [coded transmissions, wireless communications], the discourses of advertising and cinema, and even the "constellations électriques" of the recently invented neon sign (52). For Cendrars, these idioms constitute an "écriture démotique" [demotic writing], a writing, moreover, that would never have come into existence without the intervention of commerce, industry, and the application of their inexorable "principe."

Because the modern machine is responsible for these new languages of appetite and affect, man in fact *cannot* do without them. Machines give voice to elements of the human condition that more conventional aesthetic and religious languages have either sublimated or denied. The pursuit of capital cannot be rejected out of hand, reasons Cendrars, for it facilitates an expression not only of the "personnalité populaire" but also of that element of the artist or intellectual repressed by the asceticism of a purely abstract aesthetic language. As simplistic as advertising, tele-graphic, and radiophonic languages may be, they at least provide a counter to the now equally reified language of the solipsistic romantic genius, that metaphysical, hermetic, and self-indulgent discourse of the nineteenth-century aristocratic elite.[15]

Cendrars indicates clearly in a short missive of 1913 that his own goal as a poet will be to emancipate poetry from these abstract aesthetic lan-guages, and thus from its subservience to one, supposedly universal form of "taste." Troping on Kant, Cendrars claims that he is "trop sensuel pour avoir 'du goût.' J'ai tous les goûts" [I am too sensual to have "taste." I like everything (literally, "I have all tastes")].[16] The heterogeneous and contingent sensual appetites to which Kant self-consciously opposes his definition of the beautiful must become, for Cendrars, the very matter of an avant-garde verbal art. But for Cendrars writing avant-garde poetry does not require that one jettison poetic discourse or repudiate one's "taste" for the classical beauties of high art. Rather, the avant-garde poet must treat traditional poetic discourse as one among a cornucopia of other, equally significant (and often mechanically reproduced) discourses: "J'ai *tous* les goûts," he insists. Accordingly, paraliterary and nonliterary discourses are absorbed into the poet's verbal palette, just as machines, as well as the benefits they provide, are absorbed into everyday life. Poetry cannot ignore the "personnalité populaire" as it is manifested in diverse discourses of sensual appetite but must instead open its borders to these discourses previously excluded from the poetic idiolect.

However, Cendrars's goal in the poetry he writes after 1913 is not merely to enrich the vocabulary of poetic language by adding elements of the "vulgaire."[17] He also wants to demonstrate that poetic language, like popular prose, receives its very energy from the "vulgaire" and that there-fore the distinction between an autonomous lyric discourse and the heter-onomous commercial and popular discourses from which it departs can-not, in good faith, be rigorously maintained. As in romantic poetry, which depicts the poet as inspired (in the strong sense of filled with breath or energy) by a transcendent muse, divinity, or spirit, Cendrars's poetry of-fers us a speaking subject informed by a voice not fully its own. In Cen-drars's case, however, this voice is polyphonous rather than "monoto-nous,"[18] composed of a set of heterogeneous voices, sounds, and cries originating in, and transmitted from, a variety of popular domains. For Cendrars, then, it is not only the novel that is "heteroglossic," as Bakhtin has claimed;[19] the poem too retains the trace of other types of contempo-rary discursive practice upon its increasingly irregular surface.

Cendrars seeks to dramatize the heteroglossia informing his own lyric voice by integrating into his poetry discourses traditionally foreign to po-etic composition. But he does so not to replace art, in dadaist fashion, with anti-art, for these discourses *are* a form of art, a type of aesthesis (from which the word *aesthetic* is derived), an expression of the senses. At least this is what Cendrars implies in these early essays. Elsewhere, Cendrars seems to be registering an entirely different phenomenon in modern experience. This phenomenon appears in his poetic works as the substitution of a spiritual order not by a popular, colloquial order but by an overtly commercial one. If earlier poets were unable to determine where their own voice ended and the voice of a divine or natural other began, Cendrars finds himself in a similar predicament, unable to determine whether the appetites that speak through him are distorted by industry or emanate directly from his own being. Cendrars may have been capable of unambiguously celebrating modernity's "new language" in his early essays, but his poetry of the same period represents the eclipse of the subject's autonomy in more equivocal terms. The heterogeneity of the subjective voice is seen as both liberating and, at the same time, a cause for mourning. These more elegiac poems (from "Les Pâques à New York" to "La Guerre au Luxembourg") have inspired some critics to view Cendrars as a nostalgic modernist, entirely skeptical of the very economic and social transformations he seems to be applauding in essays such as "Profond aujourd'hui." There is something to be said for this view, although I believe Cendrars's approach to be far more dialectical. The poems of *Dix-neuf poèmes élastiques* in particular are exemplary of this dialectical approach. Here, even while testing out the verbal potential of the "prospectus," the "catalogue" and the "affiche" (as Apollinaire advised poets to do in "Zone"),[20] Cendrars signals his reservations concerning the legitimacy of the voices coloring his own.

Dix-neuf poèmes élastiques, Cendrars's 1919 collection of prewar and postwar compositions, constitutes his most persistent attempt to integrate paraliterary and nonliterary discourses into the poetic text. The first poem of the volume, "Journal" (Newspaper), of 1913, self-consciously weaves into its verbal texture discursive elements explicitly associated with mechanical modes of reproduction. The poem openly transgresses the frontier between the first-person discourse of the lyric and the impersonal discourses of popular forms; in doing so, it also troubles the boundary traditionally maintained between the private and the public, the profoundly subjective and the collectively shared. In "Journal" the order of the aesthetic enters into a curious dialogue with the order of the popular or the everyday; this intertwining of existential orders (and discursive registers) is typical of the volume as a whole. A brief examination of the poem "Journal" provides a sense of how Cendrars works to revise the

lyric poem by making audible within it the mechanically reproduced
voices "dont l'homme *ne* sait se passer." Cendrars stages a lyric moment
in which the autonomous subject confronts the possibility that these discourses inform its identity from within; such a possibility is experienced
as both reinvigorating and frightening, a cause for jubilation and a source
of pain.

"Journal" begins with an apostrophe to "Christ," then moves rapidly
into an anecdotal and confessional first-person narrative.

JOURNAL
Christ
Voici plus d'un an que je n'ai plus pensé à Vous
Depuis que j'ai écrit mon avant-dernier poème Pâques
Ma vie a bien changé depuis
Mais je suis toujours le même
J'ai même voulu devenir peintre
Voici les tableaux que j'ai faits et qui ce soir pendent aux murs
Ils m'ouvrent d'étranges vues sur moi-même qui me font penser à Vous.

Christ
La vie
Voilà ce que j'ai fouillé

Mes peintures me font mal
Je suis trop passionné
Tout est orangé.

NEWSPAPER
Christ
It's been more than a year now since I stopped thinking about You
Since I wrote my next-to-last poem "Easter"
My life has changed a lot since
But I'm still the same
I even wanted to become a painter
Here are the pictures I've done and which hang on the walls tonight
For me they open strange views onto myself which make me think of You.

Christ
Life
Here's what I've gotten out of it

My paintings hurt me
I'm too passionate
Everything is orange.[21]

At first, the speaker seems to be haunted by the figure of Christ, one that appears to be informing the subject's attempt at self-portraiture. The single appellative, "Christ," appears three times in the poem, effectively dividing it into three discrete sections (the fourth begins with the related term "Passion"). If at first "Christ" functions as the apostrophe of a confessional discourse, it soon begins to look increasingly like a slogan, even a newspaper caption isolated on the page. In the third section the word "Christ" does not begin the stanza but rather appears after a reference to the "Journal" of the title:

J'ai passé une triste journée à penser à mes amis
Et à lire le journal
Christ
Vie crucifiée dans le journal grand ouvert que je tiens les bras tendus
Envergures
Fusées
Ebullition
Cris.
On dirait un aéroplane qui tombe.
C'est moi.
　　(*Du monde entier*, 69–70)

I spent a sad day thinking about my friends
And reading the paper
Christ
Life crucified in the wide-open paper I hold outstretched
Wing-spread
Rockets
Turmoil
Cries.
You'd say an airplane was falling.
It's me.
　　(*Complete Poems*, 53, trans. modified)

In the lines above "Christ" functions as a hinge between two opposed semantic fields: the sacred and the popular (profane). If previously the reference to Christ suggested a confessional moment, a subject's intimate prayer, the context of this third reference produces a somewhat different impression. The allusion to how the speaker spent the day—"à lire le journal"—transforms "Christ" from a vocative, a spontaneous exclamation, into a printed word found, for instance, in a "journal." The next stanzas work to intensify the confusion between the discursive registers of the personal confession (exclamation) and the mechanically reproduced (reportage). First, through both apposition and the figure of crucifixion

"Christ" is identified with the "Life" reported in the newspaper. Further, a few lines down the name "Christ" is echoed in the noun "Cris." This "Cris" can be read either as the hortatory exclamation of the crucified subject ("C'est moi") or as a descriptive element in an appositive sequence of events narrated by the newspaper ("Fusées / Ebullition / Cris"). Thus, in this one word we hear a near homonym of the name Christ, the spontaneous cry of the subject *(cri)*, and the sounds of the newspaper (the "Cris" the newspaper is reporting). Similarly, the word "Passion" no longer seems to point to only one referent. Life, as the newspaper tells us, is full of tales of crucifixion; the speaking subject too stretches out his arms in the posture of the crucified; and finally, the newspaper takes the form of a crucified victim extended upon the cross of the subject's arms.[22] The intensity of the Passion links the speaking subject to Christ and then, in turn, to the discourse of the newspaper. The final stanzas of "Journal" reproduce in condensed form these same juxtapositions.

> Passion
> Feu
> Roman-feuilleton
> Journal
> On a beau ne pas vouloir parler de soi-même
> Il faut parfois crier
>
> Je suis l'autre
> Trop sensible
>   (*Du monde entier*, 69)

> Passion
> Fire
> Serial novel
> Newspaper
> It's useless not wanting to talk about yourself
> You have to cry out sometimes
>
> I am the other
> Too sensitive.
>   (*Complete Poems*, 54, trans. modified)

Here, the fires of the Passion suddenly reappear in a popular form: the "Feu" is resurrected in the "Roman-*feu*illeton." Meanwhile, "Passion" evokes simultaneously the Passion of Christ and the passion of the speaking subject, who confesses in the second section that he is "trop *passion*né." The repetition and embedding of one word within another— "feu" in "feuilleton," "passion" in "passionné"—produces a confusion between traditionally discrete discourses. We are, however, under no obligation to disentangle the discourses represented—the sacred ("Christ,"

"Passion," "Feu"), the personal ("crier," "passionné," "C'est moi"), and the popular ("Cris," "Journal," "Roman-feuilleton"). For as Cendrars would have it, speaking of one inevitably means speaking of all the others. "On a beau ne pas vouloir parler de soi-même." Try as one might to avoid speaking of oneself, one is nonetheless *always* speaking of oneself. Here, the self is clearly not a bounded entity; nor, the poet implies, is the discourse of the self an autonomous property. For even when speaking the language of the newspaper, one is really talking about oneself; and when talking of (or painting) oneself, one is really praying to (or portraying) Christ; and when praying to Christ, one is actually speaking the language of the newspaper ("Cris")!

Yet, despite this confusion, or perhaps even because of it, "Il faut parfois crier." Crying out, however, does not guarantee the authenticity of the subject's discourse. Instead the supposedly spontaneous cry may only serve to prove the extent to which the intimate is entangled in the public. In other words, what emerges first as a form of subjective expression, a cry of individual suffering, may in fact turn out to be the crying out of a very specific, culturally overdetermined name: the name of Christ, or, perhaps, the name of a newspaper. For Cendrars is careful to note in a related poem entitled "Contrastes" that *crier* does not mean simply to cry out, to express the self without mediation; it also means to shout out the name of a product, to hawk, to advertise, to promote. In "Contrastes" "on crie *L'Intransigeant* et *Paris-Sports*," one cries out the names of the two most popular newspapers of Cendrars's day. Anticipating the more disturbing and transgressive poems that appear later in the volume, Cendrars intimates in "Journal" that even the spontaneous self may speak in the language of the newspaper and that, further, this self's expressions ("Cris") may be a product that one can hawk.

The subject's attempt to reject the confessional mode in "Journal"— "On a beau ne pas vouloir parler de soi-même"—leads to the rather surprising revelation that all ambient discourses, commercial ones included, confess for the subject whether this subject likes it or not. Conversely, the poem indicates that a desire to cry out—"Il faut parfois crier"—fails to produce anything but the language of the (commercialized) other. Distinctions between the private and the public, the spontaneous and the commercial, are so completely undone by the end of the poem that the speaker can only acknowledge with a kind of tender regret that the subject and its language are never fully autonomous or neatly bounded. "Je suis l'autre / Trop sensible." "Journal" juxtaposes the first-person singular of lyric discourse ("Je") with discourses of the *roman-feuilleton* and the daily newspaper ("l'autre") in order to demonstrate the immanence of heteronomous languages reproduced by a machine within a supposedly autonomous, subjective language.[23] The concluding lines establish definitively that the discourse of subjectivity is penetrated not by a Nervalian unconscious or, alternatively, by the inspiration of the divine but rather by a multiplicity of popular, mechanically reproduced idioms to which the individual voice of the lyric poet is indeed "too sensitive."

The porous subject introduced in "Journal" will prove to be Cendrars's most effective instrument for opening up lyric poetry to discourses to which it has traditionally been opposed. Although several poems of *Dix-neuf poèmes élastiques* focus specifically on the example of the daily newspaper, the commercial discourses that fascinate Cendrars the most turn out to be those of the *affiche*, the *légende* (copy), and the brand name, in short, the discourses of advertising. "Journal" gives us a hint that advertising will be central to the poetics of the entire volume. The repeated, paratactic, single-word lines set in apposition in "Journal" create the impression of a list of shop signs, headlines, or slogans. Forty years earlier Rimbaud had exploited a similar technique in "Paris," the poem from the *Album zutique* composed entirely of the names of "commerçants en vogue" [chic shops], "d'assassins célèbres" [infamous assassins], and "littérateurs à la mode" [writers in fashion].[24] Apparently, Rimbaud was also too sensitive to the modern spectacle, the advertising posters, caricatures, announcements, and street signs that encumbered the Paris streets. "Contrastes," also from *Dix-neuf poèmes élastiques*, elaborates on the technique introduced by Rimbaud; in the midst of a lyric effusion the poem lists the names of Paris stations and attractions—"Montrouge Gare de l'Est Métro Nord-Sud bâteaux-mouches monde" [Montrouge East Station North-South Subway boats of the Seine crowds]—and registers the appearance of that great Parisian advertising sign, "la Samaritaine."[25]

Although "Contrastes" and "Journal" both frame lyric discourse within the context of the newspaper and the advertisement, another poem in the volume, "Aux 5 coins" (At the 5 corners), addresses even more explicitly the relation of poetry to a popular market. "Aux 5 coins," like "Journal," is concerned with the contrast between distinct cultural spaces (the private and the public) and distinct discourses (the conventionally poetic and the streetwise or idiomatic). Whereas "Journal" registers the invasion of the self by a "You" identified first with Christ and then, through apposition, with the "crucified" language of the newspaper, the "You" in "Aux 5 coins" is associated even more directly with the language of "le peuple."

The title "Aux 5 coins" refers to a *café-tabac* of the same name on the rue de Buci, where Cendrars met regularly with the painter Fernand Léger.[26] In the literary sociolect of this period the *tabac* or café represented a point of intersection between two contrasting social classes, the cultural elite of the Left Bank and "le peuple." The café can be read as a modernist chronotope in Mikhail Bakhtin's sense, a figure possessing a specific temporality (the immediate, the simultaneous) and a specific geography (the ubiquitous, the collapsed space of drunken recollection). If the conventions of the high-cultural lyric can be visualized as a room (stanza), an interior space far from the bustling crowd, and if popular and commercial forms find their spatial correlative in the street, arcade, or market, then the café, with its many windows and terrace tables, represents a site of crossing between the two. Further, in the world Cendrars inhabited, the café had literally become the spot where ideas were exchanged: heated discussions of aesthetics no longer took place in the salon or at a *mardi* but rather over the *petit vin blanc* in the local bistro. There, at least hypothetically, art rubbed elbows with the masses, expanding its reach to encompass new diction and tastes. Jean Paul Crespelle describes a similar meeting place of the early teens, La Rotonde ("the café where Cendrars went to write"), as the locale where an artist could renew contact with the proletariat: "Artists rubbed shoulders there with masons, hands from the next-door butcher, and carriage drivers."[27] If the atelier was perhaps an even more significant site of aesthetic debates, the café nonetheless figures most successfully the early avant-garde desire for a transgressive cultural practice. "Aux 5 coins" refers repeatedly to its locus of enunciation; it includes conversational idioms likely to be heard in a café as well as a reference to inebriation (the "mûr" of line 5 is slang for drunk).[28] The poem also draws attention to itself as a site of crossing, a place where traditionally opposed activities—writing and selling—and traditionally opposed domains—the lofty and isolated aesthetic and the working-class neighborhood of "crieurs" [hawkers]—work to define one another.

AUX 5 COINS

Oser et faire du bruit
Tout est couleur mouvement explosion lumière
La vie fleurit aux fenêtres du soleil
Qui se fond dans ma bouche
Je suis mûr
Et je tombe translucide dans la rue

Tu parles, mon vieux

Je ne sais pas ouvrir les yeux?
Bouche d'or
La poésie est en jeu
   (*Du monde entier*, 97, © Editions Denoël)

AT THE FIVE CORNERS

To dare and make noise
Everything is color movement explosion light
Life flowers at the windows of the sun
Which melts in my mouth
I'm ripe [drunk]
And I fall translucent into the street

You said it, buddy

I don't know how to open my eyes?
Golden tongue
Poetry is at stake [in play]
   (*Complete Poems*, 73, trans. modified)

The poem opens with a pair of futurist infinitives that imply Cendrars's debt to Filippo Marinetti's aesthetics of audacity. The first and last lines—"Oser et faire du bruit" and "La poésie est en jeu"—trace the trajectory of experimental modernism itself, a trajectory that begins with the testing of boundaries and proceeds to the endangerment or the placing at risk of aesthetic forms. Making noise ("faire du bruit") is of course the very opposite of making poetry in the traditional sense. This noise (from the street?) will increase in volume as the poems of *Dix-neuf poèmes élastiques* relinquish traditional poetic diction and a stable lyric "I" in favor of heteroglossic contrast and impersonal sources of utterance. And yet the second meaning of the idiomatic "faire du bruit"—to make a splash or to make a name for oneself—also resonates in the poem, suggesting that placing poetry "en jeu" [at stake], endangering poetry's music by producing noise, is precisely how one becomes a poet, how one makes a reputation *as* a poet. In the key image of the poem—"La vie fleurit aux fenêtres du soleil / Qui se fond dans ma bouche"— the outside ("life," sunshine, and later "the street") communicates directly with the inside, the mouth of the poet or prophet (the "Bouche d'or"). This mouth functions not as pure source but as an orifice that absorbs as well as emits; the mouth is a site of intersection rather than of immaculate conception. The poet's goal, achieved the moment he is ripe ("mûr"), is to be the space where the light crosses over (to be "translucide," from the Latin *translucere*, "to shine through"), to be a windowpane or membrane through which the "couleur mouvement explosion lumière" of the street may pass. However, the life that changes form ("se fond") on the poet's tongue is already mediated or framed ("La vie fleurit aux *fenêtres* du soleil"); the poet receives impressions from a light source through an aperture that crops, frames, and forms light just as rhetoric does experience. There is no pure sensual life outside to be absorbed by the poet; rather, there are merely framed suns, streets known only through speech, eyes that may never fully open to the sun ("Je ne sais pas ouvrir les yeux?").[29]

In "Aux 5 coins," then, poetry appears as a discourse that must open itself up to the languages of life ("bruit"), to the popular idioms that frame experience and make it available to social beings. With its nonhierarchical verbal montage, Cendrars's poetry demonstrates more vividly than most that lyric discourse is not the creation of a single subject but a confection of heterogeneous found languages, an assemblage, as Cendrars points out in a 1924 essay, of "all the neologisms; the precise, barbaric language of science and technology; foreign languages; and local dialects."[30] As in "Journal" and "Contrastes," Cendrars announces that his "style nouveau" is the antistyle of heteroglossia itself: "This new style works with all forms of language, all parts of discourse . . . often we are common *[peuple]*, vulgar *[vulgaire]*" (*Aujourd'hui*, 99, 98).

"Aux 5 coins" can be read, then, as another attempt on the part of Cendrars to follow his own mandate, "[o]ser et faire du bruit" by swelling the diction of the traditional lyric with "all forms of language and every part of discourse." The crossing-over of linguistic boundaries, one of the major themes of the poem, occurs narratively in lines 5 and 6, where the speaker falls out the window onto the street ("Je suis mûr / Et je tombe translucide dans la rue"). On the discursive level, the text also "falls" at this point, from the highly poetic, alliterative language of the first six lines ("La vie *f*leurit aux *f*enêtres du *s*oleil / Qui *s*e *f*ond dans ma bouche") into the *vulgata*, or idiomatic street dialect, of line 7. "Tu parles, mon vieux" represents ordinary language, reserving a place where "Tu"—the voice beyond the poetic text, beyond poetry itself— speaks. By seeking to designate a space within the poem (framed by line breaks) for that which lies beyond it, Cendrars effectively places poetry, as a closed and self-identical form of discourse, at stake. The foregrounded line, "Tu parles, mon vieux," associates the beyond of poetry (its outside or other) with the popular, the "peuple" and the "vulgaire." The juxtaposition of the conventional speech of the poet (emanating from "*ma* bouche") with an indeterminate "forme de langage" ("*Tu* parles") produces the impression that indeed "all forms of language" mingle here on the tongue of the poet and that it is this confusion of voices, this poetic heteroglossia, and not the seamless homogeneity of a unified poetic language, that constitutes the "Bouche d'or" of the poem. The

"Tout" of the second line, then, can be read as a self-referential description of the poem, which blends the various levels of discourse in order to create a whole. Yet if the poem is a whole, it nevertheless refrains from effacing the boundaries between the contrasting discourses it comprises. On the contrary, these boundaries are set into relief by the visual presentation of the text: the line breaks, the punctuation, the graphic incarnations of form. The blank spaces surrounding the colloquial "Tu parles, mon vieux" suggest that the difference between poetic and popular discourses, between different "formes du langage," must, finally, be maintained. As in a work of cubist collage, the borders must be marked if the poem is to achieve the sense of explosion that, paradoxically, defines it as a unified discourse, that is, as poetry. Like a ripe fruit, the poem explodes with flavor—differentiates its flavors—as it melts in the mouth and resolves into a single text.

The risk the poem has taken concerns its own generic identity, its membership in a traditional genre possessing precise lexical, formal, and thematic conventions. "Aux 5 coins" is by no means the only poem contained in *Dix-neuf poèmes élastiques* to place its identity as a poem in jeopardy by engaging in verbal collage. However, it stands out in the volume as the most ambitious poem in the sense that it aims to embrace all the languages of the "Tu," from the colloquial "Tu parles, mon vieux," evocative of casual exchange and working-class or folk culture, to discourses with distinctly commercial overtones, embedded, as we shall see, in the title and other lines of the poem. "Aux 5 coins" maintains a tension between a "Bouche d'or" understood in the traditional sense as prophetic oracle and a "Bouche d'or" in the more literal sense as a mouth whose words are worth their weight in gold. This tension will be attenuated in other poems of the volume, poems that document the increasing subordination of the colloquial to the commercial, the sensual to the commodified, the inclusive and heteroglossic to the mechanically reproduced.

Thus, the explosion of various (discursive) flavors enjoyed in "Aux 5 coins" gives way to an altogether different type of purity than that attributed to the autonomous lyric voice. In "Atelier" and "Hamac" (Hammock), for instance, the discourse of the "Tu" turns out to be composed entirely of material provided by the advertising billboard or promotional label. "Hamac" juxtaposes poetic imagery with the brand names of commodities, while "Atelier" interweaves the names of Cendrars's contemporaries (Léger, Chagall) with the prose of an advertising promise: "Nous garantissons la pureté absolue de notre sauce tomate" [We guarantee the absolute purity of our tomato sauce]. These poems imply that poetry as a modern art form must be willing to place itself at risk by embracing the very commercial discourses against which it has been defined and by situating these discourses where the lyric "I" formally was (i.e., in the "Bouche d'or"). Such a risk is necessary, Cendrars concedes in a confessional moment, not simply because poetry must self-reflexively reveal its heteronomy, the nature of the needs that compel it, but also, and even more importantly, because it must sell.

The rue de Buci, the site of the *café-tabac* named in "Aux 5 coins," was (and is today) a major commercial thoroughfare lined with shops and boasting an open-air market. It is no accident, then, that the marketplace serves as the cultural frame of poetic production in this brief, almost telegraphic poem. "Aux 5 coins" not only outlines a new aesthetic, in which noise and audacity are privileged, but also alludes to the conditions of the cultural market in which this new aesthetic must succeed. As Jean-Pierre Goldenstein points out, the title "Aux 5 coins" would remind many French readers of a childhood game called "le jeu des quatre coins," which simulates the struggle of newcomers attempting to insert themselves into what might be called a saturated market.[31] In this game, an intensified version of musical chairs, four players race from corner to corner of a room while a fifth player tries to usurp the spot of one of the others. The game obliquely referred to in the title reproduces allegorically the situation of a young poet attempting to carve out a space in the field of literary production. In fact, the vision of the literary field sketched out implicitly in "Aux 5 coins" resembles to a striking degree that proposed by Pierre Bourdieu in his sociology of literature. Portraying literary production as a highly competitive field, Bourdieu maintains that access to literary success is contingent on the author's ability to put the very definition of the literary "at stake": "The struggle to impose the dominant definition of art, i.e., to impose a style, embodied in a particular producer or group of producers, gives the work of art a value by putting it at stake, inside and outside the field of production."[32] In 1914 Cendrars was all too aware that to succeed, his poetry must "[o]ser et faire du bruit," that is, do something new, something to gain attention.[33] But the competitive field Bourdieu describes in his study of the late-nineteenth-century literary market was not the same as the field Cendrars confronted in 1914; Cendrars and other poets of his generation had to find a corner in an even more densely populated room. For the literary field Cendrars was attempting to penetrate now presented itself as a cultural field in which new media such as film, popular fiction, journalism, and advertising competed with traditional genres for public attention.

Cendrars's experimental *Dix-neuf poèmes élastiques* can be read as one set of possible responses to a competitive cultural market controlled increasingly by commercial forms. The montage character of "Aux 5 coins" and the discursive heterogeneity of "Journal" manifest the pressure exerted on high culture by mass-produced forms that were rapidly seducing the French public during the second decade of the century. Both Cendrars and his contemporary Apollinaire were aware that technologically produced popular media threatened poetry's privileged function as a "Bouche d'or," or prophetic oracle of modern civilization.[34] Poets were no longer in competition solely with other poets; their works now had to rival in interest and scope cultural products whose conventions and symbolic status had not yet been determined. In 1917 Apollinaire announced in his polemical "L'Esprit nouveau et les poètes" that if poetry intended to compete in an enlarged field of signifying practices, it would have to find a way to engage a newly created public: the crowd. To modernize itself, Apollinaire asserted, poetry would have to enter into an "apprenticeship" of the discursive and formal liberty enjoyed by more popular forms, such as the newspaper, the *roman-feuilleton*, and the advertisement (945). But Apollinaire, who died in 1918, did not have the chance to realize the projects he had outlined. Cendrars, meanwhile, continued to write poetry during the twenties; the challenge he faced was to ascertain what role poetry could play in a cultural world increasingly dominated by technological forms and commercial concerns.

Drawing attention in 1927 to what would remain a major dilemma for artists of the industrial age, the editors of the theatrical newspaper *Chantecler* asked Cendrars and a fellow poet, Fernand Divoire, to comment on whether professional writers should lend their skills to commercial enterprises such as advertising. Divoire argued that literature, as a noble calling, should remain distinct from a mere métier such as advertising; literature should not be required to lower itself in the name of a soap or a box of pills. "But *writer [écrivain]*," emphasizes Divoire, "that is a dignity, a title; it isn't simply, like 'man of letters' or 'waiter,' the name of a profession *[métier]*. . . . If you consider Art as something noble, as one of the highest forms of the expression and affirmation of the human Soul, then the evidence is overwhelming: Art must not lower itself. It lowers itself if it becomes a gimmick *[un boniment]*."[35]

As might be expected, Cendrars took the opportunity to deride the conventional view expressed by Divoire. Half in jest but also with an eye to challenging fundamental romantic assumptions, Cendrars presents poetic creation and advertising as equivalent practices. In his rebuttal, "Publicité = Poésie," Cendrars praises advertising as "an art calling for internationalism, multilingualism, a crowd psychology."[36] Invoking the example of the Russian poet Vladimir Mayakovski, Cendrars insists that poets need not isolate themselves from the larger world of industry for they possess skills vital to industrial development. Although Cendrars is impressed by Mayakovski's demotic ideals, he does not embrace the Russian poet's politics. In fact, nowhere is Cendrars's affirmation of capitalist consumer culture more clearly articulated than in his celebration of the advertisement, that "fleur de la vie contemporaine" blossoming in the public square and announcing not spring but rather the arrival of the new Model T Ford (*Aujourd'hui*, 117).

Cendrars registers the ubiquity of the advertising phenomenon and the influence of its languages in several prose pieces of the twenties and thirties. He writes in a preface to a catalog of works by the poster artist A. M. Cassandre, for instance, that "the street in Paris is surely one of the most miraculous spectacles imaginable" precisely because it is swathed from end to end in images, captions, and banners.[37] And in a 1954 interview Cendrars recalls that around 1914 the largest posters in Paris—for the enormous Baby Cadum and the shoe polish Black Lion—were Léger's richest source of inspiration.[38] Cendrars's poems of the early teens, notably "Atelier" and "Hamac," incorporate advertising slogans as if they resonated as suggestively as poetic metaphors. These poems imply that for Cendrars no hierarchy can be established between the sublimated language of the poetic and discourses of advertising that address, as he puts it, "the most vulgar needs of the senses" [(les) besoins les plus grossiers des sens] (*Aujourd'hui*, 38).

"Atelier," part 2 of the fourth poem in *Dix-neuf poèmes élastiques*, provides an evocative illustration of Cendrars's approach to the discourse of advertising. Here, the promotional copy from a jar of tomato sauce appears as a discrete line of verse nestled between a description of the artist's studio (Chagall's) and a series of protosurrealist metaphors:

Esquisses, dessins, des oeuvres frénétiques
Et des tableaux . . .
Bouteilles vides
Nous garantissons la pureté absolue de notre sauce tomate
Dit une étiquette
La fenêtre est un almanach
Quand les grues gigantesques des éclairs vident les péniches du ciel à grand
    fracas et déversent des bannes de tonnerre
Il en tombe
Pêle-mêle
    (*Du monde entier*, 79, © Editions Denoël)

Sketches, drawings, frantic works
And paintings . . .

Empty bottles
We guarantee the absolute purity of our tomato sauce
Says a label
The window is an almanac
When the gigantic cranes of lightning empty the booming barges of the sky and
    dump buckets of thunder
Out fall
Pell-mell
    (*Complete Poems*, 61)

The passage contains multiple ironies, the most obvious of which is the contradiction between, on the one hand, the "absolute purity" of the tomato sauce and, on the other, the heterogeneity of the discursive contents of the poem, the clutter of the artist's studio ("Désordre, on est en plein désordre" [Disorder, everything is in disorder]), and the variety of the visual spectacle apprehended through the window ("La fenêtre est un almanach"). In contrast to "Aux 5 coins," which underscores the social and discursive heterogeneity of an intermediary space, the café, "Atelier" reveals that the traditional site of aesthetic activity, the isolated refuge of the artist, has also been invaded by commercial and industrially generated discourses. The slogans of modern advertising now contribute to the visual environment in which the artist works. Accordingly, in the poem an "etiquette" succeeds the artist's "tableaux" with only an ellipsis to punctuate their distinction. As in "Aux 5 coins," the levels of discourse are separated typographically; the blank spaces between the lines in "Aux 5 coins" and the italic type in "Atelier" indicate the boundaries between the two types of discourse involved. At the same time, the principle of discursive juxtaposition is reiterated as a technique on the semantic level; "Atelier" contrasts two semantic fields, the industrial ("grues," "péniches," "bannes") and the organic or meteorological ("éclairs," "ciel," "tonnerre"), to produce the most highly imagistic passage of the poem: "Quand les *grues* gigantesques des *éclairs* vident les *péniches* du *ciel* à grand fracas et déversent des *bannes* de *tonnerre*." The semantic contrast between industrial and organic that composes the poetic image is structurally homologous to the "pêle-mêle" of contrasting discourses and discontinuous visual spectacles characterizing the modern landscape.

In "Atelier" Cendrars goes out of his way to differentiate the discourse of advertising from the discourse of the poetic even while juxtaposing the one with the other. But by 1927, when "Publicité = Poésie" appears, the advertisement is no longer treated simply as raw material to be drawn into contrast with poetic language; rather, advertising provides an analogy for poetic practice itself. "La poésie," begins Cendrars "fait connaître (tout comme la publicité un produit) l'image de l'esprit qui la conçoit" [Poetry introduces us (just as publicity does a product) to the image of the spirit that conceives it] (*Aujourd'hui*, 117). The modest parenthesis in Cendrars's equation effects a dramatic redistribution of symbolic capital. His "tout comme," tossed out almost casually, strips the poetic of any epistemological priority over commercial discourses and discloses the carefully concealed analogy between the aesthetic object and the commercial product of manufacture. For Cendrars, poetry introduces an image of the poet's "esprit," or mind, to an audience in the same way that an advertisement introduces a product to a potential consumer. The "esprit" appears, then, as a product that must be sold by the poem, a commodity that seduces its audience by means of promotional (rhetorical and typographic) techniques.

This vision of poetry as a promotional tool is already present in Cendrars's 1913 poem "Hamac." Here, Cendrars publicizes as a "product" his fellow poet Apollinaire. Apollinaire's resemblance to the profile on a large billboard (apparently located at the place Saint-Lazare) advertising Onoto pens serves as the conceit that organizes the poem.[39] Just as the face on the billboard sells the pens, Cendrars's poem sells the character "Apollinaire," as well as a certain variety of experimental poetic practice. This practice is inspired not only by the contemplation of fine art—"Tu as longtemps écrit à l'ombre d'un tableau" [For a long time you have written under the shadow of a painting], writes Cendrars in "Hamac"— but also by the visual stimulation of the contemporary *affiche* or advertising label. Describing Apollinaire's studio, Cendrars notes that "Oxo-Liebig fait frise dans ta chambre" [Oxo-Liebig makes a freize across your room]. According to Cendrars, the advertising iconographies of two contemporary products, Liebig meat extract and Oxo bouillon, compete for attention with paintings in the poet's studio. The hammock of the title seems to evoke the site of Apollinaire's imaginative revery, the mobile bed suspended between two manifestations—the aesthetic (tableau) and the commercial (advertisement)—of cultural modernity. The aspect of Apollinaire's practice that Cendrars celebrates in "Hamac" is his willingness to encompass the full diversity of modern cultural expression; as Cendrars hopes to do, Apollinaire draws inspiration from both the fine art "tableaux" and the promotional image, from both traditional lyric language and the idioms of the commercial enterprise. It is fitting, then, that Cendrars's homage to Apollinaire should be framed both as a portrait and as an advertisement. Cendrars is at once praising and selling Apollinaire;[40] the poem thus concludes in the manner of a promotional declaration:

Apollinaire
1900–1911
Durant 12 ans seul poète de France

Apollinaire
1900–1911
For 12 years the only poet of France
(*Du monde entier*, 86, © Editions Denoël)

To be sure, "Hamac" only revises a eulogistic genre many poets have adopted to pay homage to poetic ancestors or contemporaries. These homages serve at least as filters for reception if not as marketing tools in the recuperation of forgotten heroes. (Mallarmé's series "Hommages et tombeaux" [Homages and Epitaphs] is an obvious example.) Poets have also had occasion to use these homages as advertisements for their own works; the younger poet who praises the more famous one establishes a prestigious lineage and, it is hoped, a readership. Even intertextuality and the types of poetic misprision identified by Harold Bloom can be considered concealed or inverted forms of poetic self-promotion. What is more unusual about "Hamac," however, is that it openly offers the advertising billboard as an analogy for the poem itself, thus exploding the distinction between the symbolic market and the commodity market upon which high culture depends.

And yet this analogy between discourses does not reduce the poem to the status of a publicity brochure. For in Cendrars's poems advertising language displays a multiaccentuality that might be restricted differently in a commercial context (by an accompanying visual image, for instance, rather than by the semantic and phonetic play of the poem). This reframing of the advertisement in the context of lyric expression brings into focus the poetry in advertising, the "implicit history" (*ND*, 52) of subjectivity it contains. No longer employed to sell a product, advertising language (e.g., *"Nous guarantissons la pureté absolue de notre sauce tomate")* emerges as a discourse bearing poetic properties of its own (such as alliteration and a certain rhythmic interest). Further, in its new context the advertisement can be rendered ironical, full of a pathos generated by its obvious hyperbole (the "*absolute* purity" of a tomato sauce).

Simultaneously, the reframing of advertising in the context of poetry also reveals the advertising already contained in poetry, the self-interested, self-promotional aspect of gestures such as a virtuoso use or parody of generic conventions or a self-conscious reference to a famous literary predecessor. The fact that poetry must present itself as innovative, that is, as a distinctive linguistic practice, reveals the dependence of the poetic on self-promotion. Promotional techniques inform compositional techniques: a line such as "Oser et faire du bruit," for instance, captures the hortatory tone of the advertisement while simultaneously insisting upon the poetic difference or daring that constitutes it as a unique practice. Cendrars recognizes that such promotional strategies play a significant role in the inflation of poetry's symbolic capital or distinction. In "Aux 5 coins" and "Hamac" Cendrars even suggests that this symbolic capital cannot exist unless the poem simultaneously brings attention to itself by means of a practice that it posits, paradoxically, as its other. Cendrars thus apprehends the poem as double in nature, at once an aesthetic object and an advertisement for the value of the aesthetic *as such*. Cendrars's poetry dares to expose literary value for what it is: a commodity that, like any other, requires promotion and is therefore in part formed by that promotion. To pretend that systemic pressures, including material trans-formations in the larger field of cultural production, do not to some extent determine the actual contents of lyric discourse is, Cendrars's move im-plies, simply false. However—and this is crucial—the lyric does not thereby conform to the demands of the marketplace. Instead, poetry sets itself "in play" with other discourses, self-consciously elevating the de-mands made upon it by a new cultural market to the order of a composi-tional principle. The "elastic" poem displays an awareness of its heteron-omy through its fragmented form, its self-reflexive rhetoric, and the strained relation it sets up between an indefinable "Je" and an overdeter-mined "Tu."

On the one hand, *Dix-neuf poèmes élastiques* confesses to sharing an element with its cultural other, the commercial advertisement. By empha-sizing their self-promotional gestures, the poems openly contest the very distinction that once established lyric poetry and its subject as autono-mous entities. On the other hand, however, the poems of *Dix-neuf poèmes élastiques* reinstate the distinction that they seem simultaneously to be placing at stake. By recontextualizing the advertisement in a lyric utter-ance, these poems manage to suggest precisely what it was in the adver-tisement that originally "require[d]" its "formation" (*ND*, 11): the desire for an "absolute purity," which, in the age of the machine, can only be retrieved in the form of a "sauce tomate."

Ultimately, jeopardizing the purity of the lyric "I" while simultaneously discovering an expression of its necessity elsewhere (in the advertisement, for instance, or in the "crucified" language of the newspaper) turns out to be the very move capable of guaranteeing Cendrars's symbolic success as a poet. Cendrars is aware that discursive heterogeneity is an effective confessional tool; further, he knows that such heterogeneity is also privi-leged by the literary market of his day. Cendrars's wager is that if the

image of an autonomous lyric subject fulfills the needs of a certain bourgeois public at one point in time (if, in other words, during romanticism
the unified lyric subject captures the largest market), then the dismantling
of this same subject might reward symbolic (and eventually pecuniary)
investment several generations later.[41] And in a sense Cendrars is right,
for in the market of the early twentieth century, opening up the lyric voice,
making audible its heterogeneous melodies, is the procedure that stands
the best chance—as Cendrars acknowledges in "Aux 5 coins"—of garner-
ing symbolic success in the literary field.

In Cendrars's case a need to succeed in the literary field ends up generating a set of highly innovative strategies that directly contribute to poetry's
formal evolution. But what makes Cendrars's poetry so compelling
today—more compelling, I would argue, than that of the futurists, to
which his work has often been compared—is the highly ambivalent attitude toward the lyric "I" that Cendrars's poems express. For even while
jeopardizing the "purity" of the first-person lyric voice, the author of *Dix-
neuf poèmes élastiques* never entirely abandons this voice ("Journal," as
we have seen, insists on the traditional lyric "I"). But Cendrars presents
this voice as one discourse among others, a *produced* discourse, a kind of
advertisement for the commodity the autonomous lyric subject has become. In *Dix-neuf poèmes élastiques*, then, Cendrars manifests two distinct and self-contradictory impulses. On the one hand, the poet exhibits
a willingness to reveal the "I" 's reliance upon self-promotional strategies;
on the other, he strives to differentiate the "I" 's language from more
overtly commercial discourses. Sometimes the poet seems to confront
these conflicting impulses with good humour: the tone of "Contrastes"
and "Aux 5 coins" is for the most part cheerful.[42] In contrast, "Journal"
evokes the poet's dilemma in more tragic terms. Both the repeated apos-
trophes to Christ and the reference to the Passion suggest that the contradictory impulses involved in poetic writing produce a certain experience
of suffering. The poet's suffering derives from the fact that he knows the
"I" can never speak a thoroughly autonomous language of the self. As
"Journal" and "Aux 5 coins" indicate, this language will always be produced in response to a particular configuration of the cultural market.
The lyric subject has no pure ontological status; its manner of address
reflects, rather, the predicament of subjectivity as it attempts to resist the
commodification of itself.

It is likely, as Leroy has implied, that Cendrars became aware during the
second decade of the twentieth century that poetry did *not* know how
to "se passer [des machines]." By that time Cendrars had learned that
mechanically reproduced languages ineluctably mediate subjective discourse whether or not the subject is conscious of this mediation. Paradoxi-

cally, however, the poet also realized during this period that, as Bochner argues, poetry *could* "se passer [des machines]" insofar as it could transcend them *(les dépasser)*, insofar, that is, as it could recontextualize and thus reconstellate the languages of the machine differently. Denying the immanence of the commercial in the aesthetic, insisting upon the autonomy of the subject and its self-representations, might have resulted in a more victorious and self-righteous form of poetic expression. But such a denial would not accurately reflect the complex dynamics through which art and commerce, the self and the other, constitute and become distinguished from each other. Cendrars takes on the full burden of disclosing these dynamics. He derives the passion of his poetry from the very discourses that threaten its generic integrity, rekindling with his own breath, with the energies of his own body, the "feu" embedded in the "feuilleton."

Five

High Decoration: Sonia Delaunay, Blaise Cendrars, and the Poem as Fashion Design

AMONG the many ghostly exchanges that take place between Adorno and Benjamin in the former's *Aesthetic Theory*, a central one concerns the nature of fashion and its relation to aesthetic behavior. As Susan Buck-Morss makes clear in her presentation of the *Passagen-Werk* materials in *The Dialectics of Seeing*, Benjamin's assessment of the fashion phenomenon specific to monopoly capitalism is primarily negative. Intended to introduce the new, fashion only generates "hellish repetition," she writes (108).[1] "For fashion," says Benjamin, "was never anything but the parody of the gaily decked-out corpse, the provocation of death through the woman."[2] Instead of seeing fashion as a reflection of historicized understandings of the organic body, as Adorno might have done, Benjamin views fashion as pure reification, transforming the organic body into a commodity whose value is extinguished every season.

Indirectly taking up Benjamin's appraisal of fashion, Adorno argues in *Aesthetic Theory* that the rhythms of fashion in fact play a visible and necessary role in the field of aesthetic production. For Adorno, as for his model in this context, Charles Baudelaire, fashion constitutes the "temporal nucleus of art" (*AT*, 192). Fashion is a heteronomous principle relating art's various apparitions back to the particular historical conditions in which they were wrought. In painting as well as in poetry, fashion is the figure of the contingent, "la vie triviale, . . . la métamorphose journalière des choses extérieures" [the trivial in life, . . . the daily metamorphosis of the external world].[3] Without this contingent element the artistic monument lacks its alluring detail, its sensual image, and thus fails to address the individual in the hollow universalism of its transcendent claims.

Adorno's treatment of fashion would at first seem to be in direct conflict with Benjamin's, but this conflict is at bottom a semantic rather than an ideological one. Whereas Adorno adopts the word *fashion* as a synonym for *temporality*, thereby indicating the artwork's implication in the conditions of production peculiar to its historical period, Benjamin uses the word to designate commercial determination, evoking the more pejorative sense the word *fashion* acquired during the first quarter of the twentieth century. Because it is temporally specific, the connotative ambiguity of the word as it is used by both Adorno and Benjamin can be seen as symptomatic of a larger modernist dilemma concerning the nature of art's relation to history. In this chapter I study this dilemma with particular reference to Cendrars, whose poetry implicitly questions whether art can have a "temporal nucleus" without yielding to the dictates of commerce. Cendrars's oeuvre responds to the paradoxes generated when the capitalist fashion system infiltrates the field of high culture. Cendrars asks whether literature in the twentieth century can confess to its association with fashion, avow its submission to heteronomy, without abdicating entirely its claim to cultural distinction.

Fashion is not an abstract concept in Cendrars's work. From early on in his career Cendrars exhibits a fascination with the phenomenon of fashion, especially as it pertains to dress. The pastiche technique of *Dix-neuf poèmes élastiques* was inspired in part by the "simultaneous" dress designs of the painter and decorative artist Sonia Delaunay, whose efforts to ally fashion with art raised for Cendrars the question of art's cultural status in a modern world increasingly governed by the laws of the passing fad. When Cendrars drew an analogy between poetry and Delaunay's *robe simultanée* in "Sur la robe elle a un corps" [On the dress she has a body], of 1913, he in effect presented himself as the Baudelaire of his own day. He presented himself, that is, as a poet dedicated to locating in the visual appearance of a generation the "élément éternel, invariable," that ultimately presides over an aesthetic universe.[4] But the effect of Cendrars's hymn to Delaunay was not the same as that produced by Baudelaire's meditations on Constantin Guys. By emphasizing the parallels between poetry and *la mode*, Cendrars came close to endangering the values by which poetry has traditionally been distinguished from more popular or commercial forms. For Cendrars did not live in Baudelaire's universe; the lingering aristocratic values that in Baudelaire's day might have ensured an abiding belief in such a thing as an "élément éternel"—religious values, or simply widely recognized standards of virtue and taste—were for the most part eroded by the time Cendrars arrived on the scene. Cultural production in early-twentieth-century France was no longer divided, as it had been during the nineteenth century, between artisanal and industrial modes of production.[5] By the end of the Third Republic, industrial manufacture was rapidly replacing small workshop, craft-based production modes in a number of domains, from the decorative arts to film production.[6] Cendrars's world, in other words, was becoming one of monopoly or industrial capitalism, one in which *la mode* would come to reflect less the complexion of a particular historical moment—its "morale" or "passion" in Baudelaire's terms—than the directives of increasingly powerful entertainment and industrial monopolies. The realm of haute couture may have been somewhat protected from standardizing processes that were inexorably modifying the appearance of the everyday; however, by the early teens even this elite field of cultural production was succumbing to the demands of large-scale industrial manufacture. The general democratization of access to elite culture, the increasingly dependent relation between film stars and fashion trends, and the emergence of a middle-class "knock-off" market (a market that accelerated the alternation of models in response to a larger and more diversified clientele) all contributed to the standardization of haute couture fashion design.

Thus, the analogy Cendrars established between fashion and poetry in 1913 functioned somewhat differently from the association evoked by Baudelaire in *Le Peintre de la vie moderne*, of 1859–60. Cendrars's willingness to associate and even at times equate poetry with decorative and commercial forms threatened the epistemological claims of poetic *connaissance* in a way that even the dadaists, who continued to associate poetry with "primitive" chant and mimetic ritual, had not yet dared to attempt. Cendrars was already asking in 1913 whether poetry might not, after all, be nothing more than "sheer decoration,"[7] a play of linguistic surfaces eliciting pleasure but no deeper or more metaphysical response. If, as Cendrars would declare in 1926, "Il n'y a pas d'absolu" [There is no absolute], then poetry could boast of providing no greater access to an eternal order than could, say, the haute couture dress.[8] Even though Cendrars was careful to compare poetry to a dress made by a high modernist *painter*, he could not avoid evoking certain parallels between lyric composition and industrial manufacture. The analogy he presented in "Sur la robe elle a un corps" drew poetry inevitably into relation not with the "temporal nucleus" of all art but rather with the "hellish repetition" that fashion, according to Benjamin, had become. Apollinaire's 1913 depiction of fashion as "the mask of death" clearly indicates that by the early twentieth century the words *la mode* would have resonated quite differently than they had in Baudelaire's day.[9] To be the Baudelaire of the early twentieth century meant not only to avow the heteronomous, fashionable element immanent to poetry and the other high arts but also to place at risk the very distinctions between craft and standardization, authorship and imitation, upon which the high arts had been founded since the romantic period.

Although critics have exerted much effort attempting to clarify Cendrars's debt to Apollinaire and, conversely, Apollinaire's debt to Cendrars, the influence of Robert and Sonia Delaunay's simultaneous contrast technique upon Cendrars's work has never been properly explored. It is clear, however, that the remarkable stylistic modifications Cendrars's poetry underwent during the year 1913 can be attributed primarily to his frequent

visits to the Delaunay home. The simultaneous contrast technique introduced by Robert Delaunay and elaborated on by his wife was based on
Michel-Eugène Chevreul's theory that the perception of color values is
determined by the contrast of juxtaposed tones. The Delaunays transformed Chevreul's theory into a technique of *simultanéité*, roughly defined by Cendrars in 1914 as the process by which one entity gains its
identity through contrast with another.[10] Anticipating the postmodern fascination with surface juxtapositions, the Delaunays reinterpreted pictorial depth, or *profondeur*, as an illusion produced by surface planes of
color rather than by vanishing-point perspective. It was this reconception
of depth as a function of surface design that stimulated Cendrars's interest
in citational pastiche.

Although the simultaneous contrast theory Robert Delaunay devised
in the realm of high art clearly had a significant impact on the young
Cendrars, the decorative objects Sonia Delaunay created during the same
era were perhaps an even more decisive influence on the development
of Cendrars's literary practice. For it was specifically Sonia Delaunay's
experiments with assemblage technique in the realm of the decorative arts
that compelled Cendrars to revise his approach to verbal construction.
Encouraged (or compelled) by her domestic situation during the war, Delaunay began to transfer the modernist iconography associated with her
husband's canvasses onto a variety of decorative objects—curtains, upholstery, lampshades, bookbindings, scarves, and dresses.[11] In this way,
simultanéité evolved from a theory of color contrast into a practice of
cultural production. The goal of her visual experiments was no longer to
discover how one tone affected the perception of another; Delaunay was
now interested in bestowing upon every available surface what had become an eminently reproducible *simultanéiste* iconography, which in fact
sold quite well. The implication of her specific version of *simultanéité* was
that a visual identity between objects situated in different institutional
contexts had the potential to erase the traditional cultural distinctions
between them. Impressed by Delaunay's approach to everyday objects,
Cendrars began to apply the assemblage, or contrast, technique to the
composition of poetry, novels, screenplays, and radioplays; but he crossed
the boundary between elite and commercial realms by integrating discourses drawn from paraliterary and commercial sources. The assemblage
practices of Sonia Delaunay were thus directly responsible for what Jean-
Carlo Flückiger has aptly named the "patchwork" technique of *Dix-neuf
poèmes élastiques* and other works.[12] Cendrars's verbal "patchworks"
were a poetic response to Delaunay's *objets simultanés*.

Delaunay's first attempt to elide the decorative arts with simultaneous
contrast technique produced *Couverture*, a patchwork quilt, or assemblage, of various fabrics and furs that she stitched together for her infant

Fig. 1. Sonia Delaunay, *Couverture* [Blanket], 1911. Collections Mnam-CCI/Centre Georges Pompidou, Paris.
Copyright © L&M Services B. V., Amsterdam 980402.

son in 1911 (fig. 1). Drawing from the folk tradition of her native Russia,
Delaunay joined fur scraps with patches of "found" fabrics in order to
recreate the effect she and her husband had achieved elsewhere with varie-
gated planes of pigment. The patchwork quilt already combined three
elements of the aesthetic Delaunay would develop more fully in her fashion designs and bookbindings: the quilt suggested visually the genre of
pastiche; it juxtaposed diverse elements without creating a hierarchy of
value between them; and it created an impression of depth through the
contiguity of contrasting surfaces. Cendrars would draw attention to
these three elements in his own poem on Delaunay's *robe simultanée*,
"Sur la robe," but here the implications of Delaunay's tripartite aesthetics
for the future of poetry would be more fully explored.

Fig. 2. Sonia Delaunay, bookbinding for *Les Pâques à New York* by Blaise Cendrars, 1912. Collections Mnam-CCI/Centre Georges Pompidou, Paris. Copyright © L&M Services B. V., Amsterdam 980402.

Soon after designing the quilt, Delaunay made a series of appliqué collage bookbindings, most notably for Cendrars's *Pâques à New York* (fig. 2). Similar in this respect to the quilt, the bookbindings play with the effects of juxtaposed surfaces. Appearing frequently are rainbows and arcs, which are Russian folk art motifs, as well as the triangles and trapezoids of patchwork construction that Delaunay was using in her paintings during the same period (see figs. 3, *Bal Bullier*, and 4, *Contrastes simultanés*). Like building blocks, these motifs can be detached and reassembled in each subsequent design. Delaunay's procedure accentuates the autonomy of the unit, or building block; each shape remains distinct even while participating in a larger composition. The detachable quality of the building blocks reminds the viewer of the initial gesture of the simultaneous craft, that of assembling rather than inventing, selecting rather than originating.

Delaunay was working with the principle of simultaneous constrast on a variety of levels when she designed the *robe simultanée* in the summer of 1913. An habitué of the Bal Bullier, a popular modernist hot spot on the avenue de l'Observatoire, Delaunay arrived one evening wearing a dress that would effectively launch her new career as a fashion designer (fig. 5).[13] In her *robe simultanée* Delaunay reiterates the motifs employed

Fig. 3. Sonia Delaunay, *Bal Bullier*, 1913. Collections Mnam-CCI/Centre Georges Pompidou, Paris. Copyright © L&M Services B. V., Amsterdam 980402.

in her paintings, bookbindings, lampshades, and upholstery of the same period, such as the rainbow arc and the solar disc. The dress was formed on the principle of the quilt, sewn, in Delaunay's own words, "with small pieces of fabric that formed patches of color."[14]

Apparently, Cendrars was at the Bal Bullier on the night during the summer of 1913 when Delaunay stepped out in the first model of her patchwork *robe simultanée*. Although not a costume (Delaunay's costume designs for the Ballets Russes were far more outrageous), the dress was designed to draw attention away from the spectacle on the stage to the spectacle performed by the audience itself. In a *compte rendu* of the evening at the dance hall Guillaume Apollinaire notes that Delaunay most intentionally did not dance.[15] Her goal, according to Apollinaire, was to draw attention to the "corps *sur* la robe," the limbs dancing *on* the dress, as the title of Cendrars's poem indicates, and not to the woman's body beneath. In his poem Cendrars also confuses the distinction between surface and depth, decoration and anatomy, extending a critique of ontology that the poet finds implicit in Delaunay's practice. The first element of Delaunay's aesthetic that Cendrars chooses to thematize in his poem, then, is her tendency to destabilize the hierarchical relation between truth and appearance, eternal form and ephemeral ornamentation. Appropriately, Cendrars opens his poem with an attack on phrenology, the nineteenth-century positivist science that insists, unlike the dress, on

a one-to-one referential correspondence between surface and depth. Instead of positing an absolute correspondence between the shape of the cranium and the individual personality, Cendrars, following Delaunay, recasts identity (here the identity of the woman) as an imaginative reconstruction dependent upon the printed surfaces traditionally considered diversionary.

SUR LA ROBE ELLE A UN CORPS

Le corps de la femme est aussi bosselé que mon crâne
Glorieuse
Si tu t'incarnes avec esprit
Les couturiers font un sot métier
Autant que la phrénologie
Mes yeux sont des kilos qui pèsent la sensualité des femmes
Tout ce qui fuit, saille avance dans la profondeur
Les étoiles creusent le ciel
Les couleurs déshabillent
"Sur la robe elle a un corps"
Sous les bras des bruyères mains lunules et pistils quand les eaux se déversent
    dans le dos avec les omoplates glauques
Le ventre un disque qui bouge
La double coque des seins passe sous le pont des arcs-en-ciel
Ventre

Fig. 4. Sonia Delaunay, *Contrastes simultanés* (Simultaneous Contrasts), 1912. Collections Mnam-CCI/Centre Georges Pompidou, Paris. Copyright © L&M Services B. V., Amsterdam 980402.

Disque
Soleil
Les cris perpendiculaires des couleurs tombent sur les cuisses

ÉPÉE DE SAINT-MICHEL

Il y a des mains qui se tendent
Il y a dans la traîne la bête tous les yeux toutes les fanfares tous les habitués du
    bal Bullier
Et sur la hanche
La signature du poète

ON HER DRESS SHE HAS A BODY

A woman's body is as modeled as my skull
Glorious
If you are incarnated with spirit
Couturiers have an idiotic job
As idiotic as phrenology
My eyes are kilos that weigh the sensuality of women
All that flees, stands out moves forward into depth
Stars hollow out the sky

Colors undress
"On her dress she has a body"
Under the arms heathers hands lunules pistils when waters flow over the back
    with its blue-green shoulder blades
The belly a moving disk
The double hull of breasts passing under the bridge of rainbows
Belly
Disk
Sun
The perpendicular cries of the colors fall on thighs

SWORD OF SAINT MICHAEL

There are hands that reach
There are in the train the beast all the eyes all the fanfares all the regulars of
    the Bal Bullier
And on the hip
The poet's signature[16]

Significantly, Cendrars begins "Sur la robe elle a un corps" by mocking positivist science and its tendency to locate truth, psychic or spiritual, in the order of the organic. The pun between "sot" [idiotic] and the English word *sew* in line 4—"Les couturiers font un sot métier"—does little to dampen the blow of the accusation against traditional couturiers, who, like the phrenologists, treat the body as a privileged signified, the truth the contours of the dress must reflect.[17] In contrast, Delaunay dissociates the dress from the body it covers. The dress recreates the body not only through its abstract patterns but also through the images these patterns evoke. That is why "la femme" of line 1 is only "Glorieuse" insofar as she "incarnates" herself in a dress, or "avec esprit." Nude and unconstructed, the body of the woman is as "bosselé" as the "crâne," a word in French often associated with death, as *skull* is in English. The skull and the body of the woman are humped, differentiated surfaces, but they signify nothing—they bear neither a spiritual nor an aesthetic truth—without incarnation in fabric or text.

    If we follow Cendrars's logic, it would seem that the modern *couturière* must be freed of the obligation to follow physical contours since these contours are not in themselves the source of woman's "sensualité."[18] In "Sur la robe" Cendrars reconceives sensuality as a product of the impressions or images that the woman's reinvented (textile) body evokes. The eyes that scan the dress are, accordingly, "des kilos qui pèsent la sensualité des femmes" (and here the verb *peser* parodies the scientific discourse of the phrenologists). The organic body has been displaced as a source of sexual excitement; it is now the colors that seduce the viewer: "Les cou-

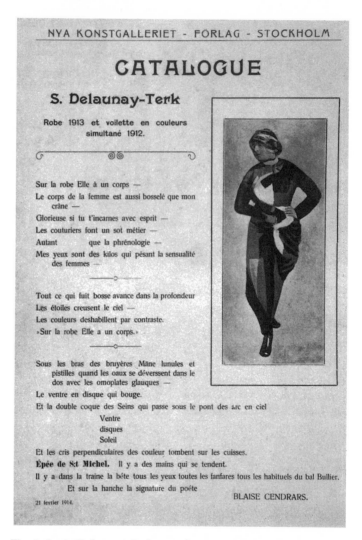

Fig. 5. Sonia Delaunay, *Robe simultanée* (Simultaneous dress),
1913. Bibliothèque nationale de France. Copyright © L&M Services B. V., Amsterdam 980402.

leurs déshabillent." Desire is stimulated by the contrast between artificial
and organic shapes rather than by the organic feminine curves alone.
These curves are rivaled as a three-dimensional construct by the depth
and volume created by the colors *on* the dress. Line 7, "Tout ce qui fuit,
saille avance dans la profondeur," refers to the colors, the contrasts between which produce the illusion of movement forward and away from
the surface plane. The traditional surface-depth relation is undermined by

the principle of composition by simultaneous color contrast: Delaunay's technique of juxtaposed surfaces creates the illusion, and rivals the physical reality, of three-dimensional depth.

Cendrars's hermeneutics of the dress shifts the location of meaning from the physical body to the surfaces that adorn it, from anatomy to the body's spectacular performance or masquerade. The remainder of the poem plays with the tension between organic and textile bodies. However, as lines 14–16 indicate, there are really three bodies evoked by the dress, each one belonging to a separate order: the organic, the textile, or the poetic. For instance, "Ventre" represents metonymically the order of the organic nude body (although it does not necessarily signify this body; the "ventre" could also be the dress's body, an ambiguity upon which the poem depends). "Disque" represents metonymically the de-anthropomorphized, or geometric, order of the designs on the fabric. And "Soleil" is a metonym for the order of the *imagined* body, what the poet makes, poetically, of what he sees. These three orders are emphatically intermingled in lines 11–13. "[B]ras," "mains" "dos," "omoplates," "ventre," and "seins" all belong to the order of the organic body; "disque" and "arcs-en-ciel" refer us back to the abstract motifs printed on the dress (the primary motifs of Delaunay's paintings), while "bruyères," "lunules," "pistils, "les eaux," "La double coque" and "le pont" all belong to the order of the poetic or imaginative discourse inspired by the abstract motifs. Meanwhile, line 11 reveals a high degree of phonetic rather than visual motivation; the /o/ of "les eaux" motivates the /o/ sounds of "dos" and "*o*moplates gl*au*ques." To attenuate even further the relation between the phenomenological truth of the body and the incarnated "spirit" in the dress, Cendrars allows the poetry of the line, the sound values of the word, to govern the longest descriptive sequence of the poem. Although it is the *eyes*, the poet tells us, that "weigh" the dress, in this case his *tongue* seems to be generating the descriptive discourse of the imaginative order. The synesthesia implied by the overlap between seeing and speaking, the visual and the poetic, is fully realized in line 17—"Les *cris perpendiculaires* des couleurs tombent sur les cuisses." This move from the eyes to the mouth as the primary organ realizing the woman's "sensualité" is highly suggestive. The semiotic activity that defines poetic writing seems to work not in the service of unveiling the human mannekin but rather in the service of veiling her yet again. And here the familiar etymological association of text and textile receives a new twist. Poetry's own artifices, the operations of paronomasia, assonance, and internal rhyme, come to resemble fashion as a method of covering the body with another body. And this imaginative poetic body, like the textile one, no longer accessorizes the organic but rather "incarnates" it. Incarnation, then, is not a matter of respecting the contours of the ontic original; rather, incarnation involves pursuing the directives of the medium concerned, ceding the "initiative" to words or, in the case of the dress, to surfaces of contrasting color.

The fashion critic Diana Vreeland has commented that Delaunay's "robes simultanées," which Vreeland calls "chromatic cocoons," were "wrapped around the body like a second skin or a mad tattoo."[19] Vreeland's allusion to the tattoo is evocative in this context, for it suggests that for Delaunay dressing is akin to a kind of writing on the body. The simultaneous dress reinvents anatomy as inscription, and the job of the *couturière* becomes one of covering the skin with a text. Delaunay in fact attempted to realize her conception of the dress as tattoo when she began in 1921 to compose designs for what she called the *robe-poème*, or poem dress. The *robe-poème* was conceived as a garment stenciled with poetic verses (as in fig. 6, *Le Ventilateur tourne dans mon coeur*, by Tristan Tzara). Although none of Delaunay's designs for the *robe-poème* were ever produced, the project itself indicates a desire on her part to reconceive fashion as a means of incarnating the "glorious" female body as language. A direct link can be drawn between Delaunay's approach to fashion as inscription and the avant-garde conviction that the artist must alter the organic body in order to perform an aesthetic (or aesthetico-political) project. When Rimbaud writes in 1871 of planting warts ("*verrues*") on his face, or when he imagines a "nouveau corps amoureux" in "Being Beauteous,"[20] he exhibits an impulse similar to that realized in Delaunay's designs. His portrait of "un homme s'implantant et se cultivant des verrues sur le visage" [a man planting and cultivating warts on his face] offers the possibility that one might make manifest or visible *(se faire voyant)* a hidden or simply abstract state of consciousness.[21] To tattoo the body is, in this context, to force *profondeur* to the surface, to make the deeper self visible, readable, and thus a subject of exhibition and performance. This visually exhibited or linguistically exteriorized self may remain a function of the self's truth; it is more likely, however, that the exteriorized self, as it enters into the pure play of surfaces, will subordinate its truth to the dynamic interaction between, in one case, the colors of the dress and, in the other, the phonetic and graphemic textures of words.

To return to Cendrars's poem, it is now clear why Delaunay's *robe simultanée* comes to serve Cendrars as a model for an aesthetic that no longer privileges organic *profondeur* over articulated surface. Delaunay's designs play with the lines of the body, treating them nonhierarchically as

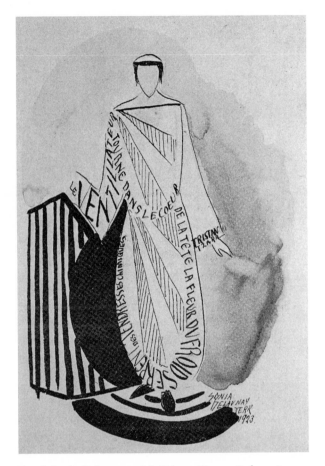

Fig. 6. Sonia Delaunay with Tristan Tzara, *Robe poème:
Le Ventilateur tourne dans mon coeur* [Poem dress: The
fan turns in my heart], 1923. Bibliothèque nationale de
France. Copyright © L&M Services B. V., Amsterdam
980402.

just another surface entering into play with the surfaces of applied and
thus artificial elements. True, Delaunay—at least according to Cendrars—
retains the order of the organic body, in contrast to the futurists, who
demand in 1909 "the total suppression of the nude."[22] However, the demotion of this nude body to pure surface design threatens to eclipse its
ontological priority and even its significance. As Cendrars's ambiguous
allusions to "ventre," "dos," and so on, indicate, there is no way to preserve the distinction either in language or in visual spectacle between a
surface that refers to an anatomical feature and one that merely serves a

function in an illusionist design. Implicit in Delaunay and Cendrars's approach is the possibility that all surfaces, all texts, behave in the manner of citations; the "ventre," for instance, refers simultaneously to the body *under* and to the visual text printed *on* the *robe simultanée*. There is no way to tell, the poem implies, which "ventre" is which.

Delaunay and Cendrars could have found no better way to signal this problem than to visually associate the *robe simultanée* with the traditional practice of quilt making. The patchwork technique Delaunay applies in the *robe simultanée* suggests that each element put into play—the "dos," the "disque," the "soleil"—exists as a kind of citation, a fragment drawn from a larger fabric or discourse. Although the elements may appear to form a whole—a dress or a poem—they are nevertheless scraps of preexisting discourses or fabrics stitched together into an assemblage. In "Sur la robe" Cendrars explicitly draws attention to the fact that the incarnation of the woman's glory requires the *cutting* of fabrics, their separation as well as their union. The repetition of the title in line 10— "Sur la robe elle a un corps"—provides a kind of *mise en abyme* suggesting the immediate citational and thus detachable or fragmented quality of all lyric utterances. The lines of a poem or a dress may claim at one point to "incarnate" the glory of the ideal, but they too are merely surfaces that can be cut out and inserted into the next arrangement. Cendrars's habit of recycling phrases from his own works as well as from works by others also adds to the impression that lyric discourse, just like the discourses of newsprint, popular fiction, and advertising, can serve as building blocks for assemblage. In an assemblage no single discourse, no single element, refers in a univocal fashion; rather, each element is continually reimmersed in a flow of attributes exchanged—phonetic, semantic, and graphic in the case of poetry, chromatic and textural in the case of the dress.

The concluding lines of the poem—"Et sur la hanche / La signature du poète"—finalize the analogy between poet and fashion designer, between "poème élastique" and "robe simultanée." In the original manuscript version of the poem Cendrars follows these lines with his own signature, rendering even more explicit the parallel between the fashion designer whose signature appears at the hip and the poet who imaginatively reconstructs and recovers the woman's body.[23] But if the poem is composed merely of clippings rearranged and reassembled, then in what ways can it be said to deserve a signature? Like the designer, Cendrars suggests, the poet can also sign because the recreated body, the incarnated ideal, depends upon the eye or the ear of a good *assembleur*. (The word *assembleur* is itself derived from textile manufacture, referring to the person who sews together the various parts of a garment.)

Further, the poet implies in "Sur la robe" that assemblage, whether in fashion or in poetry, necessarily entails violence. Cendrars refers to the violent gesture involved in assemblage in line 23, the detached and typographically emphasized "ÉPÉE DE SAINT-MICHEL." This line alludes most directly to the annunciation and the imminent incarnation of the spirit in the "glorious" flesh of Christ. But Cendrars reminds us here that in traditional iconography, Saint Michael descending to announce the Incarnation is often depicted as bearing the glinting sword with which he vanquished the dragon. To incarnate, the allusion to Saint Michael's sword suggests, one must also exert violence. In the case of Delaunay's *robe simultanée*, violence is manifested in the cutting and reassembling of swatches of fabric; on another level, however, this violence is exerted specifically on the woman's body, a body that is recut and reimagined according to the superimposed contours of artifice. Liberating the spirit, or the "profondeur sensuelle," of the woman from the chains of her anatomy is, in Cendrars's own terms, a violent as well as an imaginative gesture. The simultaneity of violence and creation is consistently foregrounded throughout the poem. We hear the victims of this violence crying in line 22 ("Les cris perpendiculaires des couleurs tombent sur les cuisses"), and we see the hands objectified in the act of cutting in line 25 ("Il y a des mains qui se tendent"). If we consider that *mains* is a term employed by the fashion industry to refer to the second-rank seamstresses responsible for *cutting* the dress form, then the line gains increased significance. Cendrars seems to be implying that Delaunay, as a fashion designer, applies (violent) hands, cutting up not only fabrics but also the natural lines of the female body in order to incarnate the glory of this body in a *robe simultanée*. But if "tous les yeux" figuratively extend their hands, then all present—"tous les habitués du bal Bullier"—are imaginatively resurrecting (recutting) the body of the woman. Cendrars depicts the violence implicated in the reconstructive gesture in the apocalyptic terms of the Annunciation. And yet here it is not God who is incarnated in the flesh, but the glory of the woman's sensuality that is incarnated in a dress. Once again, the order of the spiritual is vacated to make way for the play of sensual surfaces. These surfaces must provide an experience of depth formally ensured by allusions to a more profound (religious) order of experience.

In the manuscript of a 1945 preface composed for a volume of Baudelaire's collected poems Cendrars indicates to what a great extent the poet's relation to the spiritual has been altered since Baudelaire's time. "Comme le monde moderne a perdu la foi, mais n'a pas pu se dépouiller de la sentimentalité chrétienne," begins Cendrars, "de même j'ai n'ai [sic] plus l'amour des beaux vers et des rimes riches, mais reste tout pétri de la sensibilité baudelairienne" [Just as the modern world has lost faith but has not been able to strip itself of Christian sentiment, so I no longer care for pretty verses and full rhymes but remain awed by Baudelaire's sensibility].[24] Here Cendrars suggests that faith in divinity ("la foi") can be replaced by feeling, or "sentimentalité chrétienne," while poetic conventions, "les beaux vers et les rimes riches," can be replaced by a generalized poetic "sensibilité," without a consequent loss of aesthetic force or value. Cendrars's wager is that a feeling for the transcendent can in fact subsist even when it is not supported by any formalized or institutionalized vision of a higher order. By extension, Cendrars's post-Baudelairean poetics implies that surface decoration and its sensual appeal may take the place of a system of beliefs. This feeling without faith is like a Hegelian aesthetics without Spirit, an art without aura, or, more accurately, an art that redefines aura as a democratized experience available without initiation to "tous les yeux . . . tous les habitués du bal Bullier."

In a sense, Cendrars's privileged figure of the poem as dress merely renders literal Baudelaire's more metaphorical association of *la mode* with art's ephemeral, "modern," and contingent aspect. For Baudelaire, fashion is poetry's "élément relatif, circonstanciel," the "enveloppe amusante, titillante, apéritive, du divin gâteau" without which "le premier élément serait indigestible, inappréciable, non adapté et non approprié à la nature humaine" [the relative, circumstantial element, the amusing, titillating, and appetizing envelope around the divine confection without which the essence would be indigestible, inappreciable, inappropriate, and not adapted to human nature].[25] But what in Baudelaire appears to be a simple "envelope" rendering more palatable the suprahuman truth becomes in Cendrars's hands the very source of this truth. If for Baudelaire appearance (the "envelope" of the contingent) is present only to introduce that which is not present (the divine), for Cendrars the divine turns out to be the very function of its appearances ("envelopes"). The poet's task, according to Cendrars, is not "to detach from the fashionable whatever is poetic within it" [dégager de la mode ce qu'elle peut contenir de poétique]; nor is it "to extract the eternal from the transitory" [tirer l'éternel du transitoire].[26] *Dégager* and *tirer* are verbs that suggest an act of separation, a gesture of discernment that would cast aside the shell to reveal "l'élément éternel" inside. But for Cendrars, shells, envelopes, and appearances are precisely the locus of an experience of cosmic proportions.

The concept of depth implied in Baudelaire's poetics is far more consistent with a traditional epistemology of poetic *connaissance*, one that Jean-Pierre Richard, for instance, associates with an experience of immeasurable, inhuman depth. "The poetic adventure," states the author of *Poésie et profondeur*, consists in "a certain experience of the abyss,"[27] an experience of precisely that which is not consonant with "human nature." It is not accidental that Richard associates the end of a certain understanding of *profondeur* with the work of Rimbaud, a poet who wishes "to deny depth" [nier la profondeur]; Rimbaud "attempts to construct a world without depth [un monde sans en-dessous], a universe freed from origin and nostalgia" (11). In continuity with Rimbaud, Cendrars recasts *profondeur* as a "profondeur sensuelle," a depth located in the way the eye or ear functions, a sensual experience of the surface as origin and limit of meaning. However, as in Rimbaud's work, it is not the physiology of perception, but rather perception's *dérèglement*, that underwrites aesthetic truth. The eyes in "Sur la robe" are like "des kilos qui pèsent la sensualité des femmes" because they respond viscerally, deliriously, to a wealth of surface designs and inscriptions (to a mélange of "Ventre," "Disque," and "Soleil"). In response to these three distinct orders of phenomenal reality, the eyes "construct," to borrow Richard's verb, a world without depth ("sans en-dessous"), a world created entirely from a superfluity of nonhierarchized visual impressions. In Cendrars's poem the "ventre" becomes "un disque qui bouge" on a two-dimensional surface. The woman's glory is not, then, a materialization of her spiritual truth or even an unveiling of her physical contours. Instead, her "esprit" is fully incarnated in a designer dress.

By drawing poetry into a closer relation with apparel Cendrars not only realizes a potential inherent in Baudelaire's aesthetics of the modern; he also completes a gesture sketched out implicitly by Rimbaud. Rimbaud, even more dramatically than Baudelaire, suppresses the concept of origin and detaches appearance from necessity. "Oh! nos os sont *revêtus* d'un nouveau corps amoureux" [Oh! our bones are *clothed* with an amorous new body], writes Rimbaud ecstatically in "Being Beauteous," thereby intimating that the new world he envisions will involve, above all, a change of costume (*OC*, 181; *Ill*, 27, emphasis added). In fact *Illuminations* is full of references to costume: in "Les Ponts" the speaker glimpses "une veste rouge, peut-être d'autres costumes" [a red coat, possibly other costumes] (*OC*, 187; *Ill*, 55), and in "Parade" he witnesses a performance in which a series of "Maîtres jongleurs [Master jugglers] . . . transform le lieu et les personnes" in "des costumes improvisés."[28] The volume seems to suggest at times that the realization of Spirit, the satisfaction of the "superhuman promise made to our created body and soul" ("Matinée d'ivresse," *OC*, 184; *Ill*, 41), can occur entirely on the level of visual spectacle. "Quant au monde . . . ," Rimbaud reflects, "que sera-t-il devenu? En tout cas, rien des apparences actuelles" [As for the world . . . what will it have become? In any case, nothing like it presently appears] ("Jeunesse, IV," *OC*, 208; *Ill*, 145, trans. modified).

In a strikingly similar manner Cendrars also views the ultimate incarnation of glory as a matter of wardrobe. Consistent with the aesthetics of "simultanéité," Cendrars transforms "l'esprit," the incarnated glory, and even the woman's sensuality into a function of the surfaces presented to the eye. Because these surfaces do not need to correspond to any specific anatomy (nor do they answer to any eternal ideal) they always run the risk of falling subject to the manipulations of a contingent third party. In the case of Delaunay's *robe simultanée*, the surfaces of the dress are determined, and their patterns administrated, by a modern artist, not an industrial designer. Yet even an artist's rendering of a fashion design is still constrained by exigencies usually considered foreign to lyric composition. The author of a garment, no matter how greatly informed by a high art aesthetic, still depends extensively on available technologies of fabric production, on contemporary modes of cutting and assembling, and on the types of accessorization and color schemes privileged during a certain period. Although Delaunay belongs to a generation of artists who believe that function and fashion are not necessarily anathema to craft and aesthetic force, she herself has to admit that, in the end, the decorative arts walk a thin line between "vital, unconscious, visual sensuality on the one hand" and the "lowering [of] the costs of production . . . and the expansion of sales" on the other.[29] The fashion designer or decorator has to accept material contingencies that a lyric poet by definition would resist.

But if Cendrars's analogy holds, that is, if the poet authors a poem just as a designer authors a dress, then the implication is that poetry too "constructs" a world influenced by, perhaps even conditioned by, the contingent. "Freed" from all origins, as Richard puts it, the poet can hallucinate a new landscape of the body; however, this body, like the dress, is also a functional object, a product circulating in a market for which new bodies are always sought. Thus, because the poet relinquishes an ideal of permanence, he can only drop anchor in the shallow waters of a "profond aujourd'hui." Profound today, gone tomorrow. Cendrars is aware of this fundamental instability, this "sans en-dessous," when he describes his *Dix-neuf poèmes élastiques* as "poésies de circonstance," "inspired by the occasional meeting, friendship, painting, polemic, or reading."[30] Cendrars's "poésies de circonstance" still locate the center of insight in the speaking subject ("*Mes* yeux sont des kilos qui pèsent"), but they simultaneously displace this center by admitting that the subject can be touched, redefined by "l'occasion." In "Sur la robe elle a un corps" Cendrars takes this poetics of the occasion to its logical extreme. The accidental occasion—"a painting," "a reading"—is supplanted by contingencies of an entirely different order, such as the availability of materials, the influence of fashionable cuts, and the development of new compositional or reproductive techniques. These contingencies provide the occasion that touches and therefore alters both the subject and his or her imaginative creations. In "Sur la robe," the "je" is thus no longer an autonomous creator, but instead an *assembleur*; the lyricist belongs to that ambiguous class of artisans who must work with the given while conceding to the tastes of the contingent "other" that markets create. Rimbaud's infamous "JE est un autre" can be reread in this light as the motto of the poet as fashion designer. It is the confessional cry of a lyric subject who knows its creations—and even its self-creations—to be the contingent products of a thoroughly interactive process.

To the extent that Cendrars seeks a modern subject capable of recreating itself through a "nouveau corps amoureux," his works provide an early image of the postmodern subject as the product of masquerade.[31] And to the extent that he deflates romantic conceptions of originality and authorship he engages us in a meditation on the nature of a lyric subject deprived of its autonomy. In sum, Cendrars raises the question whether a modernist aesthetics can assert and maintain its value without relying upon an all-encompassing spiritual or institutional support (or an equally forceful ideology of the autonomous subject). Yet in his prescient manner Cendrars goes even further. He also hints at the naiveté of a project that aims to stitch together a pastiche of identities without reference to an ethical body capable of suffering. He does this in "Sur la robe elle a un corps" by continually reminding his readers of the violence inflicted—not incidentally, upon a woman—by a poetics of pastiche.

"Sur la robe elle a un corps" was published for the first time in 1916 in a catalog prepared for an exhibition in Stockholm of paintings by Robert and Sonia Delaunay. The publication was not authorized by Cendrars, and he had no occasion to revise the manuscript version he had entrusted to Robert Delaunay three years earlier. The poem appeared again in Cendrars's 1919 collection *Dix-neuf poèmes élastiques* with very few revisions. Given the poem's odd itinerary, it would be simple to dismiss "Sur la robe" as a flawed and trivial poetic effort, one lacking the rhetorical coherence and rhythmic balance of many of Cendrars's other, more carefully wrought poetic works. Indeed, critics of French poetry have neglected to provide any extended readings of the poem, consigning it in this way to an early oblivion. Departing from earlier critics, however, I will proclaim "Sur la robe elle a un corps" a centerpiece of Cendrarsian poetics, a crucial *art poétique* of the prewar generation. Cendrars's own approach to the poem suggests that it should be accorded far more attention than it has previously enjoyed.[32] Cendrars demonstrated an almost excessive concern with the publication and preservation of "Sur la robe." His wartime correspondence provides valuable evidence that the poem constituted for him a viable response to what he considered an outmoded Parisian avant-garde. For Cendrars, the poem's

significance resided in the fact that it posited a new, more dialectical relation between poetry and culture, one that his avant-garde contemporaries, as Cendrars himself stressed in 1916, had yet to envision.

During the war Cendrars wrote repeatedly to Robert and Sonia Delaunay from the front to inquire what had become of his only existing copy
of "Sur la robe." "Chers amis," begins a typical missive,

> Je n'ai pas de copie du poème de la robe—surveillez donc à ce que Canudo ne
> *perde* pas le brouillon que vous lui avez donné. Peut-être pourriez-vous me le
> faire envoyer, et je lui renverrait une copie *très lisible*. Je ne le sais pas par coeur
> et je ne saurais pas le refaire. Je tiens beaucoup à recevoir le manuscrit.

> I have no copy of the poem on the dress—so make sure that Canudo [the pub-
> lisher of *Montjoie!*] doesn't *lose* the draft you gave him. Perhaps you could get
> him to send it to me, and I would send him back a *perfectly legible* copy. I don't
> know it by heart and I wouldn't be able to write it again. I really want to receive
> the manuscript.[33]

Apparently the Delaunays did not reply, for in January 1916, while
Cendrars was recovering from the amputation of his right arm, he sent
word to Sonia Delaunay that he still longed to know where his manuscript
of "Sur la robe" might have been misplaced. That the Delaunays never
responded to Cendrars's repeated inquiries seems to have caused a rift in
their relationship: "Je m'étais juré de ne pas vous écrire tant que je n'avais
pas reçu *le poème sur la Robe*," Cendrars avows in another letter of 1916,
"que je vous réclame depuis *1 an*" [I swore I wouldn't write to you until
I got *the poem on the Dress*. I've been asking you for it for over *1 year*].[34]
Actually, Cendrars had been asking the Delaunays to return his manuscript for at least two years; in six letters written between 1914 and 1916
Cendrars reiterates the same request.

I cite this epistolary evidence of Cendrars's continuing interest in the
fate of "Sur la robe elle a un corps" to suggest how much he valued it as
a representative work of the prewar period. In general, scholars have
tended to look upon Cendrars's early poems as the somewhat careless
jottings of an author who would only find his true voice in the major
novels of the forties and fifties. But Cendrars himself seems to have considered the early poems significant in their own right; they were so radically
prescient, so beyond their own time, that all other efforts of the "so-
called" avant-garde appeared to him "foutu[s] d'avance" [already
screwed].[35] Of course, Cendrars would probably have exhibited a similar
degree of concern for any manuscript of his that had been mislaid or
placed in neglectful hands. I believe, however, that "Sur la robe" had
gained its author's affection for a very specific reason. The poem contains
many elements of what I consider to be a transitional poetics in the con-

text of twentieth-century modernism, a poetics departing from the typical modernist sense of writing as the reorganization of fragments around a new center to approach a postmodern erasure of the notion of centrality itself. "Sur la robe" can be read as a kind of *art poétique* in the rough, an inchoate manifesto of a poetics on the cusp of postmodernism. Publishing the poem was the closest Cendrars ever came to circulating a poetic manifesto on the order of Apollinaire's "Anti-tradition futuriste" or Marinetti's "Parole in libertà" (Words in freedom), both composed the same year (1913). And that is why Cendrars was so determined to locate the manuscript and to have a hand in its eventual publication.

Just what did Cendrars's *art poétique* consist of, and in what ways can it be said to constitute a point of transition between a modernist and a postmodernist aesthetic epistemology? As I have argued, "Sur la robe" draws poetic techniques into close association with the specifically *decorative* practices of Sonia Delaunay. Whereas links between the domain of painting and the decorative industries were often forged by the early-twentieth-century avant-garde, the potential continuity between lyric poetry and the decorative arts was less frequently asserted. And yet Cendrars's attempt to eliminate the hierarchy and even attenuate the distinction between the lyric and the decorative arts is consistent with the practices of a specific group of lyric poets who were exhibiting a fascination with the ornamental as early as the 1850s. Cendrars represents the culmination rather than the reversal of a trend developing within lyric modernism, one that begins with Théophile Gautier's collaboration with *La Mode* (and his claim that fashion is an art), proceeds with Baudelaire's "Éloge du maquillage" [In praise of makeup] and his analysis of the "dandy," and reappears in Mallarmé's meditations on style and self-ornament in *La Dernière Mode* [The latest style]. But whereas Mallarmé carefully preserves the distinction between poems of monumental impersonality and fashionable ephemera, Cendrars seeks to reconcile the two in "Sur la robe elle a un corps." By explicitly associating the poem with the dress, "Sur la robe elle a un corps" in effect "spiritualizes," by means of a carefully selected vocabulary of Christian allusions, an instance of apparel.

However, although Cendrars's goal may be to spiritualize the decorative, to solicit and celebrate the "profondeur sensuelle" immanent to the transient, the end result is inevitably a demotion of the poetic to the order of the decorative. For poetry's distinction no longer resides in a heightened diction (there are no more "beaux vers" or "rimes riches"); nor can such distinction be derived from a circumscribed set of themes or located in a compositional technique peculiar to poetic production (assemblage, for instance, is a procedure shared by poets and dressmakers alike). True, the demotion of the poetic to the status of the decorative is merely hinted

at rather than confirmed in the poem. Cendrars seems to enjoy the risk
he runs when he identifies the poet with the fashion designer, and yet he
retreats before celebrating the full implications of his analogy. Cendrars
in effect protects the poet from full contingency by choosing as his double
a fashion designer who is also an accomplished modernist painter. As an
artist, Sonia Delaunay hypothetically exercises greater autonomy over her
creations than would a *couturière* employed by a large firm. Cendrars
may be seen, then, as occupying the crossroads between, on the one hand,
a postmodern refusal of cultural distinctions and, on the other, a Baudelairean poetics that retains the superiority of high art over industrial products and what Baudelaire terms "leur grimace de circonstance."[36] Nevertheless, Cendrars's identification with the decorative arts, as well as his
excessive attention to surfaces, eventually implicates the lyric in a set of
conditions from which it cannot escape without recourse to a higher
order—Spirit, deity, autonomous subjectivity, or even biology.

Delaunay's efforts to harmonize her *simultanéiste* project with the exigencies of mass production highlight the dilemmas encountered by artists
or writers that sought in the twenties to establish a middle ground between a meaningful participation in the social and a strict refusal of heteronomy. It should be recalled that the theory of simultaneous contrast was
developed several years before the stock market crash of 1929 during a
period of immense enthusiasm for democratizing industries. At that time
the competitive capitalist market seemed to offer previously inconceivable
opportunities for the democratic distribution of high-quality commodities. The rapidity with which Delaunay found industrial backing for large-
scale production of her *robes simultanées* may have persuaded her that
industry could indeed provide the means for promulgating an avant-garde
aesthetic iconography previously confined to the haute couture salon.
During the second and third decades of the century Delaunay expended
a great deal of energy attempting to develop a stencil *(pochoir)* technique
that would allow her to mass-produce her simultaneous designs without
a consequent loss of tonal integrity.[37] She also invented the *tissu-patron*, a
dress pattern upon which she printed both the motifs of the *simultanéiste*
iconography and instructions for the cut and assembly of the finished
garment. All her experiments in fashion production aimed to synthesize
an "artistic conception" with "the standardization to which everything
in modern life tends."[38] Delaunay maintained that such a synthesis between pure art and industry could indeed be achieved. Denying, for instance, that her geometric patterns were proof of her compliance with
contemporary fashion trends, Delaunay defended her designs as follows:

> [Critics] have announced confidently at the beginning of each new season that
> geometric design will soon pass out of fashion and be replaced by novelties
> drawn from older patterns. A profound error: geometric designs will never be-

come unfashionable because they have never been fashionable. Bad geometric
design is the untalented interpretation of copyists and minor decorators.

  If there are geometric forms, it is because these simple and manageable elements have appeared suitable for the distribution of colors whose relations constitute the real object of our search.[39]

In contrast to the "minor decorators," responds Delaunay, the real artists of fashion, those who create the "good" as opposed to the "bad"
geometric designs, are involved in a type of scientific research. In pursuit
of truth, not profit, these "good" designers are destined to enjoy the laurels bestowed on every "lyric vision."[40] A lyric vision in the domain of
fashion is, for Delaunay, nothing less than a Baudelairean vision, one capable of discerning eternal laws in transient appearances. A talented decorator, like a pure scientist, can mobilize a fashionable geometric iconography for the purpose of discovering the profound relations established by
colors operating in a geometric design. It is only by obeying these laws
that the decorator resists the role of copyist and manages to offer an intuition of permanent (physiological) harmonies, as well as, happily, a fashionable dress.

  But if Delaunay in effect retains the Baudelairean lyric schema, if, that
is, she sustains a belief in a higher order (in this instance, the essential
truth of chromatology), then Cendrars announces the advent of an aesthetics that will place biology, physiology, anatomy, and consequently all
ahistorical orders of knowledge in serious jeopardy. Along with Baudelaire's "faith," in other words, will go the self-assured epistemology of
the chromatic scientist. No "élément éternel," no absolute science of relations, accords one geometry epistemological priority over another. In this
sense Cendrars's tentative *art poétique* leaves Delaunay's modernist preoccupations behind and advances toward the postmodern world of rela-
tivized knowledges and nonhierarchical cultural practices. By abandoning
a poetics of depth, or rather by reconceiving depth as an effect of surface,
Cendrars anticipates a postmodern aesthetics in which "tout est artificiel
et bien réel. . . . Les produits des cinq parties du monde figurent dans le
même plat, sur la même robe" [all is artificial and totally real. . . . Products from the five ends of the world appear on the same plate, on the same
dress].[41]

  Cendrars thus transforms Delaunay's dress from a scientific experiment
into a postmodern pastiche. No underlying order or chromatic law
determines the sequence or pattern of the surfaces, and any attempt to
locate a center from which to observe and hierarchize the colors of
the *robe*, or, for that matter, the "cinq parties du monde," constitutes a
baldly ideological gesture. Cendrars's decentering, similar to Rimbaud's
dérèglement, denies priority to any ontological, metaphysical, biological,
or even aesthetic order. "I'm too sensual to have 'taste,'" announces Cen-

drars. "I have all tastes."[42] The subject is thus set adrift in a world of surfaces, each of which possesses an equal claim on the subject's scattered attention.

To reiterate, Cendrars is celebrating this delirious subject and its aesthetics of decentering during a period of euphoria when Europe is only just beginning to appreciate the full consequences of capitalist expansion. As time went on, industry did eventually disappoint both Cendrars and his collaborator Sonia Delaunay. Sherry Buckberrough recounts how Delaunay abandoned all attempts to ally the decorative arts with her scientific experiments in painting during the thirties. Repulsed by the aesthetic compromises industrial manufacture increasingly imposed upon her after 1929, Delaunay retreated to the exclusive domain of the gallery exhibition.[43] As early as 1925 Cendrars also registered the failure of industry to accommodate the talents of artist-designers: "I'm especially sorry that we don't see your dresses in the street more often," he wrote to Delaunay.[44] Cendrars's mature work in particular focuses on democracy's disappointed promises; in 1949 he even concluded laconically that "today . . . we can blame capitalism"; "all that matters is cash, nothing else."[45]

"Sur la robe" introduces the dilemma that Delaunay and many artists of her generation would eventually face: the choice between the elitist pretensions of a higher order on the one hand and the dictates of an industry on the other. In a sense, the task Cendrars sets the modern artist in his *art poétique* is an impossible one: to destabilize hierarchies without homogenizing values; to retain aesthetic grandeur without the support of Kant, "objective Spirit," or conventional faith; and finally, to welcome contingency without capitulating entirely to capital. Like most of the early and most audacious members of the avant-garde, Cendrars wanted to maintain a high degree of craftsmanship (and thus preserve the categories of artist and poet) while collapsing the distinction between art objects and everyday (mass-produced) items. But Cendrars neglected to address directly the question how art is to prevent the vacant order of the transcendent from being inhabited by the interests of an industrial or military class.

In contrast, Adorno chooses to devote himself entirely to this problem in his massive study of art under capitalism, *Aesthetic Theory*. In a long digression that he was never able to integrate into the final manuscript, Adorno presents fashion in art as the dangerous hinge between self-reflexivity and submission. "Fashion," asserts Adorno, "is art's permanent confession that it is not what it claims to be. . . . Against its detractors, fashion's most powerful response is that it participates in the individual impulse, which is saturated with history. . . . If art, as semblance, is the clothing of an invisible body, fashion is clothing as the absolute" (*AT*, 316–17). Adorno's art-as-clothing metaphor could not be more *à propos*.

The important word here, however, is "absolute," which Adorno uses to refer to the phenomenon in which one aspect of an entity (such as its contingency) gains dominance over every other aspect (such as its effort to reclaim its independence). Art becomes pure fashion when it abandons all attempts at resistance to fashion. Fashion and, even more pertinently, art's confession of its fashionable aspect (its desire to please) may indeed provide "strength" to art and prevent it from "atrophy" (*AT*, 317); but "renunciation" or denial of fashion, Adorno stresses, is an equally integral part of art. For Adorno, then, fashion appears to penetrate art in two different ways, or really, to two differing degrees of depth. In a first instance, art fends off its subservience to fashion by insisting upon its own counterorder, its own set of exigencies related to an intangible and perhaps impossible ideal. In a second instance, art is penetrated by heteronomous constraints to the point where it hypostatizes—fully embodies— what previously constituted only one of its conflicting aspects. In this second case art loses its dialectical nature and comes to resemble a "piece of clothing," a thin tissue or "enveloppe . . . apéritif" that now hangs upon a body whose vulnerability, whose material existence, has become irrelevant. Fashion in art is "legitimate" since it manifests the immanence of the historical, except when it is "manipulated by the culture industry," which tears it away from "objective Spirit" (*AT*, 192).

Cendrars situates his poetics precariously between the two possibilities sketched out by Adorno. In this respect Cendrars represents a turning point between a modernist celebration of the everyday and the postmodernist commercialization of the same. Cendrars does not have recourse to an abstraction such as "objective Spirit" to defend his creations from manipulation; he can only hang his poem/dress on an unstable and utterly amorphous clotheshorse called *sensualité*. Stretching lyric form to its utmost limit, rendering lyric subjectivity as porous as it can possibly be, Cendrars asks whether a lyric poetry can in fact relinquish the principle of autonomy—confess to its incapacity to be "what it claims to be"—and still remain a counterforce to unmediated administration.

Finally, the only thing preventing "Sur la robe elle a un corps" from capitulating to radical heteronomy is the slender, nearly imperceptible barrier provided by the signature of the poet ("Et sur la hanche / La signature du poète"). In the poem this signature must take on the responsibility of fighting off the repeated assaults of technological and commercial standardization. Yet this signature is by no means the fully authoritative paraph of the romantic poet, nor is it reduced to the status of a designer brand label. Instead, this particular type of signature seems to allude to an intermediary order of subjective mastery, a hybrid state between autonomy and commercialism, absolute transcendence and purely emphemeral value. This signature belongs to an increasingly significant third field of cultural production in which one could situate a wide variety of modernist and postmodernist *pasticheurs*. Cendrars and Delaunay are typical of many artists in France, Italy, and Russia who were attempting from early on to realize hybrid creations drawing from both the decorative and the contemplative arts. It remains to be seen, however, whether the space of hybridity Cendrars helped to carve out as early as 1913 will continue to accommodate the lyric poem. As the fashion industry begins to play a greater role in funding modern art, and as publishing houses are forced by economic conditions to promote the study of visual culture over the study of poetry, the question whether "confession" can be balanced with "denial," the energy of fashion with the energy of resistance, grows ever more pressing.

———————————————————————

Six

Messages personnels: Radio, Cryptography, and the Resistance Poetry of René Char

ALTHOUGH René Char and Blaise Cendrars were born only one generation apart (Cendrars in 1887, Char in 1907), and although their literary
careers spanned approximately the same five decades of the century, their
respective poetic styles could not be less compatible. If Cendrars opens
the door to postmodern play by revealing poetry to be an assemblage of
culturally heterogeneous surfaces, Char, in contrast, attempts to homoge-
nize poetic discourse through a reduced, pastoral lexicon and a strictly
controlled network of recurring symbols. Char's lyric "I" never openly
approaches a pastiche of popular idioms but poses instead as the transmitter of transcendent truth. Thus, the famous poetic "impersonality" he
speaks of is not the impersonality of the socially formed poet but rather
that of the superhuman Absolute.

Respecting the marked differences between the two poets, critics have
invariably read Cendrars in the context of early French and Italian experi-
mentalists while placing Char in the company of more austere, postro-
mantic poets such as Hölderlin, Rilke, and Celan. In twentieth-century
French poetry studies Char is often cast as the most Heideggerian of poets
for the very reason that he aims, at least on the overt level, to produce a
poetry untainted by historically saturated discourses and the heteronomous interests they encode. On a first reading, Char would seem to fall
neatly in line not only with Heidegger's ontological poetics but also with
his programmatic rejection of material progress.[1] However, the critical
opposition between Cendrars and Char (based on the opposition between
avant-garde heteroglossia and modernist univocality) is far less definitive
than it might appear. Char's poetry is just as penetrated by historical discourses as was Cendrars's; further, his overt rejection of the technological
veils the extent to which his own language relies on technologically produced idioms.

On a pragmatic level, of course, Char emulated Heidegger's resistance
to technological constructions such as radar vanes and hydroelectric
plants along the Rhine, vigorously protesting, for instance, the implanta-
tion of nuclear reactors in his own region of southern France. Further,
Char seems to have adopted without qualification Heidegger's epistemological distinction between, on the one hand, "enterprise," or what Hei-

degger calls "Enframing" (instrumental reason and thus technological reproduction), and, on the other, *poiesis*, the supposedly more constructive
approach to the "essence of life" achieved through "staying with the
things themselves."[2] In a 1956 preface to a volume of Rimbaud's poems,
for instance, Char places poetic practice in direct opposition to "les entreprises des hommes": "la nature, encerclée par les entreprises des hommes de plus en plus nombreux . . . la nature et ses chères forêts sont ré-
duites à un honteux servage" [nature, ringed ever more tightly by human
enterprises . . . nature and its dear forests are reduced to a shameful servi-
tude]. How can nature rebel against this "servitude," asks Char in high
rhetorical fashion, "if not through the voice of the poet" [sinon par la
voix du poète]?[3]

In his essays on poetics Heidegger also mobilizes the voice of the poet
for the transmission of nature's message. The poet, in Heidegger's view,
is uniquely suited to serve as the transmitter of *physis*, for he maintains a
kind of radical receptivity, a privileged mode of contact with Being.[4] However, the transmission poetry picks up turns out not to be that emitted by
"things" but rather a transmission emitted by language itself. Still, language and "things" are not discontinuous or oppositional entities. Language can tell us about "the nature," the absolute essence or Being, "of
a thing, *provided that we respect language's own nature.*"[5] In its pure,
archaic, "high speech," language retains a link to the things it denotes,
a link that is broken by "foreground meanings," the technically precise
connotations introduced by historical usage. The "authentic" poet is he
who manages to ignore these (historically saturated) "foreground meanings" in favor of the (ahistorical) "high speech" of language (language's
"nature"), which is retrieved by listening "to what language says to us,"
by submitting to language's "appeal."[6]

Rhetorically, Heidegger often finds it necessary to define poetry in con-
tradistinction to another form of language. In his wartime and postwar
essays this other form, this "low speech" that counters the poetic, is associated not only with contaminated "foreground meanings" but also with
a specific contaminating apparatus responsible for reproducing them,
namely, the radio. According to Heidegger in "Building, Dwelling, Thinking," the poet's concentrated listening is gravely threatened by the mechanical idiom of transmitted sound. In "The Origin of the Work of Art"
Heidegger notes further that "radio sets are nowadays among the things
closest to us" but in the pursuit of Being unfortunately "of no use."[7]
Radio is Heidegger's privileged figure for a false proximity, a technological eradication of the spatial but not metaphysical distance between men
and the divinities (or the essence of "things"). Technological forms of
transmission only mime proximity, rendering even more remote man's
communication with the earth by contaminating "authentic" language,

the sole source of true "nearness" to things. "What is happening here," asks Heidegger, "when, as a result of the abolition of great distances, everything is equally far and equally near? . . . despite all conquest of distances [through telegraphic communications] the nearness of things remains absent."[8]

In an effort to distance Char from the Heideggerian poetics presented above, I want to study more closely the relation of Char's language to its "foreground meanings," paying particular attention to Char's use of the historically saturated discourse of the radio. I privilege the example of radio transmission not only because radio represents for Heidegger the opposite of "high speech" but also because the radio played a highly significant role in Char's own life and works. A reading of Char's poetry through contemporaneous discourses on—and of—the radio suggests that the very technological apparatus Heidegger taxes with distancing poetry from truth—the "unbridled yet clever talking, writing, and broadcasting of spoken words"[9]—promises for Char, in contrast, truth's conveyance and preservation. Further, the "foreground meanings" of "unbridled" talking are not alien to poetry but the very matter of which poetry is made. Radio, the technology of electronic voice transmission, emerges as an unexpected resource in Char's poetry, challenging from within the Heideggerian poetics of presence with which his works have too long been identified.

The alacrity with which critics have drawn Char into the Heideggerian fold has in effect obscured elements of his poetics that deserve greater attention. What critics have not adequately emphasized is that while Char may have parroted back Heidegger's objections to technology in his prose writings, as a practicing poet Char did not assume a thoroughly Heideggerian attitude toward either the *techne* or the historicity of poetic *language*. Char, after all, was not only a philosophical poet, an avid reader of Heraclitus, Parmenides, and Heidegger; he was also a member of the surrealist movement and exposed, therefore, to theories of the technological and its potential relationship to poetry that were decidedly not Heideggerian in orientation. When Char's works are placed within a broader discursive context, they reveal the effects of a more dialectical approach to "foreground meanings" and "unbridled" talking than the lyric theory propounded by Heidegger allows.

Avital Ronell has written persuasively on Heidegger's "naive reading of technology" with particular reference to his approach to the telephone.[10] Many of the remarks she makes concerning the telephone, however, can be applied equally well to Heidegger's treatment of radio transmission technologies. Without rehearsing what has become a familiar argument concerning Heidegger's fascism and his antipathy toward modern technology, we can single out one feature of Ronell's diagnosis that sheds considerable light on a tension also observable in Char's texts. Both radiophonic and telephonic technologies offer to Heidegger models of degraded listening; the subject is given the choice of attending either to the call of Being—embedded in the "high speech" of language—or to the call of an electronically transmitted signal capable of perverting, distorting, or scrambling the former. And yet for Heidegger as well as for Char, the distance between the call of Being and the call of the apparatus is not so easily maintained. As Ronell notes, "Heidegger *wants* to mourn technology," he wants to believe it can be set aside and overcome (16, Ronell's emphasis). However, technology "proves to be unmournable as yet, that is, undead and very possibly encrypted." It may be, Ronell adds, "that no fundamental distance establishes itself between the technical, natural, human, or existential worlds, no purity or absolute exteriority of one of these to the other" (16).

Ronell's image of technology as "encrypted" is a useful one when applied to Char's peculiar attitude toward radio transmission, an attitude deeply colored by his experience as a member of the Resistance during the German occupation of France. If Heidegger suffers from an unrelieved condition of nostalgia, a longing to reestablish an original, uninterrupted connection to language's "nature," Char recognizes this connection to be dependent upon a cryptographic writing that may have more in common with the "false proximity" of radio signals than Heidegger suspects. It is not that Char abandons the goal of proximity to Being; his writings too are suffused with a euphoria attributable only to an intense experience of poetic language as a higher form of truth. But Char's analogy for poetic language is, surprisingly, the cryptograph, the code of signals upon which radiophonically transmitted language relies. In "Impressions Anciennes," for instance, a text written specifically as an "homage of respect" and "affection" for Heidegger, Char writes that "poetry is a solitude without distance in the midst of the world's bustle"; "poetry constitutes . . . the relay *[le relais]* that permits the wounded being to recover new forces and fresh meanings."[11] Here Char appears at first to follow Heidegger (whom he is explicitly addressing) insofar as he equates the unique isolation of the poet with greater proximity to a generative source. However, for Char, the mediation constituted by Heidegger's "high speech" of language is more complexly articulated. Poetry indeed reunites fallen man ("l'être blessé") with a higher order, but poetry is itself a kind of "relais," that is, the *Petit Robert* tells us, a "device *[dispositif]* for retransmitting a radio signal *[un signal radio-électrique]*."[12] What is unusual in Char's formulation is not that he depicts the poet as a field of conversion (a "relais"), a site of crossing or transfer (for the poet in Heidegger is also a mediator), but that he uses a term to describe this transfer derived from the specialized vocabulary of telegraphic communications. "Médaillon," a short poem from the wartime volume *Seuls demeurent*, evokes this transfer in even more transparently electromagnetic terms: "qu[e le poète] sente s'élancer dans son corps *l'électricité* du voyage" [the (poet) should feel the *electricity* of the trip shoot across his body] (OC, 135, emphasis added).

It is no accident that Char metaphorically compares the poet to a receptor traversed by an electronic signal. The image of the poet as a registering device is in fact central to the avant-garde movements of the early decades of the twentieth century, movements with which Char would have been intimately familiar. We need only recall the significance of the Eiffel Tower, one of the earliest French emitters of radio signals, to the early cubists to recognize the extent to which wireless transmission facilities were construed as emblematic of imaginative labor.[13] If the romantics had envisioned the source of poetic language as a mysterious force, or "bouche d'ombre," the avant-garde identified this source with an electronic signal that the poet stood ready to intercept.

F. T. Marinetti was perhaps the first to establish openly poetry's resemblance to the T.S.F., that is, the *télégraphie sans fil*, or wireless telegraphy, in his famous "Destruction of Syntax—Imagination without Strings—Words in Freedom," of 1913; however, the figure of the poet as a *poste-émetteur* or *poste-récepteur* would be central to surrealism as well. Char was a member of the surrealist movement during his formative years in Paris (roughly, 1929–34). Char's figuration of the poet as a site of transfer was indebted not only to romanticism and its portrayal of the poet as a passive vessel for the Muse but also to the technico-medical vocabulary imported into poetics by André Breton. In "Introduction au discours sur le peu de réalité" (Introduction to the discourse on the paucity of reality), of 1924, Breton indicates how the locution *sans fil*, evoked so often by his futurist and cubist predecessors, would function in surrealist discourse. Noting that the *sans fil* had captured his generation's imagination, Breton confirms that the locution is indeed appropriate for evoking the peculiar relation of the *message automatique* to the writing subject: "Wireless telegraph, wireless telephone, wireless imagination, they even say. The inference is facile, but, I believe, legitimate."[14] In the *Manifeste du surréalisme* Breton goes even further, exploiting yet another expression associated with electronic technologies when he refers to the practitioners of surrealism as simple "appareils enregistreurs" [registering devices].[15] And again in "Le Message automatique," of 1933, Breton speaks of the surrealist as a "sujet enregistreur" [recording subject] tuned to pick up the frequency of revelation.[16]

The term *enregistreur* arrived chez Breton via dynamic psychiatry, which, in turn, had borrowed it from the technical discourse of nineteenth-century telegraphy.[17] Attracted, perhaps, to the modernist ring of *enregistreur*, Breton chose to appropriate the term to designate what he considered to be the primary creative function of the human mind. The process whereby a subject could listen without interference to an inner voice found its ideal analogy in the mechanically regulated processes of electronic transmission. Through this analogy the writing subject would be transformed into a mere receptive device, a net or screen for capturing a voice transmitted from an unnameable beyond. The task Breton set for surrealism, then, was to capture the short-wave signal, the "rayon invisible" that would ultimately facilitate the reinscription of the "imagination," the unknown, the *cryptic*, into everyday life (*OC*, 346). That the device necessary for the transmission of latent truths to human consciousness could be best represented by wireless telegraphy is one of the paradoxes of an avant-garde ostensibly antagonistic toward modern technological means.[18]

Thus, if radio transmission represented for Heidegger a contamination of "essence," a perversion of an original signal, in contrast radio transmission offered to the surrealists an ideal analogy for automatic writing. That is, radio's "appareil" served the surrealists as a concrete image for the *mécanisme psychique* by means of which access to an unknown essence could be achieved. In advancing the figure of the writer as *enregistreur*, however, surrealism was merely extending an epistemology incipient to romanticism, an epistemology that divided the self into a conscious receptive device on the one hand and an (unconscious or "inspired") emitter of curious, uncanny, and potentially undecipherable signals on the other. Surrealism identified this radio signal sent from afar, this encrypted self, with either a foreign substance inhabiting (haunting) the self or a deeper, more authentic version of the self. In both cases the encrypted self was associated with a higher reality. As in Heidegger, the poet remained the transmitter of a message emitted directly by Being.

The ending of Breton's *Nadja* presents a case in point, for here Breton identifies the subject's truth (or in Heidegger's vocabulary, its "essence") with a mysterious signal ("un fragment de message") emanating from a lost and topographically irretrievable source. "Un journal du matin suffira toujours à me donner de mes nouvelles" [A morning paper will always be adequate to give me my news], the author explains.[19] He then transcribes a contemporary *fait divers* (news item) in which, he believes, his fate is sealed:

> X . . . , 26 décembre. —L'opérateur chargé de la station de télégraphie sans fil située à *l'Île du Sable*, a capté un fragment de message qui aurait été lancé dimanche soir à telle heure par le. . . . Le message disait notamment:

"Il y a quelque chose qui ne va pas" mais il n'indiquait pas la position de l'avion à ce moment, et, par suite de très mauvaises conditions atmosphériques et des interférences qui se produisaient, l'opérateur n'a pu comprendre aucune autre phrase, ni entrer de nouveau en communication.

Le message était transmis sur une longueur d'onde de 625 mètres; d'autre part, étant donné la force de réception, l'opérateur a cru pouvoir localiser l'avion dans un rayon de 80 kilomètres autour de *l'Île du Sable.*

X . . . , December 26. —The radio operator on the *Île du Sable* has received a fragment of a message sent Sunday evening at such and such an hour by the. . . . The message said, in particular: "There is something which is not working" but failed to indicate the position of the plane at this moment, and due to extremely bad atmospheric conditions and static, the operator was unable to understand any further sentence, nor to make communication again.

The message was transmitted on a wave length of 625 meters; moreover, given the strength of the reception, the operator states he can localize the plane within a radius of 50 miles around the *Île du Sable.*[20]

In this passage from *Nadja* Breton maintains that the provenance of the mysterious signal cannot be determined: "[le pilote] n'indiquait pas la position de l'avion à ce moment"; "l'opérateur n'a pu . . . entrer de nouveau en communication." In this way he manages to suggest in Heideggerian fashion that the source of the revelatory message might be something transcendent of history or geography, that it might indeed be a lost truth such as that rendered by the "high speech" of language. Yet the very fact that Breton associates this message with radiophonic transmission, going so far as to provide details concerning the nature of the "appareil" (i.e., "Le message était transmis sur une longueur d'onde de 625 mètres"), suggests that for him the "high speech" of Being cannot be accessed without recourse to a certain technology, or, alternatively, that a technology is encrypted in the very communication of Being.

––––––––––

Char had ample opportunity to be exposed to this alternative approach to the technology of radio transmission during the period of his closest affiliation with the surrealist movement. Char's texts from the wartime period reflect his exposure to the surrealist treatment of radio, for they charge radio transmission with the task not of representing the obstruction of truth but rather of ensuring a privileged means of access to it. Although radio waves are full of "interférences," as Breton notes in the passage cited above, they nonetheless provide Char with a conduit between the writing subject and the mysterious "Île du Sable," the clandestine island of sleep, dream, and imagination that promises the purest form of "authentic" or "high speech." In Char's wartime collection *Feuillets d'Hypnos* the writing subject becomes a virtual "opérateur," fiddling with an electronic keyboard in an attempt to pick up the frequency ("la longueur d'onde") that transmits the only message with which the subject is truly concerned.

However, if radio served the surrealists as a metaphor for contact with the encrypted unconscious, during the 1930s, in a Europe increasingly in thrall to charismatic leaders, radio also came to represent an umbilical chord to national identity. While continuing to signify the intimate truth of the subject, the radiophonic message also assumed the weight of an entire nation's destiny. The significance of radio to Hitler's rapid rise to power has been well documented, as has the significance of radio to Mussolini's and, later, Pétain's regimes.[21] Jean-Louis Crémieux-Brilhac, a chronicler of the BBC's intervention in World War II, has even identified the radio with the very existence of a Gaullist Resistance within France. According to Crémieux-Brilhac, radio no longer simply established contact between a subject and its unconscious truth; it *produced* this truth in the form of a national movement. That is, during the war radio became the performative medium par excellence, virtually creating—like Heidegger's (and of course Rimbaud's) "poésie en avant"—the actions it described. "How can we help but wonder," remarks Crémieux-Brilhac,

> what the prestige and even the impact of General de Gaulle would have been *without* radio, what kind of contact the French forces outside of France could have maintained with the internal Resistants if radio had not existed? The legendary quality of de Gaulle's June 18th call to action *[l'appel du 18 juin]* disguises the unprecedented singularity of that absolute act of radio *[un acte radiophonique à l'état pur]*; for the first time in history, radio made it possible for an entire nation to meet and become familiar with *[connaître—et reconnaître]* a national hero they had never actually seen.[22]

Crémieux-Brilhac points to a remarkable phenomenon peculiar to the discursive context of World War II: during this period not only did de Gaulle make his presence known through radiophonic means but France itself existed as a sort of myth conjured forth by the BBC's *Radio France*.[23] After de Gaulle established himself in London the BBC became both the primary organ for disseminating information vital to the coordination of subversive anti-Vichy activities within France and the purveyor of a certain vision of French culture. That is, the BBC's French programming provided French citizens with a sense of "authentic" French culture, reminding them on the one hand of the uniqueness of their heritage and on the other of the foreignness of the Teutonic invader. It is worth studying this programming in greater detail, for its singular discourse—its historically specific mode of depicting "truth"—entered into Char's own poetic discourse in a number of surprising ways.

The link between radiophonic transmission and the authentic voice of freedom established by the BBC would influence the way radio as both a symbol and a discourse was treated in Char's poetry. In a sense the BBC took the place of the "Île du Sable," the irrecuperable site of the unconscious, in Char's poetic imagination. Attuned to radiophonic waves, the wartime poet became the *récepteur* of a message emanating from a very specific source, but one whose coordinates were—as in the passage by Breton—of necessity veiled. Through a sleight of hand that was at once poetic and political, the poet became the transmitter of an abstract ideal (Freedom) rather than the conveyor of a specific ideological agenda or military goal.

The BBC's French programming was actually quite diverse, including news broadcasts, interviews, music, and public-interest programs such as *Honneur et Patrie* and *Les Français Parlent aux Français*, programs that contained a good deal of anti-German propaganda. However, the most strategically important programming produced during the war was *Messages personnels*, a broadcast repeated several times a day during which a series of coded messages were transmitted with the express purpose of directing military activities within France.[24] Sentences such as "L'ange est descendu du ciel" [The angel has descended from the sky] or "Le bouquet est composé de 31 roses" [The bouquet is made up of 31 roses] were actually coded messages sent from London to specific groups of underground resistants. Aimé Autrand, who has documented Resistance activities in the Vaucluse, describes the codes as "orders corresponding to specific acts of sabotage, to guerrilla activities or parachute droppings [*parachutages*], sibylline or sometimes comic messages that could be correctly interpreted only by their authors or addressees."[25] What is most unusual and striking about the codes is that they often resembled fragments of poetry; they even operated somewhat like poetry, evoking several levels of meaning at once. Although the codes were fundamentally, in Autrand's words, "military instructions hidden under figures" (112), their formulaic syntax and their imagistic diction "invited," as Jean-Claude Mathieu has put it, their recuperation as poetic intertexts.[26]

Char obviously was not immune to the seductive qualities of the codes; in fact, in his poetry he seized and exploited the parallels that these "sibylline or comic messages" inspired between the poem and the cryptograph, the "enigmatic" imagination and the clandestine Resistance, and, most importantly, between the poet's "high speech" and the electronic frequency of truth. As a member of the FFC (Forces Françaises Combattantes, or French Forces), Char participated in the daily life of the radio.

From almost the beginning of the German occupation of France, in June 1940, to the liberation of Paris, in August 1944, Char operated as a clandestine resistant, linked to the French Forces harbored in Britain primarily through radiophonic means.

During the war Char was stationed at Céreste, near his native town, L'Isle-sur-Sorgue, where he wrote many of the aphorisms of *Partage formel* [*Formal Share*] and *Feuillets d'Hypnos* [*Leaves of Hypnos*] in 1943–44. Under the code name "Alexandre" Char entered the Section d'Atterrissage et de Parachutage de Basses-Alpes (Low Alps Landing and Parachuting Section) during the summer of 1943. He remained responsible for preparing landing fields and distributing parachuted materials until July 1944, when he was called to Algiers to train the forces of the Allied invasion. Because of the nature of his participation, Char had to be continually alert to information passing through radiophonic channels. Char's experience of the war was in fact so tied up with radio transmission that his poetry of the time could not possibly have remained unaffected either by its singular discourse or by its accessibility to symbolic figuration.[27] As opposed to Louis Aragon, Paul Eluard, and Pierre Seghers, whose Resistance work consisted mainly in editing clandestine literary journals out of Avignon, Carcassonne, and Paris, Char was directly exposed to the nonliterary discourses of military communication and to the imagistic dialect of the maquis, the bands of resistants who hid out in the mountains of the Southern Zone. The "engaged" discourse of Resistance propaganda exemplified in the poems of Aragon's *Diane française*, of 1945, for instance, was actually less vitally connected to the specific nature of the resistants' clandestine lifestyle than were the military discourses of code and pseudonym that Char absorbed into his own poetry.

Through the BBC Char received not only general news of Resistance activities but also precise instructions concerning sabotage missions and parachute landings in which he was to take part. The most persuasive evidence that these codes exerted a strong influence on Char's verse can be found in the titles he chose for poems or poetic volumes published after the war: *La Bibliothèque est en feu* [The library is aflame] is named after a radio code emitted by Char's own *réseau*; *Newton cassa la mise en scène* [Newton broke up the staging], in *Chants de la Balandrane* [Songs of the Balandrane], is a modification of the code "Darwin fera la mise en scène" [Darwin will do the staging]; and finally, *Un feu dans un bocage aride* [Fire in a dry woods], from *Sous ma casquette amarante* [Under my cap of amaranth], rewrites the code, "Le bocage est en feu" [The woods are on fire].

Unfortunately, it is now impossible to retrieve all of the codes transmitted through the *Messages personnels* during the occupation, many having been lost or destroyed. However, the BBC Radio Written Archives, in

Reading, England, does permit access to transcripts of a large number of the codes, and it is from these transcripts that I attempt to theorize Char's poetic treatment of them.[28] The file maintained by the BBC covers the period from December 1943 to August 1944, approximately the period during which the fragments of *Feuillets d'Hypnos* were composed. M. R. D. Foot, a British Secret Operations Executive, describes the inception of the *Messages personnels* in *S.O.E. in France*: "S.O.E. [Secret Operations Executive Branch] introduced also a startling innovation: a wireless communication to the field through the ordinary transmissions of the B.B.C. . . . it was an enormous convenience to reception committees to get definite information that the R.A.F. were going to attempt a drop on a particular field; in fine moonlit weather scores of messages announcing drops that night would go out each evening in the summer of 1944."[29]

Char was the captain of one of the "reception committees" mentioned by Foot. His constant exposure to the radio codes sent over the BBC (both to his unit and to others) produced two startling effects. First, Char began to depict poetic activity as a military operation, one involving a delivery of arms ("flowers") by means of a technological apparatus (an airplane or radio waves). Second, he actually started to integrate phrases from the codes into his own poetry, signaling in this way that poetic language was by no means composed of a "high speech" autonomous of history. His hidden heteroglossia indicated that even his supposedly transcendent poetic language had been penetrated by, and was dependent upon, "low," historically contaminated, ideologically implicated speech.

Fragment 97 of *Feuillets d'Hypnos* provides an illustration of the first effect of radio discourse on Char's poetry, for here he compares the poet to a technologically dependent *récepteur*:

#97

L'avion déboule. Les pilotes invisibles se délestent de leur jardin nocturne puis pressent un feu bref sous l'aisselle de l'appareil pour avertir que c'est fini. Il ne reste plus qu'à rassembler le trésor éparpillé. De même le poète . . . (*OC*, 198–99)

The plane bolts forward. The invisible pilots release their nocturnal gardens, then press a brief light under the machine's wingpits to show that all is over. Nothing remains but to collect the scattered treasure. Likewise, the poet . . . (*Leaves*, 97, trans. modified)

The analogy between Char's task as a member of a reception committee and his task as a poet is constructed by the reader in the silent space of the ellipsis: "De même le poete . . ." The poet who gathers arms is engaging in a quintessentially poetic activity: the gathering of flowers. These flowers are a treasure offered by "pilotes invisibles," emisseries transported by an "appareil" to transmit a truth from beyond (de

Gaulle!). The word *invisible* leads us back to Breton's image of the source of poetic inspiration as a "rayon invisible," but in Breton's version this "rayon invisible" never reveals the secret of its provenance. In the case of fragment 97, the origin of the "invisible" pilots and their flowers is implicitly located; the pilots, as well as their "invisible networks of signals,"[30] emanate from a very particular site indeed: the S.O.E. headquarters in London.

Through a constructed resemblance, then, a military event (the parachuting of arms) becomes emblematic of an aesthetic gesture. Weapons that kill ("[un] jardin nocturne") are, in effect, the subliminal message, the first tentative words of a poem. Char's analogy demonstrates that his imagistic vocabulary was indeed affected by the peculiar conditions of World War II. But further, the analogy he establishes in fragment 97 is overdetermined not only by structural resemblances ("invisible" inspiration = "invisible" pilot from the beyond, etc.) but also by the discursive context of Char's writings. The identification of writer and fighter, poem and weapon, was in fact central to the radio discourses to which Char was exposed during that period. (In fact, it was central to Resistance ideology as a whole.)[31] A brief survey of the *Messages personnels* confirms that the codes actively encouraged the parallel between military operations and the aesthetic imagination, cryptographs and poetic utterances, the same associations, in fact, that are repeatedly evoked by Char throughout *Feuillets d'Hypnos*. To cite the most blatant, a code transmitted on 18 August 1944 reads, "Armez les poètes" [Arm the poets]. And in an only slightly more subtle form, many other radio codes establish at least the formal similarity between literary activity and military resistance by borrowing words drawn from the discourse of the aesthetic to refer to clandestine operations:

"Auguste à César: Merci pour vos nouvelles. Abandonnez la rivière avec Pédro et vos amis et allez tous à la lecture d'André" [August to Cesar: Thanks for your news. Quit the river with Pedro and your friends and go to André's reading] (13 December 1943)

"Minos à Rhadamante: D'accord pour double lecture à partir du quinze" [Minos to Rhadamante: Agreed for the double reading after the fifteenth] (13 December 1943)

"Ce tombeau poétique reste toujours dans le bois" [This poetic tomb will remain forever in the woods] (19 December 1943)

"De Pierre à Margherite: A partir de demain nous serons dix à lire le poète" [From Pierre to Margherite: From tomorrow on, ten of us will read the poet] (24 December 1943)

"Pour M. Tartempion: Nous avons acheté les cinquante mille volumes de votre bibliothèque" [For Mr. Tartempion: We have bought the fifty thousand volumes from your library] (15 February 1944)

"Dans ma forêt normande est un grand livre" [A great book is in my Normandy forest] (25 July 1944)

"Le maquis est un rêve" [Resistance is a dream] (6 August 1944)[32]

"Une âme artiste, c'est moi" [An artist's soul, that's me] (13 August 1944)[33]

Like allegorical figures, the words *poet, artist, book, reading,* and *library* are used by the radio codes to signify various Resistance activities, such as a parachuting of ammunition, a rendezvous of resistants, or a sabotage mission. Yet another code appears to be associating a parachute drop on a cloudless night with language itself, in this case, the language of the "sublime": "L'étang est sans rides et peut-être à partir de demain le langage de la nuit sera sublime" [The pond is still (without ripples or wrinkles), and perhaps starting tomorrow the language of the night will be sublime] (8 August 1944). In retrospect, Char's treatment of parachuted arms as a "jardin nocturne" seems overdetermined by a military discourse intent upon describing military maneuvres as pastoral scenes. In tandem with the radio codes, Char draws more or less explicit analogies between poetry and resistance ("De même le poète . . .").

Paradoxically, however, Char's critics insist without reservation that the poet always erected a firm barrier between his poetic activities and his Resistance activities, between writing and military engagement. Eric Marty, for instance, has claimed that history and poetry are entirely incompatible orders in Char's work.[34] Marty distinguishes sharply the "discours exotériques" [discourses of the event] from ahistorical "discours hermétiques" such as alchemy and traditional nature symbolism, which, according to Marty, inform to a far greater extent the texture of Char's poetry. However, given the way in which Resistance discourses themselves actively dismantle the barrier between the exoteric and the esoteric, the contingent (political) and the eternal (poetic), it becomes necessary to revise the conventional approach to *Feuillets d'Hypnos,* if not to the entirety of Char's postwar production. The very fact that Char integrated the lexicon of the radio codes into his wartime and postwar poetry suggests that he seized not the absolute distinction but rather the constitutive interdependence of contingent and poetic discourses. Fragment 31, which has been used by critics to prove that Char found poetry incommensurate with action in the real world, may offer instead a key to Char's ambivalence concerning the imbrication of poetic and military discourses. "J'écris brièvement" [I write briefly], the fragment begins;

Je ne puis guère *m'absenter* longtemps. S'étaler conduirait à l'obsession. L'adoration des bergers n'est plus utile à la planète. (*OC*, 182)

I can scarcely *be absent* for long. To expatiate would lead to obsession. The adoration of the shepherds is no longer of use to our planet. (*Leaves*, 31, trans. modified)

Presumably, "L'adoration des bergers" is Char's metaphor for the celebratory discourse of the pastoral, a discourse that traditionally maintains no overt or necessary relation to the bloody realities of military retaliation. But resituated in the context of the *Messages personnels* in particular, Char's phrase acquires an entirely different resonance. In the radio codes the word *berger* returns with surprising frequency, denoting simultaneously the simple shepherd of the poetic pastoral and the resistant, who, according to the analogy, is fighting precisely for the preservation of a poetic mode of existence and address. The following codes, selected from a vast number of similar examples, provide a sense of how consistently *berger* and other elements of a pastoral discourse served to describe or incite the activities of the maquis:

"Le berger cherche ses moutons perdus dans le maquis" [The shepherd seeks his sheep lost in the woods] (14 December 1943)

"Dans la montagne la nuit lève la tête vers l'étoile du berger" [In the mountain, the night raises its head toward the shepherd's star] (21 December 1943)

"L'étoile brille la nuit" [The star shines at night] (February 1944)

"Dormir à la belle étoile; Huit amis vont dormir ce soir à la belle étoile" [Sleep under the stars; Eight friends are going to sleep tonight under the stars] (May 1944)

"Les quatre étoiles brillent la nuit; La bergère n'a pas de coeur; Dans la nuit étoilée du quatorze juillet" [Four stars shine at night; The shepherdess has no heart; During the starry night of 14 July] (May 1944)

"L'étoile de Nicole et Christophe est proche" [Nicole and Christopher's star is near] (10 August 1944)

"Tout le firmament brille à travers les ramures" [The entire firmament shines through the branches] (15 August 1944)

"Il pleut, bergère, rentre tes chiens et ton raton" [It is raining, shepherdess, bring in your dogs and your racoon] (16 August 1944)

"La bergère compte ses moutons" [The shepherdess counts her sheep] (n.d.)[35]

In light of the frequent appearance of a pastoral vocabulary in the *Messages personnels*, it becomes all the more difficult to maintain that fragment 31 and the other fragments of *Feuillets d'Hypnos* referring to stars, shepherds, sheep, herds, and so on, are necessarily distinguishing the act of the poet—"L'adoration des bergers"—from the act of the resistant. Despite his disclaimer, the *berger* would appear to be absolutely central rather than irrelevant to Resistance activity, for this *berger*, as the codes repeatedly confirm, is a figure for the maquisard himself. In fragment 216 Char once again evokes the analogy between *berger* and resistant established in the codes, employing the relation between the shepherd and the flock to indicate the nature of the relationship between the captain of a Resistance *réseau*, or network, and his "troupeau" of maquisards. "Il n'est plus question que le berger soit guide (L'Amour de son troupeau le lui défend.) Ainsi en décide le politique, ce nouveau fermier général" [There's no more question of the shepherd being guide. (The love of his herd forbids him.) Or so the politician, this new general farmer (tax collector) has decided].[36]

Here Char is referring to the increasing subordination of Resistance units to the dictates of General de Gaulle, "ce nouveau fermier général" for whom he feels little enthusiasm. On the one hand, one might justifiably assume that Char is attempting to discourage the association between the *berger* and the resistant; poetry is becoming a less credible figure for Resistance activity as this activity is increasingly dominated by the conservative nationalist politics of de Gaulle. On the other hand, the association is maintained, for the "ideal" resistant is still the one who frustrates the autocracy of command by remaining "réfractaire aux projets calculés" [resistant to calculated projects].[37] Further, pastoral discourse cannot itself be rejected as politically useless, for even while denying the pertinence of an "adoration des bergers," Char resuscitates the term *fermier général*, which only confirms the inevitable imbrication of political and pastoral discourses on another level.

The decision to derive the codes from a pastoral discourse was only part of a broader campaign conducted by the S.O.E. to associate Resistance activity with cultural distinction. The codes often evoked famous writers and philosophers overtly;[38] further, the codes' authors exploited the devices of literary language, sometimes borrowing actual verses from well-known poems. For instance, on 25 July 1944 the *Messages personnels* appropriated Lamartine's "Oh temps, suspends ton vol et vous, heures propices, suspendez votre cours" [O time, suspend your flight! And you, propitious hours, suspend your course!]. And on 1 June 1944 a modified verse of Verlaine's "Chant d'automne" served to provoke the group Ventriloquist into action.[39] Codes that relied heavily on the rhetorical devices of poetry, such as alliteration and internal rhyme, were easier to remember; meanwhile, a vocabulary of poetic figures—"bergers," "étoiles," "moutons" and so on—evoked the pastoral climate of the maquis hiding places, implicitly identifying military action with the lyric idyll and the philosophical *rêverie*.

The radio codes of the *Messages personnels* thus worked by relaying a precise message while subliminally identifying this message with a "sublime" landscape and even an aesthetic ethos. The semiotician Winfred Noth has explained that a cryptographic code assigning arbitrary numbers or ciphers to items of the message is "nonsignificant": there is no relation between the items of the message (the plaintext) and the discrete units of the code (the secondary text).[40] But "poetic" codes such as those emitted by the BBC were "significantly coded," meaning that the military directive decodable by means of a key was transmitted in a fully legible phrase (207–8). In the case of the *Messages personnels* the words of the code bore a regular and systematic relationship to the plaintext they replaced. The code "Roméo embrasse Juliette," which, when decoded, signified "the arrival in Switzerland of a courier, safe and sound, coming from Toulouse," is a good example.[41] As a unit the sentence implies the reunion that the plaintext is confirming. A safe arrival is a happy ending. This significant coding encouraged the apprehension of analogies between actions in literature and events in history and between a poetic discourse of transcendence and the functional discourse of the military. A coded message such as "Roméo embrasse Juliette" evoked Shakespeare within a military context, thereby blurring the distinction between the realm of human action and the realm of words, a tactic that was central, in fact, to Resistance ideology as a whole.[42] The *Messages personnels* were more like poetic codes than other cryptographs in that the substituted text (the secondary code) was drawn from the same sign system as the plaintext (the French language). Thus, the secondary code could be "read," just as a literary work is read, for its own qualities, and not simply in order to divulge a hidden "message." As Roman Jakobson, among others, has pointed out, literary discourse achieves its status by focusing on the text "for its own sake."[43] Of course, in the case of the radio codes it was clearly the meaning, or plaintext, that one sought to decipher. And yet the BBC radio codes presented a kind of anomaly in the history of cryptographic practice, for unlike most secondary code systems used in military or legal contexts, the radio codes behaved like a literary text in that they too drew attention to the (secondary) text "for its own sake," they too acquired what Noth calls "semiotic autonomy."[44] In this respect the *Messages personnels* were similar to a work of literature; the meaning of the substitutive code was not entirely exhausted in the plaintext or the original message into which it could, with the aid of a key (or a hermeneutics), be resolved.

Resituated within the broader context of Resistance ideology, the radio codes appear to have been sending two distinct but interrelated messages simultaneously. On the one hand, the codes had to communicate a very specific message concerning the sabotage activities to be performed. On the other, they were responsible for conveying a more general message concerning the destiny and character of French culture. For even as they sent precise orders to bands of resistants in the French countryside, the radio codes also invoked a higher order, an aesthetic order, that inevitably complicated the referential hermeneutics upon which the efficacy of a code would depend. The radio thus came to symbolize not the presence of London as the subliminal message's place of origin (and ultimate site of command) but rather the multiaccentuality of the poetic and the indeterminacy of the message's origin. That is, the secondary text implied that the military order reflected a transcendent imperative and that it emerged from an entirely ahistorical realm. The poetic was mobilized by a military force that had to disguise its geographical, historical, and ideological specificity by claiming, in a sense, to be the very voice of Truth.

Referring to the use of radiophonic transmission technologies during wartime, Gregory Whitehead has suggested that radio's distinction lies precisely in its ability to "fuse" with a nation's "mental life" while simultaneously evoking the extreme intimacy of the personal address.[45] The *Messages personnels* make the most astute use of this duality peculiar to radio, exploiting what Whitehead describes as radio's preternatural appeal, the way in which it seems to speak directly to a listener's inner ear, to his conscience, even to his soul. The name *Messages personnels* implied that the codes were missives intended for a single person or family; they thereby suggested that their origin could be located in the most intimate domain of interpersonal relations. In reality, however, the codes were intended for collectivities; their site of origin was entirely impersonal, their substance derived from a shared Continental tradition, and their precise formulation determined by exigencies having nothing to do with self-expression.

But the success of the Resistance depended upon this dissimulation of a military interest; a directive emanating from the highest seat of the FFI command had to take on the air of an "intimate communion" or of "pillow talk" (256), not simply because the directives had to be disguised in order to avoid German detection but because Resistance ideology required that they conjure forth a more profound sense of community than that provided by de Gaulle's own program. The French people had to be made to believe that they were listening to the voice of their inner conscience, the voice of their true national, ethical, and even spiritual identity. And indeed, if we are to take Char's word for it, the resistants at least did think of themselves as "poètes du tympan," poets of the inner ear, listening not for the speech of a political leader but rather for an oracular message from the Messiah, that mysterious radiophonic "visiteur que nous attendons" [visitor we await] (*Feuillets d'Hypnos*, fragment 148, OC, 211). Thus, through an ingenious manipulation of the cryptograph the *Messages personnels* assumed the status of an inner voice and acquired the authority of a subliminal message, thereby obscuring the fact that they were actually military directives transmitted from a very specific ideological and geographical "beyond."

The tension between code and poem, the reducible and the indeterminate, can be sensed in many of Char's poems. Although Char clearly encourages the association between radio code and poetic verse, he also implies the necessity of distinguishing between them. The semiotics of a poetic language, which functions by resisting a univocal interpretation, are, after all, quite different from the semiotics of a cryptograph, which, in contrast, requires a univocal interpretation. Char both forces and discourages an identification of the poet with the cryptographer; he simultaneously assimilates the language of the *Messages personnels* and denies the pertinence of historical (exoteric) discourses. In this way, he invites us to read the poems of *Feuillets d'Hypnos* doubly. On the one hand, *Feuillets d'Hypnos* constitutes a set of poetic utterances transcending their historical specificity; on the other, it is composed of a series of cryptographs leading us back to a precise event, even a precise military operation, in history.

Fragment 31, in which the poet claims that "L'adoration des bergers n'est plus utile à la planète," provides a perfect instance of how this double hermeneutic works. In one sense, the "adoration des bergers" is not, as Char insists, "useful" to the planet; as a metonym for poetry, the pastoral hymn represents precisely what the Resistance cannot afford to be: a contemplative, abstract enterprise "qui conduirait à l'obsession." At the same time, however, the type of resistance that poetry incarnates is exemplary of the "liberté . . . inextinguible" that the real Resistance seeks to retrieve.[46] If we read *bergers* as a code name for the resistants, then "[l']adoration des bergers" is indeed useful to the planet; the shepherds' "habitude des ténèbres" [familiarity with darkness] (OC, 650), their silent interrogation of the sky, is precisely what will ensure the continuing presence of a resistant force within France. And yet Char's aphorism clearly comes down on the side of the hermetic. It is as though he wanted to make sure that poetry, even as it risked being reduced to the status of a code, nonetheless retained its distinction from a cryptographic mode.

By insisting that "L'adoration des bergers n'est plus utile à la planète," Char subtly reminds us that a sabotage mission is not, after all, a "lecture" and that a bomb is not, after all, a poem. Rather, both the bombing and the mission constitute targeted interventions in history that ultimately reduce the number of human beings on the earth. If the poet is the "conservateur des infinis visages du vivant" [he who preserves the infinite faces of the living], as Char claims in fragment 83 (*OC*, 195; *Leaves*, 83), then the poet cannot also be the practical resistant who accomplishes the "Devoirs infernaux" [infernal duties] of active retaliation (fragment 106, *OC*, 200; *Leaves*, 106). Likewise, if the poem is to preserve its autonomy from historical imperatives, it cannot be confused with the military directives passing over the airwaves from London. In sum, it is clear that Char is somewhat uncomfortable with the equation of poet with resistant that at other times he seems to promote.

Yet, ironically, the military code ordaining the "[d]evoirs infernaux" only achieves its effect because it simultaneously and almost ritually evokes the vision of what it is not, namely, poetry. The poet/resistant is a clandestine liberator, a product of "LA FRANCE-DES-CAVERNES," as Char puts it in fragment 124 (*OC*, 204; *Leaves*, 124), one of those enigmatic *gens de la lune* awaiting inspiration from the beyond.[47] At the same time, however, the resistant must learn to "devenir efficace, pour le but à atteindre mais *pas au delà*" [become effective, for the end to be attained but *not beyond*] (fragment 1, *OC*, 175; *Leaves*, 1, emphasis added). The tension that resides at the heart of *Feuillets d'Hypnos* and makes the volume such a fascinating example of wartime poetics can be attributed, ultimately, to Char's inability to determine the precise nature of poetry's relation to cryptography and, therefore, of the poet's relation to the radio-controlled, ideological actor in history. Finally, it would appear that poetry both is and is not a cryptographic code: like a cryptograph, poetry depends upon an "appareil" (a rhetoric); but unlike a cryptograph, poetry tends to render problematic its own decoding. At least this is the conclusion reached by Shawn Rosenheim, a scholar of cryptographs and literary codes. The poem may indeed be a "semantic encryption," states Rosenheim, but it does not by the same token necessarily possess a "key." With respect to the resemblance between cryptography and literature, Rosenheim proposes that a truly enigmatic cryptographic writing can stand "as an affront to all master theories of the text, simultaneously producing a fantasy of reading as decipherment and undermining this promise with the possibility of further levels of encrypted significance."[48] Ideally, the poet, or "appareil enregistreur," is an apparatus in the service of the intangible; the poet-cum-*opérateur* picks up a signal but is incapable of determining definitively either what it means or whence it comes.

Rosenheim's approach to the literary suggests that the coded message the "appareil enregistreur" receives, the "électricité" by which the writing subject is traversed, must never be reducible to a plaintext, a directive for action, even if at intervals in history it comes to serve a particular ideology or national movement. During the war Char clearly wants poetry to serve a specific interest (the Resistance), but he resists the hermeneutics of service, the cryptography of the code. If his poetry is to remain poetry (and not a radio code), and if the poet is to remain "l'homme réfractaire aux projets calculés" (and not just a military machine) (*OC*, 653), then the poem must not be definitively deciphered. As an important corollary, the provenance of the subliminal message transmitted to the poet-*opérateur* also has to remain unknown. A poem cannot, that is, be reduced to the musings of a single situated subject; a set of "clefs biographiques" cannot suffice to exhaust its significance.[49] Nor can the poem be read as the crystallization of a historical discourse (decipherable by means of historical recontextualization or discourse analysis). Instead, the poem must emanate from the very mouth of Being.

Surrealism has its own version of this myth, as the passage from *Nadja* cited earlier illustrates. This passage, Breton's editors inform us, is a barely rewritten *fait divers* drawn from the 27 December 1927 issue of a contemporary newspaper, *Le Journal*: "Breton cites the article almost in its entirety," the editors explain, "leaving out, however, all anecdotal or geographical details, with the exception of the name of the island, which he stresses *[qu'il met en valeur]*. This name doesn't authorize the reader to situate the island itself, but allows the reader instead to use his or her imagination *[le rêver]*."[50] In other words, at the very moment in the *fait divers* when the original author situates the mysterious "fragment de message," Breton practices a kind of sleight of hand: "X . . . , 26 décembre. — L'opérateur chargé de la station de télégraphie sans fil situé à l'Île du Sable, a capté un fragment de message qui aurait été lancé dimanche soir à telle heure par le . . ." (*OC*, 753). In Breton's version an ellipsis is all that remains to mark the spot whence the message came. Meanwhile, the locution "à telle heure" disguises the temporal specificity of the message's appearance. Breton's omissions indicate that while a certain surrealism is willing to divulge the encrypted nature of the "fragment de message," this surrealism is not willing to take the next step, namely, to locate the geographical or temporal site of the crypt. But in fact, the crypt *is* somewhere; the message emanates from a very precise geographical and temporal origin; language never arrives at our ear relieved of its "foreground meanings."[51]

Ultimately, all we can know from Breton's account is that the mysterious message has been intercepted by another transmitter (the unconscious of the poet?) located on the "Île du Sable," the land of dream. The same phenomenon can be observed in Char's writings as well. In *Arrière-histoire du Poème pulvérisé* (The background of *The Pulverized Poem*), itself, incidentally, a kind of decoding device, Char tells us directly that the key to his own poems—and therefore the site of their origin—must remain "réservée" [unavailable]: "La clé demeure réservée." That Char eventually erases the word *réservée* and replaces it in the definitive version with an alchemical term, *vif-argent* (quicksilver), betrays a characteristic urge on his part to bury ever deeper the provenance of a particular figure or phrase.[52] In this case, the term *réservée* would have led readers back to a specific site, to Rimbaud's "Alchimie du verbe," in which the author refuses to divulge the encrypted significance of "Voyelles": "Je *réservais* la traduction" [I rendered unavailable the translation], states Rimbaud.[53] But if Char insists that his key remains "réservée," his avatar, Rimbaud, thematizes the key's existence, drawing attention in nearly every work to the "système," "méthode," "clef," or "formule" facilitating poetic composition and sometimes even confessing the historicity of the language(s) he employs. Char always maintained that he belonged unequivocally to the poetic lineage of Rimbaud; however, there are many reasons to believe that Rimbaud's true descendants are poets of quite another order, poets who understand their language to be implicated in history in ways that Char at times preferred to disguise.

Char's reticence, his refusal to provide the (intertextual or paratextual) key, indicates a compulsion on his part to actively ensure the "insolvabilité du poème" [the poem's indecipherability].[54] However, in *Feuillets d'Hypnos* the key remains more legible, especially when the fragments are resituated in their wartime discursive context. Char, a poet who valued his hermeticism very highly, obviously felt threatened by the potential "decodability" of the volume, the facility with which the poetic "crypts" might be located in a topos, a temporality, or even an ideology. Apparently, an earlier version of *Feuillets* did exist in the form of a "Cahier" in which Char originally jotted down fragmentary observations during his participation in the Resistance. These jottings must have resembled too closely the historical discourses, the radiophonic intertexts, for Char to feel comfortable about releasing them to the public. He chose to remove the "Cahier" forever from view. According to the librarian of the Fonds Jacques Doucet who composed the catalog for Char's archives, the poet marched into the library a few years after depositing the original version of *Feuillets* (the "Cahier") and withdrew it from its place on the shelf. Only a catalog card remains to indicate that the earlier version, perhaps containing the "key," ever took up space.

Rosenheim may be right after all in his view that literature, unlike the cryptographic code, resists decipherment, proffering always "further levels of encrypted significance" in place of a plaintext, a solid ground.[55] But because all language is embedded in a particular discursive environment, because all meanings include "foreground meanings," the poetic word too may eventually divulge its temporal, situated, and perhaps ideological nature. The *Messages personnels* are a kind of mock version of poetry, throwing into relief the features of a cryptographic condition that some poets—and some critics—would rather suppress. For it is possible that the poem's hermeticism is part of a game, a tactic or mechanism without which the privileged status of the poetic could not be maintained. The stakes of this game should not be underestimated, for ultimately they involve the very autonomy of the writing subject, the potential for a subject to assert its resistance to fungibility through a transformative work on language. Without doubt, all "foreground meanings," all derived discourses, are, in the hands of the poet, transformed. But this does not mean these discourses lose their historical resonances or that the poem is freed entirely from historical bonds. The problem with a Heideggerian or Heideggerian-based poetics is that it replaces the dialectical play of poetic composition with an absolute denial of the pertinence of the source. How can we measure the force of the poet's transformative powers if we do not know precisely what has been transformed?

By systematically denying us the key, by refusing to bind the "rayon invisible" of the encrypted message to a particular geographical, historical, intertextual, paratextual, or idiomatic source, the poet creates the impression that his message is indeed autonomous (as opposed to heteronomously mediated), that it emanates from a "higher" sphere of language (and owes nothing to temporally specific "foreground meanings"), and that, finally, the apparatus by which the message is transmitted is itself absolutely *sans fil* and thus incapable of inflecting the poem's line of flight ("La ligne de vol du poème"),[56] freeing it instead to circulate among the stars.

Seven

Rimbaud and Patti Smith:
The Discoveries of Modern Poetry and the
Popular Music Industry

IN the music world, the decade of the seventies belonged to Rimbaud. For a while you could flip on the radio or attend a rock concert and hear the name Arthur Rimbaud intoned earnestly by any one of a diverse group of young musicians. Lyricists such as Bob Dylan, Jim Morrison, and Patti Smith evoked Rimbaud as an important predecessor, thereby establishing their project within the paradoxical "tradition" of antiestablishment art. The assimilation of Rimbaud into certain trends of popular music during the seventies can be seen as the extension and most recent incarnation of what René Etiemble has called "Le Mythe de Rimbaud." In particular, it was punk musicians who implicitly—and in some cases explicitly—kept the torch of the Rimbaldian myth alive, viewing, as music critic Greil Marcus puts it, "the beautiful, the poetic, and the call to murder" as "all of a piece."[1] This last, or at least most recent, myth of Rimbaud throws into relief aspects of his image that were only just beginning to be detected by the interpretive communities of the first quarter of the twentieth century. Punk musicians of the seventies recognized in Rimbaud an avatar of the culturally resistant antihero, a source of destructive energy threatening to overwhelm the boundaries organizing disciplines, classes, genders, and semantic fields. That Rimbaud's poetry transformed even the confession of ambition into a force of cultural disruption must have made him irresistible to subcultural punks working to overturn systems of aesthetic distinction and economic opportunity from within.

Obviously, not all punk musicians adopted Rimbaud as a direct aesthetic or ideological forefather. It is highly unlikely that someone like Steve Jones of the Sex Pistols would have ever read Rimbaud, although his complaint "Ordinary life is so dull that I get out of it as much as possible" evokes the French poet with irreverent concision.[2] On the other hand, the direct assimilation of Rimbaud into the work of punk rock musician Patti Smith presents a particularly clear case of cultural cross-fertilization, one in which the writings of a canonized (and foreign) high-cultural figure enter into and influence a popular and, in this case, counter-cultural discourse. The disruptive potential of modern poetry, exemplified in Rimbaud's practice of *dérèglement*, anticipated and in some sense was materialized in the punk style Smith helped to create. Smith's practices of appropriation illustrate how a nonacademic reading of a canonical text could eventually produce a musical style disseminating a countercultural message of social deviance through the channels of what Adorno de-nounced—and perhaps misrepresented—as the culture industry. Here the popular music industry and its technological means of reproduction pro-vided the forum for yet another reinvention of Rimbaud as cult hero; this particular hero, however, addressed a popular audience, challenging reification (the stabilization of identities) from within the field of reifica-tion itself.

Lyric poetry, especially in the French tradition, has seldom been read through the lens of its commercial reappropriations. But if poetry is a literary genre whose evolution engages other cultural practices, then the fate of Rimbaud's text as it moves beyond the ivory tower is entirely perti-nent to an understanding both of lyric's multifarious effects and of its immanent tendencies. When the practice of quoting from *Une Saison en enfer* becomes the self-legitimating ritual of an entire generation of com-mercially successful (and sometimes not so successful) rock stars, it is time to examine the processes of appropriation in which this text is engaged, the signifying strength it possesses as cultural and commercial capital, and the relationship of this strength to what occurs in the text itself. The fact that Smith chose to focus her largely successful 1978 album *Easter* on Rimbaud points first to the great appeal of his myth; Rimbaud, the coun-tercultural rebel, provided young musicians of the seventies with a persua-sive model of antisocial innocence.[3] However, Smith's multiple allusions to Rimbaud's *text*—her appropriation of precise features of his style—suggest that there was something she found nourishing in the poetry itself.

Smith's reinvention of Rimbaud did not emerge out of a vacuum but was in fact inspired by earlier appropriations of Rimbaud and the other *poètes maudits*. The dadaists of the late teens and, even more significantly, the situationists of the fifties understood their project to be in direct conti-nuity with the history and evolution of lyric strategies, strategies pushed to their furthest and most disruptive extreme in the work of Rimbaud and the surrealists. "Clearly," the situationists wrote in 1958, "the principal domain we are going to replace and *fulfill* is poetry."[4] In a formulation that would prove decisive for the development of Smith's punk style, the situationists suggested that the textual existence of the poetic impulse did not realize the full potential of its radically anti-institutional force and that this potential could only be "fulfilled" in the realm of concrete ac-tions or "situations." While claiming that all art per se had been ex-hausted as an effective counterforce to modern consumer society, Guy Debord and Gil Wolman nonetheless maintained that the "discoveries of modern poetry" could provide a blueprint for countercultural activity, especially, if not exclusively, in arenas traditionally foreign to high culture.[5] One of these "discoveries," perhaps the most crucial, was the discovery of synesthesia as a verbal practice capable of disrupting not only semantic categories but phenomenological orders as well. Smith was particularly attuned to poetic synesthesia as practiced by the nineteenth-century *poètes maudits*. In her musical performances she aimed to fulfill the promise of poetic synesthesia in a more countercultural, but nonetheless commercial, realm.

Punk fans and practitioners may have been unaware that the sound and style of the music they appreciated owed a debt specifically to the "discoveries of modern poetry." Such a debt to combinatory techniques developed by high-cultural models was either muffled or advertised, depending upon the diverse packaging strategies of the musicians involved. Whereas the music of the Sex Pistols would maintain an attenuated relationship to the poetic tradition, Patti Smith actually foregrounded her debt, referring directly to her major poetic influence, Rimbaud, and participating in a hermeneutic activity as she transformed Rimbaud's texts into her own.

The especially close relationship Rimbaldian poetics maintains with punk culture has not received the attention it deserves. Strangely, critical works treating the intersections between popular or commercial practices and high culture have not approached the question of Rimbaud's reception by the popular music community. Even Greil Marcus's *Lipstick Traces: A Secret History of the Twentieth Century*, which comes closest to defining the links between the punk movement and high culture, refrains from addressing the role of Rimbaud.[6] Dick Hebdige's narrative of the origins of punk, *Subculture: The Meaning of Style*, is equally lacking in references to Rimbaud and the role his reception might have played, although Hebdige's analysis of punk style (influenced by Roland Barthes) evokes strong parallels between punk and the textual innovations of the French poet. Hebdige, interested only in the politics of punk, avoids discussing any impact high-cultural models may have had on the development of a synesthetic punk style, thus implying that neither Rimbaud nor any other poet played a role in the emergence of the punk phenomenon. In contrast, Tricia Henry, in *Break All Rules! Punk Rock and the Making of a Style*, pays more attention to the influence of the high-cultural lyric tradition on the evolution of punk.[7] Whereas other cultural historians, such as Hebdige and Marcus, associate the development of punk style with political movements linked to working-class causes, Henry traces punk back to the far more intellectual (and middle-class) New York rock scene of the mid-sixties. In Henry's version, punk style owes its existence less to proletarian anger than to innovations in alternative (i.e., educated

American) rock music: "When Lou Reed and John Cale founded the Velvet Underground in 1965, a series of events was set in motion that would change the direction of rock music and serve as a catalyst for the development of punk rock," writes Henry (8). By situating the origin of punk in the music of Lou Reed and glitter rockers such as David Bowie, Henry bestows upon the movement a far more self-conscious and literate heritage, one that would distance it from the image of punk promoted by the media. Henry's account suggests that, rather than a spontaneous form of expression emerging out of the lower-class British youth population, punk was actually the invention of a university-educated and highly literary community of musicians, poets, and artists congregating in the bars of downtown Manhattan.[8]

At the center of the New York rock community was Patti Smith, art student turned poet-musician, considered the most "remarkably influential" member by the editors of The "Rolling Stone" Encyclopedia of Rock & Roll, John Pareles and Patricia Romanowski.[9] Her independent single of 1974, "Hey Joe" backed with "Piss Factory," may have been, they venture, "the first punk-rock record," inspiring the work of British punk groups whose cultural capital would most likely be inferior to her own. In her work of the mid-seventies Patti Smith was establishing a hybrid genre she dubbed "rock poetry," which implicitly aligned the techniques of poetry with modern transmission technologies, a socially deviant lifestyle involving drugs, and the performance of gender ambiguity. Smith's first venues were not primarily commercial ones. She began her performance career by reading her poetry—traditionally a high-cultural activity—before the same audience that would later attend her rock concerts. Her earliest compositions grew out of attempts to set her own poetry to music, and she published song lyrics as poems in her 1978 volume, Babel.[10] That Smith began her career by writing poetry, or by confusing the boundaries between poetry and popular music, is indeed highly significant; such a blurring of cultural practices seems to have characterized not only her production but also the countercultural tradition flourishing within the popular music industry as a whole.

While Smith's work possesses the greatest number of explicit intertextual references—to Verlaine and Baudelaire as well as Rimbaud—the close relations between the high-cultural discourse of poetry and the angry rock style that would give birth to punk actually precede her. Lou Reed, one of the undisputed ancestors of both British and New York punk, was in fact a student of the poet Delmore Schwartz at Syracuse University. And Bob Dylan, one of the strongest influences on Smith, also wrote self-consciously poetic lyrics and published volumes of poetry as he achieved commercial success in the field of popular music production.[11] But the relations between poetry and popular music did not begin with the commercialization of folk music in the sixties; even during the fifties the early culture of rock music had been nourished by its association with the thriving poetic communities of New York and San Francisco. Jack Kerouac, originator of the Beats and a reader of those "renegades of high culture," Céline, Rimbaud, and Yeats, shared these influences with the poets Gregory Corso, Gary Snyder, and Allen Ginsberg, who in turn played an important role in animating the hippie-rock culture of the 1960s.[12] Given the consistently important influence poetry had on the development of rock music, it would not be unreasonable to claim that the emergence of a combative countercultural rock music tradition *within* the popular music industry—that is, produced and marketed by this industry—had everything to do with the "discoveries of modern poetry," both as a myth and as a discursive reality.

Thus, when Smith dedicated *Radio Ethiopia/Abyssinia* to Rimbaud in 1976, she was participating in a tradition firmly established by the American music industry, an industry that came into its own, as Andrew Ross has shown, when the buying power of the youth population was unleashed in the fifties. This new market sector demonstrated a surprising willingness "to cut across class-coded and color-coded musical tastes" to embrace both critical social messages and the works of the "renegades of high culture," where these messages found their formal analogies.[13] Often these analogies were loosely constructed; for instance, Rimbaud's "*dérèglement de tous les sens*" was interpreted by Jim Morrison in the late sixties not as a poetic directive, a formula for writing lyrics, but as a license to hallucinate on stage. Bob Dylan's "you're gonna make me lonesome when you go," from the 1974 album *Blood on the Tracks*, also evokes the *poètes maudits*, but although Dylan compares his amorous relationships to that of Rimbaud and Verlaine, the impact of Rimbaud's attack on conventional lyric form, vocabulary, and figuration is not registered. Certainly the myth of the poet as antihero played a large role in the construction of Smith's public identity as well, but what is most original in her work, and what differentiates her from earlier folk rock musicians as well as from her punk rock contemporaries, is her insistence upon Rimbaud's poetic texts. Smith openly identifies her project not only with the stated themes of his poems but also with the conception of verbal art they embody. Her success in carving out a unique position within the rock-and-roll community is due to the attention she drew to poetic textuality as a medium capable of subverting a whole set of distinctions between the high-lyric tradition and popular music, academic criticism and countercultural reappropriation, music and social change.

Smith's proximity to the Rimbaldian text and the unique position her music holds in the field of cultural production as a result are both related to her rather remarkable success in sustaining her visibility simultaneously in the arenas of poetry publishing and popular music recording. By the time *Wool Gathering* was finally published, in 1992, Smith had produced only one major book of poetry, the 1978 volume *Babel*;[14] however, it would be incorrect to say that in the interim she had ceased pursuing her career as a poet. Smith's entire career has been characterized by an attempt to elide the two cultural fields, to create a product that could transgress the boundaries between them. She did in fact create a hybrid form—as well as a hybrid public—by publishing her poems on the jackets or notes of her record albums in the place where the song lyrics would normally be. These "jacket poems" can be seen as constituting part of her effort to transport the cultural capital as well as the verbal complexity of the written word to the arena of popular music. Since the jacket poems receive no musical representation on the album, they are more like poetry than song lyrics, but a poetry, nonetheless, that cannot be separated either from the musical compositions performed on the album (and that bear the same names as the poems) or from the album format and its conditions of production. In the jacket poem Smith manages to appropriate the high-cultural conventions of poetic textuality while reproducing them for a large youth audience and packaging them as countercultural, part of a rebel's essential iconography.

Smith's 1975 album, *Horses*, for instance, carves out its unique position within the field of popular music by mixing and thus transgressing a series of hierarchical codes established in order to distinguish popular from high culture. At least three distinct subcultures are juxtaposed by the iconography of the album cover: the title *Horses* alludes to heroin and the drop-out youth counterculture associated with its use; a black-and-white photograph of Smith in a suit shirt and tie juxtaposes images of formality, the workplace, and radical androgyny or cross-dressing; and the back of the album jacket serves as a publication venue for a strophe of unsung lyrics celebrating not self-destruction, low-life cool, and marginality but their conventional contrary: aesthetic canonization. The jacket reads, "only history (gentle rocking mona lisa) seals . . . only histoire is responsible for the ultimate canonnizing [*sic*]." The French "histoire," made legible through the appearance of its English equivalent in the preceding line, provides a heterogeneous element signifying cultural capital of a very precise variety. Smith's heavy use of French words (another line on the album jacket reads "me the memoire of me racing thru the eye of the mer") may seem awkward and somewhat pretentious, but it serves the function of associating the harsh punk rock sounds of the album with the prodigious aesthetic ancestry of the French avant-garde.[15]

While Smith alludes frequently to other members of the French avant-garde, it is clear that Rimbaud offers the most credible archetype of subversive behavior and that his texts provide the richest source for the development of innovative aesthetic practices. Smith devoted an entire poem to Rimbaud in her 1994 volume, *Early Work: 1970–1979*, a fantasy of an erotic encounter with the poet entitled "dream of rimbaud." But while the poem follows the traditional itinerary of Rimbaud's life—Charleville, Roche, Abyssinia, Aden—its discursive tone does not directly indicate the influence of his poetry. The extent of her aesthetic debt to his poetry can be sensed elsewhere, in the multiple references she makes to the themes and strategies of his work on the albums themselves. Most of these references appear, not surprisingly, in the unsung lyrics, the hybrid poems, printed on the album jackets or sleeves. The album notes to Smith's 1978 *Easter*, for instance, reveal Smith's debt on both thematic and stylistic levels. Of all her albums, *Easter* is most clearly influenced by Rimbaud, containing implicit readings of his poems, references to his life, and even a photograph of the poet with his brother on communion day.[16] The words to the title song, "Easter," as printed on the album cover constitute a kind of elegy to Rimbaud to which the lugubrious, liturgical musical accompaniment corresponds. These words differ from the lyrics as they are sung by Smith on the album, although at one point near the end of the song Smith does recite the italicized riming couplet printed on the notes: "i am the sword/the wound/the stain/ scorned transfigured child of cain." The rest of the poem, which reads as follows, is not integrated into the music.

I am the sword/the wound/the stain
scorned transfigured child of cain

the word cain means worker . . . slayer . . . smith. a smith is one most wretched and blessed. picture two such smiths in the faces of arthur and frederic. one a vagrant and one a vagabond.both of them condemned to babble and battle. thru the heart of a map or the stop of a bottle.

one morning about a hundred years before little richard baptised america with rock 'n roll, arthur and frederic and their sisters isabelle and vitalie labored thru the streets of charleville in white ribbons and cloth of blue to receive their first communion. close to the church it was arthur who broke formation and called to the other rimbaud children to come run with him thru the field, past the chapel off a bridge into the cold and finite waters of a river that led to the warm and infinite blood of christ.[17]

Smith's poem-song begins with Cain and ends with Christ, tracing a trajectory of sin and redemption that Smith will repeatedly evoke in relation to Rimbaud's poetic practice. Smith's references to biblical figures set up the theme of religious revisionism, a theme consistent with Rimbaud's portrait of a redeemed Cain in "Mauvais Sang" and a materialized, corporealized Christ at the conclusion of "Adieu." The allusion to Cain turns out to be a particularly rich and useful one for Smith, for it serves to

mythologize not only the poet but also his double in the poem, that originator of rock and roll, Little Richard. Reminding her audience that Cain
is the "scorned" and repulsed laborer of the biblical myth, Smith identifies
him, through the etymology of his name (*Cain* means "smith"), with other
stock figures of the Rimbaldian repertoire: the title character of "Le Forgeron" [The smithy] and the "Paysan" [Peasant] hurled back to the earth
in the final movement of *Une Saison en enfer*. That Smith's name associates her with Rimbaud's privileged revolutionary figure, the smithy, is
only a happy coincidence, but one she knows how to exploit. Just as Little
Richard "baptised" America and "arthur" baptises his siblings in the
river, Smith resacralizes the world through music produced in her own
smithy's forge. In "Le Forgeron," a smithy who represents the revolutionary proletariat leaves his toil to join the masses challenging the monarchy
at the Bastille. The smithy's move from labor to provocation as recounted
in the Rimbaud poem is evoked by the narrative progression of Smith's
"Easter": "arthur . . . *labored* thru the streets of charleville," only to
break "formation" and produce a call for general revolt against, here, the
institutional structures of the church: "it was arthur who broke formation." The references to the smithy as "worker" and "slayer" and the
expression "labored thru the streets" suggest a familiarity not only with
the Rimbaud myth—the poet as rebel almost without historical specificity—but also with the precise modes of figuration (and their political context) deployed in his texts.

   In the jacket poem, "Easter," the theme of transgression, of breaking
formation, is also elaborated on in the figures of "babbling" and "battling." Smith claims that by means of "babbling" and "battling" Arthur
and Frederic manage to pass "thru the heart of a map or the stop of a
bottle," that is, through a material or conventional block to an unknown
territory. That Smith associates going beyond the "stop"—the ultimate
law of closure—with both babbling and battling indicates once again her
close relation to Rimbaud's texts (remember, Smith's first poetry volume
is named *Babel*). The effort to go beyond, to pass through, is staged in
both *Une Saison en enfer* and *Illuminations* as a kind of babbling: a "musique sourde" in "Being Beauteous" and a pagan tongue in "Mauvais
Sang"—"quelle langue parlais-je?" [What language did I speak?].[18] This
babbling or production of incoherent speech corresponds to an aggressive
battling, as in "Guerre," where the poet dreams of a war "aussi simple
qu'une phrase musicale" [as simple as a musical phrase] (*OC*, 205), and
in *Une Saison en enfer*, where a "bataille d'hommes" [a battle of men] is
identified with spiritual combat (*OC*, 244). The barely sublimated rage
of Smith's music—her exaggerated, sardonic twisting of vowels, the dissonance of her orchestrations—also implicitly associates violence and pre-
linguistic glossolalia with an art of liberation and salvation.

The aspects of Rimbaud's poetry that Smith accentuates in the lyrics of "Easter," such as the association of primitive expression with violent revolt, the emphasis on racial inferiority and lower-class origins (the race of Cain), the perversion of Christian symbolism, and the celebration of self-mutilation ("wounds," "stains"), all correspond to features of the punk aesthetic that will become more pronounced as time goes on. It could be argued that these features would all have been available to Smith and the punks through the influence of Rimbaud's myth rather than that of his texts. Extratextual material certainly serves as a filter between Smith and the Rimbaldian corpus, as her references to Isabelle and Vitalie confirm. Yet despite the mythical or biographical superimpositions, Smith does manage to articulate in "Easter" an identity between Rimbaud's revolutionary project and her own through the appropriation of poetic figures privileged by Rimbaud himself. Another song on the album, "rock n roll nigger," corroborates the theory that Smith is influenced both by the privileged figures of the poetry—Cain, the smithy, the "nègre"—and, more broadly, by the textual practices his poetry celebrates. In continuity with "Easter," the figure of the smithy is once again central to "rock n roll nigger"; in this poem Rimbaud is "beating" or forging art out of "soft solid shit," like an alchemist transforming primitive matter into gold. Again, the words printed on the album notes are not actually sung in the musical version; rather, as an accompaniment to the frenetic, throbbing music we hear the refrain "Outside of society" alternating with an enumeration of artists Smith considers part of the avant-garde canon: "Jackson Pollock was a nigger" is followed by "Jimmy Hendrix was a nigger," and so on. But in the verses printed on the album notes Rimbaud is central: "the word (art) must be redefined—all mutants and the new babes born sans eyebrow and tonsil-outside logic-beyond mathmatics . . . any man who extends beyond the classic form is a nigger-one sans fear and despair-one who rises like rimbaud beating hard gold rythumn outta soft solid shit-tongue light . . . "[19]

The sociopolitical rebellion evoked in "Easter" is presented in "rock n roll nigger" in directly aesthetic terms. Here it is "the word (art)" that "must be redefined," not the religious (social) order that must be disrupted. Smith makes explicit this time the opposition between the artist who remains within a classical vocabulary of forms and the author of the "Livre nègre" (Rimbaud's first title for *Une Saison en enfer*): "any man who extends beyond the classic form is a nigger," she insists. The "nigger," Rimbaud's stock figure for the pre-Christian pagan or primitive, is drawn from a nineteenth-century colonialist rhetoric.[20] Smith uses the word very much as Rimbaud did: to represent the social reject, the deviant, the scorned "lower" race that turns out to be the source of creative energy and spiritual truth. In the politicized aesthetic discourse of the

1960s and early 1970s the word *nigger* undergoes a transvaluation, just as it had in Rimbaud's text: the negative epithet becomes a word of praise. In Smith, as in Rimbaud, a "nigger" artist is "sans fear and despair," the ultimate alchemist of modernity, the great Nietzschean redefiner of values. The project of redefinition that a "nigger" art involves is one that transforms the physical as well as the aesthetic realm; that is, not only words but human beings themselves are reborn, this time as "mutants," "new babes born sans eyebrow and tonsil-outside," subject to a new logic "beyond mathmatics." The punctuation of the line—the parentheses surrounding "art"—also suggests that the "word" itself requires redefinition. The verbal register, Smith implies, can no longer be understood as self-contained, a safe place for social deviance; the word impacts the world, its redefinition produces material effects. Thus, in "rock n roll nigger" to transgress the boundary of the word is to transgress material boundaries as well: excrement becomes "hard gold rythumn," a new "mathmatics" makes art (words) "outta soft solid shit."

However, even as Smith represents the transgression of phenomenological orders, she draws attention through the very orthography of the passage to the distinction between word and song, text and matter, "art" and "shit." Smith's (mis)spelling of *rhythm* in "hard gold rythumn" demonstrates the crucial importance of the textual grapheme in her punk practice, for as excrement is transformed into gold, the conventional *rhythm* becomes "ryth*umn*" on the lyric page (Smith adopts the French suppression of the first *h* as in *rythme*, but the ending is her own). The idiosyncratic spelling evokes the religious origin of music in the *hymn* through the doubling of the nasal consonants, *mn*; but simultaneously, through the replacement of the *y* with a *u*, the spelling directs us toward the nonsemantic and decidedly nonreligious "hum" of Rimbaud's ubiquitous "bourdonnement," the vibrating insect noise he refers to directly in "Chanson de la plus haute tour" and "Enfance, II." This "hum" is the presemantic music that will gain increasing volume in *Illuminations* as "les sifflements mortels et les rauques musiques" [the deadly hissings and the hoarse music] of the creative operation ("Being Beauteous," *OC*, 181; *Ill*, 27).[21] In Smith's verse this "hum," or elemental sound, is redefined as, drawn into phonetic proximity with, the sacralized "hymn." As in the Rimbaud text, the "hum," or white noise of human corporeality, the excremental or purely physical base of *aesthesis*, is resacralized, repoeticized, as it discards the restrictions—and definitions—of "classic form."

Smith is also attempting to imitate spoken language, as in "outta" and "mathmatics." But a phonetically motivated orthography foregrounds the disparity, rather than the identity, between textual and aural realms. On the one hand, voice and text are drawn together by the *u* (one naturally pronounces *rhythm* as "ryth*um*"); on the other, they are drawn apart by the *n*, which is merely textual or graphic, never phonetic or voiced. Thus, the crossover from *rhythm* to *hymn* to *hum* is accomplished on the level of the text, through the graphic rather than the phonic material of the sign. The grapheme works, paradoxically, to suggest the reduction of all graphic marks and signifying structures to the level of a "hum," the pure undifferentiated noise Smith's music approaches incrementally as "rock n roll nigger" nears its raw conclusion. That is, only the grapheme, the textual difference, can recall the sacred "hum" of the body, pure noise before signification, art's return to its pretextual origin. "Rock n roll nigger" asserts the performativity of language, its ability to produce material effects, even while demonstrating the unique qualities of the written sign. Smith's mobilization of a textual excess, a polyvalence produced by the grapheme, draws her work closer to the poetic tradition she emulates.

It is when Smith foregrounds the proximity of language to noise, and of noise to corporeal transformation, that she is most Rimbaldian, not because the French poet actually wrote noise or transformed his body but because such a dream was obsessively evoked by the textual operations of his poems. Noise ("hard gold rythumn" in "rock n roll nigger," "babble" in "Easter") is for both Smith and Rimbaud the first product of the newly defined aesthetic operation (Rimbaud's "nouveau travail"), a kind of brute matter to which the aesthetic—in the defining dream of the twentieth-century avant-garde—is ordered to return. This return, in Smith's and Rimbaud's parallel worlds, depends upon a process of pulverization requiring the expenditure of a kind of primal negative energy. To create, to return to the source of creation in the primal, physical noise of the resacralized body, one must *beat*, as one might beat one iron object in order to forge another. Beating produces the "coup de doigt sur le tambour [qui] décharge tous les sons et commence la nouvelle harmonie" [rap of your finger on the drum (which) fires all the sounds and starts a new harmony] in "À une raison" (*OC*, 183; *Ill*, 39). Beating also produces the "bruit de l'oeuvre dévorante" [noise of the consuming work] of "Jeunesse, IV" (*OC*, 207; *Ill*, 141) and the "musique sourde" [deafening or inaudible music] of "Being Beauteous."

This last poem can be read as an archetype of the scene in which a creator "beats" out a new transgressive music, a scene inspiring the narratives Smith will rehearse in her own jacket poems. The central event of "Being Beauteous" is, as in "rock n roll nigger," the physical transformation of an animated figure; in both, moreover, the physical mutation recounted coincides with a call to redefine art. In "rock n roll nigger" "the word (art) must be redefined," while in Rimbaud's "Being Beauteous" it is against the "canon" of all previous literary efforts that the speaker must struggle. While a fully elaborated reading of "Being Beauteous" is not required here, a glance at the vocabulary of figures deployed in the poem can help us understand the nature of Smith's debt to this primal scene and to the poems that, with slight variations, repeat it ("Parade," "À une raison," "Matinée d'ivresse," "Villes [I]," "Fleurs," "Métropolitain," "Barbare," "Hortense," and "Génie").

BEING BEAUTEOUS

Devant une neige un Être de Beauté de haute taille. Des sifflements de mort et des cercles de musique sourde font monter, s'élargir et trembler comme un spectre ce corps adoré; des blessures écarlates et noires éclatent dans les chairs superbes. Les couleurs propres de la vie se foncent, dansent, et se dégagent autour de la Vision, sur le chantier. Et les frissons s'élèvent et grondent, et la saveur forcenée de ces effets se chargeant avec les sifflements mortels et les rauques musiques que le monde, loin derrière nous, lance sur notre mère de beauté,— elle recule, elle se dresse. Oh! nos os sont revêtus d'un nouveau corps amoureux.

X   X   X

O la face cendrée, l'écusson de crin, les bras de cristal! le canon sur lequel je dois m'abattre à travers la mêlée des arbres et de l'air léger!

BEING BEAUTEOUS

Against snow a Being of high-statured Beauty. Whistlings of death and circles of muted music make the adored body, like a specter, rise, expand, and quiver; wounds of black and scarlet burst in the superb flesh.—Life's own colors darken, dance, and drift around the Vision, in the making *[sur le chantier].*— Shudders rise and rumble, and the delirious savor of these effects clashing with the deadly hissings and the hoarse music that the world, far behind us, hurls at our mother of beauty,—she recoils, she rears up. Oh, our bones are clothed with an amorous new body.

O the shy face, the crined escutcheon, the crystal arms! the cannon on which I must cast myself in the tangle of trees and of light air![22]

While Smith's "Easter" and many of the other poems in which Rimbaud figures prominently illustrate her debt to the popularized myth of his life (and this myth's textual anchor in *Une Saison en enfer*), the scene of physical mutation depicted in "rock n roll nigger" points unequivocally to the influence of poems such as "Being Beauteous." As Anne-Emmanuelle Berger, among others, has noted, the expression "être de beauté" designates an ideal of aesthetic beauty that must be exploded, a canon of literary conventions that must be reforged, by the activity of the words on the page (the white "neige" of the first line).[23] To put it in Smith's terms, a "classic form" must be replaced with a "nigger" art, an "Être de Beauté" (upper case) returned to its origin in the "mère de beauté" (lower case)—corporeal experience, primal noise of the world. Thus, "Being Beauteous" describes a scene in which a feral, fatalistic music (a "musique rauque") seems to cause a body—the body of the poetic text, of language, of the speaker himself—to explode: "Des sifflements de mort et des cercles de musique sourde *font* monter, s'élargir et trembler comme un spectre ce corps adoré" (emphasis added). Realizing what will become the quintessential punk dream of total material transformation, the first stanza concludes as "nos os sont revêtus d'un nouveau corps amoureux," the very skin seemingly peeled off the plural subjects as they are reclothed in a new (singular) body. The second stanza, or the fragment added after the Xs, implies that this "nouveau corps amoureux" produced by the cacophonous music is not an integral unity, a single entity, but rather a jumble of synecdochic fragments—a face, a shield, arms—suggesting no whole to which we can attach them. "Being Beauteous" is in this sense an antiportrait, a dismantling of the descriptive elements that compose a portrait; the "couleurs propre à la vie" in the poem are not reassembled to produce a new, identifiable life form but instead intensify, girate, and break off ("se foncent, dansent, et se dégagent"), liberated by the energy of the music from the confines of "classic form."

Rimbaud's poem thus proposes creation as a fundamentally negative process, and the objects or subjects that undergo and result from this process are not described so much as labeled, simply, by the adjective "new": "*nouveau* corps," "travail *nouveau*," "*nouvelle* harmonie," and so on. "Being Beauteous" seems to suggest that the "Vision," the "new," is too radically discontinuous to be poetically reconstructed in positive terms. Thus, what we witness at the conclusion of poems like "Being Beauteous" (or "Barbare," for that matter) is never the animation of a perfected Galatea but rather the disarticulation of a physical body, a scene that Rimbaud describes in "Génie" as "le dégagement rêvé, le brisement de la grâce, croisée de violence *nouvelle*" [the dreamed-of release, the shattering of grace crossed by *new* violence] (*OC*, 206; *Ill*, 137, emphasis added). In "rock n roll nigger" Smith approximates this vision of the "new" with her mutant "new babes" whose features have been inverted or effaced, while the logic of these mutations has become inexplicable, a "logic-beyond mathmatics." Like Rimbaud's "Être," Smith's version of the mutated being does not, in the end, constitute an identifiable entity but rather is realized in "hard gold rythumn," that is, in a sound, an energy, the "violence nouvelle" registered by the repeated phoneme /o/ concluding the first stanza of "Being Beauteous" and initiating the second.

The visual spectacle ("la Vision") in "Being Beauteous" is resolved, finally, into an aural experience; the "musique sourde" of the beginning turns out to be not inaudible but deafening. Such a move from the visual to the aural register, from a spectacle to a vibration that produces sound, is implicit in the first lines of "Being Beauteous," where shivers groan ("frissons . . . grondent"), death whistles ("sifflements de mort"), and wounds burst out, as visual spectacle or as sound, on the superb body ("des blessures écarlates et noires *éclatent* dans les chairs superbes"). This move from the visual to the aural is made explicit, moreover, in Smith's derivation of "hard gold rythumn" from an operation in which the "classic form" is extended (trembles convulsively and bursts apart to become noise in Rimbaud's rendering). Ultimately, these attacks on the "word (art)," allegorized as a scene of mutilation, implicate the subject instigating them as well. In an effort to produce "un concert d'enfers" [a concert of hells] the speaker of "Nuit de l'enfer" swallows poison (OC, 227); in Smith's version, singing ("beating") itself causes damage. Smith's line in "rock n roll nigger," "beating hard gold rythumn outta soft solid shit-tongue light," suggests both making a rhythmic sound *with* the tongue and actually doing damage *to* the tongue, striking it with a blunt instrument. Like Rimbaud in his famous letter to Paul Demeny of 15 May 1871, Smith insists that a new form of music, a new aesthetic, involves an attack on and a mutilation of the physical body. "Imaginez un homme s'implantant et se cultivant des verrues sur le visage" [Imagine a man planting and cultivating warts on his face], Rimbaud suggests to his friend (OC, 270). A century later, Rimbaud's vision of the smithy at his "chantier," beating and mutilating both his art and his self to achieve a new art, a new self, becomes for Smith an analogy for the transgressive experimental musical practice to which she, and other punk musicians, will aspire.

Once again, however, this vision of an aesthetic practice that transforms the physical world (here, the body) is rendered textually, not phenomenologically. The "musique sourde" of the poem turns out to be *sourde* in the other sense: not deafening but inaudible, a textual music one hears through the eyes. Smith may attempt to realize this textual vision in the deafening music of her albums, but she simultaneously retains a memory of its earlier textual incarnation through the jacket poems that frame her music. Smith's insistence upon the transgressive force of a textual tradition transforms high culture into a rich source of countercultural strategies susceptible, nonetheless, to popular reappropriation.

———————

Smith seems to have intuited that Rimbaud's primary rhetorical means for figuring the transgressive is the trope of synesthesia. Not only do Smith's own lyrics rely heavily on synesthetic metaphors ("beating hard *gold rythumn* outta soft solid shit-tongue light"), but her entire punk aesthetic seems to be based on a pattern of synesthetic transfer between disparate realms. Most of Rimbaud's synesthetic metaphors involve a transfer of attributes associated with sight to the order of the ear, or vice versa.[24] Synesthesia is essential to Rimbaud's practice because it suggests linguistically the transgression of phenomenological orders his poems thematize. Synesthesia is in a sense the purest, most paradigmatic of rhetorical figures, one that, as Paul de Man has observed, demonstrates in extreme form what all figures would like to do: allow a word to cross from one semantic field to another, unbounded by any logical or conventional or even grammatical limitations whatsoever.[25]

On the level of the synchronic verbal system, synesthesia achieves a true *"dérèglement* de *tous les sens"* by juxtaposing elements of discrete semantic fields that have been organized around the concept of mutually exclusive sense organs and their vocabularies. The end point of a perpetually synesthetic poetic language would be the destruction of the notion of semantics or semantic fields altogether (as well as the notion of individuated sense organs), since at least hypothetically any signifier could serve for any other, undermining, finally, the differences between them. Practiced relentlessly, synesthesia would bring about the death of language as a communicative tool or the birth of language as pure, all-encompassing noise. Rimbaud's poems evoke this full noise repeatedly. His task in *Illuminations* is to replace the "ancienne inharmonie" of the world as it is ("Matinée d'ivresse," *OC*, 184) with "la nouvelle harmonie" ("À une raison," *OC*, 183), consisting, paradoxically, of all notes, all riffs, played at once. This noise is full or pregnant because it contains "toutes les possibilités harmoniques et architecturales" in one brief but eternal second ("Jeunesse, IV," *OC*, 208; *Ill*, 145). Noise and chaos—synesthesia as both a linguistic practice and a phenomenological model—are thus valorized in Rimbaud's corpus because they figure a massive totalization of, *and thus an escape from*, the cultural and linguistic institutions guaranteeing the persistence of old forms of work, art, physical sensation, and, finally, love.

Roland Barthes once complained that Rimbaud's poetic practice, "so opposed to the social function of language," was terrorist in nature, that it led not to a euphoric paradise, a reinvention of love, but rather to a social desert.[26] The disruption of all social units, of all communities based on traditional distinctions, is indeed one of the dangers of what Barthes calls Rimbaud's "terrorist" poetic practice, a danger perceived almost instinctually by countercultural musicians of the late sixties and seventies. It is likely that Rimbaud's significance for these musicians lay in the fact that he, perhaps more than any other poet, explored and exploited what is most *poetic* about poetry, what makes poetry distinct from other linguistic practices, namely, the extensive use of figures displacing elements from one semantic field to another. Poetic figuration is in this sense paradigmatic of the type of cultural displacements, odd juxtapositions, and forced ambiguities promoted by punk subculture. The punk practice of appropriating and rearranging fragments of integrated sign systems suggests, as does poetic figuration in general, the possibility of a more active participation in the production of social meanings. The fragments that punk manipulates (high-cultural references, low-life paraphernalia, crosses, swastikas, and lingerie) evoke the very systems of overdetermination from which they have been wrenched; but the practice of rearranging these fragments works ultimately to scramble the systems to which they belong, including the hierarchical system governing cultural production, thereby annulling their power to determine meaning and value.

Because Rimbaud practiced more deliberately than most the desocialization, or radical displacement, of the word, he became emblematic of the poetic function in its most extreme manifestation and, hence, available for appropriation by groups for whom this function served as a paradigm for post-Marxist social deviance. Further, Rimbaud was influential in the domains of literary and nonliterary counterculture precisely because he left poetry behind. For musicians less familiar with his texts the myth of Rimbaud's life, rendered typically as a rejection of the poetic in favor of the geographical "unknown," suggested a continuity between aesthetic resistance and the exploration of alternative realities. For those who knew Rimbaud's work more intimately, such as Smith, Rimbaud's poetry exemplified a textual practice that performs—through its radical processes of figuration—acts of transgression in the linguistic realm that suggest, all the while, their homologies in the material. As Edward Ahearn has observed in concert with many of Rimbaud's academic and nonacademic admirers, "The dislocations of the economy of [Rimbaud's poetic] text [reach] beyond themselves to propose impossible/substantial transformations of person and world. . . . [Rimbaud's] explosions of experience, self and discourse [are] not explosions that can be contained within the notion of discourse alone."[27] It is this vision of a transgressive aesthetic experience, impossible to contain "within the notion of discourse [or music] alone," that Smith and the punks emulate when they thematize—and actually perform—chaos and noise.

Up to this point I have been concerned exclusively with enumerating and analyzing the similarities between Rimbaud and Smith, or between Rimbaud and the punk style Smith's work informed. However, it is still possible, and even desirable, to ask how Rimbaud's poetry and the practices of punk *differ*, how, even if they are related, they materialize a similar impulse in different ways. It is clear that Patti Smith's music, although more tame and certainly more literate than that of the Sex Pistols, will probably never stimulate anything like the scholarly discussions stimulated by a single lyric of Rimbaud's. But what still demands to be articulated is what makes Rimbaud, at least in the eyes of the academy, more persuasive and more durable. For the purposes of comparison I have been associating punk with Rimbaud on the grounds that both describe and perform the disarticulation of socially constructed meaning systems in order to transgress their categories and envision new possibilities of linguistic, corporeal, and social organization. It must be noted, however, that Rimbaud's poetry, while on one level performing semantic undecidability, on another level maintains a consistent and highly regular signifying system based on phonetic resemblance (internal rhyme, assonance, paronomasia) and diacritical markers (uppercase characters, punctuation, ellipses). Even a poem like "Being Beauteous," which I have presented as an extreme articulation of punk dynamics, possesses, as James Lawler has cogently argued, a "unique coherence"; "focus is achieved by means of phonetic coherence, firmly articulated syntax, [and] sharp spatial reference."[28] Lawler points to what he calls the "stage directions" in "Being Beauteous," which, far from disrupting theatrical *vraisemblance*, produce a recognizable and consistent spatial background. Lawler's example is the opening expression "Devant une neige un Être de Beauté," but we might add the precisions "sur le chantier" and "derrière nous," as well as the flat descriptive narration "elle recule, elle se dresse." The paronomastic play of the signifiers, such as the repetitions of phonetic chains in the lines "des blessures *écarlates* et noires *éclatent*," "la *saveur forcenée* de *ces effets*," "Oh! n*os os*," and so on (Lawler's examples), also contributes to the sense we have of the poem as a polished whole. There is, further, the phonetic play that Lawler does not note but that determines in part the richness of the text and the plurality of the readings it inspires, for example, the embedding of *ne* and *je* in "neige," suggesting an initial negation of self that the process of poetic creation effects and then potentially reverses. In another instance, phonetic resemblance itself seems to generate the flow of signifiers: the fragment "la *vie se foncent*" motivates phonetically the entire sequence of the sentence (the soft *c* of "foncent" motivates the *s* of "dansent," whose *d* in turn motivates "se *dégagent*," while the *v* of "*vie*" is realized in "*V*ision," and so on). These complex sonorities do not, finally, evoke the chaotic noise the poem describes; we might say, in keeping with Rimbaud's language, that they are "sifflements de vie," sounds giving birth to semantic plurivalence, rather than "sifflements de mort," sounds eliminating sense.

Jean-Marie Gleize's reading of Rimbaud's "incohérences de surface" [superficial incoherencies] also assures us that even though the unity of a Rimbaud text might appear to be at risk, a tight prosody, a systematic return of figures and themes, and self-reflexive and self-allegorizing gestures maintain coherence at another, more hermeneutically demanding level. "In sum," Gleize concludes, "we must not take the strategies of 'chaos' [the grammar of discontinuity] as the only rules of the system."[29]

Rimbaud's poems may at first seem to be miming the disarticulating energy they represent, but their own phonic and semantic coherence is not, finally, disarticulated by this energy. It would be wrong, then, to conflate the "musique sourde" evoked in a poem like "Being Beauteous" with the poem itself. The "nouveau travail" to which so many of Rimbaud's poems allude may indeed *not* be conceived by the poet as a set of texts possessing a "unique coherence," "composed" and "musically rigorous" [musicalement tenu].[30] On the other hand, neither can the texts Rimbaud actually produces be read as realizations of their own figures for the transgressive antiaesthetic practice they seem to want to achieve.

Rimbaud may have been the first to celebrate such a practice, however, and for this reason his experiments in that direction remain an essential source of inspiration for an avant-garde tradition increasingly critical of the political limitations of textuality. Rimbaud's figures for noise and chaos are reanimated and put to a different use by movements attacking art even more violently than does Rimbaud, movements such as punk rock, dada, and the futurism of Luigi Russolo's "Art of Noises." Either as a figure or as sensually experienced "aural emotions," "noise" comes to play the role of the antiaesthetic, assuming a set of specific significations in the history of avant-garde practice.[31] Richard Huelsenbeck, for example, will see in the creation of noise "a direct call to action,"[32] thereby recognizing, and in some instances realizing, the connection Rimbaud had only pre*figured* but could not perform. Thus, even Rimbaud's most aesthetically radical poems would be assimilated into the French literary canon more easily than dada *Merzgedicht* (shit poetry) or punk screaming not only because the poet imposed a rigorous system of organization on the texts but, more to the point, because they remain texts and they depend upon their textuality to represent precisely that which transgresses textuality. For as much as Rimbaud's poems must sing to make sense (i.e., they depend upon phonetic, potentially audible elements of the signifier), they must also make marks, diacritical (silent) marks, to furnish a system of *renvois*, a grammar of hierarchies, that aids us in our largely successful exegetical enterprises. It is, then, this dialectic between disarticulation and composition on a higher level, a call for noise and yet a brilliant control of assonance, a vision of transgression and yet a strict adherence to, as well as dependence upon, the rules of typography and the grapheme, that produces what we may still be permitted to call "high" art.

A century after Rimbaud, Smith will also exploit the semantics of inscription to produce meaning on one level even while subverting it on another. That is, she will maintain in Rimbaldian fashion the distinctions between text and world, lyric and body, "art" and "shit," even while figuring the effacement of these distinctions at the representational (mythic) level of the lyrics. Although this may not make her a poet due the laurels of a Rimbaud, it does place her in a kind of intermediary position between high culture and the far less literate noise of punk. The position she carved out in the field of cultural production is in this sense unique. She drew attention to the Rimbaldian contradiction in which a form of cultural expression struggles to be more than a form, a text more than a text, a band performance more than a musical experience, all the while exploiting the rules governing the publication, commodification, and distribution of the particular cultural form involved. That this contradiction summed up the transgressive desires of an entire market sector and could accordingly be expressed in a musical shorthand requiring few allusions to its origin was merely the apprehension of a very astute businessman, Malcolm McLaren.

If the punk music of McLaren's Sex Pistols is a renewed evocation of a tradition much older than itself—a tradition Greil Marcus traces all the way back to the twelfth-century Assassins through to dada and the Situationist International—it is nonetheless an evocation deprived of the kind of critical self-consciousness and craft we witness to varying degrees in the works of Smith and Rimbaud. For Marcus, groups like the Sex Pistols are important because they rekindle the agon lying dormant beneath the craft and doctrine of the earlier groups; we seize once again the fire "in the *words* they [dada, Debord, Rimbaud] left behind because of the *noise* the Sex Pistols made."[33] According to Marcus, then, the true colors of Rimbaud's "Visions" and "Illuminations" fully appear only when flooded from behind by Smith's "hard gold rythumn" and punk's hard metal racket. And to be sure, a particular version of Rimbaud does emerge, a particular need for transgression does make itself more clearly heard, when he is read against the background of his contemporary appropriations. However—and this is a point Marcus fails to pursue—what also becomes clear when the juxtaposition is performed is the *difference*, the textual difference and therefore all the phenomenological differences and barriers, separating *Illuminations* from "Anarchy in the UK," textual inscription from self-mutilation, the creation of metaphors from the ejaculation of spit. This difference, despite Rimbaud's warning in "Solde," keeps his poems from being consumed utterly by fashion. For while "Solde" testifies to Rimbaud's awareness that all ideas, all cultural strategies, can be appropriated and commodified as myths, it also makes sense only as a member of a printed volume, a volume that profits from a potentially infinite number of textual connections capable of retaining the reader's interest even after the passing of a hundred years.

On the one hand, the much-touted plurivalence, the semantic instability associated with textual inscription, can become a myth in itself, an "auratic" element to be appropriated by poet-musicians like Smith. One could indeed read "Solde" as Rimbaud's premonition that resistance to com-

modification conforms brilliantly to commodification, that social deviance articulated through signs *sells*. The history of Rimbaud's reception
confirms in many ways that a disruptive use of rhetoric, coupled with a
myth of its extension into the phenomenal realm, can become a highly
profitable commodity to be manipulated by cultural producers in aesthetic, commercial, and even academic fields. For this history reveals that
Rimbaud's name did not first become a successful marketing device when
it was cited by Smith. Rimbaud was a bestseller from the time the first
edition of his *Oeuvres complètes* appeared in 1912. The consistently high
sales of this volume allowed its publisher, Le Mercure de France, to remain solvent for many years while continuing to publish less popular
fare.[34] From the start, then, Rimbaud's textual dream of the text's transgression produced a set of cultural myths that still find reiteration elsewhere: the myth of the poet as "nigger," the myth of the poet as disruptive
influence or agent of social change.

On the other hand, however, the textual strategies Smith assimilates
into her own style do not merely *signify* "high culture" or "aura"; Smith
is too textual to merely exploit textuality as a commodified attribute. Her
lyrics and jacket poems actually encourage fans to exercise interpretive
faculties (and perhaps to gain new areas of competence) rarely appropriate to the appreciation of more mainstream commercial fare. The demanding hermeneutic work required of the reader or listener to make
(provisional) sense of Smith's work prevents the "myths" she appropriates from hardening into definitive forms (especially if the "word [art]
must be redefined"). Textuality is both a mark of symbolic distinction in
Smith's work and the operative mode of resistance to imposed meanings,
unified subjects, symbolic hierarchies, and predetermined cultural codes.
Smith's graphemic play may indeed win her a certain number of adher-
ents, but, markedly cerebral, it also acts as a deterrent to greater audience
interest.

Whereas the Sex Pistols sought to gain "Cash from Chaos,"[35] economic
capital from synesthetic style, Smith attempted to produce a serious middle ground between immediate co-optation and elitist high culture. It is
unlikely that Smith could have predicted the enormous popular success
of the punk bands she inspired or the profitable collusion between musical
primitivism and social deviance she helped to evolve. Smith's music was
distinct from that of later punk bands in a variety of ways. For one thing,
her albums were never as popular (commercially successful) as those of
the Sex Pistols. *Rolling Stone* rated the Sex Pistols' album *Never Mind
the Bollocks Here's the Sex Pistols* the second most popular rock album
in history, after the Beatles' *Sergeant Pepper's Lonely Hearts Club Band*.[36]
And yet, as a commodity packaged and distributed by Arista Records,

Smith's work reached a much larger public than did the tracts of the situationists, whose debt to high culture was greater than her own. In sum, an inverse ratio can be seen to exist between the proximity of the cultural form to the high-cultural text and the degree of commercial and popular success this form achieves. What Smith's case reveals is that resistance to commodification (and thus to immediate commercial success) may well reside in the foregrounding of textuality itself, in the retention of a textual difficulty or inaccessibility associated with the avant-garde, in an exploitation of a semantic excess generated by the way the grapheme works. A cultural form's susceptibility to commodification, then, can be said to vary according to its proximity to, and its dependence for effect upon, the high-cultural text from which it departs. Smith defines her place in the cultural market precisely by refusing to relinquish the very cultural form her popular format seems to oppose, the high-cultural lyric and its textual conventions. Because semantic density does have more cultural durability after all, Smith—and not the Sex Pistols—has continued to gain recognition over the years both as a poet and as a musician whose seminal influence has not yet been measured.[37]

When Adorno composed "The Culture Industry: Enlightenment as Mass Deception" in collaboration with Max Horkheimer in 1944, he could not have foreseen that the youth culture of the sixties and seventies would seek to revise its relation to high art in such a radical and ultimately fruitful manner.[38] To be sure, the extent of Smith's experimentation was probably reigned in and qualified by profit-minded producers anxious to broaden her audience appeal. Nevertheless, Adorno's contention that everything in the culture industry, "down to the last detail," is shaped by commercial interests and totalitarian ideology seems, when applied to Smith's case, both theoretically overdetermined and hermeneutically limiting (128). The itinerary of Rimbaud's synesthetic subject and its reconstructed body is evidence that exchanges between high art and popular culture can be more complex than Adorno's model allows us to envision. Rimbaud's itinerary repeatedly crisscrosses the boundary between traditionally discrete cultural forms. For instance, the protean subject that Rimbaud employs to burst open the lyric "I" is imported into poetry from the domain of the mechanically assisted *féerie*. A hundred years later this disruptive poetic subjectivity returns to the popular stage, incarnated this time in the guise of a "mutant," a babe "born sans eyebrow," a rock-and-roll queen. In this second moment of what might be an endless repartee between poetry and popular culture, Smith derives her own vision of the countercultural subject not from industrial sources but rather from a textual machine, a graphemic technology she "discovers," as did the situationists, in Rimbaud's work. Rimbaud's textual machine allows Smith to resist the gravitational pull of the music industry toward standardization while creating a viable subgenre within that industry, namely, the countercultural lyric.

Finally, the Smith-Rimbaud connection suggests that popular culture can indeed manifest needs that at times enter into direct conflict with the standardizing requirements of an industry, such as the need to explode the confines of the self, for instance, or the need to disrupt hardened cultural values, hierarchies, and meanings. It is these needs—not just for the new but, even more importantly, for the ambiguous, the unstable, and the unpredictable—that Adorno fleetingly detects in a distorted form within capitalism itself. In *Negative Dialectics* at least, Adorno comes surprisingly close to elaborating a theory that would locate the struggle *against* reification (the need for deviance) within reifying industries themselves. Adorno leaves room, that is, for the possibility that art's immanent historicity, its reluctant bow to fashion, is matched by the immanent historicity of the need that popular culture also encodes, the legitimate or authentic need, in Adorno's terms, that required the invention of a particular image or machine in the first place.

Too often, however, Adorno opposes "heteronomy," the historical mediation of artistic expression, to "administration," the unmediated, ahistorical reproduction of the same. In "The Fetish Character of Music and the Regression of Listening" (1938), for instance, Adorno considers the "false need" addressed by the product of administration to be one created entirely by capital; instead of responding mimetically to social conditions, the culture industry merely manufactures needs, micromanaging the popular form to the point where its function as a conveyor of legitimate longing (in however distorted a form) is utterly expunged.[39] This latter, more familiar theory of industrial culture denies the possibility that resistance against administration might occur within the commercial domain. The emergence of a countercultural lyric in the late sixties challenges the strict opposition between mediation and administration, modernity and postmodernity, that underpins most of the cultural analytics that have been proposed. It may be, as Jim Collins has argued, that Adorno's vision of an "all-devouring consciousness industry" is unreflectively elitist, too dependent upon avant-garde models and high modernist values.[40] And yet at the same time it must be remembered that cultural deviants such as Smith only succeed in expressing their deviance by resuscitating a *textual* complexity peculiar to the historical avant-garde.

Eight

Laurie Anderson: Confessions of a Cyborg

In "A Cyborg Manifesto" Donna Haraway urges her reader to reject the traditional ideal of a unified, organic self in favor of a vision of the self as penetrated by technology, a self "committed to partiality, irony, intimacy," and the "perverse."[1] In a rhetorical move similar to that deployed by the iconoclastic performance artist Laurie Anderson, Haraway concludes, "I would rather be a cyborg than a goddess" (181). In this way, Haraway indicates that a cyborg identity promises greater possibilities for personal self-realization than do mythic figures associated with more traditional feminist ontologies (149). Haraway criticizes feminism's demonizing of technology and suggests that there are "great riches" to be found in "the breakdown of clean distinctions between organism and machine" (174). "What might be learned from personal and political 'technological' pollution?" asks Haraway. How can a refusal of "anti-science metaphysics" (181) stimulate the creation of new networks, new

Fig 7. Laurie Anderson, *The Pillow Speaker*, 1979. Courtesy Laurie Anderson.

couplings that, while jeopardizing the privileges of autonomy, nevertheless liberate the imagination to realize "a world without gender," "a world without end"? (150).

I cite Haraway's groundbreaking manifesto here in order to suggest a link between, on the one hand, Adorno's interpretation of the role of the technological in the works of the early-twentieth-century avant-garde and, on the other, Haraway's explicit support for the imaginative techno-projects of postmodern feminist art. When Adorno suggests (hesitantly, to be sure) that the machine aesthetic should be embraced insofar as it reveals a truth about the human that human languages of meaning cannot articulate, he in effect prefigures what will become a highly antifoundationalist reading of the human subject in postmodernist discourse.[2] Adorno's vision of a mediated subject (one formed in large part by its material conditions) and Haraway's celebration of fictions in which "no character is 'simply' human" (179) are points on a single trajectory leading away from the cult of the autonomous, bounded, organic subject toward a reimagining of the subject as cyborg. When Adorno is most daring, when he is most willing to consider the "human" as just another provisional historical construct, he comes closest to providing an approach to the technological that anticipates both the theoretical paradigm proposed by Haraway and the inventive performance pieces of an artist like Anderson. However, Adorno provides something that Haraway does not, namely, a sense of the risks incurred when one abandons entirely a suspicious attitude toward technology, a theory of the autonomous subject, and discourses of "human meaning" in favor of a politics of the cyborg. Although Adorno claims that art derives its "power" from disclosing the human encounter with technology, he nonetheless qualifies this encounter as a "crisis." Art gives "expression" to this "crisis of experience" (*AT*, 34); it registers suffering and vulnerability even as it capitalizes on the increased sophistication of its tools.

In this chapter I argue that Anderson's works convey the sense of danger signaled by Adorno but muted in Haraway's own formulations. Anderson combines what Haraway calls an apprehension of "intense pleasure in skill, machine skill" (180), with an intimation of the crisis of subjectivity that an encounter with technology may entail. Both a poet and a popular culture heroine,[3] Anderson extends the lyric tradition I have been delineating in vital ways. She perpetuates the vision of the subject as a "maître de fantasmagories" (Rimbaud); she confesses heteronomy through a manipulation of heterogeneous paraliterary and nonliterary discourses (Cendrars); she imagines intimate speech as always electronically filtered (Char); and, finally, she merges the self-reflexivity and textual density of avant-garde lyricism with a skilled use of technology and an astute exploitation of promotional strategies (Smith).

Just as Adorno's essays glossed the artworks of the early European avant-garde, so Haraway's "Cyborg Manifesto" offers a kind of discursive accompaniment to Anderson's polemical performance pieces. Haraway expresses in the high speech of poststructuralist technotheory what Anderson demonstrates visually and musically through the manipulation of familiar icons, voices, and words. For Anderson as for Haraway, there is no route back to a thoroughly organic state; accordingly, the task of the contemporary artist is to reconfigure identity as cyborg identity, to take control of and exploit all the possibilities offered by various modes and degrees of technological intervention. "The cyborg is a kind of disassembled and reassembled, postmodern collective and personal self" that implicitly undermines "the [Western] myth of original unity," writes Haraway. "This is the self," she states emphatically, that "feminists must code."[4]

Much of Anderson's work could be read as a response to Haraway's call for feminists to critique "the [Western] myth of original unity" by actively working to "code" the self. For instance, Anderson begins an episode included in *Collected Videos*, "Tour of Laurie's Home," by juxtaposing a traditional approach to technology (technology is threatening) with an approach that assumes instead the immanence of electronic codes to more traditional fictive and lyric forms of self-expression.[5] The episode begins with a shot of Anderson's sneakered feet walking across the wooden floorboards of her studio. A voice-over track of Anderson speaking accompanies the visual image: "I went to an acupuncturist," recounts Anderson, "and he said, 'Do you work with electronics?'" At this point the camera switches to a frontal shot of Anderson's studio-home in which we find an electronic keyboard flanked by all manner of recording devices: synthesizers, voice filters, microphones, and so on. "And I said," continues Anderson, now positioned solidly in the center of the frame, "'yeah, I happen to [work with electronics],' and he said, 'Well, let me polarize your watch for you because *electronics can really be dangerous*'" (emphasis added).

Cut. The camera now focuses on an on/off switch, which Anderson clicks on (a red light is illumined); then we see a sequence of brief shots of a sound recording and mixing panel, a reel-to-reel tape recorder, and a stack of electronic voice filters. Anderson proceeds: "And [the acupuncturist] offered to come over and polarize my house, but I kept picturing these shelves of blank masters [*the camera pans left to right down shelves of labeled audiotape boxes*] and I said, 'uh . . . maybe let's skip the polarization of my house.'"

Here, in the guise of a simple narrative, Anderson outlines not only a theory of electronics and its role in her own work but also a theory of technology in general and its relation to human forms of expression. All the elements of a Laurie Anderson performance piece are in place. First, a modest, yet powerfully photogenic figure identified as the author recounts a short narrative in everyday speech; the brevity of the monologue, as well as its enigmatic character, invite the spectator/reader to interpret this monologue as poetry. Second, shots of this human figure and of electronic apparatuses, with or without their users, are spliced together at rhythmic intervals, suggesting the impossibility of determining which element—electronic or corporeal—is responsible for the emission of the sounds we hear. Third, a comic foil, here an acupuncturist, provides Anderson the opportunity to poke fun at a naive but popular cultural paradigm; in "Tour of Laurie's Home" the acupuncturist who tells Anderson that "electronics can really be dangerous" promulgates the idea maintained by practitioners of diverse forms of holistic medicine that the body has to be protected from an invasion of the invisible—radio waves, electronic signals, theta waves, and so on. And fourth, an electronic medium serves to represent its supposed contrary, the more "natural" instrument of classical art. Instead of using a violin as the symbol of high art (as Anderson almost invariably does in works dating from the seventies all the way to the 1995 *Puppet Motel*), Anderson selects the word *masters* to introduce the difficulty of distinguishing conventional print forms from electronic forms of cultural preservation.

A "master" is an original tape recording of a song, speech, or sound. Of course, on the most immediate level, when Anderson says "masters" she is referring to the audiotapes filed neatly in labeled boxes on the shelves of her library–electronics studio. But Anderson intentionally does not specify that these "masters" are *tape* masters. She does not say, that is, "I kept picturing these shelves of blank *tape* masters," but simply, "I kept picturing these shelves of blank masters," thereby introducing a kind of ambiguity that belies the simplicity of the monologue she presents. For these files of "masters" could just as easily be editions of the Masters and her electronic sound bank a library of Great Works. Anderson is indirectly pointing to the necessary mediation of a technology of inscription and therefore to culture's dependence upon a machine for the conservation and transmission of knowledge, experience, and art. Electronics may "really" be dangerous but no more so, the monologue implies, than the printing press. And the danger, one begins to realize, lies not so much in the electronic ions that may be silently pulsing through the tissues of the human body but rather in the facility with which the cultural inscription might suddenly be erased, "polarized" out of existence in the name of the body's health.

An emphasis on the problematics of inscription is not new to Anderson's work. Even Anderson's earliest sculptures of the 1970s are concerned with the technologies of print, with their ability to code or "filter," as she puts it, human experience and sensation.[6] What is particularly interesting about "Tour of Laurie's Home," however, is the attention it draws to the interaction between bodies and signals, the organic and the electronic. Through the metaphor of polarization Anderson explores the contact, at once dangerous and facilitating, between the body and the machines that express its impulses. She reiterates humorously, and with a certain amount of irony, a theme that runs throughout her work, namely, the difficulty of distinguishing the body from its apparatuses, subjective expression from its discursive and mechanical mediations.

In order to approach the question of the self's relationship to its machines Anderson focuses on two processes: the process by which the self is invaded by the outside world and the process by which this self projects itself out into representational space. Sometimes Anderson posits the body as an essentially porous container allowing the ambient world access to the individual mind (or "inner" self) through a multiplicity of orifices or vulnerable surfaces. At other times the body appears to be an originary source, an emitter of sounds and impressions that achieve voice or form by passing through a series of filters, both organic (the body's attributes) and technological (the attributes of the apparatus). Many of Anderson's works combine both processes; indeed, the works often problematize the distinction between what is intrinsic (internal to the self) and what is extrinsic (technology, institutions, politics, the media, etc.). The border between inside and outside is negotiated most frequently on the surface of the body, especially through narratives or images that thematize this body's contact with machines. For the purposes of clarity, however, it is useful to distinguish one theme from the other, to distinguish, that is, works that thematize the permeability of the psyche from those that seek to stage its vocal or plastic instantiation.

As an M.F.A. student at Columbia University, Anderson began her idiosyncratic career by dramatizing the vulnerability of the self to penetration by some external force, understood variously as a text, a discourse, an institution, or a machine. In *Institutional Dream Series* of 1972 Anderson directly takes on the problem not only of the body's vulnerability but of the vulnerability of the unconscious to its immediate surroundings. *Institutional Dream Series* is a multimedia piece comprising both an ephemeral component—Anderson slept in various civic buildings and public spaces—and a documentary component—Anderson photographed herself sleeping and afterwards recorded the dreams she had while asleep (figs. 8 and 9). In a 1992 interview with John Howell, Anderson explained her project in the following terms:

At that time I was also doing my "Institutional Dream Series," which came from falling asleep in art history class. I would drift off and have dreams that mixed my personal life with art history. I'd get them very deeply confused, so I did this whole "Institutional Dream Series." I'd go to different places, like night court, or a boat that was docked in the South Street Seaport, or a women's bathroom, or the library at Columbia University and fall asleep. I'd write down the dreams, you know, whether they had any association with that institution and how those things can seep in. . . . A lot of these things were about how to be vulnerable in a bureaucratic situation.[7]

As Anderson indicates here, *Institutional Dream Series* was intended to thematize the way in which elements of the external world "seep in" to the unconscious, providing what Freud calls "manifest content"—and thus a kind of filter—through which the most intimate obsessions or concerns of the self can be expressed. The impetus for the project derived from the artist's own observation that if she fell asleep in art history class, her dreams tended to mix personal life with art history. In other words, Anderson's lived experience of the contingent hybridity of consciousness, of the entanglement of the "personal" in extrasubjective narratives, suggested the issues to be pursued in the piece.

Anderson's works repeatedly return to the theme of the penetration or invasion of the self. In *It Depends on Who You're Talking To*, a project Anderson initiated in the seventies but never documented, the artist "say[s] the same thing to various people" and then "work[s] with the slight changes in inflection and tone that result."[8] Relying upon a low degree of technical sophistication (the piece merely requires a tape recorder), in *It Depends On Who You're Talking To* Anderson is already working with the problem of filters and external interference, with the degree, in this case, to which expression is marked by "occasion." Like Cendrars's "poésies de circonstance," engendered after a chance "meeting" with a person, painting, or book, Anderson's works are inspired either by interpersonal contacts (whom one is "talking to") or by more ominous and static "bureaucratic situations." But whether Anderson concentrates on the interpersonal or the personal-public mediation, she always brings to the fore the consciousness that vocal "inflections" and "tones" are altered, mental images and sounds are redesigned, by the filters through which they are passed. Anderson is consistently interested in analyzing the ways the self is invaded, informed, and perhaps even "polluted" by what the self, at least as traditionally conceived, is not.

For Jessica Prinz, this interest is related to a politics of resistance: "Anderson's art, like [William] Burroughs's, involves the use of creative techniques for allowing artists to dissociate, to manipulate, and hence gain more personal control over language[s]"—and bureaucratic situations— "that would otherwise 'control' them."[9] However, control and manipula-

Fig. 8. Laurie Anderson, *Institutional Dream Series (Sleeping in Public), Night Court, 100 Centre St. 10:30 p.m.–1:00 a.m., December 29, 1972.* Courtesy Laurie Anderson.

Fig. 9. Laurie Anderson, *Institutional Dream Series (Sleeping in Public), South Street Seaport, L. G. Howard starboard berth, 11:00 a.m.–2:00 p.m., December 10, 1972.* Courtesy Laurie Anderson.

tion constitute only one aspect of Anderson's concern with the phenomenon of penetration. Although Anderson's debt to Burroughs is obviously very great, her work does not always produce the sense that the invasion of the self by an external "virus" is necessarily ominous or threatening. To make oneself "vulnerable" in a bureaucratic situation may also be a means of changing consciousness, one as useful, and potentially as revelatory, as experimentation with psychedelic drugs. In brief, it is the mechanism itself that fascinates Anderson. At least in its early stages, Anderson's is not a paranoid art. Containing moments of caustic cultural criticism and even of apocalyptic vision, Anderson's early works nevertheless constitute *studies* rather than condemnations of the phenomenon of penetration. That the mind is vulnerable to the body's situation (as in *Institutional Dream Series*), or that self-expression is influenced by occasion (as in *It Depends on Who You're Talking To*), is a fact that must be accepted, explored, and even exaggerated for the purposes of aesthetic self-realization.

Anderson, one might say, enjoys being a medium. She is more at home as an impressionable surface than as a singular or consistent essence. As Craig Owens contends, Anderson's entire project is designed in such a way that she might become "the medium which so many corporeal voices require in order to communicate with us, the body they temporarily assume."[10] Anderson's art depends not so much on the ability to control and manipulate the self's mediations as on the ability to bring attention to the fact that mediations do indeed occur. Accordingly, she does not offer us merely one alternative to the enculturated, constructed, manipulated selves we are forced to adopt; rather, she offers us the possibility of multiple selves, multiple inner voices, that emerge through dialectical confrontation with institutional discourses, media images, and even structures adopted from high culture, filters we can never entirely exorcize from our consciousness.

A 1978 installation at New York City's Museum of Modern Art (MOMA) entitled *Handphone Table* exemplifies how Anderson attempts to capture the process by which "external" information permeates both the body and the mind. *Handphone Table*, inspired by Anderson's observation that the arms of the body can themselves serve as audioelectronic conductors, involves channeling prerecorded sound directly into the eardrums. The effect of the installation, as Anderson herself notes, is to alter the mind's sense of its own autonomy, to produce a confusion between internal and external stimuli. "I got the idea for The Handphone Table when I was typing something on an electric typewriter," explains Anderson. "It wasn't going very well and I got so depressed I stopped and just put my head in my hands. That's when I heard it: a loud hum coming from the typewriter, amplified by the wooden table and running up my arms, totally clear and very loud."[11]

For the MOMA installation Anderson built a table with two pairs of slight indentations, where human subjects were intended to place their elbows. Connected to these indentations under the table were steel rods that led to cassette decks containing prerecorded material. When the subjects put their elbows in the indentations, "the sound rose through [their] arms via bone conduction." If the subjects placed their hands over their ears, "it was like putting on a pair of powerful stereo headphones." The head, in other words, became a "speaker," producing in the subject the impression that he or she was hearing lyrics generated from memory or the imagination: "I wanted to make songs that were more like remembering than listening. So it would seem like you'd heard them somewhere before. . . . [The music's] not out here in the air, you know, it's inside your head" (48).

Other aspects of the installation were also significant. Anderson designed the table so that two people could be seated there at the same time, and the lyrics she chose were borrowed from a love poem by the seventeenth-century metaphysical poet George Herbert. As the subjects sat at the table, their arms conducting the music to the skull, they heard the line "Now I in you without a body move." By using a stereo system, one pickup for each elbow, Anderson managed to convey the impression that the musical line was actually passing from one side of the brain to the other. She gradually lowered the volume transmitted to one elbow while gradually raising the volume transmitted to the other. In *Stories from the Nerve Bible* (48) Anderson reproduces a graph of how the Herbert line traveled that looks something like this:

NOW I   IN YOU
        WITHOUT   A BODY
                        M   O   V   E

Anderson's graph clearly emphasizes the word "move" over the words "I," "you," and "body." Movement, in this case the movement of the electronic signal, is dynamic, whereas the "you" and even the "I" are both static, situated, reduced to the status of a mechanical apparatus. Meanwhile, the lyric signal that "moves" across the brain is incorporeal ("without a body") yet active, living parasitically (like a virus) off the cerebral tissue and cranial cavity each human subject provides. *Handphone Table* exemplifies one extreme of Anderson's practice; it dramatizes the manner in which the body can be reconceived as a pure receptive device, invaded by messages—including poems—that potentially become elements (memories, structures of understanding) belonging to the mental network that in other contexts we designate as "the self."

During the eighties Anderson would continue to experiment with methods of implanting electronic information in the brain. In *Talking Pillows*, for instance, Anderson placed small speakers inside of white bed pillows that transmitted to listener-subjects short poetic narratives intended to replicate dreams. Anderson's hypnotic songs of the same period also aimed to "get under the skin" with their repetitive rhythms, simple rhymes, and dreamlike orchestration. In mixing the themes of love and intimacy with a dramatization of the active invasion of the body by an electronic signal, *Handphone Table* and *Talking Pillows* prefigure the menace and beauty of songs such as the hit single "O Superman," which also juxtaposes the theme of intimacy ("Mom") with the theme of nuclear threat ("Here come the planes. / They're American planes"). The repetition of the word *arms* emphasizes the uncanny proximity of the physical embrace and the military weapon:

> 'Cause when love is gone, there's always justice.
> And when justice is gone, there's always force.
> And when force is gone, there's always Mom. Hi Mom!
>
> So hold me, Mom, in your long arms. So hold me,
> Mom, in your long arms.
> In your automatic arms. Your electronic arms.
> In your arms.
> So hold me, Mom, in your long arms.
> Your petrochemical arms. Your military arms.
> In your electronic arms.[12]

The sense of vulnerability to external messages and environments created in "O Superman" is anticipated in many performance works of the seventies. In a work like *Handphone Table* Anderson is on the one hand mimicking what she sees as the manipulations of the American culture industry; she infiltrates the mind with lyrics in a manner that imitates the way mass media subliminally penetrate consciousness. On the other hand, however, poetic lines such as "Now I in you without a body move" or lyrics such as "So hold me Mom, in your long arms . . . your electronic arms" from "O Superman" simultaneously thematize what they enact. *Handphone Table* and "O Superman," as different as they might seem on the surface, both draw attention to the same observation, one usually repressed in media culture: that the self is not autonomously constructed but rather pastiched together out of the heteronomous voices (from the most nurturing to the most destructive) by which it is penetrated. The individual psyche may filter the messages coming from the outside, but, as Anderson often implies, this psyche is dependent upon organic apparatuses, such as the ear and the eye, that are ceaselessly vulnerable to impression. The linguistic confusion

between Mom's arms and military arms suggests that even the most intimate source of the subject's identity—the maternal order from which the
unconscious emerges—may encrypt a frightening, destructive, and entirely impersonal directive. The vision of the self repeatedly invoked in
Anderson's work is one in which the receptive organs are entirely passive,
composed of a series of channels ("conductors") merely transferring—
without significant alteration—objective information. As Anderson illustrates in *Words in Reverse*, ears, for instance, can be blank surfaces
upon which the world inscribes. "I can draw you so that you have no
ears," she writes; "I can draw you so that you have no ears at all. So that
where your ears would be, *there is only blank paper.*"[13] Or again from
Words in Reverse,

> I read about a rabbit in a laboratory. The experimenters held the rabbit's
> head, eyes open, pointed towards an open window. For twenty minutes,
> staring at the bright window. Then they took a knife and cut the rabbit's head
> off, peeled the tissue off its eyes, dyed it, and under the microscope, like
> film, the tissue developed. *There were two windows imprinted on the rabbit's
> eyes.* And they said, "Look! This rabbit has windows on its eyes. (emphasis
> added)

In both of these early narratives the organs of perception are rendered
even more vulnerable than they appear to be in *Handphone Table*. Ears
and eyes are unable to close, prevented from returning to some kind of
imaginative inner world, idiosyncratic set of memories, or unconscious
network through which the external stimulus might be filtered, interpreted, interjected with subjectivity. Organs of perception are victims of inci-
sion or inscription, comparable to blank pieces of paper or light-sensitive
photographic plates. Thus, in Anderson's most radical vision of the
human subject's vulnerability the sense organs are technologized, depersonalized, reconceived as simple registering machines. It is almost as
though Anderson were returning to an eighteenth-century epistemology
of perception as "sensations 'imprinted' on a white page,"[14] for the implication of her images is that there is no *moi profond* that manifests itself
through idiosyncratic modes of framing, synthesizing, and processing information. Finally, in an early work entitled *Eight Standing Figures* (fig.
10) Anderson projects an image of the self that implicitly undermines any
ontology of its essence. The work comprises eight upright polyester resin
cylinders "conceived," Anderson tells us, "as self-portraits"; "all [are]
approximately my height."[15] Here the spectator is invited to imagine the
space within the body—represented by the thin membranes of resin—as
containing any matter whatsoever; meanwhile, the warping, bubbling,
scraping, and even reflections on the resin's surface suggest the membranes' vulnerability to inscription. Such is Anderson's most devastating

Fig. 10. Laurie Anderson, *Eight Standing Figures*, 1972. Courtesy Laurie Anderson.

imagination of the vulnerable self: the self as a mere surface, a hollow sounding board or instrument, entirely passive with respect to the information it receives and, like a computer, encodes.

However, these images of the body as permeable, vulnerable to inscription, or punctuated by orifices should be contrasted with another image central to Anderson's work, one that has proved the most memorable to audiences and critics alike. This is the image of the body as car. During the years when she was creating works such as *Talking Pillows* and *Handphone Table*, works that treat the body as a passive receiver of codes, Anderson was also playing with the idea that the body might instead be a kind of apparatus possessing its own code. The relationship between the body and the inner self (the "I") that Anderson posits in what is perhaps her most famous aphorism, "I am in my body the way most people drive in their cars,"[16] is different in significant ways from that established by the works already examined. In this formulation the body appears not merely as a surface of inscription but as analogous to a complex machine capable of a certain number of functions subject to variation and extension within a limited range. Anderson's car analogy suggests that the body can be conceived or experienced as a detachable part, a membrane that encloses the "I" (as in *Eight Standing Figures*) but simultaneously provides the "I" with its means of locomotion.

Further, the syntax of the aphorism presupposes that there is indeed an "I" that can be distinguished from the body; the "I" is "in" the body, just as people drive "in" their cars. Thus, the line seems to support a theory of subjectivity in which the subject—the "I" "inside"—*comes first*. The subject's priority does not promise its transcendence but nonetheless allows it to manipulate and, ultimately, control its own machines. Such a vision of the subject's relation to the body is implicit in Haraway's treatment of the cyborg. If "we," as feminists, can seize "the tools to mark the world that marked [us] as other," if "we" can transform these tools into more strategically self-expressive devices, it is because "we" already exist in some form that is not entirely overdetermined by these tools.[17] Logically, in order for Haraway's (and Anderson's) formulations to make sense we must posit an excess of subjectivity beyond that which is coextensive with a preformed discourse or fused with a particular technology.

Of course, there is an extent to which the properties of the body/car we are forced to use determine and delimit the nature and range of the "I" 's self-invention. How "I" can move, what "I" can do, is in large part conditioned by the preprogrammed functions of the body/car. Similar in this respect to engine components or performance meters, the sensory organs and appendages of the body are technological givens, incapable of registering or achieving movements for which they have not yet been programmed (for instance, as Anderson notes with some dismay, the ears cannot close). From this recognition of the appliance's defects comes Anderson's insatiable need to bend technologies (and bodies) to the will of her expressive impulses. The body may be a machine (as she suggests in *Handphone Table* and *Words in Reverse*), but it is a machine that can be retooled—and "someone," some kind of "I" beyond the machine, has to do the retooling. In an attempt to represent a part of the "I" that has not yet achieved expression, the "I" mobilizes all its means, including its receptive sensory organs, its voice, its facial features, its gender attributes, and its various prosthetic devices. In this way the "I" comes to redefine the dimensions of its own being.

For Anderson, then, the body is merely another prop, an instrument, like the violin or synthesizer, that can be altered to service the varying needs of the subject who will "play" it.[18] Anderson's ultimate fantasy is in this respect not dissimilar to Rimbaud's. She also strives to be a "one-person opera,"[19] and she searches to recreate or at the very least rewire the body in such a way that it might express modes of subjectivity that a more familiar discourse of the subject fails to express. Because Anderson conceives of the body as an apparatus, she can interface this body with other types of apparatuses in a search for the perfect machine. She can fuse it, that is, with a "machine aimée." Through an inventive use of masks, electronic synthesizers, and so on, Anderson extends the body beyond the limits of its surfaces; as she repeatedly demonstrates, "natural" orifices can provide the perfect plugs into which other instruments may be inserted. In "Monkey's Paw" (1989) Anderson even suggests that the body can be sent back to the "shop" and upgraded with new instruments in the same manner as one might upgrade an older model of automobile:

> Well I stopped in at the body shop
> Said to the guy:
> I want stereo FM installed in my teeth.
> And take this mole off my back and put it on my cheek.
> And uh . . . while I'm here, why don't you give me some of those high-heeled feet?[20]

Anderson's imagery is only partially fantastic, since the retooling she orders is not far from what she herself is able to accomplish. In *United States, II* (1980), for instance, Anderson attaches a microphone to her skull so that the sound of her teeth clicking together can actually be channeled through a stereo amplifier. The first image of "Monkey's Paw" ("I want stereo FM installed in my teeth") refers, then, to a technological intrusion or alteration of the body that Anderson chooses to practice on herself. The next two images, however, evoke the mediations of a plastic surgeon; moving a mole from one part of the body to another or remodeling the feet to conform to the standards of fashion are merely slight exaggerations of the kinds of additions, reconstructions, and transfers regularly performed by modern cosmetic medicine. "Monkey's Paw" thus captures Anderson's ambivalent attitude toward the postmodern cyborgization of the body. The trite rhyme scheme of the lyric ("teeth," "cheek," "feet") suggests a tone of mockery, and yet the "body shop" pun also possesses some serious implications. The menacing refrain "Nature's got rules and Nature's got laws," which recurs in each stanza of the song, seems to imply that tinkering with the body can produce negative consequences ("electronics," after all, "are dangerous").

Clearly, however, for Anderson, a world in which corporeal transformations can take place is not entirely dystopic. The transformation of the body can be directed by an impersonal, menacing force, such as the fashion industry or the military-industrial complex, but it can also be accomplished by a unique "I" who also refuses "Nature's" rules. Manifesting her ambivalence, then, Anderson juxtaposes an allusion to her own idiosyncratic project (to amplify the face) with allusions to alterations that merely adapt the body to general fashion trends; she suggests in this way that challenging Nature's laws can lead to both oppression and self-expression, greater conformism and more radical experimentation. Anderson's dialectical approach to the "body shop" is reminiscent of Haraway's conclusions concerning the techno-body: "Technological determination is only one ideological space opened up by the reconceptions of machine and organism," writes Haraway. "For us, in imagination and in other practice, machines can be prosthetic devices, intimate components, friendly selves."[21]

To the degree that Anderson rejects a totalizing view of the self as unified, impenetrable, and singular her works reflect a postmodern theory of the genderless, culturally constructed subject. However, to the degree that she insists syntactically upon an "I" as distinct from a "body," she supports a more traditional paradigm of subjectivity associated with the first-person, confessional lyric. The lyrics of "Monkey's Paw," similar in this respect to the formulation "I am in my body the way most people drive in their cars," place an unexpected emphasis on the first-person subject, an emphasis that belies Anderson's other portrayals of this subject's vacuity or vulnerability to penetration. "*I* stopped in at the body shop," says Anderson; "*I* want stereo FM installed in my teeth"; "while *I*'m here, why don't you give me some of those high-heeled feet?" Granted, "Monkey's Paw" is presented in the format of the popular song and must depend upon traditional notions of the subject in order to reflect its audience's expectations. As Anderson stated in a 1986 interview, "Being pop is about consolidating, about going 'I'm me.' "[22] But there are more complex reasons why Anderson insists upon the first-person singular, reasons having to do with the presence of a significant autobiographical strain in her work that has not yet received the attention it deserves.

As an emerging presence on the New York art scene of the seventies Anderson in fact belonged to a group of artists dedicated to exploring the aesthetic potential of an autobiographical, even confessional discourse. A *compte rendu* of the 1976 art community by Peter Frank indicates the extent to which an autobiographical impulse was shaping the most visible experimental works not only in New York but also in Los Angeles and in major cities in Europe as well. Rejecting conceptual art's "totally intellectualized procedures" as well as minimalism's stringent and limited vocabulary, artists of the seventies were turning, according to Frank, to "personal, idiosyncratic, poetic content," generating mini-movements such as autobiographical art, autogeography, self-transformational art, life art, and body art. Frank groups all these various mini-movements together under the term *auto-art*, which he distinguishes from more traditional forms of "confessional" art insofar as it approaches the self not as a known and identifiable entity but as primary material to be exploited and performed.

"The phenomena [the auto-artists] wish to explore," writes Frank, "are not those of their tools but of themselves"[23]—themselves *as tools*, one might add.

Anderson is Frank's first case in point. Identifying a strong "poetic" streak running through Anderson's work, Frank argues that Anderson "establishes a distinct persona for herself, communicating with her audience in a low-keyed, confessional, almost abashed manner that accentuates her vulnerability" (44). The curious contradiction Frank establishes here is between a "confessional" tone and the "distinct persona" this tone projects. Anderson takes a mode of being that is familiar and intimate to her—the "shy, dreamy girl" from the Midwest (44)—and objectifies it, transforms it into an artistic principle or tool, and then uses it to generate the formal features and technological apparatuses of the work. In a 1974–75 performance piece entitled *Duets on Ice*, for instance, Anderson tells a story about the day her grandmother died that does more than simply accentuate the author's vulnerability: the autobiographical narrative also suggests the use of certain props and requires the development of specific technical innovations.

For *Duets on Ice* Anderson froze her ice skates into blocks of ice, strung a violin with audiotapes of prerecorded cowboy songs, and traveled to various public sites in Genoa, Italy, and Manhattan (fig. 11): "In awkward Italian, I told a group of people in Genoa that I was playing these songs in memory of my grandmother because the day she died I went out on a frozen lake and saw a lot of ducks whose feet had frozen into the new layer of ice."[24] On the one hand, Anderson's body became in this piece merely another prop (stuck in ice), while her personal anecdote became objectified in the displacements it inspired (bird's feet were transformed into skates, a lake was transformed into blocks of ice, a violin became a tape recorder. But on the other hand, although Anderson's intimate memory was processed as artistic material objectified as a form of performance, the link between the "distinct persona" who performed and the subject of the autobiographical tale remained intact. The tone Anderson adopted in *Duets on Ice* was intended to establish a connection of trust and intimacy between audience and performer that even the objectifications of the narrative could not disturb. Anderson desired this intimacy, one that seems to have depended upon a kind of *pacte autobiographique*, in Philippe Lejeune's terms, because it added a dimension of risk to the performance project.[25] The self, as a unique set of memories and associations, was certainly a sort of tool, another prop that could be made to signify within the signifying system of the piece; however, this self also remained a vulnerable entity interacting with a group of spectators whose race, class, politics, and gender composition could never be controlled. In other words, self-exposure in *Duets on Ice* was

Fig. 11. Laurie Anderson, *Duets on Ice* (*A Series of Performances* in Genoa, Italy, and NYC, 1974–75). Courtesy Laurie Anderson.

both a performed element of the piece (an objectifying tool) and a reaffirmation that the "I" of the artist exists at a particular place and time, that it can be drawn into conversation by the audience, influenced, and perhaps even harmed.

Anderson's move into confessional performance art was encouraged by one of her most important mentors, the confessional poet Vito Acconci. In Acconci's pieces aesthetic distance was ground down to its bare minimum: the "self" that appeared on what was frequently not a stage but rather a site was one in search of an experience of total exposure. Acconci taught Anderson how to play with the border between persona and person to blur the distinction between an artistic objectification (a performed self) and an artistic subject (the vulnerable self). *Institutional Dream Series* in particular was inspired by Acconci's efforts to place objectified forms of the self—the self's performed "personas"—at risk. Anderson's decision to place her sleeping body in a public place actively produced the vulnerability of the human subject that Acconci and other body artists of the seventies were also seeking to produce through staged but entirely unpredictable encounters. Not only was Anderson's mind vulnerable to the subliminal influences of the spaces in which she planted herself but her body too was exposed to attack. The insistence of the body in *Institutional Dream Series*, achieved by means of a photographic documentation that focuses in every instance on her prone or slumped form, challenges the viewer to dissociate the persona from the person of the artist. Because the photographs were taken when the female subject was asleep their subject appears truly vulnerable, unable to consciously organize or control her own representation. Likewise, in *Duets on Ice* Anderson plays a role, performs a musical composition that she herself did not write (prerecorded cowboy songs); however, the outdoor performance venue serves to provoke contacts—and thus incite (spontaneous) dialogues—that the author cannot foresee or script in advance. The author accentuates the self's vulnerability and places the body in a public space in order to dramatize in visceral terms the self's intangible yet implicit alterity with respect to its objectified forms, its incarnation as stage prop or machine. In a manner reminiscent of Adorno's confessional dialectics, Anderson's self is reified as a persona at the moment it is disclosed (objectified), and yet this objectification simultaneously resituates the reified self within a space—a historical flux—in which it can be modified, in which it can evolve.

Whether Anderson is working with words, violins, the body, electronic synthesizers, computer technologies, or even personal memories, her goal in every case is to impose these apparatuses like objectifying filters on the "I" 's expression.[26] Clearly, the "I" to be expressed remains inarticulate until processed through a filter. The filter, or to use an *echt* Anderson analogy, the "speaker system," inevitably processes and thus "administrates" the subjectivity it is meant to express.[27] But at least the presentation of the filter *as filter* predicates the existence of a not yet reified subjectivity—an energy, vibration, or impulse—that must pass through the filter in order to achieve amplification. Although one could argue, in typical poststructuralist fashion, that the impulse, or "I," does not necessarily precede its filtration, such a rendering of the chronology of expression fails to do justice to Anderson's own formulations. It is this unnameable impulse that ultimately exerts its will in the dialectical exchange with apparatus or occasion.

Anderson's restlessness, her implicit refusal to accord any one machine, rhetoric, or filter the privilege of expressing finally and exhaustively that which the subject is capable of emitting, is ultimately the most potent sign of her autonomy, an autonomy manifested negatively as that which technology is *not*. Her interest in exploring technology's outer limits can be attributed to her need to exploit the entire range of a given apparatus, to enlarge its expressive possibilities as a vehicular and revelatory medium. Perhaps, as Adorno has written, "it is as labor, and not as communication, that the subject in art comes into its own" (*AT*, 166). If this is the case, then the labor Anderson exerts on the expressive device, and not necessarily the content it expresses, is the gesture that most eloquently betrays the presence of a unique subjectivity. Such a position is tacitly endorsed by Haraway, who also tries to redefine subjectivity as work on the given. In Haraway's technofeminist utopia, "intense pleasure in skill, machine skill, ceases to be a sin" and becomes "an aspect of embodiment."[28] Through the development of a skill, one embodies the self in a new form, according to a new aesthetic, discursive, or technological configuration. In Adorno's terms, the subject makes itself into a tool in order to actualize a latent content that languages of subjectivity fail to express. Yet it must be remembered that the self actualized (objectified) is not prescriptive or definitive but rather "contradictory," "partial," and "strategic," always susceptible to further revision.[29]

The thematic and structural elements linking an early work like *Duets on Ice* to a more recent effort such as "Monkey's Paw" should now be evident. But to insist too adamantly on the continuities between the early and the late works would be an error, for the discontinuities that keep these works temporally and conceptually apart also deserve consideration. There are still salient distinctions to be made between the more intimate and autobiographical works of the seventies, those that skillfully expose the subject to penetration, and the more tightly packaged, technologically dependent, and commercially successful works of the eighties and nineties. While it is true that "technological determinism" is, in Haraway's words, only "one ideological space opened up by [recent] reconceptions of machine and organism,"[30] it is also highly likely that the technology or filter applied in the individual work plays more than a neutral role in determining the range of expressive possibilities available to the creative subject as well as the types of audience before which the work may be exhibited. The Tape Bow Violin and the Viophonograph (souped-up instruments Anderson employs in early performance pieces such as *Duets on Ice*) demand a rather different performance space than that required by a full band with its host of synclaviers and amplifiers. The dimensions of the audience and even its class, race, and gender composition are in part determined by the technology involved in the piece's preparation and performance. It is still clear (at least to many artists) that particular technologies (means of production) are linked to particular markets. The question that must be raised, then, is whether there is any qualitative difference between a violin and an electronic sound mixer, between poems mediated by occasion (and printed by small presses) and poems filtered through industrial processes (and distributed by commercial monopolies)? Is the modern lyricist's confession of mediation the same as the postmodern pop artist's confession of mediation? How is the content of the given work conditioned by what the chosen technology allows the subject to say?

Two of Anderson's most recent projects, each of which employs advanced technological media, can help provide provisional answers to these questions. *Home of the Brave*, released as a feature film in 1986, exploits advanced video technologies and complex electronic voice-altering devices to present its author as a virtual automaton. Meanwhile, Anderson's 1995 *Puppet Motel* adopts exploratory hypertext technologies in order to engage users in a game of hide and seek that can only metaphorically be termed a performance. Both pieces (or products) change in telling ways the relation of the author to her personas, redefining the nature of subjectivity in significant ways.

Home of the Brave is a kind of technofest that constantly surrounds the speaking subject with "masks and mechanical stuff."[31] If *Duets on Ice* relies upon audience interaction, exposing the speaking subject to unpredictable interventions and inciting different responses each time it is performed, *Home of the Brave* presents a static, prerecorded spectacle in which a media star sings pop songs and recounts brief narratives that have the flavor of stand-up comedy routines. The author persona of *Home of the Brave* is first introduced in the guise of a genderless robot whose entire head is enveloped in a white mask with black holes placed at the site of the eyes and nose as well as a set of exaggerated red lips (fig. 12).

During the robot routine Anderson processes her voice through an electronic synthesizer in order to speak in what she calls her "voice of authority," an unctious, masculine tone that mimics the intonations and clichéd self-promotional strategies of a public official or media personality.[32] After performing a brief song Anderson returns to address the audience in her natural speaking voice. Although Anderson is no longer wearing a mask or distorting her vocal identity, the anecdote she recounts still aims to undermine, albeit in a new way, the integrity of the unified subject. She explains that she recently had her palm read by two different people who both said the same thing about her past lives: "Your first life on this planet you were a cow," recounts Anderson, "and then you were a bird, and next you were a hat." In her subsequent life she was "hundreds and hundreds of rabbis." "This is my first life as a woman," Anderson concludes,

Fig. 12. Laurie Anderson, *Talkshow: Lower Mathematics*, 1986. Courtesy Laurie Anderson.

"which explains quite a few things." Both the opening segment, with the gesticulating automaton, and the fourth segment, involving the palm reader and the narrative of past lives, create the impression that the person speaking on the stage is only incidentally a woman, one of Haraway's "contradictory, partial, and strategic" subject constructions.[33] The implicit assumption is that gender ("This is my first life as a woman") is accessory to a self that is manifested but never fully incarnated in the body, mask, or voice in which this self provisionally appears.[34]

Anderson's use of masks and voice-altering devices corresponds to a motif that returns incessantly in *Home of the Brave*, the motif of technification, the substitution of body and voice by mechanical apparatuses such as the telephone answering machine and the ubiquitous video image. Although in earlier works Anderson had already imitated "Computerese," "newsspeak," and other technologically generated discourses, they were less commonly foregrounded as mediations of subjectivity than the "homey" discourses of the everyday, such as "shy-Midwestern-girl-tells-all," New York slang (as in *New York Social Life*, of 1977), and small-town bureaucratese. Each one of these discourses may be traced back to a certain aspect of Anderson's lived experience, a specific locale, institution, or even family environment. But the voices she appropriates in *Home of the Brave* are discourses simultaneously available to (almost) everyone and, at least hypothetically, produced by no one, and from no place, in particular. In *Home of the Brave* Anderson seems to be dramatizing the self's increasing exposure (and subjection) to widespread hegemonic discourses rather than regional-, gender-, or class-based ones. The poetic or narrative passages common to her earlier works also reappear in *Home of the Brave*, but here they compete more strenuously with entirely impersonal slogans emanating from video screens and slide projectors apparently lacking any connection to an individual voice.

There is thus nothing gratuitous or incidental about Anderson's shift away from personal or community-generated discourses toward those that are mechanically produced and transmitted. This shift reflects, rather, a contemporaneous cultural phenomenon that Anderson obviously wants to document, namely, the invasion of media and computer technologies into daily life and hence a homogenization (and reduction in number and variety) of the processes and "occasions" by which individual subjects are mediated and through which they achieve voice. A similar evolution can be witnessed in Anderson's *Puppet Motel*, which, like all CD-ROMs, plugs the user-subject into a network of nodes (segments or rooms), each of which produces another narrative or sequence of images determined by the user-subject's improvised selections. Anderson places in relief the act of "plugging in" to cyberspace by choosing the socket as a kind of signature that introduces the menu and permits egress from the individual nodes. By plugging into the cyber-socket, the user-subject fuses his or her identity with a set of images, narratives, and lyrics that are both limited in number and eminently vulnerable to rearrangement.

Anderson's *Puppet Motel*, however, is more exploratory than interactive, for although the user-subject is responsible for the sequence of events, he or she cannot add anything to the screen nor create his or her own "room." Except for a few segments in which the user-subject is permitted, for instance, to "enter sounds" or leave a message on the answering machine, the hypertext technology employed focuses on sequence rather than addition. The user-subject floats in a limited space of options that sometimes seem claustrophobic or redundant. As the user-subject enters each room he or she becomes in a sense Anderson's "puppet," pulled by the strings of the auditory and visual information, sutured to the screen along the umbilical cord of the mouse.

Not only does the subject feel somewhat like a puppet executing preprogrammed motions, but the "Laurie Anderson" who is anthologized and celebrated by the CD-ROM begins to appear somewhat reified as well. *Puppet* is in fact a word Anderson has used to describe her own personas, many of which are "present" in *Puppet Motel* in hypertext form. *Puppet Motel* thus elaborates on a possibility first presented in *Home of the Brave*, the possibility that all subjectivities are merely "puppets," states of mind that can be assumed like costumes in any order whatsoever. The user-subject of *Puppet Motel* creates a kind of patchwork out of familiar Anderson materials, rescripting her performances in a somewhat aleatory process of discovery that depends upon the user-subject's own interests, instincts, and at times mistakes.

The back cover to *Puppet Motel* invites the user-subject to "navigate a world saturated with Laurie Anderson's presence and interact directly with her intelligence and art."[35] However, just what "presence" means in this context is anything but clear. If "presence" in *Duets on Ice* presupposed an interaction that confronted the author directly with a group of individuals, "presence" in *Puppet Motel* has been reinterpreted in cyberspace to mean a kind of memory file, a compendium of elements from Anderson's past works that now represent in a fully reified form her "intelligence and art." *Puppet Motel* expands on the anthology model that Anderson uses to compose most of her performance pieces.[36] Although some of the images are new, produced just for the CD-ROM, a large percentage are drawn from earlier works. There is even a function that allows the user to access an attic filled with debris or Anderson memorabilia; by clicking on an item of the debris, the user-subject enters or reenters yet again one of the rooms associated with that item. Rummaging through an attic of miscellaneous but by now familiar objects becomes a kind of analogy for accessing the memory of the program, which in turn is a figure for the memory of the author herself ("her intelligence and art"). The user-subject can create new associations between different elements of Anderson's past, interacting, in a sense, with a subject's mnemonic material in order to assume new "puppet" identities. Moving from "room" to "room," from one "puppet" to the next, the user-subject ventriloquizes—but without altering or mediating in any way—each figure of the Anderson hypertext lexicon.

In both *Home of the Brave* and *Puppet Motel*, then, the speaking subject is radically disembodied either as a result of masks, costumes, harmonizers, and the feature-film format or through the computer, which definitively absents the author from her own stage. Meanwhile, the spectator or user-subject is supplanted by the "puppet," plugged into a technology that leaves little room for improvised response. While Anderson has frequently insisted that she aims to provide her audiences with "choice" (of where to look, what to listen to, how to assemble the various elements of the performance, when to intervene), the interactive model of her former performance pieces is clearly not operative to the same extent in either *Home of the Brave* or *Puppet Motel*. These works seem to allegorize Anderson's entire project, referring the reader continually to earlier texts, earlier images of the Anderson repertoire. Although the works are confessional insofar as they deploy advanced technologies to demonstrate the subject's constructedness and artificiality, they simultaneously reify "Laurie Anderson" as a recordable "presence," an author whose "intelligence and art" we not only recognize but also thoroughly exhaust (at least in its CD-ROM incarnation). *Puppet Motel* presents the spectacle of Anderson as invulnerable technocreation; it admits the artifice of personality but offers no play, no way out.

It is tempting to construe Anderson's high-tech performance pieces as negative commentaries on subjectivity in the age of high capitalism. This subjectivity appears as totally constructed, a building-block persona made up of homogenizing, industrially produced images and discourses shuffled into different patterns according to a limited number of options. The claustrophobic aspect of both *Home of the Brave* and *Puppet Motel* has been noted by Anderson herself; in conversation with John Howell, for instance, Anderson has admitted her frustration with technospectacles, claiming that soon after completing *Home of the Brave* she felt a strong need to return to more intimate performance venues, to less repetitive (and less commercially successful) incarnations of herself.[37]

Finally, the most telling indication of Anderson's discontent with industrial processes and commercial venues can be found in the lyrics she wrote for a song bearing the same title as her CD-ROM. "The Puppet Motel," produced in 1994 (a year before the CD-ROM appeared) provides a strange commentary on her own efforts to employ hyperspace imaginatively, proleptically suggesting the CD-ROM's obsolescence even before its release:

THE PUPPET MOTEL

I live on the highway
Near the Puppet Motel
I log in every day
I know the neighborhood well.
Now about the residents
Of the Puppet Motel
They're more than a little spooky
And most of them are mean.
They're runnin' the numbers
They're playin' cops and robbers
Down in the dungeons
Inside their machines.
. . . .
So if you think we live in a modern world
Where everything is clean and swell
Take a walk on the B side of town
Down by the Puppet Motel

Take a whiff. Burning plastic.

I drink a cup of coffee I try to revive
My mind's a blank I'm barely alive
My nerves are shot I feel like hell
Guess it's time to check in
At the Puppet Motel.[38]

In the course of the song Anderson describes the "puppets" of cyber-space as "Down in the dungeons," "in this digital jail," "havin' virtual sex," with their minds "out on bail." They live on the "B side of town" and "don't know / What's really real now." These descriptions evoke the seedy-hotel-room atmosphere of the CD-ROM *Puppet Motel*, an atmosphere that Anderson explicitly associates with William Burroughs and lowlife subculture. (Photos of Burroughs tinted à la Warhol hang on the walls of one of *Puppet Motel*'s "rooms.") The newest technology—"if you think we live in a modern world / Where everything is clean and swell"—turns out to resemble the thirties landscape of film noir, which relies on images of urban decay, moral decadence, and outdated forms of sophistication. The association Anderson makes between the radically new and the irremediably outmoded recalls Walter Benjamin's notion of the dialectical image, the image of an object that reveals its humanity, its story of disappointed need. As a critical historian of the new, Anderson seems to be employing the means provided by large entertainment indus-tries like Warner Brothers Communications to mock the pretensions of modern technology; she resists the pressures of standardization by focus-ing light on postmodernity's hidden industrial wastelands, plugged-in zombies, and ghosts. Yet as a dialectical philosopher of the outmoded, Anderson seems simultaneously to be striving to identify a sensuous ele-ment "Down in the dungeons," inside the machines. In the lyrics of "The Puppet Motel" the very seediness of hyperspace, even the industrial smell of "Burning plastic," gains an erotic or hallucinogenic charge ("Take a whiff"). The "virtual sex" of jailbirds in "search of the Holy Grail" is experienced as pleasurable, as full of a latent, "inhuman" appeal. The final verse of the song reiterates this erotics of alienation:

Boot up. Good afternoon. Pause.
Oooo. I really like the way you talk.
Pardon me. Shut down.

"The Puppet Motel" thus appears to present alienation not as reifying but as auratic, full of pulsing energies from plugged-in, coffee-adled nerves. The ending—"Pardon me. Shut down"—suggests a kind of guilty confession, but whether this confession refers to the subject's mediated nature (the subject "log[s] in every day") or, alternatively, to the pleasure the subject takes in artificial mediation is a question the reader or listener cannot resolve. If there is no longer any resistance to, but only pleasuring in, technological saturation, if the "I" enjoys merging entirely with the "they" of the virtual "neighborhood" and requires no further instantiation, no alternative form, then an admission of guilt terminates only in the subject's "Shut down," canceling out any voice (any subjectivity) other than the computer's own. The erotic relationship with technology ("Oooo. I like the way you talk") seduces the subject entirely, ending its existence at the moment this subject enters the network and participates in digital reality. And this seduction is successful because real life (life before booting up) is anything but appealing: in the song, "Blank" minds, "shot" nerves, and minimal signs of life ("I'm barely alive") mark the spot where the subject used to be, the spot where a full, autonomous subject not limited by computer functions has disappeared into the flickering space of a precontact "Pause."

On the one hand, the concluding, prefabricated syntagm of "The Puppet Motel"—"Shut down"—seems to refer to the turning off or cancellation of subjectivity that occurs once full objectification has been completed, that is, once the subject-user has been successfully plugged in. Yet another reading, however, could generate the opposite conclusion, namely, that by participating in a confessional moment ("Pardon me") the subject-user actually manages to confuse the computer with contradictory commands and thus causes a computer crash (a computer "Shut down"). In this second scenario the subject's inappropriate conduct, its breathy "Oooo" of pleasure and pain, explodes the system upon which all reified languages are predicated. The system has to stall—shut down—when there is only a visceral rather than a cognitive thing to express.

But Anderson does not merely show the limits of her machines by eroticizing them to the point where they shut down. She also places them on the "B side of town." Certainly, this gesture of relocation associates the new with the seedy, but it also suggests the possibility of a "B" way of using technologies, an alternative, subcultural way of manipulating them for subversive ends. A "B" approach to the computer might bring out its less socially acceptable, instrumental, or predictable ways of processing information. This subversive approach would be linked not to a vision of the "modern world / Where everything is clean and swell" but rather to a guilty memory of the computer's less palatable history, the smell of burning plastic recalling the substandard working conditions under which computers are made.

Clearly, in *Home of the Brave* Anderson is not concerned with technology's grimy underbelly. She presents her technologies as spanking new, top-of-the-line, shiny, and hard. There is no "B" movie tone here, no allusion to emptiness or suffering. But "The Puppet Motel" shows us another aspect of Anderson's work, one that brings her closer in line with the Rimbaldian tradition I have been delineating in this book. The poets of this tradition strive to confess mediation, even to eroticize it, while simultaneously challenging mediation's limits, placing it into new constellations, plugging it into different currents. Anderson seems to suggest that the lyric impulse, the investment in human subjectivity as indeterminate, mobile, and evolving, not only survives but thrives within industrial culture when it is allowed to appropriate, for its own journey of self-discovery, industrial means.

Coda _____

THE question whether technology determines its subjects or is determined by them is one that has animated debates in both humanistic and scientific communities for years. (It is the question at the very heart of Adorno's opus and probably at the heart of Marx's as well.) When Apollinaire urged poets to take technological means of production into their own hands in 1917, he had not thought through the implications of this act in any meaningful way. He neglected to inquire whether technologies, once freed from the exigencies of profit, would in fact be able to overcome their mechanical limits and expand their epistemological grids. He thus left an enigmatic legacy to his heirs, signaling the necessity of engaging with the new but failing to indicate how technology might alter a lyric aesthetics dedicated to the expression of the self. Subsequent poets, philosophers, and critics have had to struggle to determine whether the promises of the lyric have been disappointed or realized by the machine.

Entering a lively debate that Apollinaire and the avant-garde helped to initiate, Mark Poster has recently attacked the question of technology's influence on subjectivity and subjective discourses with particular regard to electronic writing. As opposed to an enthusiastic proponent of computer technologies such as Michael Joyce, Poster comes down more heavily on the side of technological determinism; for him, not only the conditions in which technology is developed and exploited but technology itself is restrictive. Poster argues that although the electronic mark merely radicalizes "tendencies inherent in all writing," it nonetheless constitutes the writing subject—and thus, implicitly, the subject of lyric writing as well—in a new and troubling way.[1] Subjects, Poster claims, "are constituted in acts and structures of communication" (11); thus, the communication system that "disperses" and "destabilizes" the subject poses a serious threat to models of embodied subjectivity. A potential risk of cybernetics that Poster sketches out implicitly is that the disembodied subjectivity ushered in by computers may ultimately grow immune to context, unable to retrieve its form in the here and now and thus *less conscious of its capacity to inflict and experience pain.*[2] The computer "institutes a factory of postmodern subjectivity," writes Poster (128). It is a generator of "puppet" personalities, dispersed and encountered only in separate "rooms."

It is useful to contrast Poster's dystopic vision of computer writing as constitutionally incapable of registering suffering with that of Gabriele Schwab, who writes on the cyborg and on cybernetic fiction from the far less pessimistic perspective of Haraway. "Poets of all time," declares

Schwab, "have known how to use technologies of writing and print against the codifying force inherent in them."[3] Schwab's position is compelling; her words suggest that however functional and "codifying" a technology might be, a poet could always find ways to transform codes from within, to find their indeterminacies and embedded contradictions. While one might be momentarily reassured by Schwab's confidence, the question still remains why Anderson's technospectacles and incursions into cybernetic writing have as yet failed to yield more self-conscious, hermeneutically demanding, and culturally resistant fruits.

It is possible that Anderson is less successful in subverting filmic and cybernetic technologies because they are less easily extricated from large industry backing. The production and distribution of videos and hypertext software require huge sums of investment; thus, these forms often demand greater subservience to norms as defined by the capitalist market. One could speculate that within a different market these same technologies might indeed replicate the troubling sense of intimacy and ambiguity Anderson achieves in works such as *Duets on Ice* or *Handphone Table*. Ultimately, Anderson's most recent works leave our questions unanswered, for they do not indicate how the subject—as "congealed" in technology but also as technology's excess—can be actualized as anything other than a blank surface, a current to be "plugged in" or "shut down." On the one hand, these works seem to suggest that as impersonal, global media increasingly penetrate the subject's inner life, creating myths, providing manifest content for dreams, and producing memories, the existence of a subjective excess, a unique body and "mental filter," becomes ever more difficult to discern. On the other hand, however, they hint at a future project in which the most advanced technology might still offer a dialectical image, a project in which the apparatus could divulge a forgotten, repressed, or previously inarticulate impulse at odds with the dominant definitions of human being.

In conclusion, I would suggest that Poster and Schwab (and before them, the more pessimistic Adorno and the sanguine Haraway) represent two positions in an argument that can be only provisionally resolved. These two positions define the parameters of a field in which the work of contemporary poets evolves. Many of these poets still challenge the given technology to work in subversive ways, tacitly accepting what Apollinaire proposed almost a century ago and what Michael Davidson recently confirmed in the following terms: "Prophecy no longer emanates from some inner visionary moment [if it ever did, one might add] but from a voice that has recognized its inscription within an electronic environment, a voice that has seized the means of reproduction and adapted it to oppositional ends."[4]

To what extent this opposition remains effectual, however, may depend upon how it is received by later cultural producers. For opposition, resistance to technological determinism, can itself only appear in an objectified and potentially commodifiable form. The subjectivity "congealed" in technique is the oppositional force that must be freed by future artists who will transform but also mentally congeal this force once again. There is no moment when the resistant force of the unique, the particular, the subjective, simply flashes out in a pure, unmediated form. For this reason all art objects require interpretive work, the interpretive work of a spectator or reader able to bring out the artwork's traumatic element in a different light. A confessional dialectics demands a hermeneutics, a method, that reads reality for the embedded "oppositional" meanings that haunt it.

Hal Foster has written persuasively on the recuperative gesture involved in the transmission of oppositional meanings from work to work, objectifying form to objectifying form. Pondering the relation between the "neo-avant-garde" and the historical avant-garde, Foster proposes that aesthetic inheritance is similar to a variety of Freudian *Nachträglichkeit*, the interpretive process involved in reviving a traumatic event. Just as a significant event in our lives only obtains meaning by being "registered through another that recodes it," so, surmises Foster, the works of the historical avant-garde only reveal their latent subjectivity, their repressed and unsatisfied desire, when revived in the works of the next generation. "We come to be who we are only in *deferred action*, in *Nachträglichkeit*," states Foster.

> I believe historical and neo-avant-gardes are constituted in a similar way, as a continual process of protension and retension, a complex relay of reconstructed past and anticipated future—in short, in a deferred action that throws over any simple scheme of before and after, cause and effect, origin and repetition.
>
> . . . the avant-garde work is never historically effective or fully significant in its initial moments. It cannot be because it is traumatic: a hole in the symbolic order of its time that is not prepared for it, that cannot receive it, at least not immediately, at least not without structural change.[5]

Foster's description of the avant-garde work as a "hole in the symbolic order" implicitly draws this work into comparison with the subject itself, whose irreducible alterity also frustrates symbolic systems and mediating forms or technologies. The oppositional action of the avant-garde, it would seem, is similar to, or even coextensive with, the "deferred action" of the unconscious relayed through the work of art. This action is a force that is "inhuman" (in Adorno's terms) insofar as it refuses to be captured *definitively* by any human category or form of objectification.[6] "Structural changes" (technological upgrades, the invention of new techniques, etc.) do manage to "receive" previously unvoiced aspects of the work (or subject), but, Foster implies, such changes will never exhaust the force of the trauma that motivates them.

Foster's comments on the relation between the "neo-avant-garde" and the historical avant-garde characterize appropriately the relations between the avant-garde and popular cultural producers as well. For if Adorno's claim concerning the "implicit history" embedded in things is accurate, then reproductive technologies and their commodified products also contain the "deferred action" of a "hole in the symbolic order." Artists of the historical avant-garde discovered that they could indeed locate and reanimate the energy of the traumatic encoded not only in high art forms but also in cultural products of an entirely different order. In every case, the "complex relay of reconstructed past and anticipated future" connecting different generations of high-cultural producers—or different types of cultural producers—has occurred because these producers accorded a specific type of attention to human creations. This attention, a hermeneutic activity I will call "reading," allows cultural producers to locate the "hole in the symbolic order," to discern the as yet unrealized subversive or traumatic element in contradiction with the surface properties of the product or work. The process of *Nachträglichkeit*, in other words, requires a reader, a subject that approaches all cultural forms as a text. Adorno (here with Horkheimer) calls this type of reading or attention a "dialectic," a practice disclosing the other within the self, the self within the other: "Dialectic . . . interprets every image as writing. It shows how the admission of [the image's] falsity is to be read in the lines of its features—a confession that deprives it of its power and appropriates it for truth."[7]

In the tradition I have been tracing, dialectics, the resolution of image into writing, nature into mechanics, is an interpretive practice taught by the lyric text itself. Lyric language presents itself as inspired effusion but then, paradoxically, demands the acquisition of the most sophisticated of interpretive skills. Textual clues, such as agrammaticalities, lexical infelicities, conflicts between discourses, and rhetorical undecidabilities, urge the reader to look deeper, to return repeatedly to words never "historically effective or fully significant in [their] initial moments."[8] But because lyric engages a definition of the self, it goes further than most idioms, impelling readers to place "natural" images of selfhood at stake, to recognize them as objectifications and yet to continue probing their traumatic content. I would not want to claim that when we stop reading lyric, we stop learning how to read in the strong sense of the term I have been evoking. After all, lyric has consolidated images of autonomous subjectivity as much as it has helped to explode them. The question we now face, though, is whether the technopoems of the future will continue to "refine themselves," as Apollinaire once predicted, or whether they will succumb instead to the simple, celebratory visions of technification that industry, by and large, supports. One day, to borrow from Apollinaire, when advanced versions of "the phonograph and the cinema" have become "the only remaining forms of transmission," will poets realize "a liberty unimaginable until now"?[9] Or, conversely, will poets be constrained to abandon the semantic complexities, the self-reflexive rigors, and the rhetorical resistance exemplified by a lyric tradition no longer experienced firsthand?

Notes

All translations from the French are my own unless otherwise noted. I have, however, made extensive use of Louise Varèse's beautiful translations of Rimbaud's *Illuminations*.

Introduction

1. Guillaume Apollinaire, "L'Esprit nouveau et les poètes," in *Oeuvres en prose complètes, II*, ed. Pierre Caizergues and Michel Décaudin (Paris: Gallimard, 1977), 944, hereafter abbreviated as *OC*.

2. Apollinaire's *Les Mamelles de Tirésias, Drame surréaliste en deux actes et un prologue*, written in 1903 but not performed until June 1917, anticipates many of the innovations introduced in Anderson's performance works. Apollinaire employed a revolver, an accordion, different types of drums, sleigh bells, castanets, breaking dishes, and other inventive devices as both aural and visual props (see Guillaume Apollinaire, *Oeuvres poétiques*, ed. Marcel Adéma and Michel Décaudin, preface by André Billy [Paris: Gallimard, 1959]). For details on the original production and its revolutionary use of sound, see Christopher Schiff, "Banging on the Windowpane: Sound in Early Surrealism," in *Wireless Imagination: Sound, Radio, and the Avant-Garde*, ed. Douglas Kahn and Gregory Whitehead (Cambridge: MIT Press, 1994), esp. 142–48. Apollinaire also wrote the program notes for Jean Cocteau's *Parade*, another innovative multimedia piece, presented in May 1917, that brought together the talents of Erik Satie, Diaghilev, Léonide Massine, and Pablo Picasso. *Parade* not only looked forward to Anderson's technospectacles but also self-consciously allied itself with the poetics of Rimbaud, a point that will take on greater relevance in a moment. For an account of Rimbaud's influence on *Parade*, see Pierre Brunel, "Jean Cocteau et *Parade*," *Oeuvres et critiques* 22, no. 1 (1997).

3. See Margareth Wijk's summary of the critical reaction to "L'Esprit nouveau et les poètes" in *Guillaume Apollinaire et l'esprit nouveau* (Lund, Sweden: Gleerup, 1982).

4. Heideggerian critics such as Gabriel Bounoure lost an important opportunity to develop one of the more provocative aspects of Heidegger's thought when they emphasized the discontinuity between technology and *poiesis* instead of exploring their shared relation to *techne*. In "The Question Concerning Technology" Heidegger posits the origin of both technology and art in the act of "revealing" implied by the Greek term *techne* (Martin Heidegger, *Basic Writings*, ed. David Farrell Krell [New York: Harper & Row, 1977], 294). Adorno explores more fully the implications of this shared etymology in *Negative Dialectics* and *Aesthetic Theory* but, for reasons I will address later, neglects to give Heidegger the credit he is due.

5. The principle proponents of Poésie Sonore (also known as Poésie Action) are Bernard Heidsieck and Henri Chopin. Influenced by dada and Fluxus (a

movement animated by John Cage and Jackson Mac Low), Poésie Sonore sought in the early sixties to create a broader audience for poetry by reading in alternative performance spaces. According to Heidsieck, the group established "another mode of circulation for poetry" by combining the recitation of poems with theatrical gestures, innovative lighting, and audio technologies (Bernard Heidsieck, interview by author, 1 July 1996, Paris). A further study could explore the ways in which poetic strategies have suggested innovative techniques in the cinematic domain. Early-twentieth-century poets such as Jean Cocteau and poetry critic Jean Epstein both began with poetry but then went on to pursue filmmaking (as Blaise Cendrars also—unsuccessfully—attempted to do). For a meditation on the continuity between poetry and filmmaking see Jean Epstein, *La Poésie d'aujourd'hui: un nouvel état d'intelligence* (Paris: La Sirène, 1921).

6. OULIPO did produce one performance poet, Michèle Métail, who employs formal and semantic constraints to produce oral poetry before live audiences. As far as I know, Métail has not moved beyond oral recitation into the sphere of high-tech performance.

With respect to the popularization of poetry, an argument could be made that the French tradition of *poètes chansonniers* constitutes an advance of poetry into the popular realm. The distinction between a poet like Smith and a *chansonnier*, however, is that the former transforms a poetics (in this case, Rimbaud's) into a subcultural musical form requiring electronics (electronic guitars and complicated feedback and voice-over techniques), whereas the latter remains within a voice-based, acoustic, and traditional melodic format that never draws attention to the conflict between the lyric address and commercial modes of transmission and distribution.

7. The art critic Peter Frank points out, however, that such experimentation was only made possible in the 1960s, when corporations began to sell technological hardware at prices affordable to working-class American consumers. On the increasing availability of technological means and its effect on the American culture industry, see Frank, "The Next Song You Hear on the Radio Might Well Be Art," *Art News* 80, no. 10 (1981): 74–76.

8. Guy Debord and Gil J. Wolman, "Preliminary Problems in Constructing a Situation," in *Situationist International Anthology*, trans. and ed. Ken Knabb (Berkeley: University of California Press, 1989), 44.

9. In this way Rimbaud comes close to anticipating Walter Benjamin's perspective toward nonauratic cultural forms as presented in his well-known essay "The Work of Art in the Age of Mechanical Reproduction" (in *Illuminations*, ed. and intro. Hannah Arendt, trans. Harry Zohn [New York: Schocken, 1969]). Rimbaud also seizes that "sense perception . . . has been changed by technology," as Benjamin puts it (242). And yet Rimbaud discovers a potential in capitalism to create new technologies and thus new, emancipatory modes of vision that Benjamin attributes solely to a demotic socialist program.

10. Andreas Huyssen, *After the Great Divide: Modernism, Mass Culture, Postmodernism* (Bloomington: Indiana University Press, 1986).

11. See, e.g., the debates conducted in *The Anti-Aesthetic: Essays on Postmodern Culture*, ed. Hal Foster (Seattle: Bay Press, 1983).

12. Bürger neglects to study the relations between technology and art in sufficient detail in part because he believes that "the latter [art] cannot be derived from the former [technology]" (*Theory of the Avantgarde*, trans. Michael Shaw, with a foreword by Jochen Schulte-Sasse [Minneapolis: University of Minnesota Press, 1974], 32). Bürger's warning against a reflection theory of art is salutary, but it also blocks certain avenues of research that have only recently begun to be pursued with meaningful results by theorists such as Michael Davidson, Hal Foster, and Marjorie Perloff.

13. Kirk Varnedoe and Adam Gopnik, *High and Low: Modern Art and Popular Culture* (New York: Museum of Modern Art, 1990); Jeffrey Weiss, *The Popular Culture of Modern Art: Picasso, Duchamp and Avantgardism* (New Haven: Yale University Press, 1994); Robert Jenson, *Marketing Modernism in Fin-de-Siècle Europe* (Princeton: Princeton University Press, 1994); Johanna Drucker, *The Visible Word: Experimental Typography and Modern Art* (Chicago: University of Chicago Press, 1994); Thierry de Duve, *Pictorial Nominalism: On Marcel Duchamp's Passage from Painting to the Readymade*, trans. Dana Polan and Thierry de Duve, with a foreword by John Rajchman (Minneapolis: University of Minnesota Press, 1991), originally published as *Nominalisme pictural: Marcel Duchamp, la peinture et la modernité* (Paris: Minuit, 1984); Hal Foster, *Compulsive Beauty* (Cambridge: MIT Press, 1995).

14. Marjorie Perloff, *Radical Artifice: Writing Poetry in the Age of Media* (Chicago: Chicago University Press, 1991); Michael Davidson, *Ghostlier Demarcations: Modern Poetry and the Material Word* (Berkeley: University of California Press, 1997).

15. Richard Terdiman, *Discourse/Counter-Discourse: The Theory and Practice of Symbolic Resistance in Nineteenth-Century France* (Ithaca: Cornell University Press, 1985).

16. Apollinaire does allude indirectly to the significance of Mallarmé's typographical play for futurist experimentation in "L'Esprit nouveau et les poètes" (*OC*, 944). And it would be absurd to deny the immense importance of Mallarmé's poetics on the generation that followed him. Yet in his notes to the manuscript, Apollinaire makes it clear that the poetry of *l'esprit nouveau* will be under the sign of Rimbaud and *not* Mallarmé: "Arthur Rimbaud (who belonged neither to Parnasse nor to Symbolisme) is perhaps the first poet who can realistically claim to have embodied the new spirit" ("Notes," *OC*, 1687).

17. Walter Benjamin, "One-Way Street," in *One-Way Street and Other Writings*, trans. Edmund Jephcott and Kingsley Shorter (London: Harcourt, 1979), 63. Benjamin is referring here to the increasingly graphic nature of the script employed in advertising. Benjamin suggests that poets, "first and foremost experts in writing" (62), will one day manipulate graphs (developed in statistics, for instance) in eloquent ways.

18. Walter Benjamin, "A Small History of Photography," in *One-Way Street and Other Writings*, 249, emphasis added, and 243.

19. Guillaume Apollinaire, *The Cubist Painters: Aesthetic Meditations, 1913*, trans. Lionel Abel (New York: George Wittenborn, 1962), 11.

20. See, e.g., Lambert Zuidervaart, *Adorno's Aesthetic Theory: The Redemption of Illusion* (Cambridge: MIT Press, 1991); and Jim Collins, *Uncommon*

Cultures: Popular Culture and Post-Modernism (New York: Routledge, 1989). For a more nuanced reading of Adorno's position, see Peter Uwe Hohendahl, "Reading Mass Culture," in *Prismatic Thought: Theodor W. Adorno* (Lincoln: University of Nebraska Press, 1995).

21. In chapter 3 I discuss the significance of lyric poetry to Adorno as both a mode of knowing and a type of language. The most stimulating discussion of Adorno's language is provided by Fredric Jameson in *Late Marxism: Adorno, or, The Persistence of the Dialectic* (New York: Verso, 1990). Jameson locates a narrative tendency in Adorno's prose but completely ignores his debt to poetry as a compositional practice based on affinity (mimesis), confession, and the sacrifice of the subject's authority in the face of the objective other.

Chapter One

1. René Etiemble, *Le Mythe de Rimbaud*, vol. 2, *La Structure du mythe* (Paris: Gallimard, 1952), 435.

2. Stéphane Mallarmé, for instance, describes Rimbaud as a cosmic phenomenon: "éclat, lui, d'un météore," extinguishing itself without precedent or following ("issu seul et s'éteignant") (see Mallarmé, "Arthur Rimbaud," in Mallarmé, *Oeuvres complètes*, ed. Henri Mondor and G. Jean-Aubry [Paris: Gallimard, 1945], 512).

3. Mikhail Bakhtin, *The Dialogic Imagination: Four Essays*, ed. Michael Holquist, trans. Caryl Emerson and Michael Holquist (Austin: University of Texas Press, 1981), 279. Bakhtin speaks of the "internal dialogism of the word" with reference primarily to the novel, but throughout this book I question the distinction he makes between novelistic and poetic languages.

4. The inaugural issue of *La Nouvelle Revue Française*, hereafter abbreviated as *NRF*, was published in 1909. Jacques Rivière was the editor in chief. The *NRF* was not the only arbiter of literary taste. A wide variety of viewpoints were available to literary consumers at the beginning of the century. However, the *NRF* possessed the strongest ties to the Sorbonne and to the university-sanctioned discourse on literature. For an account of the different positions taken by reviews such as Charles Péguy's *Cahier de la quinzaine*, *Le Mercure de France*, and avant-garde journals such as Apollinaire's *Les Soirées*, André Salmon and Paul Fort's *Vers et prose*, and Ricciotto Canudo's *Montjoie!*, see *L'Année 1913*, vol. 1, *Les Revues internationales*, ed. Liliane Brion-Guerry (Paris: Klincksieck, 1971).

5. Henri Ghéon, quoted in Michel Décaudin, " 'La N.R.F.' et les débats sur la poésie, 1909–1914," *Revue d'histoire littéraire de la France*, no. 5 (September–October 1987): 806.

6. Michel Arnauld, "Du Vers Français," *NRF* 2 (1909–10); André Gide, "Baudelaire et M. Faguet," ibid. 4 (1910).

7. Albert Thibaudet, *Paul Valéry* (Paris: Grosset, 1923).

8. Henri Brémond, *La Poésie pure avec Un débat sur la poésie par Robert de Souza* (Paris: Bernard Grasset, 1926), 75.

9. For Bergson's influence on French literary culture, see Romeo Arbour, *Henri Bergson et les lettres françaises* (Paris: José Corti, 1955); and Mark Antliff, *In-*

venting Bergson: Cultural Politics and the Parisian Avant-Garde (Princeton: Princeton University Press, 1993). On the French reception of German idealism, see Gene H. Bell-Villada, *Art for Art's Sake and Literary Life: How Politics and Markets Helped Shape the Ideology and Culture of Aestheticism, 1790–1990* (Lincoln: University of Nebraska Press, 1996).

10. Paul Claudel, "Arthur Rimbaud," *NRF* 8 (1912).

11. Rimbaud "abdique sa raison, proscrit tout processus logique" (Henri Ghéon, "Les Poèmes," ibid., 347). For a broad treatment of the *NRF*'s prewar policies on poetry, see Décaudin, " 'La N.R.F.' et les débats sur la poésie." For an account of Rimbaud's reception prior to 1909, see André Guyaux, "Aspects de la réception des 'Illuminations' (1886–1936)," *Revue d'histoire littéraire de la France*, no. 2 (March–April 1987).

12. Jacques Rivière, "Rimbaud," *NRF* 12 (1914), reprinted in Rivière, *Rimbaud: Dossier, 1905–1925* (Paris: Gallimard, 1977).

13. Jacques Rivière, "Rimbaud, Deuxième Partie," *NRF* 12 (1914): 227. In *Le Poème en prose de Baudelaire jusqu'à nos jours* (Paris: Nizet, 1959) Suzanne Bernard studies the same drafts, remarking astutely that "very often Rimbaud accords such importance to words, he has such faith in their evocative power, that, contrary to what one might think, he starts with the words themselves; he starts from words to arrive at the idea instead of starting with the idea and finding the appropriate words" (169). She concludes that "Rimbaud corrects his first draft just like any other artist . . . his hatred of literature doesn't stop him from 'making literature' " [ne l'empêche pas de 'faire de la littérature'] (170).

14. Rolland de Renéville, *Rimbaud le voyant* (Paris: Au Sans Pareil, 1929); André Breton, "Arthur Rimbaud," in *Anthologie de l'humour noir* (1940; reprint, Paris: Pauvert, 1966); Albert Béguin, *L'Ame romantique et le rêve: Essais sur le Romantisme Allemand et la poésie française* (Marseille: Editions des Cahiers du Sud, 1937). Béguin traces a double lineage dominated on the one hand by Mallarmé, the king of "artifice," and on the other by Rimbaud, who prefigures the surrealists through his "abandon passif à la rêverie" (406–7).

15. See also Jean Paulhan's *Les Fleurs de Tarbes; ou, La terreur dans les lettres* (Paris: Gallimard, 1941), in which Rimbaud is portrayed as the forefather of a (surrealist) poetry that disdains technique in favor of free, spontaneous self-expression.

16. Jules Monnerot, *La Poésie moderne et le sacré* (Paris: Gallimard, 1945), 14.

17. Guillaume Apollinaire, *The Cubist Painters: Aesthetic Meditations, 1913*, trans. Lionel Abel (New York: George Wittenborn, 1962), 14; Blaise Cendrars, "Modernités: Braque," in "Peintres," *Aujourd'hui, 1917–1929, suivi de Essais et Réflexions, 1910–1916*, ed. Miriam Cendrars (Paris: Denoël, 1987), 67.

18. Jacques Rivière, May 1912, quoted in Décaudin, " 'La N.R.F.' et les débats sur la poésie," 810.

19. Henri Ghéon, "Les Cubistes contre le salon d'Automne," *NRF* 6 (November 1911), quoted in Décaudin, 809; Léon-Paul Fargue, in *NRF* 12 (January 1914), quoted in ibid., 811.

20. Apollinaire, *The Cubist Painters*.

21. André Gide, "Contre Mallarmé," *NRF* 1 (1909): 97.

22. Technology and commerce go hand and hand in the futurist consciousness. See, e.g., Umberto Buccioni, Carlo Carrà, Luigi Russolo, Giacomo Balla, and Gino Severini, "Futurist Paintings: Technical Manifesto 1910," in *Futurist Manifestos*, ed. Umbro Apollonio, trans. R. W. Flint, J. C. Higgitt, and C. Tisdall (New York: Viking, Documents of Twentieth-Century Art, 1973).

23. Jacques Copeau, " 'Poesia' and Futurism," *NRF* 2 (August 1909): 82.

24. Paul Verlaine, "Rimbaud," *Lutèce*, October–November 1883, reprinted in Verlaine, *Les Poètes maudits* (1884; reprint, Paris: Slatkine, 1979).

25. Paterne Berrichon's *La Vie de Jean-Arthur Rimbaud* appeared in 1897, and Isabelle Rimbaud's *Reliques* in 1921. See also Isabelle Rimbaud's letters to Berrichon republished in Arthur Rimbaud, *Oeuvres complètes*, ed. Rolland de Renéville and Jules Mouquet (Paris: Gallimard, 1954), hereafter abbreviated as *OC*.

26. René Etiemble, *Le Mythe de Rimbaud*, vol. 1, *Genèse du mythe* (Paris: Gallimard, 1954), 66.

27. Robert Jouanny, "Moeurs et stratégies littéraires de l''avant-siècle,' " in *L'Esprit nouveau dans tous ses états en hommage à Michel Décaudin*, ed. P. Brunel, J. Burgos, C. Debon, and L. Forestier (Paris: Minard, 1986), 31. Verlaine, adds Jouanny, "cleared the path for this kind of promotion through biography with his *Poètes maudits*" (33).

28. Ferdinand Brunetière, "Symbolistes et décadents," in *La Revue des deux mondes*, 1 November 1888, cited by Etiemble in *Le Mythe de Rimbaud*, 1:57.

29. Georges Izambard, *Arthur Rimbaud à Douai et à Charleville* (Paris: Simon Kra, 1927), 57.

30. Steve Murphy, *Le Premier Rimbaud, ou, l'apprentissage de la subversion* (Lyon: CNRS Presses Universitaires de Lyon, 1990). Murphy's subtle readings establish that Rimbaud had, so to speak, done his homework: Rimbaud knew which authors were published in which journals and what kind of poems these authors tended to write. Murphy unravels the tangle of imitation and subversion, confession and parody, that together compose Rimbaud's earliest efforts. But the question of the relation of parody to success in the literary market is barely touched on in Murphy's work. Michele Hannoosh's *Parody and Decadence: Laforgue's "Moralités légendaires"* (Columbus: Ohio State University Press, 1989) suggests that parody became the dominant and commercially most successful mode of the 1880s.

31. *OC*, 255; Arthur Rimbaud, *Rimbaud: Complete Works, Selected Letters*, trans. with intro. and notes by Wallace Fowlie (Chicago: University of Chicago Press, 1966), 297, trans. modified.

32. *OC*, 256. The poem was ultimately rejected.

33. *OC*, 288; Fowlie, *Rimbaud*, 317, trans. modified.

34. *OC*, 288 (the letter was published for the first time, with two others, in "Trois lettres inédites de Rimbaud," *NRF* 12 [1914]: 53). "Nôress," according to Claude Jeancolas, is Rimbaud's way of phonetically imitating the Ardennais pronunciation of *Nord-Est*, the name of a literary review in which Rimbaud had tried unsuccessfully to publish a poem (*Le Dictionnaire Rimbaud* [Paris: Balland, 1991], 193). Fowlie, *Rimbaud*, 317–19, trans. modified.

35. Kristin Ross, "The Right to Laziness," in *The Emergence of Social Space: Rimbaud and the Paris Commune* (Minneapolis: University of Minnesota Press, 1988), 50. In *Une Saison en enfer* Rimbaud may indeed have rejected "the social division of labor" and its alienation of the product from the worker; nonetheless, it is clear that he also participated in the literary trade. Ross wants to identify the work of writing not with apprenticeship but with a nonalienated practice such as vagabondage. Writing may be a *less* alienated activity, but it is by no means unmediated by practical concerns. For a rigorous discussion of nineteenth-century poetry and its relation to the theme of work, see Richard Terdiman, "The Dialectics of the Prose Poem," in *Discourse/Counter-Discourse: The Theory and Practice of Symbolic Resistance in Nineteenth-Century France* (Ithaca: Cornell University Press, 1985). Terdiman claims that the image of the strike *(la grève)* in Rimbaud's correspondance "registers the determined self-conception of the artist as a *producer*, constrained despite himself to investigate the conditions of his production" (331).

36. Rivière, *Rimbaud*, 46–47.

37. *OC*, 271; Fowlie, *Rimbaud*, 309, trans. modified.

38. See, e.g., Bernard's treatment of the "Lettre du voyant" in *Le Poème en prose de Baudelaire*, 152–58. An exception to the general rule would be W. M. Frohock's attentive reading of the letter's ironies in *Rimbaud's Poetic Practice: Image and Theme in the Major Poems* (Cambridge: Harvard University Press, 1963).

39. Anne-Emmanuelle Berger, *Le Banquet de Rimbaud: Recherches sur l'oralité* (Seyssel: Champ Vallon, 1992), 157.

40. Charles Baudelaire, "Conseils aux jeunes littérateurs," in Baudelaire, *Oeuvres complètes*, ed. Y.-G. Le Dantec, rev. Claude Pichois (Paris: Gallimard, 1961), 479, hereafter abbreviated as *OC*.

41. Jouanny, "Moeurs et stratégies littéraires de l'"avant-siècle,' " 28.

42. Pierre Bourdieu, "The Field of Cultural Production," in *The Field of Cultural Production*, trans. and intro. Randal Johnson (New York: Columbia University Press, 1993), 55.

43. Ross considers Rimbaud's trajectory to be "part of the massive displacement of populations from the provinces to the city, that vagabondage whereby thousands of peasants, workers, and middle-class people learned of exile for the first time" (Ross, *Emergence of Social Space*, 20). Ross may be conflating Rimbaud's ambition with the sheer need to survive experienced by many peasants of the countryside. Rimbaud, after all, was not forced to leave home in order to earn his keep. Rimbaud's journey to Paris follows a literary rather than a demographic model. Jouanny also observes that a large number of "enthusiastic provincials" and "naive foreigners" conducted their own "Charleville–Paris" escapade in order to satisfy their "desire to make it" [une volonté de parvenir] ("Moeurs et stratégies littéraires de l'"avant-siècle,' " 28–29).

44. Alfred de Musset, "Voeux stériles," in Musset, *Oeuvres complètes*, ed. Philippe Van Tieghem (Paris: Seuil, 1963), 85.

45. Charles Marie Leconte de Lisle, "Les Montreurs," quoted in Murphy, *Le Premier Rimbaud*, 281.

46. Murphy, *Le Premier Rimbaud*, 280.

47. Charles Cros and Tristan Corbière, *Oeuvres complètes*, ed. Louis Forestier and Pierre-Olivier Walzer (Paris: Gallimard, 1970), 47.

48. Maurice Blanchot, "L'Oeuvre finale," in *L'Entretien infini* (Paris: Gallimard, 1969), 430. Blanchot is glossing Yves Bonnefoy's *Rimbaud par lui-même* (Paris: Seuil, 1961), in which the poet is depicted as attempting to "transmuer la dépossession en richesse" (93).

49. Current French criticism on Rimbaud continues to follow the model established by the *NRF.* See, e.g., Jean-Marie Gleize's *Arthur Rimbaud* (Paris: Hachette Supérieur, 1993), a sampler of Rimbaud criticism for Hachette's "Portraits Littéraires" series, which fails to include a single text investigating the context of Rimbaud's poetic production. Gleize makes no reference to the three most exciting works on Rimbaud to appear in the last decade: Kristin Ross's *Emergence of Social Space*, Steve Murphy's *Le Premier Rimbaud*, and Antoine Raybaud's *Fabrique d' "Illuminations"* (Paris: Seuil, 1989).

50. Shoshana Felman, "Tu as bien fait de partir, Arthur Rimbaud," in *La Folie et la chose littéraire* (Paris: Seuil, 1978), 100.

51. Berger, *Le Banquet de Rimbaud*, 38.

52. Michael Baxandall, *Patterns of Intention: On the Historical Explanation of Pictures* (New Haven: Yale University Press, 1985), 30.

53. On the emergence of popular culture in France, see Claude Bellanger, *Histoire générale de la presse française*, vol. 3 (Paris: Presses Universitaires de France, 1972); Theodore Zeldin, *France, 1848–1945: Taste and Corruption* (Oxford: Oxford University Press, 1979); Rosalind Williams, *Dream Worlds: Mass Consumption in Late Nineteenth-Century France* (Berkeley: University of California Press, 1982); Anne Friedberg, *Window Shopping: Cinema and the Postmodern* (Berkeley: University of California Press, 1993); and Vanessa Schwartz, *Spectacular Realities: Early Mass Culture in Fin-de-Siècle Paris* (Berkeley: University of California Press, 1998).

54. Charles Baudelaire, "Le Public moderne et la photographie," in *Salon de 1859, OC*, 1035.

55. Bourdieu, "Field of Cultural Production," 55, emphasis added.

56. See, e.g., Christopher Beach, *Poetic Culture: Contemporary American Poetry Between Community and Institution* (Evanston: Northwestern University Press, 1999). In France, poetry critics tend to be deeply suspicious concerning modern technology's contributions to the dissemination and evolution of contemporary poetry. For a typical treatment of the problem, see Yves Chamet, "Malaise dans la poésie: Un État des lieux," *Littérature: De la poésie aujourd'hui*, no. 110 (1998): 13–21.

57. Bourdieu, "Field of Cultural Production," 49.

Chapter Two

1. Jacques Gengoux, *Le Symbolique de Rimbaud: Le Système des sources* (Paris: La Colombe, Editions du Vieux Colombier, 1947). Gengoux writes: "Literary criticism, under the influence of a surrealist bias, has until now emphasized the role of the unconscious to such an extent that the second and perhaps more important role of lucidity has been forgotten" (16). Gengoux attempts to reveal

the various "formule[s]" (52) underlying Rimbaud's compositional practices, from Kabbalistic and alchemical equations to Hegelian dialectical paradigms. The publication in 1949 of Bouillane de Lacoste's *Arthur Rimbaud et le problème des "Illuminations"* (Paris: Mercure de France) also focused attention on Rimbaud's technique.

2. Theodor W. Adorno, "The George-Hofmannsthal Correspondance, 1891–1906," in *Prisms*, trans. Samuel Weber and Shierry Weber (Cambridge: MIT Press, 1992), 190.

3. Antoine Raybaud, *La Fabrique d' "Illuminations"* (Paris: Seuil, 1989).

4. Friedrich Kittler, *Discourse Networks, 1800/1900*, trans. Michael Metteer, with Chris Cullens (Stanford: Stanford University Press, 1990).

5. Guillaume Apollinaire, "Notes," in *Oeuvres en prose complètes, II*, ed. Pierre Caizergues and Michel Décaudin (Paris: Gallimard, 1977), 1687.

6. Fernand Léger, "The Machine Aesthetic: Geometric Order and Truth," in *Functions of Painting* (New York: Viking, Documents of Twentieth-Century Art, 1973), 65–66.

7. Years before Marinetti encouraged the union of man and machine, early French avant-garde poets such as Nicolas Beaudoin and Jules Romain were already exploring poetic equivalents for the mechanical rhythms of the steam engine and the electric motor. Members of the early avant-garde collective l'Abbaye de Créteil (René Arcos, Georges Duhamel, Charles Vildrac, Henry-Martin Barzun, and the painter Albert Gleizes) also considered science and technology more akin to poetry than opposed to it. Beaudoin's *paroxysme*, Romain's *unanimisme*, and the Bergsonian-inspired poetics of the Abbaye each contributed to some extent to Apollinaire's *esprit nouveau* and to Marinetti's futurism. However, these earlier movements did not thematize the links between modern technology and capitalism, nor did they propose that poets make use of industrial means. Apollinaire's greater exposure to cinema may have played a part in his reevaluation of both popular culture and industrial technologies. On early-twentieth-century avant-garde movements in France, see Léon Somville, *Dévanciers du surréalisme: Les Groupes d'avant-garde et le mouvement poétique, 1912–1925* (Geneva: Droz, 1971); Michel Décaudin, *La Crise des valeurs symbolistes, 1895–1914* (Geneva and Paris: Slatkine, 1981); and Rosalind Williams, "Jules Romain, *Unanimisme*, and the Poetics of Urban Systems," in *Literature and Technology*, ed. Mark L. Greenberg and Lance Schachterle (London and Toronto: Associated University Press, 1992).

8. Guillaume Apollinaire, "L'Esprit nouveau et les poètes," in *Oeuvres en prose complètes*, 2:954.

9. Ibid. Apparently, the idea that poets should set about mechanizing poetic expression was anything but appealing to the future leader of surrealism. Breton suspected that Apollinaire's program would hasten the alienation of the poet from his own labor, an alienation Rimbaud had abetted by his own example. For Breton, Rimbaud's later involvements in colonization, industry, and commerce were not inconsistent with the particulars of his earlier career; Rimbaud had merely realized a potential—the potential to become a "marionnette," as Breton put it—always discernible in his behavior and in his work (André Breton, "Arthur Rimbaud," in *Anthologie de l'humour noir* [Paris: Pauvert, 1966], 213).

10. Adorno, "George-Hofmannsthal Correspondance," 191.

11. Paul Dermée, Amédée Ozenfant, and Charles-Edouard Jeanneret (Le Corbusier), "Domaine de l'esprit nouveau," *L'Esprit nouveau*, no. 1 (1920): 2. See also "L'Esthétique mécanique," in which the editors state: "Nous sommes . . . quelques esthéticiens qui croyons que l'art a des lois comme la physiologie ou la physique" (3).

12. Victor Basch, "Esthétique nouvelle et une science de l'art," ibid., 12. Basch taught aesthetics and German literature at the Sorbonne. He was assassinated by the French militia at the close of World War II. His efforts to reconcile Kant and the automatism of Pierre Janet and Théodule Ribot reflect a deeper contradiction inherent in the purist program. Purists sought at once to respect the Freudian psychology of the unconscious (represented on the editorial board by Dr. Allendy) and to adhere to what they considered technology's grounding principles: reason and efficiency.

13. On psycho-physiological theories of automatism and their influence on aesthetic thought, see Hal Foster, "Beyond the Pleasure Principle?" in *Compulsive Beauty* (Cambridge: MIT Press, 1995); Anna Balakian, *Surrealism: The Road to the Absolute* (New York: Noonday Press, 1959); and Michel Carrouges, *Les Machines célibataires* (Paris: Arcanes, 1954). For an account of how models of man as a machine influenced early-twentieth-century thought in general, see Anson Rabinbach, *The Human Motor: Energy, Fatigue, and the Origins of Modernity* (New York: Basic Books, 1990).

14. Paul Dermée, "Découverte du lyrisme," *L'Esprit nouveau*, no. 1 (1920): 34–37. Dermée created a tension in the first issue of *L'Esprit nouveau* when he insisted on the noninstrumentality of the lyric utterance, whereas purists typically called for the reconciliation of form and function (3). See also "Poésie = Lyrisme + Art," ibid., no. 2 (1920). Dermée was probably influenced by the Bergsonian Tancrède de Visan, whose *L'Attitude du lyrisme contemporain* of 1911 advocated a poetry of pure intuition. Dermée was also in dialogue with Paul Valéry; during the twenties Valéry was devising a theory of lyric creation that depicted writing as an effort on the part of the intellect to suspend its habitual responses and observe its own proceedings in order to gain access to "l'esprit," a space of free and infinitely evolving associations that critics have associated with *la durée* (see, e.g., "Introduction à la méthode de Léonard de Vinci" and "Première leçon du cours de poétique," in Paul Valéry, *Oeuvres*, vol. 1, ed. Jean Hytier [Paris: Gallimard, 1957]). A complete analysis of the early avant-garde's approach to lyricism would have to include a study of the multiple intersections between Bergsonism, orphic cubism, Le Corbusier's purism, Reverdy's poetics as presented in *Nord-Sud*, and the rationalism or scientism of the Puteaux cubists. In this regard, see Mark Antliff, *Inventing Bergson: Cultural Politics and the Parisian Avant-Garde* (Princeton: Princeton University Press, 1993); Christopher Green, *Léger and the Avant-Garde* (New Haven: Yale University Press, 1976); and Kenneth E. Silver, *L'Esprit de Corps: The Art of the Parisian Avant-Garde and the First World War, 1914–1925* (Princeton: Princeton University Press, 1989).

15. Paul Dermée, Amédée Ozenfant, and Charles-Edouard Jeanneret, "L'Esprit nouveau," *L'Esprit nouveau*, no. 1 (1920): 1.

16. "Quelle fut la leçon de Rimbaud, de Mallarmé, précisément et techniquement?" ask Paul Dermée, Amédée Ozenfant, and Charles-Edouard Jeanneret in "Pour la littérature," ibid., iv.

17. Stéphane Mallarmé, "Crise de vers," in "Variations sur un sujet," *Oeuvres complètes*, ed. Henri Mondor and G. Jean-Aubry (Paris: Gallimard, 1945), 366.

18. Jean-Jacques Thomas has wittily summarized the popular critical commonplaces of the early twentieth century that established Mallarmé and Rimbaud at opposite extremes of the lyric spectrum in "Impasse Mallarmé, . . . Porte Rimbaud," *French Literature Series* 18 (1991): 55. Albert Thibaudet exemplifies the tendency described by Thomas in "Réflexions sur la littérature: Mallarmé et Rimbaud": "The influence of Rimbaud was as different from that of Mallarmé as the two poets were different from each other" (*NRF* 18 [1922]: 202). An exception to the rule is Pierre Reverdy's *Self-Defence: Critique-Esthétique, 1919*, in which Rimbaud and Mallarmé are brought together under the sign of *l'esprit nouveau*: "When one refers to the influence of Mallarmé and Rimbaud, one is speaking about what they brought to literature: a new spirit *[un esprit nouveau]*" (Reverdy, *Nord-Sud, Self-Defence et Autres écrits sur l'art et la poésie, 1917–1926* [Paris: Flammarion, 1975], 104–5). For a broad view of Mallarmé's influence during the prewar period, see Raymond Bellour, "1913: Pourquoi écrire poète?" in *L'Année 1913*, vol. 1, *Les Formes esthétiques de l'oeuvre d'art à la veille de la première guerre mondiale*, ed. Liliane Brion-Guerry (Paris: Klincksieck, 1971), 527–632.

19. Adorno's critique of Bergson is based on the difference between a historical model of consciousness and a transcendent one. In *Negative Dialectics* Adorno calls Bergsonism "a cult of irrational immediacy" (*ND*, 8). Bergson's division of the psychic apparatus into two parts, a "causal-mechanical" part governing "pragmatic knowledge" and an "intuitive" part productive of transcendental experience, is regressive and undialectical; it fails to take into account the historicity (or instrumentality) that, according to Adorno, affects every psychic operation.

20. Richard Terdiman, *Discourse/Counterdiscourse: The Theory and Practice of Symbolic Resistance in Nineteenth-Century France* (Ithaca: Cornell University Press, 1985), 294, Terdiman's emphasis. Terdiman, who has analyzed Mallarmé's relation to modernity in greater depth, proposes that Mallarmé's poetry may indeed reject its cultural antagonist, journalism, but nonetheless "continues to inscribe the power which its antagonist retains" (289). Terdiman nuances Adorno's account of Mallarmé, demonstrating that he "grudgingly acknowledges as a condition of the creation of avant-garde discourse the existence of the referent whose discourse he would wish to separate from his own." Mallarmé too adopts a form associated with popular culture as a figure for poetic practice: pantomime. This form, however, does not rely on an advanced technology. A richer area of investigation would be the relation between Mallarmé's poetics and the emerging field of photography. Gayle Zachmann has begun to work in this promising area; see her "Developing Movements: Mallarmé, Manet, the 'Photo' and the 'Graphic,' " *French Forum* 22 (May 1997).

21. Rimbaud to Georges Izambard, 13 May 1871, in *Oeuvres complètes*, ed. Rolland de Renéville and Jules Mouquet (Paris: Gallimard, 1954), 268, hereafter abbreviated as *OC*.

22. On Rimbaud's visits to the London Exposition, the Crystal Palace, Royal Albert Hall, indoor light shows *(éclairages)*, Christmas *féeries*, and weekly fireworks displays *(illuminations)*, see V. P. Underwood, *Rimbaud et l'Angleterre* (Paris: Nizet, 1976); and H. Matarasso and P. Petitfils, *La Vie d'Arthur Rimbaud* (Paris: Hachette, 1962).

23. Arthur Rimbaud, "Délires, II: Alchimie du verbe" (Delirium, II: Alchemy of the Word), in *Une Saison en enfer, OC,* 232.

24. See Raybaud's discussion of theatrical imagery in "Visions d'Hélène," in *Fabrique d' "Illuminations,"* 133–56.

25. See James Lawler, *Rimbaud's Theatre of the Self* (Cambridge: Harvard University Press, 1992).

26. Roger Munier, *"Génie" de Rimbaud* (Paris: Traversière, 1988).

27. Atle Kittang, *Discours et jeu: Essai d'analyse des textes d'Arthur Rimbaud* (Grenoble: Presses Universitaires de Grenoble, 1975), 220. In true structuralist form, Kittang reads the "machine aimée" as a self-reflexive reference to the linguistic machine generating the text (224). The question to be asked, though, is why Rimbaud, *at this point in history,* would figure genius, or the procedure generating the text, as a machine.

28. Raybaud, *Fabrique d' "Illuminations",* 9, Raybaud's emphasis.

29. Anne-Emmanuelle Berger, *Le Banquet de Rimbaud: Recherches sur l'oralité* (Seyssel: Champ Vallon, 1992), 179. "Génie" could conceivably be a rewriting of Honoré de Balzac's *La Peau de chagrin* or "La Fille aux yeux d'or."

30. Bruno Claisse, " 'Barbare' et le nouveau corps amoureux," *Rivista di letterature moderne et comparate* 41 (April–June 1988).

31. Jean-Louis Baudry, "Le Texte de Rimbaud," *Tel Quel* 36 (winter 1969).

32. See Tzvetan Todorov, "A Complication of Text: The *Illuminations,*" in *French Literary Theory Today: A Reader,* ed. Todorov, trans. R. Carter (Cambridge: Cambridge University Press, 1982).

33. Jonathan Crary, *Techniques of the Observer: On Vision and Modernity in the Nineteenth Century,* 6th ed. (Cambridge: MIT Press, 1995), 6. See also Michel Foucault, *Power/Knowledge: Selected Interviews and Other Writings, 1972– 1977,* ed. Colin Gordon (New York: Pantheon, 1980), for an analysis of how modes of vision and thus subjects are fabricated by historical conditions.

34. I am indebted to Raybaud's discussion of theatrical spectacles and the influence of Wagner's synesthetic opera on Rimbaud's poetry (see Raybaud, *Fabrique d' "Illuminations",* esp. 107–56).

35. The word *féerie* appears again in "Angoisse," "Métropolitain," and "Scènes," also in *Illuminations.* In "Mauvais Sang" Rimbaud alludes to "mille féeries profanes" *(Une Saison en enfer, OC,* 221).

36. Raybaud, *Fabrique d' "Illuminations",* 111.

37. On the *fête foraine* and its contribution to the development of the *féerie,* see Katherine Singer Kovács, "Georges Méliès and the 'Féerie,' " *Cinema Journal* 16, no. 1 (1976). Although the *féerie* emerged on the local fairground, by the early nineteenth century it had found a place in Parisian theaters as well. The directors of *féeries* soon learned that the more a play depended upon advanced technologies of stagecraft, the more commercially successful it would be. Thus, technological innovation was in part motivated by pecuniary interest. Kovács also traces how

the *féerie* influenced technical innovations in the filmmaking of Méliès's "cinema of attractions." See also Tom Gunning, "The Cinema of Attraction: Early Film, Its Spectator, and the Avant-Garde," *Wide Angle* 8, nos. 3 and 4 (1986); and Erik Barnouw, *The Magician and the Cinema* (New York: Oxford University Press, 1981).

38. The *féerie* is a variety of phantasmagoria to which Marx and Marxist critics refer when theorizing the process of ideological mystification through visual technologies. Walter Benjamin, for instance, ascribes particular importance to the *féerie* as an industrial technology capable of informing structures of understanding. Apparently, he even entertained the idea of calling his *Passagen-Werk* a "dialectical *féerie*" [dialektische Feen] (see Margaret Cohen, *Profane Illumination: Walter Benjamin and the Paris of Surrealist Revolution* [Berkeley: University of California Press, 1993], 235–39, 251–59; and Susan Buck-Morss, *The Dialectics of Seeing: Walter Benjamin and the Arcades Project* [Cambridge: MIT Press, 1989], 49, 271–75).

39. Théophile Gautier, *Histoire de l'art dramatique en France depuis vingt-cinq ans*, vol. 1 (Paris: Edition Hetzel, 1858), 101–2; emphasis added.

40. Théophile Gautier, review of *Le Cheval du diable*, an adaptation of Balzac's *La Peau de chagrin*, staged at the Cirque-Olympique, in *Histoire de l'art dramatique en France depuis vingt-cinq ans*, vol. 4 (Paris: Editions Hetzel, 1859), 210.

41. Ibid., 30.

42. Ibid., 210.

43. Kittang, *Discours et jeu*, 43.

44. Marjorie Perloff, "Trouver une langue; The *Anti-paysage* of Rimbaud," in *The Poetics of Indeterminacy* (Princeton: Princeton University Press, 1981), 51.

45. See, e.g., Charles Baudelaire, "Un Voyage à Cythère," in *Les Fleurs du mal, Oeuvres complètes*, ed. Y.-G. Le Dantec, rev. Claude Pichois (Paris: Gallimard, 1961), 111–12.

46. Leo Bersani, "Rimbaud's Simplicity," in *A Future for Astyanax, Character and Desire in Literature* (Boston: Little, Brown & Co., 1976), 257.

Chapter Three

1. *ND*, xii; Theodor W. Adorno, *Negative Dialektik* (Frankfurt: Suhrkamp, 1966), 9.

2. The relation between the lyric and the idealist project is discussed with particular respect to the "crisis" of the subject in Jean-Luc Nancy and Philippe Lacoue-Labarthe, *The Literary Absolute: The Theory of Literature in German Romanticism*, trans. Philip Barnard and Cheryl Lester (Albany: State University of New York, 1988).

3. See esp. Adorno's critique of the "lyrical subjectivism of Heine" in *Minima Moralia*. Heine's subjectivism "does not stand in simple contradiction to his commercial traits," for "the saleable is itself subjectivity administered by subjectivity" (215). In *The Jargon of Authenticity*, trans. Knut Tarnowski and Frederic Will (Evanston: Northwestern University Press, 1973), Adorno is even more critical of lyric poets who refuse to question whether their words, "gathered from culture,

at all cover the experiences whose objectification is the central idea of such lyric. . . . [a lyric] which makes believe it could be capable of transcendence" (86).

4. The discourse of confession emerges as a central mode of subjective expression early on in the development of French romanticism, Rousseau being, of course, the most obvious example. Alfred de Musset's *La Confession d'un enfant du siècle* and Benjamin Constant's *Adolphe* focus plot development even more narrowly on the exposure of a hidden part of the subject, exploring the epistemological potential of a meditative form returning incessantly to a protagonist's moral weakness or fault. Further, confession is a genre significant not only to Adorno but to other students of humanism as well. For Michel Foucault the confessional mode constitutes one of several "technologies of subject production," a set of integrated discourses that fortify the ideology of humanist individualism emerging at the end of the eighteenth century in Europe. Confession is a "lyrical outpouring," one of "the West's most highly valued techniques for producing truth" (Michel Foucault, *The History of Sexuality*, vol. 1, *An Introduction*, trans. Robert Hurley [New York: Vintage, 1990]).

5. "*Homo sum*," writes Hugo. "On ne s'étonnera donc pas de voir, nuance à nuance, ces deux volumes s'assombrir pour arriver, cependant, à l'azur d'une vie meilleure" [The reader will not be surprised to find that, little by little, these two volumes get increasingly darker until they arrive, nonetheless, at the azure regions of a better life] (*Les Contemplations* [Paris: Gallimard, 1967], 28).

6. Stéphane Mallarmé, "Le Tombeau de Charles Baudelaire," in *Oeuvres complètes*, ed. Henri Mondor and G. Jean-Aubry (Paris: Gallimard, 1945), 70.

7. The self, once hypostatized, becomes a "lie, because for the sake of its own absolute rule it will deny its own objective definitions" (*ND*, 277). According to Adorno, the art of modernity "innervates" precisely this aporia.

8. In the openly autobiographical *Minima Moralia* Adorno is so uncomfortable with the idealist implications of the first-person pronoun that he consistently emphasizes the objective content of the "I" 's most intimate memories: "In a real sense, I ought to be able to deduce Fascism from the memories of my childhood" (*MM*, 192).

9. Charles Baudelaire, *Oeuvres complètes*, ed. Y.-G. Le Dantec, rev. Claude Pichois (Paris: Gallimard, 1961), 69.

10. Arthur Rimbaud, "Matinée d'ivresse," in *Oeuvres complètes*, ed. Rolland de Renéville and Jules Mouquet (Paris: Gallimard, 1954), 184, hereafter abbreviated as *OC*.

11. *ND*, 13; *Negative Dialektik*, 9.

12. The resemblance between Adorno's approach to method and Georges Bataille's approach to the calculated *projet* deserves mention. A full comparison would show how each philosopher recuperates Hegelian negativity to destroy the insularity of systematic thought (see esp. Bataille's *L'Expérience intérieure* [Paris: Gallimard, 1954]).

13. "Like one confessing compulsively, Hegel deciphers his previously taught affirmative identity as a continuing break and postulates the submission of the weak to the more powerful" (*ND*, 324). Confessing "compulsively" or "involuntarily" (*AT*, 10) would appear to be the impulse shared by most of the major thinkers included in Adorno's pantheon. In the context of Wagner, for instance,

Adorno writes: "With a genius's compulsion to confess, [Wagner] laid bare the whole process [of the culture industry] in the scene of the 'Ring' " (*MM*, 201). Likewise, Kant confesses in footnotes (*AT*, 10) and "Freudian slips" (*ND*, 195).

14. *Negative Dialektik*, 28–29.

15. Whereas philosophers from Plato to Philippe Lacoue-Labarthe understand *mimesis* to refer to the practice of copying, Adorno uses the term in the anthropological sense, to mean the direct assimilation of an essential force or attribute. Adorno derives his theory of mimetic conduct largely from Marcel Mauss and Henri Hubert's study of sympathetic magic, *A General Theory of Magic*, trans. Robert Brain (New York: Norton, 1972), originally published in *L'Année sociologique*, 1902–3. Martin Jay studies Adorno's use of the term *mimesis* in "Mimesis and Mimetology: Adorno and Lacoue-Labarthe," in *The Semblance of Subjectivity: Essays in Adorno's Aesthetic Theory*, ed. Tom Huhn and Lambert Zuidervaart (Cambridge: MIT Press, 1997). To my mind, Jay pays too much attention to poststructuralist treatments of mimesis and too little to the works of Mauss, which influenced Adorno's own approach.

16. The gap is a significant philosophical category for Adorno. See the section entitled "Gaps" in *Minima Moralia* (80–81).

17. *ND*, 214. Adorno discerns a "convergence of Kantian morality with the ethics of property" (*ND*, 275). Terry Eagleton pursues Adorno's line of argument further in *The Ideology of the Aesthetic* (Oxford: Basil Blackwell, 1990).

18. "The system is the belly turned mind," Adorno states dramatically (*ND*, 23). "All mental things are modified physical impulses" (*ND*, 202).

19. "Das Bedürfnis, Leiden beredt werden zu *lassen* [to *let* itself be voiced], ist Bedingung aller Wahrheit" (*ND*, 27).

20. *ND*, 56; *Negative Dialektik*, 64.

21. Constellating is Adorno's metaphor for setting concepts into relations, into contexts, that reveal the historicity of the objects they designate. "The history locked in the object can only be delivered by a knowledge mindful of the historic positional value of the object in its relation to other objects. . . . As a constellation, theoretical thought circles the concept it would like to unseal, hoping that it may fly open like the lock of a well-guarded safe-deposit box: in response, not to a single key or a single number, but to a combination of numbers" (*ND*, 163). "The model" for this constellating, says Adorno, "is the conduct of language" (*ND*, 162).

22. The most recent attempt to unravel Adorno's debate with Benjamin can be found in Margaret Cohen, *Profane Illumination: Walter Benjamin and the Paris of Surrealist Revolution* (Berkeley: University of California Press, 1993). Although stimulating, Cohen's treatment of the Adorno-Benjamin debate does not take seriously enough Adorno's critique of Benjamin's immanence, the entanglement of his (Freudian) concepts in a historical framework. Nor does she sound the impact of the debate on Adorno's own evolution. For a full rehearsal of the issues, see Adorno's letter to Benjamin of 2 August 1935 in Theodor Adorno, Walter Benjamin, Ernst Bloch, Bertolt Brecht, and Georg Lukács, *Aesthetics and Politics*, trans. and ed. Roland Taylor, afterword by Fredric Jameson, 4th ed. (New York: Verso, 1990). See also Shierry Weber Nicholsen, "*Aesthetic Theory*'s Mimesis of Walter Benjamin," in Huhn and Zuidervaart, *Semblance of Subjectivity*.

23. *Le Petit Robert* (Paris: Société du Nouveau Littré, 1969), 1140. The *Dictionnaire de l'Académie Française*, 6th ed. (Paris: Firmin Didot, 1823), also associates an early meaning of *entreprendre* with invasion, aggressive attack; *entreprendre* was used with the preposition *sur* as a synonym for *empiéter sur* (to encroach, to infringe upon).

24. Baudelaire also uses *entreprise* in a similar way in "Comment on paie ses dettes quand on a du génie" (How one pays one's debts when one has genius) of 1845: "C'était bien lui, la plus forte tête commerciale et littéraire du dix-neuvième siècle; lui, le cerveau poétique tapissé de chiffres comme le cabinet d'un financier; c'était bien lui, l'homme aux faillites mythologiques, aux entreprises hyperboliques et fantasmagoriques dont il oublie toujours d'allumer la lanterne; le grand pour-chasseur de rêves, sans cesse à la *recherche de l'absolu*" [It was indeed he, the best commercial and literary head of the nineteenth century; a poetic mind papered over in numbers like the office of a financier; the man of mythic bankruptcies, hyperbolic and fantasmagorical enterprises, which he always forgot to get going; the great chaser-after of dreams, forever in *quest of the absolute*] (OC, 467; Baudelaire's emphasis).

25. The *Trésor de la langue française: Dictionnaire de la langue du XIXe et du XXe siècle (1789–1960)* (Paris: Editions du CNRF, 1979) records an increase in the use of *entreprendre* and *entreprise* in commercial and industrial contexts over the course of the nineteenth century. In the seventh edition of the *Dictionnaire de l'Académie Française* (Paris: Firmin Didot, 1879) the expression *l'esprit d'entreprise* appears for the first time.

26. Karen J. Dillman, " 'Aube': The *Je* in Process," in *Arthur Rimbaud*, ed. Harold Bloom (New York: Chelsea House, 1988), 169.

27. Jacques Plessen, *Promenade et poésie: L'Expérience de la marche et du mouvement dans l'oeuvre de Rimbaud* (Paris: Mouton, 1967), 324.

28. The examples of hydraulics and metallurgy are chosen advisedly. See the multitude of references to all varieties of engineering in the correspondence from Aden and Harar (OC, 320ff.). Just as Rimbaud earlier asked his friends to send him volumes of poetry from Paris, he later exhorts his family to send him technical manuals on mechanics, engineering, and agriculture.

29. By exploiting the multiaccentuality of the word *Produziertes* throughout *Negative Dialectics* Adorno manages to draw philosophy into proximity with industrial manufacturing through a kind of poetic shorthand or semantic *dédoublement*.

30. "No theory today escapes the marketplace," writes Adorno (*ND*, 4).

31. Adorno's exact word is "befangenen," suggesting the paradoxically self-imprisoning (death-desiring) nature of the very instinct that is meant to render humanity more powerful, more free (*Negative Dialektik*, 291).

32. The critique of self-preservation that reaches its crescendo in "After Auschwitz" is Nietzschean as opposed to Hegelian in orientation. If at bottom Hegel advocates the "primacy of the subject" (*ND*, 7), Nietzsche, in contrast, allows Adorno to laugh sardonically at this subject's thinly veiled attempts to save itself. Nietzsche is useful to Adorno because he is "the irreconcilable adversary of our theological heritage in metaphysics" (*ND*, 169). Adorno echoes the Nietzsche of *Le Gai Savoir* when he attacks reason, "bourgeois individualism,"

the "transcendental subject," and "the ego principle" on the grounds that they are nothing more than advanced forms of a primitive survival instinct.

33. As Adorno points out, the principle of self-preservation underlying a philosophy of the autonomous subject is implicated in a survival mechanism that necessarily sacrifices the other in the name of the self: Adorno suffers from the "guilt of a life which purely as a fact will strangle other life" (*ND*, 364).

34. The locution "it may have been wrong" signals the presence of a confession embedded within a confession. Adorno's defense of lyric poetry (as the expression of "perennial suffering") corrects an earlier essay entitled "Cultural Criticism and Society," in which Adorno wrote that "to write poetry after Auschwitz is barbaric" (*Prisms*, trans. Samuel Weber and Shierry Weber [Cambridge: MIT Press, 1992], 34).

35. *ND*, 362–63, trans. modified; *Negative Dialektik*, 353–54. I have changed Ashton's prose to reflect Adorno's impersonal constructions. For example, where Ashton translates "ob nach Auschwitz noch sich leben lasse" as "whether after Auschwitz *you* can go on living" (emphasis added), I write "whether after Auschwitz it is permissible to go on living [life *lets* itself be lived]." Many of Ashton's pronouns ("you," "him," "his") do not appear in the original German.

36. "Thinking men and artists have not infrequently described a sense of being not quite there, of not playing along, a feeling as if they were not themselves at all, but a kind of spectator. . . . The inhuman part of it, the ability to keep one's distance as a spectator and to rise above things, is in the final analysis the human part, the very part resisted by its ideologists" (*ND*, 363).

37. As Adorno puts it, "The living have a choice between involuntary ataraxy [objectifying life by standing apart from it] . . . and the bestiality of the involved [acting as a subject, seeking one's own self-preservation]. Both are wrong ways of living. But some of both would be required for the right *désinvolture* and sympathy" (*ND*, 364).

38. On the discursive context of Adorno's early reaction to fascist "authenticity," see Jeffrey Herf, *Reactionary Modernism: Technology, Culture, and Politics in Weimar and the Third Reich* (Cambridge: Cambridge University Press, 1984).

39. My characterization of de Man as dark is, as Andrzej Warminski has pointed out, a critical commonplace (see Warminski's "Introduction: Allegories of Reference," in Paul de Man, *Aesthetic Ideology*, ed. and intro. Andrzej Warminski [Minneapolis: University of Minnesota Press, 1996], 8–10). But de Man's tone is indeed gloomy, even acerbic (*brutal* is the word Warminski repeatedly uses), especially in those instances when his deconstructive exercise ends up reducing all readings deriving coherent meaning from the text to naive and slightly foolish mistakes. Adorno's embrace of naiveté in *Negative Dialectics* stands in stark contrast to de Man's rejection of the same. To the extent that Adorno valorizes the cognitive moment, he indeed appears more affirmative than de Man. One might easily reverse the evaluation, however, and say that de Man is far more affirmative where his own methodology is concerned. De Man rarely questions his own tactics, his founding concept of rhetoric, or his inherited taxonomies, and he certainly never analyzes the immanence of his model to a historical situation "after Auschwitz." (Demonstrating that his language performs what it describes, that it depends upon the referential function even while undermining it, does not constitute

a critique or historical recontextualization of the methodology itself.) In this regard it is Adorno who might be regarded as the truly gloomy or tragic theorist, for the authenticity of his insight is bought at the price of his system's integrity.

40. Paul de Man, "The Rhetoric of Temporality," in *Blindness and Insight: Essays in the Rhetoric of Contemporary Criticism*, intro. Wlad Godzich, 2nd ed. (Minneapolis: University of Minnesota Press, 1983), 214.

41. De Man writes: "At the moment that the artistic or philosophical, that is, the language-determined, man laughs at himself falling, he is laughing at a mistaken, mystified assumption about himself. . . . The Fall, in the literal as well as the theological sense, reminds him of the purely instrumental, reified character of his relationship to nature. Nature can at all times treat him as if he were a thing" (ibid.).

42. De Man's late essays on the "materiality" of inscription are, however, highly pertinent to a reading of avant-garde poetry. His intuition that a pure, nonteleological optics underlies aesthetic vision is consistent with observations made by Benjamin, Adorno, and poets of the avant-garde concerned with the a-subjective, material, depthless play of the letter, the "blind spot" (*AT*, 20) of lyricism. See "Phenomenology and Materiality in Kant," in de Man, *Aesthetic Ideology*: 70–90.

43. For Breton the street is the locus of the *rencontre*, the encounter with history, with the unconscious, with Nadja: "la créature toujours inspirée et inspirante qui n'aimait que d'être dans la rue, pour elle seul champ d'expérience valable, dans la rue . . . celle qui *tombait* . . ." [the creature always inspired and inspiring, who liked nothing better than to be in the street, for her the only valid field of experience, in the street . . . that one who *fell* . . .] (*Nadja*, in André Breton, *Oeuvres complètes*, vol. 1 [Paris: Gallimard, 1988], 716; Breton's emphasis). On the encounter in the street with history, see Cohen, *Profane Illumination*, 173ff.

44. Johanna Drucker, *The Visible Word: Experimental Typography and Modern Art* (Chicago: University of Chicago Press, 1994), 149, emphasis added.

Chapter Four

1. Arthur Rimbaud, "Paris," in *Oeuvres complètes*, ed. Rolland de Renéville and Jules Mouquet (Paris: Gallimard, 1954), 113–14, hereafter abbreviated as *OC*.

2. Alain Jouffroy discusses Cendrars's changing attitude toward capitalism in "Cendrars 1990," *Revue des sciences humaines* 92, no. 216 (1989). See also Marjorie Perloff's insightful discussion of Cendrars in *The Futurist Moment: Avant-Garde, Avant-Guerre, and the Language of Rupture* (Chicago: Chicago University Press, 1986), esp. 3–13. Perloff claims that Cendrars was swept up in the "Futurist Moment," a brief but exhilarating period before World War I when engineering and industry seemed to offer limitless resources for the creative mind.

3. F. T. Marinetti claims to oppose "the obsessive *I* that up to now the poets have described, sung, analysed, and vomited up" ("Destruction of Syntax—Imagination without Strings—Words in Freedom, 1913," in *Futurist Manifestos*, ed. Umbro Apollonio, trans. R. W. Flint, J. C. Higgitt, and C. Tisdall [New York: Viking, Documents of Twentieth Century Art, 1973], 100).

4. Jay Bochner, "Blaise without War: The War on Anarchy in Blaise Cendrars' *Moravagine*," trans. Rima Canaan Lee, *Modernism/Modernity* 2, no. 2 (1995).

5. Jean Epstein, *La Poésie d'aujourd'hui: un nouvel état d'intelligence* (Paris: La Sirène, 1921).

6. Blaise Cendrars, "Lettre en guise de postface," in ibid., 214, reprinted in Bochner, "Blaise without War," 62, emphasis added.

7. Claude Leroy, "Inédits et documents," *Revue des sciences humaines* 92, no. 216 (1989): 181.

8. Blaise Cendrars, *Le Lotissement du ciel* (Paris: Denoël, 1991), 281. The book has recently been translated as *Sky* by Nina Rootes, intro. Marjorie Perloff (New York: Paragon, 1992).

9. *La Peinture sous le signe de Blaise Cendrars, Robert Delaunay et Fernand Léger*, ed. Louis Carré (Paris: Louis Carré Gallery, 1965), from an interview conducted in 1954. See also Cendrars's text for *La Banlieue de Paris* (1949; reprint, Paris: Denoël, 1983), an album of photographs by Robert Doisneau in which Cendrars condemns the industrial aesthetic responsible for the sterile landscapes Doisneau captures on film.

10. Blaise Cendrars, "Le Principe de l'utilité," in Cendrars, *Aujourd'hui, 1917–1929, suivi de Essais et Réflexions, 1910–1916*, ed. Miriam Cendrars (Paris: Denoël, 1987), 51.

11. Kirk Varnedoe, "Advertising," in Kirk Varnedoe and Adam Gopnik, *High and Low: Modern Art and Popular Culture* (New York: Museum of Modern Art, 1990), 231. Cendrars's positive attitude toward advertising language and iconography should be considered not only in the context of futurism's romance with typography but also with respect to the enthusiasm toward the printed word expressed by artists of leftist orientation such as Fernand Léger, Pablo Picasso, and Robert Delaunay. Conservative opposition to posters and billboards grew during the 1910s, encouraging members of the avant-garde to experience advertising as a sort of revolt against city planning and overadministration. However, the dadaist position, that commercial languages manipulate human beings for the benefit of capital, is echoed by Cendrars in his later, more critical works, such as *L'Or* (1925) and *Le Lotissement du ciel*. On dada's approach to advertising, see Varnedoe, "Advertising," 253–84.

12. Cendrars, "Le Principe de l'utilité," 50.

13. On the reaction of the cultural elite to advertising, see Marjorie A. Beale, *The Modernist Enterprise: French Elites and the Threat of Modernity, 1900–1940* (Stanford: Stanford University Press, 1999). For a paradigmatic study of the relations between art and advertising in the American context, see Michele H. Bogart, *Artists, Advertising, and the Borders of Art* (Chicago: University of Chicago Press, 1995). Bogart confirms that "late-nineteenth-century developments in publishing and advertising widened the confines of art to include illustration and posters. Initially, practitioners in these fields met with a favorable reception. Enthusiasm faded in the second decade of the twentieth century; many observers perceived the forces of commerce to be adversely affecting the intents and practices of artists and to be encroaching inappropriately into realms of experience once deemed private" (4).

14. Cendrars, "Le Principe de l'utilité," 50.

15. To put Cendrars's claim for popular discourses in perspective, it is worth noting the presence in early-twentieth-century France of a Bergsonian discourse linking the rhythms of the machine to the authentic rhythm of human experience *(la durée)*. On the widespread acceptance of this discourse (by both the right and the left), see Mark Antliff, *Inventing Bergson: Cultural Politics and the Parisian Avant-Garde* (Princeton: Princeton University Press, 1993).

16. Blaise Cendrars, "Lettre à Smirnoff," in *Aujourd'hui*, 193.

17. Blaise Cendrars, "Les Poètes modernes dans l'ensemble de la vie contemporaine," in ibid., 98.

18. In "Les Pâques à New-York," Cendrars's farewell to romantic and symbolist poetics, he writes that the "bonnes paroles" of the Holy voice are "doucement monotones" (Cendrars, *Du monde entier, Poésies complètes: 1912–1924*, with a preface by Paul Morand [Paris: Gallimard, 1989], 15, hereafter abbreviated as *Du monde entier*). Editions Denoël has published the complete works of Blaise Cendrars, but I have chosen to quote from the Gallimard edition.

19. On the univocality of poetic discourse, see Mikhail Bakhtin, *Dialogic Imagination: Four Essays*, ed. Michael Holquist, trans. Caryl Emerson and Michael Holquist (Austin: University of Texas Press, 1981). According to Bakhtin, only the novel contains "languages that serve the specific sociopolitical purposes of the day, even of the hour" (263).

20. Guillaume Apollinaire, *Alcools*, in *Oeuvres poétiques*, ed. Marcel Adéma and Michel Décaudin, with a preface by André Billy (Paris: Gallimard, 1959), 39. For an example of Cendrars's poetic use of a *prospectus*, see the advertisement for Denver reproduced in "Le Panama ou les aventures de mes sept oncles" (*Du monde entier*, 59).

21. Blaise Cendrars, "Journal," in *Du monde entier*, 69, © Editions Denoël; "Newspaper," in *Blaise Cendrars, Complete Poems*, trans. Ron Padgett, intro. Jay Bochner (Berkeley: University of California Press, 1992), 53, trans. modified; hereafter references appear in the text.

22. A further resonance should also be noted: this speaking subject with "bras tendus" is also identified with the falling airplane ("on dirait un aéroplane qui tombe"); "les bras tendus" assume the same form as the wingspread ("envergure") of a plane. The image of poet as airplane is entirely typical of the period; it can be found in the works of Apollinaire, Marinetti, Marius de Zayas, and Francis Picabia, among others.

23. It should be noted that Cendrars wrote "Journal" during the period when Pablo Picasso was also testing the potential of newsprint to convey subjective moods in collage works such as *Bottle and Newspaper on Table* (1912) and *Still Life with Bottle of Vieux Marc, Glass, Newspaper* (1913). Cendrars was certainly exposed to these canvasses, both of which play with variations on the word *journal* (*urnal, jour, jou*, etc.). For an excellent treatment of Picasso's use of the word *journal* in his *papiers collés*, a treatment that also sheds light on Cendrars's procedure, see Robert Rosenblum, "Picasso and the Typography of Cubism," in *Picasso in Retrospect*, ed. Roland Penrose and John Golding (New York: Praeger, 1973).

24. Rolland de Renéville and Jules Mouquet, "Notes et variantes," in Rimbaud, *OC*, 697; see also Rimbaud to Demeny, 17 April 1871, ibid., 266.

25. Once again Cendrars seems to be playing with the religious connotations of commercial names, in this instance "la Samaritaine." Cendrars was probably influenced by Apollinaire's "Zone," which also juxtaposes the commercial and the sacred: "Et toi que les fenêtres observent la honte te retient / D'entrer dans une église et de t'y confesser ce matin / Tu lis les prospectus les catalogues les affiches qui chantent tout haut / Voilà la poésie ce matin et pour la prose il y a les journaux" [And you whom the windows observe shame holds you back / From entering a church and confessing this morning / You read ads catalogs posters that sing aloud / That's poetry this morning and for prose there's newspapers] (*Oeuvres poétiques*, 39).

26. In a 1950 radio interview with Michel Manoll, Cendrars recalled how he used to meet Léger "every day at happy hour at the corner of the rue de Buci, with the pimps, the whores, all the young punks of the neighborhood" (*Blaise Cendrars vous parle*, ed. Michel Manoll [Paris: Denoël, 1952], 113). Apollinaire also devotes a story to the rue de Buci, "so dear to my generation," in *Le Flâneur des deux rives* (Paris: Gallimard, 1975), quotation on 40.

27. Paul Crespelle, *La Vie quotidienne à Montparnasse à la grande époque 1905–1930* (Paris: Hachette, 1976), 96.

28. "Aux 5 coins" should be compared to Apollinaire's "Les Fenêtres" and "Lundi rue Christine" (both of 1913), *poème-conversations* integrating in a similar manner the conversational idioms heard in a café (Apollinaire, *Oeuvres poétiques*, 168–69, 180–82).

29. This reading is in direct conflict with those of earlier critics, who tend to depict Cendrars as a poet of "life." See, for instance, Jay Bochner, *Blaise Cendrars: Discovery and Recreation* (Toronto: University of Toronto Press, 1978).

30. Cendrars, "Poètes modernes dans l'ensemble de la vie contemporaine," 98–99. Yvette Bozon-Scalzitti claims that this essay, composed for oral presentation during a 1924 visit to São Paulo, Brazil, is in large part an assemblage of citations from Joseph Vendryes, *Le Langage: Introduction linguistique à l'histoire* (Paris: Renaissance du Livre, 1921). See Yvette Bozon-Scalzitti, *Blaise Cendrars ou la Passion de l'écriture* (Lausanne: L'Age d'homme, 1977), 348–49.

31. Jean-Pierre Goldenstein, *"Dix-neuf poèmes élastiques" de Blaise Cendrars* (Paris: Méridiens Klincksieck, 1986), 83.

32. Pierre Bourdieu, "The Production of Belief: Contribution to an Economy of Symbolic Goods," in *The Field of Cultural Production: Essays on Art and Literature*, ed. and trans. Randal Johnson (New York: Columbia University Press, 1993), 80.

33. Cendrars's "Notule d'histoire littéraire" (A little note on literary history), appended to the *Dix-neuf poèmes élastiques*, suggests that he was indeed concerned with his career when he published the volume: "The older writers, the established poets, and the so-called avant-garde rejected my work," Cendrars complains (*Du monde entier*, 106; *Complete Poems*, 369). Although Cendrars lacked the promotional backing of respected magazines like the *NRF* until 1918, he did manage to publish in all the major avant-garde journals of his time. In response to what he perceived to be mainstream neglect, Cendrars developed promotional techniques to sell editions of his 1913 *La Prose du transsibérien et la petite Jehanne de la France*. Cendrars and his collaborator Sonia Delaunay not

only distributed a subscription "Bulletin" in the form of a postcard (a common practice at the time) but also produced a flier resembling a commercial leaflet and an *affiche publicitaire* that they intended to reproduce in bulk (see Antoine Sidoti, *Genèse et dossier d'une polémique: 'La prose du transsibérien et la petite Jehanne de France', Blaise Cendrars—Sonia Delaunay, nov.–dec. 1912–juin 1914*, Archives des lettres modernes 224 [Paris: Lettres Modernes, 1987], 33–35).

34. In "L'Esprit nouveau et les poètes," for instance, Apollinaire notes the advantage modern technology now has over poetry in the domain, specifically, of prophecy (Guillaume Apollinaire, *Oeuvres en prose complètes, II*, ed. Pierre Caizergues and Michel Décaudin [Paris: Gallimard, 1977]).

35. Fernand Divoire, "Littérature et publicité," *Chantecler*, 26 February 1927, 1. *Chantecler*'s survey was inspired by a call (in the 15 February 1927 issue of *La Revue de la Femme*) for writers to submit advertisement copy to a competition, the Grand Prix Beaumarchais, organized by Henri Lemeunier, director of the advertising agency Encartage.

36. Blaise Cendrars, "Publicité = Poésie," *Chantecler*, 26 February 1927, 1. Part of the text is reprinted in *Aujourd'hui*, 117.

37. Blaise Cendrars, *Le Spectacle dans la rue: Présentation des affiches de A. M. Cassandre par Blaise Cendrars* (Montrouge/Seine: Draeger, n.d.), unpaginated.

38. *La Peinture sous le signe de Blaise Cendrars*, 18. For discussions of the impact of advertising billboards on modern artists, see Fernand Léger, "Contemporary Achievements in Painting," in *Functions of Painting*, Documents of Twentieth-Century Art (New York: Viking, 1973); Varnedoe and Gopnik, *High and Low*; and Johanna Drucker, *The Visible Word: Experimental Typography and Modern Art* (Chicago: University of Chicago Press, 1994). Drucker analyzes Tristan Tzara's use of advertising typography in his poster poems; strangely, she does not mention that many of the strategies employed by Tzara after 1916 are anticipated by Cendrars in 1913–14.

39. Goldenstein, *Dix-neuf poèmes élastiques" de Blaise Cendrars*, 60.

40. For a reading of "Hamac" that explores Cendrars's desire at once to praise and to replace Apollinaire as the "seul poète" of the generation, see Susan Horrex, " 'Modernity' in the Poetry of Blaise Cendrars" (Ph.D. diss., University of Reading, 1969).

41. Jane M. Gaines argues in *Contested Culture: The Image, the Voice, and the Law* (Chapel Hill: University of North Carolina Press, 1991) that the romantic image of an autonomous lyric subject (possessing a unified voice) was itself fabricated in response to the encroachment of commodifying structures into the domain of authorship. "The Romantics countered the commodification of the work," writes Gaines, "by elevating the artist"—and the artist's voice—to the status of origin (59). Ironically, however, as artists "resisted commodification by projecting the personal traits of the author onto the work, the Romantics effected a reification of their own," namely, the reification of authorship, personality, signature, and voice. On the relation between the development of print culture and the ideology of autonomous artistic creation, see Raymond Williams, *Culture and Society, 1780–1950* (New York: Columbia University Press, 1983); idem, *Keywords* (Oxford: Oxford University Press, 1976); and Roger Chartier, *The Order of Books*, trans. Lydia G. Cochrane (Stanford: Stanford University Press, 1994).

42. It should be noted, however, that "Contrastes" ends with a set of ambiguous images. As the machine is transformed into high art, human beings become reified as factory smoke stacks: "L'aérodrome du ciel est maintenant, embrasé, un tableau de Cimabue/ Quand par devant/ Les hommes sont/ Longs/ Noirs/ Tristes/ Et fument, cheminées d'usine" [The aerodome of the sky is now, aflame, a painting by Cimabue / When in the foreground / Men are / Long / Black / Sad / And smoking, factory chimneys] (*Du monde entier*, 76).

Chapter Five

1. Susan Buck-Morss, *The Dialectics of Seeing: Walter Benjamin and the Arcades Project* (Cambridge: MIT Press, 1993), esp. 97–101, quotation on 108.

2. Walter Benjamin, *Das Passengen-Werk*, quoted in ibid., 101.

3. Charles Baudelaire, "Le Croquis des moeurs," in *Le Peintre de la vie moderne*, *Oeuvres complètes*, ed. Henri Mondor and G. Jean-Aubry (Paris: Gallimard, 1945), 1155.

4. Charles Baudelaire, "Le Beau, la mode, et le bonheur," ibid., 1154. In " 'Modernity' in the Poetry of Blaise Cendrars" (Ph.D. diss., University of Reading, 1969) Susan Horrex reports that Cendrars considered his nom de plume to be a partial anagram of the name Charles Baudelaire.

5. On the persistence of artisanal modes in the France of the Second Empire, see Whitney Walton, *France at the Crystal Palace: Bourgeois Taste and Artisan Manufacture in the Nineteenth Century* (Berkeley: University of California Press, 1992).

6. For accounts of increasing standardization in turn-of-the-century and early-twentieth-century France, see Debora L. Silverman, *Art Nouveau in Fin-de-Siècle France: Politics, Psychology, and Style* (Berkeley: University of California Press, 1989); Rosalind Williams, *Dream Worlds: Mass Consumption in Late Nineteenth-Century France* (Berkeley: University of California Press, 1982); and Richard Abel, *The Ciné Goes to Town: French Cinema, 1896–1914* (Berkeley: University of California Press, 1994).

7. Fredric Jameson, *Postmodernism, or, The Cultural Logic of Late Capitalism*, 2nd ed. (Durham: Duke University Press, 1992), 7.

8. Blaise Cendrars, "Eloge de la vie dangereuse," in *Aujourd'hui, 1917–1929, suivi de Essais et Réflexions, 1910–1916*, ed. Miriam Cendrars (Paris: Denoël, 1987), 26.

9. Guillaume Apollinaire, *The Cubist Painters: Aesthetic Meditations, 1913*, trans. Lionel Abel (New York: George Wittenborn, 1962), 18. A certain self-consciousness concerning the links between fashion and avant-garde art characterizes the literary world of Apollinaire's time. Many writers of Apollinaire's circle, including André Salmon, Blaise Cendrars, and later André Breton, were supported by the famous couturier Jacques Doucet. On Doucet's intervention, see François Chapon, *Mystères et splendeurs de Jacques Doucet, 1853–1929* (Paris: J. C. Lettes, 1984).

10. Blaise Cendrars, "Modernités: Delaunay," in *Aujourd'hui*, 71–72.

11. Delaunay lost all of her Russian properties during World War I. Finding herself in a precarious economic situation, she extended her field of operations beyond the domestic sphere, opening a Casa Sonia in Madrid, an Atelier

Simultané in Paris, and a Boutique Simultanée at the 1925 Exposition des Arts Décoratifs.

12. Jean-Carlo Flückiger, *Au coeur du texte: Essai sur Blaise Cendrars* (Neuchâtel: A la Baconnière, 1977), 176. Cendrars was working under the sign of the simultaneous contrast technique when he collaborated with Sonia Delaunay in 1913 to create *La Prose du transsibérien et la petite Jehanne de France*, a two-meter-long poem stenciled with Delaunay's designs and folded in the manner of an accordian.

13. Although Delaunay may not have admitted it at the time, her "robe simultanée" was very much a response to moves made on the competitive chessboard of avant-garde art. As several commentators have noted, the competition between the futurists and Sonia and Robert Delaunay was quite intense during the years just before the war (see Elizabeth Morano's introduction to *Sonia Delaunay: Art into Fashion*, with a foreword by Diana Vreeland [New York: George Braziller, 1986]; and Emily Braun, "Futurist Fashion: Three Manifestos," *Art Journal* 54 [spring 1995]).

14. Sonia Delaunay, "The Poem 'Easter in New York,' " in *The New Art of Color: The Writings of Robert and Sonia Delaunay*, ed. Arthur A. Cohen, trans. Arthur A. Cohen and David Shapiro (New York: Viking, Documents of Twentieth Century Art, 1978), 198.

15. Guillaume Apollinaire, "La Femme Assise" (The Seated Woman), of 1914, in Jean-Pierre Goldenstein, *"Dix-neuf poèmes élastiques" de Blaise Cendrars* (Paris: Méridiens Klincksieck, 1986), 54.

16. Blaise Cendrars, *Du monde entier, Poésies complètes: 1912–1924*, with a preface by Paul Morand (Paris: Gallimard, 1989), 83–84, © Editions Denoël.

17. It is very likely that Cendrars intended this pun. The poet had just returned from six months in New York, where he had worked for the Butterick pattern company (see Jay Bochner's detailed account of Cendrars's life in New York in "Cendrars Downtown," in *La Revue des lettres modernes. Blaise Cendrars 2: Cendrars et l'Amérique*, ed. Monique Chefdor [Paris: Minard, 1989]).

18. *Sensualité* is Cendrars's modernist synonym for spirituality. A follower of Remy de Gourmont's theory of the aesthetic as the spiritual life of the senses, Cendrars substitutes "sensuality" for more traditional poetic values, such as spirituality, divinity, beauty, or truth. Cendrars's "profondeur" is a "profondeur sensuelle" (see "Lettre à Smirnoff," in *Aujourd'hui*, 193), an arousing visceral experience involving the five senses.

19. Diana Vreeland, foreword to *Sonia Delaunay: Art into Fashion*, 10.

20. Arthur Rimbaud, "Being Beauteous," in *Oeuvres complètes*, ed. Rolland de Renéville and Jules Mouquet (Paris: Gallimard, 1954), 181, hereafter abbreviated as OC.

21. Arthur Rimbaud, "Lettre du voyant," 15 May 1871, in OC, 270.

22. Boccioni, Umberto, Carlo Carrà, Luigi Russolo, Giacomo Balla, and Gino Severini, "Futurist Painting, Technical Manifesto, 1910," in *Futurist Manifestos*, ed. Umbro Apollonio, trans. R. W. Flint, J. C. Higgitt, and C. Tisdall (New York: Viking, Documents of Twentieth Century Art, 1973), 31.

23. See Goldenstein, *"Dix-neuf poèmes élastiques" de Blaise Cendrars*, 52.

24. This quotation is found in a marginal comment not included in the published preface to *Baudelaire* (Paris: Union Bibliophile de France, 1946). See the unpublished manuscript preserved in the Fonds Blaise Cendrars, Bibliothèque Nationale Suisse, Berne, dossier O 236.

25. Baudelaire, "Le Beau, la mode, et le bonheur," in *Le Peintre de la vie moderne*, OC, 1154.

26. Baudelaire, "La Modernité," ibid., 1163.

27. Jean-Pierre Richard, *Poésie et profondeur* (Paris: Seuil, 1955), 10.

28. OC, 180; *Ill*, 23 and 21. For further references to apparel, see Arthur Rimbaud, "Métropolitain," and "Ouvriers," OC, 186.

29. Sonia Delaunay, "Survey of Artists on the Future of Fashion (1931)," in Delaunay and Delaunay, *New Art of Color*, 208.

30. Cendrars, *Du monde entier*, 106.

31. The now classic version of the theory of identity as masquerade may be found in Judith Butler, *Gender Trouble: Feminism and the Subversion of Identity* (New York: Routledge, 1990). In response to Joan Rivière's "Womanliness as a Masquerade," Butler asks provocatively whether masquerade "serve[s] primarily to conceal or repress a pregiven femininity . . . [o]r is masquerade the means by which femininity itself is *first* established?" (48, Butler's emphasis). I am suggesting here that once an organic, "essential" femininity is eliminated as a possibility, any female identity one creates may be susceptible to other, equally reifying forces (such as commodification).

32. In *La Main de Cendrars* (Paris: Presses Universitaires du Septentrion, 1996) Claude Leroy provides an exhaustive treatment of this period in Cendrars's career. He does not, however, recognize the significance of "Sur la robe elle a un corps," nor does he link the poetics it advocates to Cendrars's later works.

33. The archivist of the Fonds Delaunay, Bibliothèque Nationale, Department of Manuscripts, suggests an approximate date of June 1914 for this letter, which is located in dossier mf. 7022 25650. The emphasis is Cendrars's.

34. Cendrars to Sonia and Robert Delaunay, 1916, ibid.

35. Cendrars to Robert Delaunay, c. 1916, ibid.

36. Charles Baudelaire, "Le Public moderne et la photographie," in *Salon de 1859*, OC, 1034. This "grimace de circonstance" results from "la grande folie industrielle" (1036), the subservience of painting to the mechanical processes of photography.

37. See Burr Wallen, "Sonia Delaunay and Pochoir," *Arts Magazine* 54, no. 1 (1979).

38. Sonia Delaunay, "The Influence of Painting on Fashion Design" (lecture delivered at the Sorbonne, in Paris, in 1926, reprinted in Delaunay and Delaunay, *New Art of Color*, 206). On Delaunay's desire to democratize access to haute couture, see Sherry Buckberrough, "Delaunay Design: Aesthetics, Immigration, and the New Woman," *Art Journal* 54, no. 1 (1995).

39. Sonia Delaunay, "Influence of Painting on Fashion Design," 207.

40. Sonia Delaunay, "Rugs and Textiles" (1925), reprinted in Delaunay and Delaunay, *New Art of Color*, 201.

41. Blaise Cendrars, "Profond aujourd'hui," in *Aujourd'hui*, 12. At this point in his career Cendrars anticipates postmodernism in another way as well:

he celebrates globalization without regard for the often inequitable conditions of the workers producing these multinational products.

42. Cendrars, "Lettre à Smirnoff," 193.

43. See Sherry Buckberrough, "An Art of Unexpected Contrasts," in *Sonia Delaunay: A Restrospective*, with a foreword by Robert T. Buck (Buffalo, N.Y.: Albright-Knox Gallery, 1980), 105.

44. Cendrars to Sonia Delaunay, quoted in Goldenstein, *"Dix-neuf poèmes élastiques" de Blaise Cendrars*, 55.

45. Blaise Cendrars, *Le Lotissement du ciel* (Paris: Denoël, 1991), 286, 285.

Chapter Six

1. Char seems to have recognized in Heidegger a significant intellectual ally despite the German philosopher's affiliations before World War II. Char repeatedly encouraged the association between Heidegger's work and his own; he even hosted Heidegger's visits to southern France in the summers of 1966, 1968, and 1969, during which the philosopher presented the Thor seminars on pre-Socratic philosophy (collected in Martin Heidegger, "Les Séminaires du Thor," in *Heidegger: Questions III et IV*, trans. Jean Beaufret et al. [Paris: Gallimard, 1990]). Heidegger also exhibited an interest in Char, dedicating his *Acheminement de la parole* to the French poet. On Char's relation to Heidegger, see Jean-Pol Madou, " 'La poésie ne rythmera plus l'action. Elle sera en avant' (Char, Heidegger, Hölderlin, Rimbaud)," *Cahiers du SUD* (Marseille), 1984, ed. Daniel Leuwers.

2. Martin Heidegger, "Building, Dwelling, Thinking," in *Poetry, Language, Thought*, trans. Albert Hofstadter (New York: Harper & Row, 1975), 156.

3. René Char, "Arthur Rimbaud" in Char, *Oeuvres complètes* (Paris: Gallimard, 1983), 731, hereafter abbreviated as *OC*.

4. On this peculiarly poetic act of "listening," "concentrated perception," or "gathered taking-in," see Heidegger's ". . . Poetically Man Dwells . . . " in *Poetry, Language, Thought*, 223.

5. Heidegger, "Building, Dwelling, Thinking," 146, emphasis added.

6. Ibid., 148.

7. Martin Heidegger, "The Origin of the Work of Art," in *Poetry, Language, Thought*, 21.

8. Martin Heidegger, "The Thing," in ibid., 166. Heidegger is clearly reacting to the massive invasion of radio into the home that occurred during Hitler's rise to power. On Nazism's use of radio, see Alice Yaeger Kaplan, *Reproductions of Banality: Fascism, Literature, and French Intellectual Life*, foreword by Russell Berman (Minneapolis: University of Minnesota Press, 1986), 134–39.

9. Heidegger, "Building, Dwelling, Thinking," 146.

10. Avital Ronell, *The Telephone Book: Technology, Schizophrenia, Electric Speech* (Lincoln: University of Nebraska Press, 1989), 16.

11. René Char, "Impressions anciennes," in *Recherche de la base et du sommet*, OC, 742.

12. *Le Petit Robert* (Paris: Société du Nouveau Littré, 1969).

13. See René Duval, *Histoire de la Radio en France* (Paris: Moreau, 1979). Some of the first radio announcers were in fact poets or actors drawn from the

"Théâtre d'Avant-Garde" (96). Paul Dermée, the resident lyricist of *L'Esprit nouveau*, also worked as a radio announcer.

14. André Breton, *Point du jour* (Paris: Gallimard, 1970), 7.

15. André Breton, *Manifeste du surréalisme*, in *Oeuvres complètes*, vol. 1 (Paris: Gallimard, Pléiade, 1988), 330, hereafter abbreviated as *OC*.

16. André Breton, "Le Message automatique," in *Point du Jour*, 184.

17. Breton would have been familiar with dynamic psychiatry through his medical training at the Centre neuro-psychiatrique of Saint-Dizier in 1916 (see Jennifer Gibson, "Surrealism before Freud: Dynamic Psychiatry's 'Simple Recording Instrument,' " *Art Journal* 46 [spring 1987]: 56–60). According to Christopher Schiff, French dynamic psychiatry transformed the human subject, in the name of clinical research, into a kind of "stenographer of internal sound" ("Banging on the Windowpane: Sound in Early Surrealism," in *Wireless Imagination: Sound, Radio, and the Avant-Garde*, ed. Douglas Kahn and Gregory Whitehead [Cambridge: MIT Press, 1994], 172). Breton modeled surrealist practice after dynamic psychiatry because in the dynamic paradigm (as opposed to the Freudian) "the patient *personally* transcribed and appraised interior speech" (ibid., Schiff's emphasis).

18. Hal Foster has sounded the depths of this paradox, locating in surrealism's ambiguous attitude toward the machine a sometimes overt, sometimes repressed inquiry into the nature and provenance of the subliminal message. See Foster's *Compulsive Beauty* (Cambridge: MIT Press, 1995).

19. Breton, *Nadja*, in *OC*, 753, translated into English under the same title by Richard Howard (New York: Grove Press, 1960), 160.

20. Ibid.

21. Gérard Miller contends in *Les Pousse-au-jouir du maréchal Pétain* (Paris: Seuil, 1975) that the Vichy government was primarily "une histoire de radios" (226). According to Miller, Petainism was primarily "un phénomène d'audition" (44).

22. Jean-Louis Crémieux-Brilhac, *Ici Londres! Les voix de la liberté* (Paris: Editions de France, 1982), xiii, Crémieux-Brilhac's emphasis.

23. Originally the BBC was used as a means to control what were feared to be independent, rebellious (i.e., Communist) forces forming within France. On the British effort to transform the Resistance into an Allied organization, see M. R. D. Foot, *S.O.E. in France* (London: Her Majesty's Stationery Office, 1966).

24. According to Jacques Gaucheron, these codes were composed by Pierre Dac, a French radio announcer and novelist working for *Les Français Parlent aux Français* during the German occupation of France (*La Poésie, la Résistance: Du Front populaire à la Libération* [Paris: Messidor, 1991], 202). See also Pierre Dac, *Un Français libre à Londres en guerre* (Paris: Editions France-Empire, 1972). The librarian at the BBC Radio Written Archives in Reading, England, could provide no proof that the codes were written by Dac. It is likely that Dac read the codes over the radio, but they were probably written by S.O.E. officers.

25. Aimé Autrand, *Le Département de Vaucluse de la Défaite à la Libération—mai 1940–25 août 1944* (Paris: Aubanel, 1965), 112.

26. Jean-Claude Mathieu, *La Poésie de René Char ou le sel de la splendeur*, vol. 2 (Paris: José Corti, 1988), 203.

27. In his wartime volume *Feuillets d'Hypnos* Char makes a direct allusion to the significance of the BBC transmissions. Fragment 75 reads: "Assez déprimé par cette ondée (Londres) éveillant tout juste la nostalgie du secours" [Rather depressed by that thundershower (word from London) awakening only the yearning for help] (*OC*, 193; *Leaves of Hypnos*, trans. Cid Corman [New York: Grossman, 1973], 75, hereafter abbreviated as *Leaves*).

28. The codes preserved at the BBC Radio Written Archives Centre are located in a file titled "French Service: Code Messages to the French Resistance Movement; Acc. 10190." All further references to the BBC radio codes are to this file. I also consulted Mathieu, *La Poésie de René Char ou le sel de la splendeur*, vol. 2; Jean Garcin, *De l'Armistice à la Libération dans les Alpes de Haute-Provence 17 juin 1940–20 août 1944* (Digne: B. Vial, 1983); Autrand, *Le Département de Vaucluse*; Crémieux-Brilhac, *Ici Londres!*; and Jean Fernand, *J'y étais* (Cavaillon: Association des Médailles de la Résistance de Vaucluse, 1987).

29. Foot, *S.O.E. in France*, 110. The S.O.E. was created by Winston Churchill in July 1940. Although the procedure for transmitting coded messages through the BBC's airwaves was established in the summer of 1941, the greatest production and transmission occurred during the latter part of the war. Increased repression in the Southern Zone, occupied by the Nazis in November 1942, emphasized the need for covert radio communication; the frequency and the number of codes transmitted during this period, both from London and between French-based units, increased accordingly (see also Musée de la Résistance, *La Résistance en Vaucluse: Documents et témoignages*, Recueil no. 8 (Fontaine-la-Vaucluse, 1980); and Pierre Lorain, *Armements clandestins: France, 1941–1944* (Paris: Presses de l'Emancipatrice, 1972).

30. Lorain, *Armements clandestins*, 19.

31. On the self-representations of the Resistance and the crucial significance of the literary, see Harry Roderick Kedward, *Resistance in Vichy France: A Study of Ideas and Motivation in the Southern Zone* (Oxford: Oxford University Press, 1978).

32. "Le maquis" is untranslatable. It refers to the clandestine units of resistants that hid out in the rural areas of southern France. Literally, *maquis* means a kind of scrubby woods found in Corsica. The French maquis were named after the Corsican resistants who hid out in these woods.

33. *La Bibliothèque est en feu* should be reread in the context of the radio codes and their use of the word *bibliothèque*. It may also be significant that Aragon, Eluard, and Seghers named their wartime publishing house La Bibliothèque Française in 1942. The word *bibliothèque* came to signify a repository of French culture.

34. See Eric Marty, *René Char* (Paris: Seuil, 1990), 24–26. Likewise, Jean-Claude Mathieu has argued that for Char, participation in the Resistance meant silencing his own voice as a poet: "nécessité pour l'action: le mutisme" [to act one must be mute] (*La Poésie de René Char*, 241).

35. The repetition of certain words and their consistent relationships rendered many of the codes virtually transparent to the gestapo, which intercepted them. According to M. R. D. Foot, by the end of March 1944 almost all the codes had been deciphered by the enemy (*S.O.E. in France*, 105).

36. *OC*, 226; *Leaves*, 216, trans. modified. The second sentence—"L'Amour de son troupeau le lui défend"—is found only in the original manuscript, not in the printed or the translated version.

37. René Char, "Bandeau de *Fureur et mystère*," in *OC*, 653.

38. For example, "Raison règne au pays de Descartes" [Reason reigns in the land of Descartes] (7 February 1944); "Je pense donc je suis" [I think, therefore I am] (12 January 1944); "Relisez la Nouvelle Héloïse" [Reread the New Heloise] (11 February 1944); "Cultivons notre jardin" [May each man cultivate his own garden] (n.d.). Codes evoked foreign luminaries, such as Shakespeare and Darwin, in an attempt to associate the Resistance not only with French culture but with the notion of culture itself.

39. Crémieux-Brilhac, *Ici Londres!*, xxx.

40. Winfred Noth, *Handbook of Semiotics* (Bloomington: Indiana University Press, 1990), 209.

41. See Crémieux-Brilhac, *Ici Londres!*, xxi; and Foot, *S.O.E. in France*, 110.

42. For instance, the *parachutage* landing fields in the north of France were given names such as Rimbaud, Balzac, La Fontaine, Lamartine, Saint-Simon, Vigny, Apollinaire, Montaigne, and so on (Henri Noguères, *La Vie quotidienne des Résistants de l'Armistice à la Libération* [Paris: Hachette, 1984], 140).

43. Roman Jakobson, "Linguistics and Poetics," in *The Structuralists from Marx to Levi-Strauss*, ed. Richard De George and Fernande De George (Garden City, N.Y.: Doubleday, 1972), 93.

44. Noth, *Handbook of Semiotics*, 208.

45. Gregory Whitehead, "Out of the Dark: Notes on the Nobodies of Radio Art," in Kahn and Whitehead, *Wireless Imagination*, 256–57.

46. The quotation is from a piece by an anonymous author entitled "La poésie, conscience de la France" in the emphemeral Resistance leaflet *Les Lettres françaises*, no. 13 (February 1944).

47. *Gens de la lune*, roughly translated as "the moon's children," was the idiomatic way of referring to Resistance fighters during the occupation.

48. Shawn James Rosenheim, *The Cryptographic Imagination: Secret Writing from Edgar Poe to the Internet* (Baltimore: Johns Hopkins University Press, 1997), 4.

49. As Marty insists, "One has to set aside . . . all biographical keys *[les clefs biographiques]* in order to elucidate the difficult poem" (*René Char*, 120).

50. Marguerite Bonnet, with Philippe Bernier, Etienne-Alain Hubert, and José Pierre, "Notes," in *OC*, 1563.

51. I am obliquely in conversation here with Jacques Derrida's "Fors," preface to *Cryptonymie: Le Verbier de L'Homme aux Loups*, by Nicolas Abraham and Maria Torok (Paris: Aubier Flammarion, 1976), in which he argues for the "non lieu" (the no-place, or not taking place) characterizing the cryptographic. For a meditation on the unlocalizable crypt as a Derridian figure for literature, see J. Hillis Miller, "Derrida's Topographies," in *Topographies* (Stanford: Stanford University Press, 1995).

52. René Char, *Arrière-histoire du "Poème pulvérisé"* (Paris: Hughes, 1953). The original version (i.e., the printer's manuscript) is housed in the Fonds Jacques Doucet, Bibliothèque Sainte-Geneviève, Paris.

53. Arthur Rimbaud, "Alchimie du verbe," in *Une Saison en enfer, Oeuvres complètes*, ed. Rolland de Renéville and Jules Mouquet (Paris: Gallimard, 1954), 233.

54. Char, "Bandeau de *Fureur et mystère.*"

55. Rosenheim, *Cryptographic Imagination*, 4.

56. In fragment 98 of *Feuillets d'Hypnos* Char writes suggestively: "La ligne de vol du poème. Elle devrait être *sensible* à chacun" [The poem's line of flight. It should be within the power of each to *feel*] (*OC*, 199; *Leaves*, 98, Char's emphasis).

Chapter Seven

1. Greil Marcus, *Lipstick Traces: A Secret History of the Twentieth Century* (Cambridge: Harvard University Press, 1989), 17.

2. Steve Jones, quoted in Dick Hebdige, *Subculture: The Meaning of Style* (New York: Methuen, 1979), 27.

3. See, e.g., Wallace Fowlie's *Rimbaud and Jim Morrison: The Rebel as Poet* (Durham: Duke University Press, 1993), in which the author traces some rather broad parallels between Morrison's "testing [of] the boundaries of reality" (19) and Rimbaud's rejection of Second Empire society. According to Fowlie, it was "the legend of Rimbaud that attracted Morrison" (70).

4. Guy Debord and Gil J. Wolman, "Preliminary Problems in Constructing a Situation," in *Situationist International Anthology*, trans. and ed. Ken Knabb (Berkeley: University of California Press, 1989), 44, original emphasis.

5. Guy Debord and Gil J. Wolman, "Methods of Detournement," ibid., 9.

6. At one point Marcus elaborates a connection between the energy that generated the Sex Pistols in 1975 and the energy that produced the Paris Commune of 1871 (*Lipstick Traces*, 125), but he mentions neither the Commune's role in Rimbaud's work nor Rimbaud's influence on dada, a movement he considers central to the punk phenomenon.

7. Tricia Henry, *Break All Rules! Punk Rock and the Making of a Style* (Ann Arbor: University of Michigan Press, 1989).

8. Malcolm McLaren invented the Sex Pistols a year after he was exposed to the New York scene (he came to manage the New York Dolls in 1974). This fact confirms the significance of American punk rock for the development of the British punk movement. According to Dan Graham, "After the Dolls had disbanded, McLaren, who had been influenced by the emerging New York City 'punk rock' scene—the Ramones, Richard Hell and the Voidoids, Patti Smith—decided to apply the 'punk' style to a more English political context" ("Malcolm McLaren and the Making of Annabella," in *Impresario: Malcolm McLaren and the British New Wave*, ed. Paul Taylor [Cambridge: MIT Press, 1988], 61–62).

9. See John Pareles and Patricia Romanowski, eds., *The "Rolling Stone" Encyclopedia of Rock and Roll* (New York: Rolling Stone Press / Summit Books, 1983), s.v. "Patti Smith."

10. See Patti Smith, *Babel* (New York: Putnam's Sons, 1978).

11. On the importance of Bob Dylan, see Simon Frith, *Sound Effects: Youth, Leisure, and the Politics of Rock & Roll* (New York: Pantheon, 1981).

12. Paul S. George and Jerold M. Starr, "Beat Politics: New Left and Hippie Beginnings in the Postwar Counterculture," in *Cultural Politics: Radical Movements in Modern History*, ed. Jerold M. Starr (New York: Praeger, 1985), 192.

13. Andrew Ross, "Hip and the Long Front of Color," in *No Respect: Intellectuals and Popular Culture* (New York: Routledge, 1989), 77.

14. Smith published several chapbooks at small presses between *Babel* and *Early Works*.

15. Patti Smith, *Horses* (Arista Records AL4066, 1975).

16. Smith's 1976 album, *Radio Ethiopia/Abyssinia* (Arista Records 115143), also pays homage to Rimbaud's myth, evoking the latter part of his life in Ethiopia (Abyssinia) on the album jacket.

17. Patti Smith, *Easter* (Arista Records AB4171, 1978). The text is by Smith; the song is by Smith and Jay Dee Daugherty. On the album itself Smith ventriloquizes the voice of Rimbaud, chanting a set of refrains against the musical background of descending scales. One refrain is "Isabella, all is glowing; Isabella, all is knowing; Isabella, we are dying; Isabella, we are rising." Another is "Frederic and Vitalie, the Saviour dwells inside of thee." Smith is obviously playing with Isabella's apocryphal story of Rimbaud's conversion.

18. Arthur Rimbaud, "Mauvais Sang," *Une Saison en enfer*, in *Oeuvres complètes*, ed. Rolland de Renéville and Jules Mouquet (Paris: Gallimard, 1954), 220, hereafter abbreviated as *OC*.

19. Patti Smith, "rock n roll nigger," *Easter*. This song was recently used by Oliver Stone in his 1994 film *Natural Born Killers*.

20. See Christopher Miller, *Blank Darkness: Africanist Discourse in French* (Chicago: University of Chicago Press, 1985).

21. For an explication of the importance of the *bourdonnement* in Rimbaud, see Kristin Ross, "The Swarm," in *The Emergence of Social Space: Rimbaud and the Paris Commune* (Minneapolis: University of Minnesota Press, 1988), 100–122.

22. *Ill*, 27, trans. modified. The relation of the first strophe to the second, shorter one has long been a subject of debate among Rimbaud critics. I follow James Lawler and Antoine Raybaud (and not André Guyaux) when I consider the two fragments to be related. My reasoning is that the question the dividing Xs raise—are they separate fragments or parts of a totality?—is a major theme of the poem itself (see James Lawler, "The Unity of 'Being Beauteous,' " *French Studies* 40 (April 1986); and André Guyaux, *Poétique du fragment: Essai sur "Les Illuminations" de Rimbaud* (Neuchâtel: A la Baconnière, 1985).

23. For a reading of "Being Beauteous" as a parody of lyric conventions, see Anne-Emmanuelle Berger, *Le Banquet de Rimbaud: Recherches sur l'oralité* (Seyssel: Champ Vallon, 1992), 51–62. Rimbaud's "anti-blasons" are also treated by Michael Riffaterre in *La Production du texte* (Paris: Seuil, 1979), 95–97.

24. See, e.g., "Les Ponts," where "les accords mineurs se croisent, et filent" (*OC*, 187), or "Vagabonds," where "la campagne [est] traversée par des bandes de musique rare" (*OC*, 190).

25. Paul de Man writes in "Reading (Proust)": "The crossing of sensory attributes in synesthesia is only a special case of a more general pattern of substitution that all tropes have in common" (*Allegories of Reading: Figural Language in*

Rousseau, Nietzsche, Rilke, and Proust [New Haven: Yale University Press, 1979], 62).

26. Roland Barthes, *Le Dégré zéro de l'écriture* (Paris: Seuil, 1972), 38.

27. Edward J. Ahearn, "Explosions of the Real: Rimbaud's Ecstatic and Political Subversions," *Stanford French Review* 961 (spring 1985): 71, 76. See also Charles Dobzynski, "Une Ethique de l'action," *Europe: Revue littéraire mensuelle*, January–February 1988: "What one calls Beauty is obviously not, for Rimbaud, purely aesthetic" (55). Again, Ross: "The true program of such a language [as Rimbaud's] is, like that of Artaud's theater of cruelty, to verge *beyond* representation" (Kristin Ross, "The Right to Laziness," in *Emergence of Social Space*, 66, Ross's emphasis).

28. Lawler, "The Unity of 'Being Beauteous,' " 167, 172.

29. Jean-Marie Gleize, "D'ailleurs il n'y a rien à voir là-dedans" (Besides, there's nothing to see in there), *Revue des sciences humaines*, no. 193 (1984): 37.

30. Ibid.

31. Luigi Russolo, "The Art of Noises (extracts) 1913," in *Futurist Manifestos*, ed. Umbro Apollonio, trans. R. W. Flint, J. C. Higgitt, and C. Tisdall (New York: Viking, Documents of Twentieth Century Art, 1973), 87.

32. Richard Huelsenbeck, *"En avant Dada*: A History of Dadaism," in *The Dada Painters and Poets: An Anthology*, ed. Robert Motherwell (Boston: Hall, 1981), 26.

33. Marcus, *Lipstick Traces*, 443, emphasis added.

34. See Fowlie, *Rimbaud and Jim Morrison*, 8.

35. Slogan by Malcolm McLaren, quoted in Paul Taylor, "The Impresario of Do-It-Yourself," in *Impresario*, 12.

36. Patti Smith's albums hit the charts five times in America: *Horses* was number 47 in 1975; *Radio Ethiopia* was number 122 in 1976; *Easter* was number 20 in 1978; *Wave* was number 18 in 1979; and *Dream of Life* was number 65 in 1988. Only two of her singles hit the charts: "Because the Night," number 6 in 1978; and "Frederick," number 90 in 1979. Although the Sex Pistols never appeared on the American charts, they did far better than Smith on their own soil (see *Billboard Magazine*'s *Top Singles* [Menomonee Falls, Wis.: Record Research, 1991]. Paul Gambaccini, Tim Rice, and Jonathan Rice's *British Hit Albums* (Middlesex: GRR Publications, 1992) indicates that *Never Mind the Bullocks* was number 1 in 1977; *The Great Rock n' Roll Swindle* was number 7 in 1979; *Some Product* was number 6 in 1979; and *Flogging a Dead Horse* was number 23 in 1980. Their singles were on the charts twelve times between 1976 and 1992 (two of these were re-releases), with "Anarchy in the UK" hitting number 3 in 1976 and "God Save the Queen" number 2 in 1977. Smith also appeared on the British charts but always significantly further down, as low as 70 in 1988 and as high as 16 in 1978. The charts register the number of sales and the quantity of airplay for singles, whereas they only register the number of sales for albums.

37. In the fall of 1995, to cite just one instance, Smith was an honored guest at the Long Beach Spoken Word Festival, "When Words Collide," a festival that featured Laurie Anderson as well. In recent years Smith has also presented poetry readings at libraries and other high-cultural venues.

38. Theodor W. Adorno and Max Horkheimer, "The Culture Industry: Enlightenment as Mass Deception,"in *Dialectic of Enlightenment*, trans. John Cumming (1944; reprint, New York: Continuum, 1995), 120–67.

39. Theodor W. Adorno, "The Fetish Character of Music and the Regression of Listening,"reprinted in *The Culture Industry: Selected Essays on Mass Culture*, ed. J. M. Bernstein (New York: Routledge, 1991). In response to Adorno's pessimism, Bernstein notes that the "culture industry is no longer the purveyor of a monolithic ideology but, however unwittingly or unintentionally, includes moments of conflict, rebellion, opposition and the drive for emancipation and utopia" (18).

40. Jim Collins, *Uncommon Cultures: Popular Culture and Post-Modernism* (New York: Routledge, 1989), 10.

Chapter Eight

1. Donna J. Haraway, "A Cyborg Manifesto: Science, Technology, and Socialist-Feminism in the Late Twentieth Century," in *Simians, Cyborgs, and Women: The Reinvention of Nature* (New York: Routledge, 1991), 151.

2. According to Adorno, "Radicalized, what is called reification probes for the language of things. . . . Emphatically modern art breaks out of the sphere of the portrayal of emotions and is transformed into the expression of what no significative language can achieve" (*AT*, 60).

3. On Anderson as a poet, see Marjorie Perloff's introduction to *Postmodern Genres*, ed. Marjorie Perloff (Norman: University of Oklahoma Press, 1987), 5; and the fine article by Jessica Prinz, " 'Always Two Things Switching': Laurie Anderson's Alterity," *Genre* 20, no. 3–4 (1987), reprinted in ibid. Prinz argues that although Anderson "transgresses both the 'laws of genre' and gender" (388), poetic language is undeniably central to her hybrid constructions. See also Michael Davidson's analyses of Anderson's "Tapevoice" poetry in *Ghostlier Demarcations: Modern Poetry and the Material Word* (Berkeley: University of California Press, 1997).

4. Haraway, "Cyborg Manifesto," 163, 151, 163. Michael Davidson also evokes Haraway in relation to Anderson in *Ghostlier Demarcations*, 214. In reference to the practices of American contemporary poets, Davidson writes, "Rather than search for forms of presence in peasant shoes or the windowless monad of aesthetic autonomy, these writers have heard in the tapevoice, to adapt Wallace Stevens, 'ghostlier demarcations, keener sounds' " (223).

5. Laurie Anderson, "Tour of Laurie's Home," *Collected Videos* (Warner Bros. Videos, 1990), camera by Michael Lesser.

6. In 1971–72 Anderson created a series of sculptures out of newspaper print. "New York Times, Horizontal / China Times, Vertical," for instance, weaves a quilt out of thin strips of identical issues of the two newspapers named in the title. Janet Kardon comments on Anderson's interest in typography and other types of sign systems in "Laurie Anderson: A Synesthesic Journey," in *Laurie Anderson: Works from 1969 to 1983*, ed. Janet Kardon (Philadelphia: Institute of Contemporary Art, 1983), 25–26.

7. Laurie Anderson, "Artist in Dialogue," interview by John Howell, in John Howell, *Laurie Anderson* (New York: Thunder's Mouth Press, American Originals, 1992), 41.

8. Laurie Anderson, interview, in notes to *New Music for Electronic and Recorded Media: Women in Electronic Music, 1977*, compact disk produced and edited for 1750 Arch Productions by Charles Amirkhanian, 1996), 19. *It Depends On Who You're Talking To* belongs to Anderson's Wittgenstein phase. On the significance of Wittgenstein to Anderson, see Prinz, "Always Two things Switching," 391–93.

9. Prinz, "Always Two Things Switching," 393. On Burroughs's immense influence, see also Victor Bockris, *With William Burroughs: A Report from the Bunker* (New York: Seaver Books, 1981); and Robin Lydenberg, "Sound Identity Fading Out: William Burroughs' Tape Experiments," in *Wireless Imagination: Sound, Radio, and the Avant-Garde*, ed. Douglas Kahn and Gregory Whitehead (Cambridge: MIT Press, 1994).

10. Craig Owens, "Amplifications: Laurie Anderson," *Art in America* 69 (March 1981): 123.

11. Laurie Anderson, *Stories from the Nerve Bible: A Retrospective, 1972–1992* (New York: HarperCollins, 1994), 47.

12. "O Superman (For Massenet)," *Big Science* (Warner Bros. Records 3674-2, 1982).

13. Laurie Anderson, *Words in Reverse* (Buffalo, N.Y.: Hallwalls, 1979), unpaginated, emphasis added. *Words in Reverse* is composed of extracts from two performance pieces, *Like a Stream* (1978) and *Americans on the Move* (1979). The latter piece was integrated into *United States, Parts I–IV*, performed in 1983 at the Brooklyn Academy of Music.

14. See Jonathan Crary, *Techniques of the Observer: On Vision and Modernity in the Nineteenth Century*, 6th ed. (Cambridge: MIT Press, 1995), 55.

15. Anderson, *Stories from the Nerve Bible*, 88.

16. *Words in Reverse*. This sentence is reiterated in Anderson's later works as well, such as *United States, Parts I–IV*.

17. Haraway, "Cyborg Manifesto," 175.

18. In "Confessions of a Street Talker" (1975) Anderson insists that all instruments—her violin, her synclavier, her gendered body—are props to be creatively transformed: "What I really want to say is that if instruments are props, then human bodies are too" (*Stories from the Nerve Bible*, 35).

19. Anderson, "Artist in Dialogue," 45.

20. "Monkey's Paw," *Strange Angels* (Warner Bros. Records 9 25900-2, 1989).

21. Haraway, "Cyborg Manifesto," 152, 178.

22. Laurie Anderson, "Laurie Anderson: Dancing about Architecture," interview by Michael Dare, *L.A. Extra*, July 1986, 9, quoted in Prinz, "Always Two Things Switching," 404.

23. Peter Frank, "Auto-art: Self-indulgent? And How!" *Art News* 75, no. 7 (1976): 43.

24. Anderson, *Stories from the Nerve Bible*, 44.

25. See Philippe Lejeune, *Le Pacte autobiographique* (Paris: Seuil, 1975).

26. The mind is a filter in its own right, what Anderson calls the "mental filter." At times it would seem that the "mental filter" is no less "tilted," no less distorting, than those introduced by journalese, advertising, the popular song, or television. Anderson makes this argument in *Laurie Anderson: An Interview*, an audiotape recorded on 11 October 1981 at Riverside Studios in London.

27. That the poet "administrates" subjectivity for the purposes of expressing and then packaging it is proposed by Adorno with respect to the lyric poet Heinrich Heine in *MM*, 215.

28. Haraway, "Cyborg Manifesto,"180.

29. Ibid., 155.

30. Ibid., 152.

31. Anderson, "Artist in Dialogue," 69.

32. "Lower Mathematics" is the name of the skit, which concerns the possibility of transforming everything—the Gettysburg address, the author's phone number, Anderson's song "Sharkey's Day"—into the code of cybernetics.

33. Haraway, "Cyborg Manifesto," 155.

34. According to Anderson's own testimony, in an interview published in 1992, the electronic distortions in *Home of the Brave* reflected her need to "get out" of herself (Anderson, "Artist in Dialogue," 22). Apparently, Anderson found the risks of the earlier, intimate formats too great. As audience demand for her work grew, she increasingly turned to more distancing performance venues, such as the stadium, the prerecorded video, and the CD-ROM. Technological gadgets began to serve as her "defense"; "There was a time when I thought, 'I'm going to get eaten alive' " (60–61).

35. Laurie Anderson with Hsin-Chien Huang, *Puppet Motel* (New York: Voyager, 1995).

36. *United States, Parts I–IV* (1983), *Natural History* (1986), *Home of the Brave* (1986), and *Empty Places* (1990) are all partial anthologies of past works, containing recycled versions of songs, fragments of prose poems presented earlier, as well as some new material.

37. Responding to this need, Anderson radically stripped down her set for *Empty Places*, of 1989–90. Her next show, *Voices from the Beyond*, of 1991, was even less dependent on high-tech equipment. See the glossy book that emerged from the experience, also entitled *Empty Places* (New York: Harper Perennial, 1991), in which Anderson tells several stories that focus on her interactions with various audiences.

38. Laurie Anderson, "The Puppet Motel," *Bright Red* (Warner Bros. Records 9 45534-2, 1994).

Coda

1. See Michael Joyce, *Of Two Minds: Hypertext Pedagogy and Poetics* (Ann Arbor: University of Michigan Press, 1955); and Mark Poster, *The Mode of Information: Poststructuralism and Social Context* (Chicago: University of Chicago Press; Cambridge: Polity Press, 1990), 123.

2. See Poster, *Mode of Information*, 124–28. This is part of his argument with Jacques Derrida concerning the relation of utterance to context and surface.

3. Gabriele Schwab, "Cyborgs and Cybernetic Intertexts: On Postmodern Phantasms of Body and Mind," in *Intertextuality and Contemporary American Fiction*, ed. Patrick O'Donnell and Robert Con Davis (Baltimore: Johns Hopkins University Press, 1989), 210.

4. Michael Davidson, *Ghostlier Demarcations: Modern Poetry and the Material Word* (Berkeley: University of California Press, 1997), 206.

5. Hal Foster, "What's Neo about the Neo-Avant-Garde?" *October* 70 (fall 1994): 30, Foster's emphasis.

6. "The self is what is inhuman" (*ND*, 299).

7. Theodor W. Adorno and Max Horkheimer, *Dialectic of Enlightenment*, trans. John Cumming (1944; reprint, New York: Continuum, 1995), 24. This formulation's debt to Benjamin's theory of the dialectical image should be clear.

8. Foster, "What's Neo about the Neo-Avant-Garde?" 30.

9. Guillaume Apollinaire, "L'Esprit nouveau et les poètes," in *Oeuvres en prose complètes, II*, ed. Pierre Caizergues and Michel Décaudin (Paris: Gallimard, 1977), 944.

General Index

Index of Primary Sources Cited